MW00527645

LEONARD SWEET

*For Jeremiah Luke Sullivan, a seven year-old Endkeeper
who reminds us daily of the chief end for which God
created humans: "to glorify God and enjoy God forever."*

LEN WILSON

*Shar Leigh Wilson
Kaylyn Love Wilson
Christian Wayne Wilson
Joslyn Grace Wilson
Austin Wade Wilson*

... who show me daily the joy of telos living.

TELOS

TELOS

The Hope of Heaven Today

LEONARD SWEET
LEN WILSON

invite
ACADEMIC

Plano, Texas

TELOS

The Hope of Heaven Today

Copyright © 2022 by Leonard Sweet and Len Wilson

All rights reserved.

No part of this work may be reproduced or transmitted in any form or by any means, electronic or mechanical, including photocopying and recording, or by any information storage or retrieval system, except as may be expressly permitted by the 1976 Copyright Act or in writing from the publisher. Requests for permission can be addressed to Permissions, Invite Press, P.O. Box 260917, Plano, TX 75026.

This book is printed on acid-free, elemental chlorine-free paper.

Hardcover: 978-1-953495-38-9; Paperback: 978-1-953495-39-6; eBook: 978-1-953495-40-2

All scripture quotations unless noted otherwise are taken from the New Revised Standard Version of the Bible, copyright 1989, Division of Christian Education of the National Council of the Churches of Christ in the United States of America. Used by permission. All rights reserved.

Scripture quotations marked CEB are taken from Common English Bible (CEB) Copyright © 2011 by Common English Bible.

Scripture quotations marked ESV are taken from The Holy Bible, English Standard Version. ESV® Text Edition: 2016. Copyright © 2001 by Crossway Bibles, a publishing ministry of Good News Publishers.

Scripture quotations marked KJV are taken from the Holy Bible, King James Version (public domain).

Scripture quotations marked NIV are taken from THE HOLY BIBLE, NEW INTERNATIONAL VERSION®, NIV® Copyright © 1973, 1978, 1984, 2011 by Biblica, Inc.™ Used by permission of Zondervan. All rights reserved worldwide.

22 23 24 25 26 27 28 29 —10 9 8 7 6 5 4 3 2 1

MANUFACTURED in the UNITED STATES of AMERICA

CONTENTS

ACT TWO | THE BEGINNING OF THE END: THE AGE TO COME

THE END

Men perish because they cannot join the beginning to the end.

—Aleman of Croton, 5th century BCE

LONG TIME COMING: THE STORY

....

What happens in the end?

....

Everybody wants to know what happens in the end.

Everybody yearns for something that can't be assuaged in this life. There is something inside each of us pulling toward a happy ending.

By the end, we mean of everything—the end of the world, the end of time, the end of the story. It's a question for all people, a question of how God's kingdom comes. Jesus' first disciples asked the question long before we did. But twenty-first-century culture has made predictions of "the end" an end in itself.

Six possible endings offer competing visions of the future in culture and church today, creating a powder keg of conflict. They're all wrong. Jesus has already told us how it's going to play out, though we've misunderstood him. Act 1, the Present Age, considers each false ending. In an interlude, we explain why they fail. Then, in act 2, the Age to Come, we will talk about the promised true ending of our collective story: our telos.

Everyone needs to know their natal story. But the biggest questions in life are best pursued not by looking at the beginning, but by looking at the never-ending end.

0.1 | When Is the End of the Age?

In my beginning is my end . . .
. . . In my end is my beginning.

—T. S. Eliot, "East Coker" (1943)

Christians have been obsessed with the end since the beginning. You can't blame the earliest disciples. After a series of sunny teachings and healings, Jesus sent his twelve out to offer the same. In the middle of his instructions, Jesus reframed their future in a much more ominous light: "You will be hated by all because of my name. But the one who endures to the end will be saved" (Matthew 10:22).

It was a lesson they learned quickly. The Twelve returned from their first excursion with the grim news that Jesus' cousin John had been murdered. They clearly did not forget Jesus' portent but waited to bring it up again until much later, on what turned out to be the last week of Jesus' life. After he had taught on the destruction of Jerusalem, they saw their chance and came to Jesus privately with two urgent questions: "When is the end of the age?" and "How will we know the signs?" (see Matthew 24:3).

These are questions Jesus followers—and anyone seeking the common good—have never ceased to ask. We look at the pain, suffering, and chaos of the present age, and we desire comfort, peace, and order for all people. We want a better end. We want to understand how to read the signs to get there.

All want to know: What happens at the end of this story called life?

The reason we keep asking questions about the end is that when we look around us, we see a story still unfolding. The denouement has yet to occur. Or in the phrasings of comparative mythologist and story guru Joseph Campbell's monomyth (one myth),[1] we are still on a hero's journey and have yet to return home. Who is "we"? "We" are the main characters of our lives on an individual level. "We" are the collective protagonists of our shared culture. "We" are members of the body of Christ, who, just as the first disciples did, wait and wonder about the end. "We" ask and wonder and wait for the last act to unfold. In short, the persistent power of story comes from the ongoing uncertainty of now.

And what is the end we seek?

Storytellers use the same language preachers use—transformation. Or to use Jesus' language from the Gospels—*metanoia*, transfiguration, metamorphosis, a changing of image. Every good story is about an inside-out changed life. Always the consummate storyteller, who aims for participation over performance, Jesus answered the disciples' questions by showing them the end, rather than telling them the end (see Matthew 17:1–10). To turn an inquiry into a journey was both his genius and his intention. As master screenwriter and "storynomics" consultant Robert McKee observes, "the storyteller's selection and arrangement of events is his master metaphor."[2] Jesus was always taking his disciples on a journey—not a hero's journey but a disciple's journey.

The conclusion of the journey is the moment when with unveiled faces reflecting the glory of the Lord, we will be changed, transfigured, into the image of God (see 2 Corinthians 3:18). The light of the Transfiguration foreshadows events to come. But alas, we get ahead of ourselves. First, we must go on that journey.

Storytellers use structure to take the viewer/reader/participant—we prefer "storyreceiver"—on the journey. Structures are form, not formula.[3] They help us understand the life we are living and the story we are telling. Campbell outlined an archetypal structure—the aforementioned monomyth—which all great narratives share. Campbell proposed seventeen stages to the journey, which can be summarized in a "too-long-didn't-read" version as three: departure, initiation, and return. Each of us begins in a comfortable status quo. An event shakes us out of our stupor and forces us to go on a journey. We go through a trial of initiation and challenge. Then we return, changed. If you have seen *Star Wars*, you have experienced Campbell's structure at work.

Other story structures exist as well. Aristotle had one. Shakespeare had one. Contemporary variations include structures from presentation theorist Nancy Duarte,[4] screenwriter Christopher Vogler,[5] and marketer Don Miller.[6] Novelist Kurt Vonnegut, who took satire and irony as far as it would take him, reduced all stories to a set of graphs for his master's thesis in anthropology at the University of Chicago. The university rejected it for being too simple; he later said it was the best thing he ever did.[7]

"Time will tell" when it comes to things of this earth. But when it comes to Jesus and the kingdom of God, only eternity will tell. Time is story: a sequence of events with a beginning, middle, and end. We cannot know what happens in the end without going on the journey. We are going to take you to the deep end of the pool. Are you ready to be pushed? Are you open enough to put last things first?

> *What we call the beginning is often the end*
> *And to make an end is to make a beginning.*
>
> **—T. S. Eliot, "Little Gidding"**

Historian Martyn Whittock, in his enlightening book *The End Times, Again? 2000 Years of the Use & Misuse of Biblical Prophecy* (2021), tells the following anecdote:

There is a story told—which may be apocryphal—that, in the seventeenth century, a very dark day caused the members of a New England assembly to think that the end of the world was upon them. Their debating chamber was deep in premature shadows. A motion was presented, that they should disperse to their homes and await events with prayer. At last, the speaker made his ruling. It allegedly went as follows: "Either this is the end of the world, or it is not. If it is not, then we have business to attend to. If it is, then I would have it that Christ finds us attending to our duties. I rule, let lights be brought."[8]

Let the lights be brought.

And let the lights be brought on our journey to "The End." Every time we step out under the stars for that midnight rush of being alive and that nightfall thrill and fill of wonder, the blackness of the night sky reminds us that the universe had a beginning. God created that Beginning with an End in mind.

0.2 | The End Is about Story

To ask about "the end" is to seek the resolution or denouement of a story. Questions about the end require a view of history as story. We must place ourselves into the grand story, the overarching narrative.

The value of understanding history as story has been either sent packing or brushed scoffingly aside by an academy raised on the deconstructionist tendencies of critical theories that came in multiple forms but were all true to trope: linguistic, Marxist, postcolonial, gender studies, queer theory, structuralism, poststructuralism, new historicism, cultural materialism, to name but a few. Might the time be overdue to deconstruct deconstruction?

Secular philosophy has tried to separate theology from story, and story from science. But even philosophy is obsessed with the end. The political movement once called the New Left started a journal dedicated to story and used the Greek word for the end as its title: *Telos*. Pretend though some might, story is inescapable.

Oxbridge scholar C. S. Lewis wrote that the miracle of the Jesus story is that myth became fact, and by becoming fact it did not cease to be a myth.[9] A scholar of medieval and early modern literature, Lewis approached the study of God using the lens of story and ended up on many lists of the best theologians of the twentieth century. In response to criticism for his fondness of story, Lewis once remarked in *Christian Century*, at the time the mediated center of mainline religion, that "if the real theologians had tackled this laborious work of translation about a hundred years ago, when they began to lose touch with the people (for whom Christ died), there would have been no place for me."[10] Lewis's *Christian Century* barb rebutted a commenter, but his real nemesis was philosophical—the rise of criticism in nineteenth-century England, which took over theology and literature alike. It became a standing joke that everyone had two professions: one's own and that of a critic.

The question of story is not mere conjecture or children's bedtime ritual, as the deconstructionists tried to claim. It has real-world consequences. Although the question of the end is often framed as cosmic and spiritual—what will happen one day—it is also a question for the here and now. The stories we tell ourselves shape our destiny, for good or ill. Stories tell us who we are and bind us to one another. They are the heart of our identity as humans.

The loss of story has been devastating to both church and culture, especially in a world that runs on stories. The world no longer runs on words or economics. The world runs on icons and signs and stories. This is an iconomic world. Not economic. Iconomic. The major cultural currency is no longer words but narratives and metaphors, icons and stories.

Corporate executives get it wrong when they emphasize a vision for the future. The truth is that each of us already has a vision of the future. The story we tell ourselves is the vision we are living now. Cognitive scientists tell us that the mind is made of metaphors and stories. Psychologists have documented how we live our nows based on the images we carry of our destinations, and on the stories we tell ourselves about what will eventually happen, for good or ill.

The second-century theologian Irenaeus lived within generational reach of Jesus' resurrection. He battled endlessly against gnostic preferences for a more sophisticated, secret knowledge. Irenaeus is generally credited with being the first in the church to recognize the narrative sequence of what we now call the Bible as a single, unified narrative from Genesis to Revelation. This understanding was customary throughout Christian history until the rise of "criticism" in nineteenth-century Europe. The critical approach was simple: there was story, and there was the meaning behind the story, which could be pieced together like an artifact, and the meaning behind the story was better.[11]

The culture of critique and check, over celebration and affirmation, became deeply embedded in the "modern" critical mindset. How many of us grew up in classrooms the majority of which took attendance by checking names off a list rather than by affirmation of presence? A fundamental tenet of critical theory, that you "size up" something by taking it apart, meant that the modern era looked at "wholes" (from Shakespearean sonnets to the Bible) as intelligible only if dissectible, decomposable, and deconstructable into their constituent parts.[12] Our identity as Christians went from being well-storied to well-versed.

> It will never cease to amaze me that a biblical studies academy that lauds diversity functionally requires an epistemology rooted in the European enlightenment that only allows itself to be criticized using the tools of North American and European skepticism and cynicism.
>
> **—biblical scholar Esau McCaulley**

To be sure, the rise of criticism offered benefits. Expeditions to discover the meaning behind the story led to an explosion of innovative thinking in a variety of disciplines, one of which was literary criticism. For example, German writer Gustav Freytag spotted patterns common to stories and created a pyramid to describe them.[13] Sometime later, Cornish writer Sir Arthur Thomas Quiller-Couch distilled all stories into one of seven basic plots. Literary criticism provided new insight and application, and the story we tell in this book is a descendant of this approach. But when you look at the Pietà, or the *Mona Lisa*, or *Guernica*, do you cut it up into its component parts? Or is the essence of art its wholeness and ability to move you? The priority of celebrate then cerebrate, praise then appraise, commend then condemn, assess positively then negatively, say yes then no, was upended.

We all need criticism. Every writer needs an editor. In 1948 Thomas Merton wrote to his new epistolary friend Evelyn Waugh, "I need criticism, the way a man dying of thirst needs water."[14] We are to be open to correction (Proverbs 18:18), but when we criticize others, we are to do so in a loving manner (Eph. 4:15). Tongues of fire meant to inflame fires of encouragement, love, and hope can quickly turn into pyromaniacs of criticism and complaint, hate and negate.

The default mode of "critique" created a host of problems for people of faith. When a people can no longer praise, when the default mode of a people or a culture is to negate or denigrate the praiseworthy, can that culture long survive? Isn't prayer primarily praise? Isn't singing another word for being? Here is Marianne Moore's poetic interpretation of the first psalm:

> Blessed is the Man
>   who does not sit in the seat of the scoffer—
>   the man who does not denigrate, depreciate,
>   denunciate;
> (Ah, Giorgione! There are those who mongrelize. . . .)[15]

For our purposes, the biggest problem was not the guillotine blade of critique that hung over everything in the modern world. It was that the story behind the story took over the story itself, to the place where we no longer trusted the story or could even tell the story in the first place. As we say today, we became "meta." We no longer saw heroes and villains—only people with differing views and alternative perspectives. Hollywood screenwriting guru Robert McKee, lamenting the loss of good storytellers in Hollywood, identifies the deconstruction that criticism has wrought. He describes the impact of critical theory as creating a shift of locus from inside the story to outside the story.[16]

What was called "higher" criticism attempted to discover truth as universal, scientific axioms hovering outside the context of story. Maybe it is "higher" in the sense that it has tried to occupy a void, outside and above story. But this ambition has been an Icarus errand, for we cannot escape the ground out of which we are born. Trying to escape narrative has simply divided loyalties, split identities, and amplified anxieties.

We have become masters of form but illiterate to meaning. We have swapped truth for verisimilitude, believing that the more precise our observations, the more truth we tell. But fact, no matter how minutely observed, is truth with a small *t*. Big-*T* Truth is located behind, beyond, inside, below the surface of things, holding reality together and tearing it apart, often indirectly observed and unheralded, as we will see.

The result is that late-twentieth-century and early-twenty-first-century intellectual life has been set adrift by the "Great Refusal" of negation.[17] Devoid of material life, the sacred cow of "critical thinking" has reduced its dancing disciples to hedonists and nihilists trying to snatch an identity off the racks of a Gucci store or locate it on the marble floor of a Bentley showroom. Critical theory has also facilitated a nadir of culture, a game of thrones with no heroes or villains, simply a never-ending struggle for power. All this despite the striking fact that there is almost no discussion about what "critical thinking" is.

From the perspective of history, the denial of the dynamics of story and the illusion and sterility of the critical vantage point reinforces that story has been present from pre-time to the present time. You can't cancel history: history knocks down every door, no matter how hard we try to lock it out and keep it away. History seeps into the soul; it beats in every heart. Being and history go together. Church cannot escape culture and culture cannot escape context.

There is no history—something that was, is, but never stays—without myth—something that never was but always is. Or at least, never was in the sense that you can prove its facticity with absolute certainty. History needs myth, and myth needs history. For example, it is hard to forgive Sigmund Freud for what he did in 1939, and we repeat 1939, when he demythologized the origins of Judaism in his *Moses and Monotheism*. He argued that Moses descended from the Egyptians. At the very moment the Jewish people needed myth the most, an identity rooted in story and time, culture got Freud's version of history.[18]

The Apache word for "myth" literally means "to tell the holiness."[19] How did we get to the place where, for some, history does not exist, not to mention "the holiness"? Perhaps this was the unforeseen consequence when philosophy reduced meaning to an artifice of our own agency and endowment. Science replaced myth with agency, at least according to philosopher of science Karl Popper, who wrote that history itself has no meaning outside of our own will and determination.[20] If meaning is entirely an intellectual construct, it is up to us to find meaning, even if that meaning is found in meaninglessness.[21] And if "us" is an increasingly global, multicultural mashup of different cultures and dissimilar histories, unable to share a common myth, the only conclusion left is that there is no universal meaning, but a fragile construct of "your truth" and "my truth" (phrases we detest).

This is the heart of the oft-confusing concept of critical race theory. In the pursuit of truth, modern philosophy tried to replace myth with unfalsifiable propositions, and then unfalsifiable propositions with somewhat coherent opinions. In the end we killed the thing we sought to capture. We killed truth to save truth. Once we realized we had killed the truth, we attempted to suggest the truth never existed to begin with, only perspective, and markers. All these identitarian markers are a part of who we are . . . but none of them are who we are.

The lens a photographer uses to see life can make or break the story he or she is telling. "The lens is everything," photographers say. The aperture you use to see life can make or break the quality of your story. The best lens for life? In this book we suggest the Jesus lens. Not the lens of gender, generation, class, race, religion, or sexual orientation. The Jesus lens.

Behind this carnage of crusading crit, myth remains. Like the dolphins that returned to the clear canal waters in Venice during the COVID-19 shelter month of April 2020, what was once lost returns when given the chance. In the same way, story has returned. But in truth, it never left. While the value of history understood as story has been under attack, story remains never-ending. We cannot escape it, only engage it.

0.3 | Starting with the End in Mind

Begin with the end in mind... Know what God wants you to do.

—Rick Warren, in his last sermon as senior pastor of Saddleback Church

There is an aphorism that says, "Start with the end in mind," which is both bromide and brilliant. We all have a set of assumptions or convictions we make about the world. These assumptions are not an exercise we solve on a whiteboard; they are already held. We don't see our own deepest convictions because we live inside them. They are the story we tell ourselves. A good writer or detective can tell a person her story based on the dialect in her voice, the dirt under her nails, and the device sticking out of her pocket. Our convictions are our religion.

The Declaration of Independence of the United States of America is remarkable in part because of the story it tells: life, liberty, and the pursuit of happiness. We lose sight of the context of these revolutionary words. When a people group was subject to the whims of an absolute authority, "life" was not something to be taken for granted. Yet, amid existential threat, the writers dared to tell one another, and the world, a different story.

Their revolutionary action is also remarkable because its authors knew that the end they named would drive the behavior that followed. Our story is our guide: where we think we are going in life determines the actions we make today. We make our most significant life decisions based on the truths we hold to be self-evident. One naturally follows the other. You live what you believe about the end; our end becomes our purpose. Thus, this book is about both what will happen at the end of the age and about what is happening in the world today. You cannot separate one from the other.

In the old days, an intellectual "dialect" was known to the learned as *theology*, where theology simply means the study of "God," whether understood to refer to the God of the three monotheistic religions or symbolically and anthropologically to represent questions of ultimate value. Theology was once known as the "queen of all sciences" because the highest form of debate was the discussion of questions of ultimate value and importance. Theology was the "why" of life; science was lesser because it was simply the "what" of life.

Beginning in the mid nineteenth century, as we will discuss, this began to change. Empirical thinking became so dominant that for many, it was not only the *what* of life but a *way* of life. We developed a philosophy of science. Of course, not every scientist understands science as the means to answer questions of ultimate value. Stephen Hawking, for example, argued that there is no longer any such thing as a philosophy of science.[22] Yet in our world today, for the most part, science has replaced theology as the umbrella epistemology and academic discipline over which we analyze every other discipline or means of knowing. Meanwhile, theology has been relegated to the broom closet. Most people no longer think of theology when they consider the ultimate questions of life. Instead, we use the milquetoast term "worldview." But the consequences are the same.

Some will say religion is dangerous and should be abolished, but this is a "religious" statement, if religion is shorthand for the story we tell ourselves. To paraphrase political analyst Ross Douthat, what we have today is not so much no religion as bad religion, or religion that tries to hide behind scientific sunglasses and a hat.[23] Empiricism is a religion because it has become for many not a methodology but a life story. There was a recent period, a supposed end of history, when some tried to claim that questions of ultimate meaning had become less important, but the events of the early twenty-first century have proven once again that theology never ceased to matter. In fact, it matters now more than ever.

The story we hold to be self-evident is important because it is public. Our varied purposes affect one another, and all of creation. If your story has a bad end, the decisions you make today are not only dangerous to yourself, but destructive and harmful to society. It is no small anecdote, for example, to find a US presidential adviser citing apocalyptic literature. While the story for some ends with nothing but decaying personal possessions, the worst characters of history operated from something far more dangerous: false endings of entire civilizations. Hitler used the German church to justify his dark vision. ISIS believes they are interpreting the Koran properly. The worst actors, no matter how monstrous, are merely seeking the end of their story.

Thus, the most important thing we can do is to name the end properly. Shakespearean plays end in comedy or tragedy, depending on the ends the actors have in mind. False endings lead down rough roads to tragic denouements; good endings come from right stories, which lead to life-giving visions. Let us take the right road toward a good end.

0.4 | The End Is Completion

O Lord,
Give us the vision to dream the unknowns—
the naivete to believe they exist,
the faith of first steps forward thrown
in paths of resolute grace: to stay the course
when, even to revision the vision,
brings collision, division, and derision.
Amen.

To ask about The End is also to ask about the future. What sets humans apart from animals is a concept of past, present, and future. What sets Christians apart from the pack is a concept of how God comes to us from the future, through the past, into the present. Christians have spilled a lot of ink trying to go the other way and predict the future, both of which are invariably wrong for one reason: we extrapolate current trends and trajectories outward in linear fashion. The reality is, events function more like a network, or a sine wave, or a spiral.

Case in point: the development of modern medicine in fighting pathogens. In 1979 the World Health Organization announced that smallpox had been eradicated worldwide, save for a single strand of virus locked away in a lab behind double-paned glass and guarded by professionals in hazmat suits. Global media declared infectious disease a sign of some previous, less enlightened age. Forty years later, the world has dealt with a pandemic that wouldn't quit mutating, with rising fears about a new era of super-resistant strains. Disease, as it turns out, has not gotten on board with our rosiest views of progress. There is no end to endemic.

As we will point out, the end is not just about the future. A future-only focus is as incomplete as a future-ready bluster is fallacious. The end is the future, but it is also the past and the present. The more accurate way to think about the end is not the future, but the denouement—the resolution or the completion of the story.

I'll tell you . . . one thing that no Cabinet has ever had is a Secretary of the Future, and there are no plans at all for my grandchildren and my great grandchildren.

—novelist Kurt Vonnegut

All stories share a basic framework, which we can at the least agree includes a beginning, a middle, and an end. As you read the story of this book, you are somewhere in the middle of your life. Our sense experience confirms only the infinite present. Being stuck in a perpetual act 2, it is quite natural for us to wonder what happens at the end. Like the disciples, this book asks questions about the end of the story—the grand, cosmic story, which we as Christians find in the stories of the Scriptures. Thus, this book is for those with faith in Jesus, although our analysis of culture may find resonance with others, as well.

One piece of advice storytellers give to budding writers is: when creating a story, begin at the end, and work backward: "Mapping out your destination first allows you to navigate the rest of the story as you write."[24] This brings us to the end. All of us know someone who starts a new book by peeking at the last page first, because he or she must know what happens in the end. We think that spoils the fun, but it reveals a basic truth: we all want to know what happens in the end. With a peek at the end, we can navigate the journey with assurance.

Hence the pressing pertinence of the disciples' question to Jesus, "When is the end of the age?" The disciples' questions are not without answers. We already know the end, because Jesus has revealed it: the end is the presence of God and our transfiguration into a new humanity, when we, with unveiled faces, contemplate the Lord's glory and are changed into ever-increasing glory (see 2 Corinthians 3:18). This new humanity, this new body, is what we become in the kingdom of God.

The end is also a question of destination. The end isn't about future or place, per se, but about purpose, about mission, about presence. The church's ongoing obsession with eschatology isn't wrong so much as it is irrelevant. If we name and live our purpose, we find our destination. So, the question about what happens in the end begs a beginning question: What is our purpose? or What is our mission?

It may be the devil or it may be the Lord
but you're gonna have to serve somebody.

—Bob Dylan, "Gotta Serve Somebody"

The answer to the question of purpose is found in authority. The end of authority is authorship. Every story has an author. That author is your authority. To whomever you give authority, you give authorship to write your life story. We have a choice—to give authority to our fears, to our technology, to our traditions, to our celebrities, to our escapist fantasies, or we can give authority to Jesus to author our story. The making of the self is one way, the Jesus way; the making up of the self is a world away, the world's way. Jesus has all authority on heaven and earth. The question of the future comes down to a question about Jesus. Do we let him author our life story? If the answer is yes, then we already know the future.

Thus, this book is ultimately about the kingdom of God: the presence of God, our purpose as humankind, and the authority of Jesus Christ.

0.5 | The End Is Our Beginning

The End is our beginning. The endgame of life is a paradox.

The good news is that we get to see how it all ends. We get to be a part of the end. We will be there for the finale of the last act of God's story. Longing for "the life of the world to come" is what inspires us to live for "the life of the world."

The gospel invitation is addressed to the individual in community. Jesus introduces and welcomes the individual into a community whose fulcrum and fulfillment is an End called Jubilee. If Jubilee is the goal and end of history, the Bible still insists that Jubilee is present with us now. The kingdom of God, prophesied in the past, is here now: "I am the one who is, who always was, and who is still to come—the Almighty One" (Revelation 1:8).

The essence of Christianity is teleology. The end is not just near, but now. The end is among us, within us, around us. Jubilee is an event, and Christianity is the presence and process of that event, the completion of all events, even of history itself. The fulfillment of time is not limited to the end of time. The fulfillment of time can be experienced in here-and-now moments, little glimpses of eternity, little tastes of the heavenly banquet where Jesus hosts the table.

Jesus is Jubilee, and the church is the presence of Jesus as Jubilee in the here and now. Jesus began his mission with a teleological declaration and a teleological meal. The declaration came when "the scroll of the prophet Isaiah was handed to him" (Luke 4:17 NIV).

> Unrolling it, He found the place where it was written: The Spirit of the Lord is on Me, because He has anointed Me to bring good news to the poor. He has sent Me to proclaim release to the captives and recovery of sight to the blind, to set free those who are oppressed, to proclaim the year of the Lord's favor. (Luke 4:17b–19)

That phrase "to proclaim the year of the Lord's favor" was a teleological one pointing to the end-time reign of God. In the Jewish calendar, Jubilee falls in the fiftieth year. The ram's horn is blown, everyone goes home, debts are forgiven, prisoners are released, relationships are restored, and the grace of God covers every iota of the universe.

Jesus began his ministry announcing The End, the Year of Jubilee. He himself was The End, the Alpha and Omega, the Beginning and the End (Revelation 22:13). He promised to be with us "to the end" (Matthew 28:20).

Jesus also began his ministry with a teleological meal. The whole of Jesus' mission with the Twelve, in fact, was framed with teleological meals.

Jesus began his mission with the Twelve by conducting his first miracle, a provision of a feast. Jesus ended his mission with the Twelve by presiding at the Last Supper with the provision of a feast. Jesus spent the bulk of his mission with the Twelve teaching and eating at meals. During the Last Supper ("while they were eating," Matthew 26:26), which was a full dinner (Gr., deipnon)—bean stew, lamb, olives, bitter herbs, a fish sauce, unleavened bread, dates, and aromatized wine—Jesus took the bread and said, "This is my body" (Luke 22:19), after which ("after the supper," v. 20) Jesus took the cup and said, "This is my blood." Then he told the disciples, "I confer on you a kingdom, . . . so that you may eat and drink at my table in my kingdom" (vv. 29–30 niv).

Jubilee is a time of feasting and drinking at the banquet table of heaven (see Isaiah 25:6–8; Revelation 19:9). Every meal is a festivity of the future and an earnest of The End in the Here and Now. If Jesus is Jubilee, then the heart and soul of Christianity is teleology. The end of our common story is comedy, not tragedy, but comedy where the tragic and the trifling run cheek by jowl. The kingdom is Jubilee. Jubilee is the goal and end of history, its *telos*.

In this book, we ask three core questions: First, what happens at the end of our present age? Second, since for Christians this is so closely tied to our understanding of "the kingdom of God," what exactly is the kingdom of God? Third, like the disciples, we ask, what are the signs? What makes this book different is that most books on the kingdom ignore Jesus' most important word in describing the kingdom: *telos*. *Telos* is Greek for "the end." The kingdom is The End, the summation, the consummation, the completion, the purpose of human history. It is the end of the never-ending story.

The first miracle and the Last Supper are earnests of The End. The marriage banquet at the start, the marriage of the Passover Lamb at the end, are foretastes of the future when Jesus returns to the Table. "For whenever you eat this bread and drink this cup, you proclaim the Lord's death until he comes" (1 Corinthians 11:26). The Greek basis for "until" is unusual: *achri bou* means grammatically keeping an end in mind. The moment of the church's highest remembrance of the past is also its moment of greatest focus on the future. In every eucharistic experience, we are less pressed or pressurized by the past than incentivized and inspired by the future. Worship itself is a foretaste of future, a participation in the cosmic liturgy of heaven, which revolves around the Lamb (Jesus Christ). Here "on earth" we are enacting eternity, "as it is in heaven" (Matthew 6:10).

> *The very word paradox is paradoxical. Let the paradox be. Remember, after all, the Gospel is full of paradoxes, that man is himself a living paradox, and that according to the Fathers of the Church, the Incarnation is the supreme Paradox.*

> **—French Jesuit priest and theologian Henri de Lubac**

The Aramaic prayer "*maran atha*" literally conveys the three past-present-future tenses at once: Our Lord has come, our Lord is come now, our Lord will come. No wonder "maranatha" was connected to the eucharist by the church's earliest believers.[25] It may also be why Paul's first letter to the church at Corinth ends with "Maran atha." It was a segue to the fellowship meal that would have followed the reading of Paul's letter.[26]

"The End is our Beginning" is the paradox of Christian life. Where there is no paradox, there is no true Christianity. Orthodoxy is paradoxy. But paradox only works if there is an overarching higher mission, a metanarrative that can embrace and embed both opposites. The unified life has two sides to a single, living reality. We must be able to both separate and connect the ends.

All individuals need community.

Fire needs a fireplace.

Diversity needs unity.

Openness needs orderliness.

Innovation needs consolidation.

Liberal needs conservative.

Old needs new and new, old.

The earthly needs the heavenly.

The ethereal needs the eternal.

The end needs a beginning.

> A revelation is signaled by mystery, happiness by suffering, the certainty of faith by uncertainty, the ease of the paradoxical-religious life by its difficulty, the truth by absurdity.
>
> **—Soren Kierkegaard's footnote in Concluding Unscientific Postscript**

Jesus is always saying two contradictory but complementary things. The shadow of the cross is a paradox. The teleological heart of Christian faith is the union of the transcendent and the immanent, the vertical and the horizontal, the otherworldly and the this-worldly. To put any rift between them, or to divide them, is to push the self-destruct button.

Writing another book on the kingdom may seem redundant, or reckless, or really stupid. Yet despite the richness of our theological tradition, the church's understanding of the kingdom remains incomplete.[27] We are emboldened by the fact that the vast majority of what is written about the kingdom comes either from a perspective where kingdom is king, or from a future orientation where king is kingdom. Jesus is very clear that not only is the kingdom the end, but the kingdom is also now. The kingdom is present with us now in the risen Lord. Jesus is risen, rising, regnant: "It is finished" (John 19:30). Jesus is also very clear that the kingdom is wherever the king is. In short, the call and challenge to redefine "kingdom" is great.

The kingdom is come. The End is our beginning.

0.6 | The Story of This Book

To the disciples, it seemed that all Jesus offered them was a peek ahead, which perhaps is an indication that Jesus knew that if they knew, they would lose interest. Andrew Stanton, the Pixar director, says that stories make a promise. The promise is, they're going to take you to a great ending. Stanton has created some of the best films of the century on the premise that audiences want to work for their story; they don't just want to go through the paces. He says, "Don't give them four; give them two plus two."[28] If the plot goes static, the story dies. The formula for moving the plot forward is anticipation and uncertainty. Because we are human, it is the *not knowing* that keeps us glued to the screen. Curiosity is a defining human trait. Just ask Adam and Eve.

It also means that our orientation is toward a future from the present, not to the present from the future. Since the best way to find out the end is to go on the journey, this book is structured as a story. The plural protagonist of our book is us, and the thing we desire is a better world. We want The End to come with the promise, as John wrote in Revelation, that we will finally be free of mourning, tears, suffering, and pain. So, we go on a journey seeking The End.

Our book begins as all good stories do: with action. The action at hand is the cultural turmoil we collectively face. While interest in "The End" waxes and wanes over time, you, the storyreceiver, do not need us to tell you that we are now living through a time of peak wax. Google Trends reports that searches for "the end" in the United States are at 100 on a scale of 1 to 100, and this was before Russia's invasion of Ukraine.[29] There is an ongoing apocalyptic strain in Russian history, literature, and thought that combines politics, pragmatism, sectarianism, utopia, and apocalypse. You can hear it in Putin's comment in 2018 contending that MAD (Mutually Assured Destruction) was not reciprocal between Russia and the West, because Russians would immediately go to heaven as martyrs, but the Wicked West wouldn't have the time to repent, so they would be sent directly to hell.

There are also apocalyptophiles aplenty in the US. While digital mogul Elon Musk fires off new rockets to the moon from his private city, Starbase, Texas, to fulfill fantasies of a techno-utopian future, economic and political turmoil rock the globe. Book printing requirements render it impossible to provide a recent enough example, as dystopian stories seem to appear on our Twitter feeds and television screens each day. In fact, as we write this, it is impossible to know with any degree of certainty what sort of future you will be living in as you consider these ideas. The dawn of the third decade of the twenty-first century has been a time in which political and social developments come with shocking speed and surprising severity.

As disciples of Jesus, we already know the end. Yet, we continue to chase alternate endings with tragic, dead-end consequences. Throughout the first act of the book, we describe our cultural turmoil, and then engage in a little backstory—how we got to where we are. Then, as with all stories, we go on a journey. But we must explore several stops in pursuit of the end, each of which will result in frustration, but each of which, like every heresy, is based on an important truth. We will explore six false narratives with tragic endings. In brief, here they are:

apocalypticism—the false ending that we are headed toward disaster

utopianism—the false ending that we are creating a perfect world

traditionalism—the false ending that we should return to the beginning

ahistoricism—the false ending that there is no story at all

millennialism—the false ending that we can escape the journey or build the kingdom ourselves

messianism—the false ending that a strong man will save us from living through the story

Each results in a tragic ending. We use each story line to identify what the kingdom is not.

You may come to this book with a sense of urgency and fear about current events, which is quite understandable. The fear you feel is because of rising tension in our shared story. The church has participated in each of these false endings to varying degrees, and we have been the masters of some (or none, as it were). Each offers a false ending because, bluntly, we are imperfect storytellers. We keep trying to craft the story ourselves, and it never works. Like a Spielbergian drama that stretches the tension to unimaginable lengths, each seems to be rising along with the others into one giant superstorm today. Any one of the six has the power to disrupt the fragile frames of society and shake its scaffolding. But together they may be unprecedented in their strength, the winds of change a rare F5, with power to raze and uproot entire civilizations.

After the rising tension of these six false narratives, we reach the midpoint of our story. In story structure, the midpoint is where a major event happens. For our journey, the midpoint is the realization that we have been listening to bad guides. Why do we keep getting the story wrong? We keep acting on bad advice. In story structure, the protagonist's journey is guided by a mentor or sage, an Obi-Wan–like character who provides us the path for our journey. If the sage is wise and good, the story ends well. If the sage is not good, the story ends poorly.

The problem is that we've been on bad paths with bad guides. How do we find the one true guide who will lead us to a good ending? In other words, who authors the story? This is a question of truth. To understand the ending of our shared story, we must return to a very basic question, once thought solved. As Pontius Pilate asked, what is truth? From truth we decide what is authoritative, or who authors our lives. The common problem that drives each false ending is the lie that truth is a proposition. Truth is in fact a person: Jesus.

When we get this right, then we can begin to name what the kingdom is. Each of the six false narratives ultimately fails because each is a poor understanding of Jesus' signs, stories, and teachings to his disciples. In none of the church's visions of the kingdom realized does Jesus fully occupy the throne of the "author of Life" (Acts 3:15) and the "author and finisher of our faith" (Hebrews 12:2 KJV). Jesus is the author, not we, the one to whom God gives all authority in heaven and on earth. The second half of the book fleshes out six answers to the false narratives: the kingdom is under Jesus' authority, it is the fullness time, it is material and real, it gives us hope, it gives us joy, and it gives us peace. We close with some applications and suggestions for living the Jesus story.

Write on my heart every word . . .

—Fanny Crosby, "Tell Me the Story of Jesus" (1880)

A caveat: from the kingdom of God to eschatology to millennialism and everything in between, the field in which this book plays is massive, and it is inevitable that we will shortchange something. We approached the subject more culturally than theologically, though we did address theological implications throughout. We have tried to address all the traditional doctrines, even the harrowing of hell. At some point, space constraints must come to bear.

For the follower of Jesus, understanding these forces is of great theological, pastoral, ethical, and ecclesiological value. Jesus' answer to the disciples' question provided hints of the age to come. He described the struggles of nation-states against one another, a state of emergency, and the emergence of a new state. As political analyst Martin Gurri observes, authority is a variable of power, which is a relationship between the governor and the governed, and depends on matters of trust, faith, and fear, "appointed variously but involving both sides."[30] So who or what is authoritative in your life? The perpetual waxing and waning of history is symptomatic of the rising and falling action of story itself, which is the same as the rising and falling of a single human life. When we put people—ourselves and one

| Prologue | Long Time Coming: The Story

another—in positions of power, we become subject to the same tragic story line of human life. We choose our own adventures, and the plot goes on in a perpetual act 2, like a bad soap opera, always waiting for denouement.

Authority cannot be forced in any kingdom. It needs the faith of the people to exist, and we the people—inside and outside the church—have tried to do kingdom without a king. Thus, our participation and practice—our faith—is a key component of the story. We participate in and practice the coming of the kingdom, not through our works and engineering, but through our faith in the author of life. Authority is a question of authorship. Who authors your life story?

Jesus answered the disciples' final questions about the end with a description of the age to come. Contrary to popular belief, the end of the story is not *eschaton*, but *telos*. *Eschaton* is plot, but *telos* is resolution, or what storytellers call the *denouement*. Near the fulfillment of Matthew's gospel, the author offers a cutaway shot from the protagonist Jesus to Peter, lurking in the shadows (see Matthew 26:57–58). Despite all that had happened, Peter needed to know the end of the story. It has been said that in the writing process all storytellers have but one task, to answer the basic question of the reader: What happens? Radio announcer Paul Harvey made this question famous by offering "the *rest* . . . of the story." The whole story of God as captured in the Bible boils down to this one question: What happens in the end? Life is a story, and we want to know the end.

The only way to know the end is to know the author, Jesus. Before his ascension, Jesus said, "All authority in heaven and on earth has been given to me" (Matthew 28:18). The one to whom is given all authority is the one to whom authority best be given. There is always one place you set up on, stand on, and step from. That "place" or "standpoint" is authoritative in one's life story. We all launch propositions from a place of presupposition. The only question is, what is your place or position? Phrased another way, what is your "standpoint?" What is your authority? What is your presupposition from which a conversation or confession is launched? Everyone stands somewhere to see. Everyone has a "stand" from which they point. Why you stand where you're standing is the answer to the question, who is your authority? Everyone needs an alpha and vaunts an alpha. Even if the alpha is yourself, and no one else, you still have an alpha. Humans were designed for the Alpha and Omega alpha.

The 1994 Disney animated musical *The Lion King* boasts a moment where the King of the Pride Lands, Mufasa, says to his son, Simba, Wherever the light hits, there is the kingdom.[31] Exactly. Wherever the light of the world falls, there is the kingdom. To live in the kingdom is to live in Jesus' light. We lift up the "good news" of a kingdom above brought to us below in the story of Jesus' birth, death, resurrection, and ascension. The one to whom you give authority becomes the author of your life. It is only when we assign authorship to Jesus, and let him write the story of our lives, that we can end the vicious cycle of false narratives that lead to suffering and destruction in our lives and in the world today.

```
5   1   5       6   9               6   8   9   8       4   7   3                   5
2       8       7               8       7       1   5       4   4                   3
    2   9   3   6   7   5   8   1       8   3   9       5       6   2   3
    3   6   7       8       8           1       1           8   5   1   6       8   2   4   5
5       2   3   1   8       8       7           8           5   1       5   5   1   5   2   4
    1   9   8   3   3       6   3   1   2   7   9       8   2       8   8   9       8   6   9
1   1       7   1   4   8               1   2       8   9   6   8   7   1           1   8   8
9       2       9           3   9   6       2       8           1   4           4       6   8
8   1       7   5   3       7           1   4       4           9   4   5       4   9   3       7   9
9   5       6           7   8   8   9       7                   7   9       8       7   8   1
```

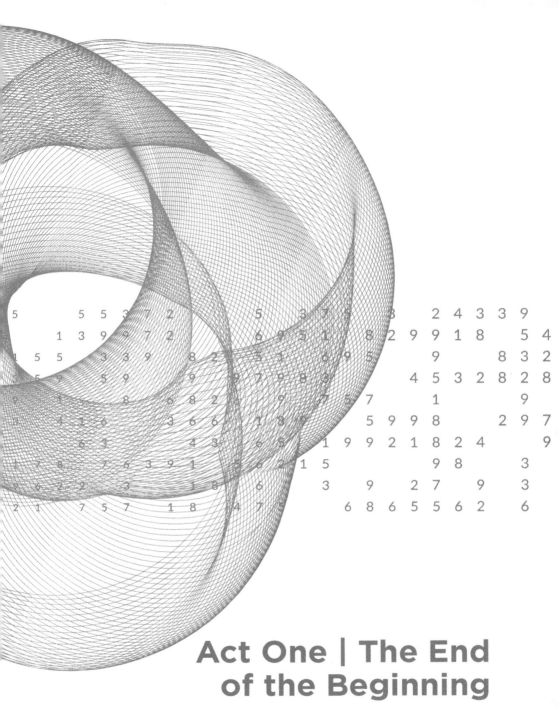

Act One | The End
of the Beginning

The Present Age

| CHAPTER 1 |
OUT OF TIME: THE FALSE ENDING OF APOCALYPTICISM

Is the world going to be destroyed?

In its most common understanding, apocalypticism is reading current events considering biblical prophecy to discern signs of the "end times." In all ages, you can find clear-and-present-danger warning signs that the world is falling apart if you look hard enough. Apocalyptic fervor is high today because you don't have to look hard to find those signs. The Doomsday Clock is currently set to 100 seconds to midnight, or global catastrophe. Some seek to accelerate the end through tearing down the political and economic structures of civilization, from nihilistic or eschatological motivation. But what would happen in the void?

The story of the Black Death has already shown that an apocalyptic end neither destroys the age nor inaugurates a more glorious future. Whenever culture seems to be in decline and the future uncertain, or the future is certain with technology our savior, interest in the "end times" mushrooms. Jesus talks about the end, too, and promises that those who endure to the end will be saved. But he is also clear that the kingdom of God is not birthed by destruction or evil.

Apocalypticism, as it is commonly known, is a false ending because it is self-defeating. Properly understood, "apocalypse" is not an eschatological destruction but the revelation of God's social order. This begs the question, what does Jesus mean by "the end"?

1.1 | The Great Mortality

The first warning sign was a large bubo, usually in the groin or armpit depending on where the flea had bitten you. It would grow rapidly, perhaps as big as a tennis ball. When it started making strange gurgling sounds, high fever followed, accompanied by vomiting, diarrhea, and a strange sensitivity to light. You would also develop "God's tokens," or bruise-like blotches on the skin, as your capillaries burst. Your extremities might turn black. As the disease coursed through your body, you might become delirious, with episodes of manic shouting or laughing. A pervasive stench would ooze from your breath, sweat, urine, and pus that expelled from your body.[32] Within a week, you would be dead.[33]

The bubonic plague was a merciful kind of affliction. More sinister variations infected the lungs or blood and brought almost certain death within hours. Some people went to bed healthy and never woke up.

Entire villages died. In the end, no one knows how many or what percentage of people succumbed to the beckoning of what we now call the Black Death of 1347–1352. Estimates range from 40 to 60 percent of all people living in Europe, the Middle East, and North Africa.[34] Florence, Italy, a center of culture and a city in which nine out of every ten people perished, did not recover its population for five hundred years. Bodies stacked up in the streets, and the reckless made a fortune as impromptu gravediggers. Ships floated on the open seas with no living souls to guide them. It was a catastrophe beyond our imagination, the closest recorded history has come to a true "apocalypse" of the sort imagined in film and on television.

Pandemics come in two varieties: influenza and plague. The COVID-19 pandemic is influenza. Whereas influenza is the light tank of natural warfare, covering lots of ground but with lesser guns, plague is the heavy tank, which comes over the horizon slowly but with devastating force. Plague pandemics are believed to take decades to ferment and arise from a confluence of destructive factors.[35]

While the Hebrew Scriptures and other ancient texts hint at outbreaks (see, for example, 1 Samuel 5:6), the Black Death is one of three recognized global plague pandemics in history. The first occurred during the century after the fall of Rome, and the third during the nineteenth century. The Black Death was by far the worst of the three. According to the Foster scale, a sort of Richter scale of human suffering, two of the three highest disasters in human history were the two world wars of the past century. The third was the Black Death.[36] A quarter of the world's population died within four years. Were it to occur with today's global demographics, this fourteenth-century pandemic would kill 1.9 billion people.[37]

The plague was so devastating it seemed like an "apocalypse," or a surreal, end-of-the-world experience. A common understanding of plague in the fourteenth century was that it was the judgment of a wrathful God. Agnolo di Tura, an Italian tax collector and shoemaker, recorded the feeling of many of his neighbors when he wrote, "It is the end of the world."[38] With the death rate so high, the "apocalypse" of death and dying became a dominant cultural theme of fourteenth century Europe. For example, though it is now seen as the prime agent of a new dawn of human civilization and flourishing, the printing press was originally a sort of photocopier for existing texts, and one of its early bestsellers was *The Art of Dying* (Ars Moriendi), which achieved 100 editions in fifteenth-century Germany. Dante wrote his famous *Inferno*, from which we get our contemporary images of hell, during this period.

The Black Death subsumed what had been a three-century period of revival, prosperity, and flourishing for medieval Europe. Coming out of the "Early Middle Ages," a moniker questionably better than the former "Dark Ages," new technologies were emerging, resource production was improving, and the population of Europe quadrupled. The positive vibes coincided with what is known as the *little climactic optimum*, a period of global warming that began around 950 CE. But the summer effect was wearing off by 1300. Europe would not surpass its population again until the year 1850.

Periods of prosperity tend to mask problems that bite back. For example, the prosperity of the Early Middle Ages led to an increase in trade.[39] The resulting mobility increased intercultural exposure. People—and germs—found new travel hosts. The bacterium, which originated in modern-day north Kyrgyzstan in the late 1330s, eventually made its way to western Europe.[40] The only thing more feared than the contagion of plague during the medieval period was the contagion of being slain in the Spirit, where the contortions of dancing and shouting and writhing quickly spread from traveling bands of penitents to whole villages and families.[41]

One way to understand both the social and scientific cultural context for the Black Death, and perhaps discover clues for other crises, is through the lens of a Malthus catastrophe. English cleric and economist Thomas Robert Malthus (1766–1834) is credited with observing that population growth, which is exponential, always outpaces resource growth, which is linear.[42] The resulting imbalance inevitably leads to what social scientists call "corrections in population," a euphemism for really bad times. Corrections are never clean or seemly; they come through famine, disease, and war, sometimes swiftly and violently.

Innovations such as agronomist Norman Borlaug's Green Revolution may exponentially increase resource production and mitigate the imbalance for a period.[43] But this does not last, as the resulting resource abundance triggers additional (exponential) population growth. The effect is akin to an overly leveraged household that spends a sudden financial windfall on new goods and services that require additional expense to maintain, which make its long-term financial situation even worse. As narrative historian John Kelly writes, "explosive growth always comes with a price."[44]

Though they missed the signs and did not know it, Europeans in the year 1300 were due for a Malthusian "correction." In the decades before the arrival of the bubonic plague, warning signals pointing to an overextended culture were popping up in many places. Foremost was an overextension of resources. But other signs were present, including a high degree of violence and what would be, to modern sensibilities, an outrageously onerous level of filth and waste. Medieval urban environments were cesspools of garbage and excrement, to the point that street names in Paris were inspired by *merde*, the French word for feces. Personal hygiene was no better. One historian reports a disregard for the body that is shocking to modern ears:

> Friar Albert, a monk in Boccaccio's Decameron, displays a more typical medieval attitude toward personal hygiene. "I shall do something today that I have not done for a very long time," the friar announces cheerfully. "I shall undress myself." When the assassinated Thomas à Becket was stripped naked, an English chronicler reports that vermin "boiled over like water in a simmering cauldron" from his body.[45]

Between resource overextension, environmental stress, stratified social conditions, violence, and ignorance about personal hygiene, the onset of a period of plague is unsurprising.

The Great Mortality was as apocalyptic an event as recorded history has known. Yet, the Black Death wasn't a black swan, but a gray rhino.[46] In fact, black swans really don't exist. Their arrival is obvious, for those who can read the signs and see through the fog. Is our current world exhibiting similar warning signs? Are we nearing the end of the world, a moment in which we are going to be destroyed?

1.2 | American Carnage

The Black Death was a nadir of humankind's ability to respond to pathogens. The New World was conquered not by soldiers but by smallpox; not by guns but by germs, such as the bubonic plague, measles, influenza, and other biological weapons that functioned as mass killers. The native Mayans, Incas, Aztecs, and Floridians fought off the first European invaders but were helpless against the diseases they brought with them. At least half the populations of Mexico and Peru were killed by infectious weapons of mass destruction.[47] In the early seventeenth century (between 1616 and 1619), visiting fishermen brought bubonic plague to New England, killing off as many as 90 percent of its inhabitants. When the Pilgrims arrived in Massachusetts, they encountered not thriving native communities but vacant dwellings and empty fields.

As we noted in the prologue, since that time, medicine has exponentially increased our knowledge and improved our quality of life. Yet despite the triumphs of modern medicine, such as the eradication of smallpox, COVID-19 is a clear sign that diseases do not fade away easily. While COVID-19 has been in many ways the global pandemic predicted by prognosticators such as Bill Gates, it is not the deadliest outbreak of the century. That dishonor belongs to the Ebola virus. Compared to COVID-19's mortality rate of around 2 percent,[48] Ebola's hovers around an unbelievable 50 percent. While Ebola was first recognized in the 1970s, the West African outbreak of 2013 was a worst-case scenario, as it appeared and spread through one of the poorest, most underdeveloped, and war-torn areas of the world. The spread was so terrifyingly fast that in September 2014, Liberia's defense minister, Brownie Samukai, told the UN Security Council that his country was on the brink of collapse.[49] People lay in the street dying in a country with inadequate infrastructure and professional expertise to deal with the virus.

Of the three West African countries most affected by Ebola, Liberia had the most challenging situation. Long one of the most impoverished countries on earth and devastated by a civil war that had ended a decade earlier, Liberia had practically no transportation system and only fifty doctors serving a population of 4 million people. With the small network of health-care workers dying, and with little attention from the outside world, Western relief agencies, such as Doctors Without Borders and Samaritan's Purse, were forced to the front lines of the epidemic.[50] Corruption, hunger, poverty, local custom, and distrust of industrialized medicine were all factors that led to 11,000 Ebola cases in a country of just over 4 million people.[51]

What kept the virus from spreading out of control was its limited contagion window. Spread occurred only in the exchange of bodily fluids, and the most contagious patients were those sweating profusely just before death. The small heroic crew of medical workers were able to overcome custom and control the environment. The West African Ebola epidemic was finally officially declared over in June 2016, forty-two days after the last known case was reported negative.[52]

Yet flare-ups continue. Distrust of industrialized medicine combined with a lack of medical modernization in areas traditionally affected by corruption, hunger, and poverty have set the stage for further outbreaks. In February 2021 the World Health Organization deployed a medical team to respond to a new outbreak reported in Guinea, near where the 2013 outbreak began.[53]

To the Western world, the reemergence of deadly diseases has seemed like a "latter-day plague," not to mention a drag on the lofty promises of modern medicine. For centuries before and after the Black Death, deadly diseases had been commonly understood as a part of life. Plagues ripped through cities with ruthless regularity. Shakespeare wrote *King Lear*, *Macbeth*, and *Antony and Cleopatra* in a single year while quarantined from the London plague of 1606.[54]

Surely, we have progressed past such dystopian medieval scenes. We were not supposed to find so familiar the words found in Daniel Defoe's *A Journal of the Plague Year* (1722), where the narrator ends his account with the woozy wonder of survival, the thrill of coming out of lockdown, walking the streets again, and going out to eat in late 1665 and 1666. One by one, Londoners emerged from their houses, jubilant and vociferous after months of seclusion. "These were all strangers to one another. But such salutations as these were frequent in the street every day; and despite loose behavior, the very common people went along the streets giving God thanks for their deliverance."[55]

The reemergence of destructive forces once thought vanquished has startled and shifted the public mindset. Disease is just one example. Rather than things getting better, it seems in many ways that things are getting worse and may even be falling apart. The effect goes far beyond the field of medicine. Indeed, a defining theme of the still-young century is the imminent demise of Western civilization. Pew Research polling for the summer of 2020 showed widespread anger and fear. Only 12 percent of Americans were "satisfied with the way things are going in this country."[56] No wonder we are a scratchy, itchy, thin-skinned, on-edge people, on the prowl for things to fall out over rather than to fall in around or get behind.

Every day it seems there is a new doomsday drama, an end-of-world movie, a horror or deathliness series, or science-fiction disaster novel. The zombification of the culture may be the most obvious apocalyptic symbol and symptom of domicide that dominates our existence. We project on zombies our mindlessness, placelessness, speechlessness, and heedlessness.

Could it be that humankind is now so alienated from itself, as German philosopher Walter Benjamin noted in his classic essay "The Work of Art in the Age of Mechanical Reproduction" (1936), "that it can even experience its own annihilation as a supreme aesthetic pleasure"?[57]

Dissatisfaction with the status quo has peppered public discourse for most of the century. President Donald Trump's inaugural address in 2016 was dark, with language of "rusted-out factories," "tombstones," and "American carnage."[58] (Compare this to Reagan's appropriation of Puritan leader John Winthrop's 1630 "city on a hill" imagery fewer than forty years earlier.) Trump's vision of America could even be described as politically nihilist, in that his description of Washington, DC as a "swamp" suggested nothing in the existing order was worthy of saving.

But cries about the end of America and the Disuniting States of America are not just characteristic of the political Right. While Trump is brusquer and more of a bull in a china shop than his predecessor, President Barack Obama seemed to be no fan of the existing order either. His administration's take on American political life was deconstructive at best, nihilistic at worst, inasmuch as its goal was to "agitate, aggravate, fray, and separate."[59] In recent years, more and more people on the right and on the left, populists and progressives, seem willing to put the end of the world on the table and gamble all human life upon it.

The destructive mood of the age belies facile political analysis. While USAmericans have remained remarkably consistent in self-identifying as "conservative" and "liberal,"[60] dissatisfaction has remained remarkably high, regardless of which party holds the presidency.[61] "Declaring 'The End of America' has become a parlor game for thermostatic social media pundits," says Miami Herald columnist Leonard Pitts Jr., who collates the thoughts of several who claim the end of America is nigh and suggests it is ending because it couldn't get the race question right.[62] The race question is as embedded in the apocalyptic mood as it is into the history of America. Initially, racial protests in the wake of the murder of George Floyd in April 2020 seemed inchoate and without strategic purpose. The protests in and of themselves were enough. Online, many shared a line from Martin Luther King Jr.: "a riot is the language of the unheard."[63] Gradually, the protests changed to a focus on police brutality and the removal of statues. But the protesting public seemed less interested in policy than in deconstructing culture. Political nihilism finds nothing good in the existing social order and seeks destruction itself as an aspirational ideal.[64]

Of course, deadly disease, political turmoil, and ongoing frustrations about racism and inequality aren't the only triggers. Existential angst is rising with the threat of climate change, the rise in global population, and other seemingly intractable problems facing global civilization. In 1977, President Carter directed thirteen federal agencies to predict the future for long-range planning. *The Global 2000 Report* gave this summary of their findings:

> The time: the year 2000. The place: Earth, a desolate planet slowly dying of its own accumulating follies. Half the forests are gone; sand dunes spread where fertile farmlands once lay. Nearby, a million species of plants, birds, insects, and animals have vanished. Yet man is propagating so fast that his cities have grown as large as his nations of a century before. The bleak scenario is not science fiction, but a detailed look at the real worlds' future.[65]

A lot of what was predicted here has come true. But consider our situation now: less than 150 years ago, the world population was fewer than 2 billion people, and there were only forty-seven nations. Now, with the world population near 8 billion, there are almost two hundred nations. Six new nations have developed in the last decade alone. The increase in the number of nations correlates to an increase in the number of wars between nations. A new study shows that war is steadily increasing along with the rise of the number of nations.[66] The drug crisis is pervasive and perverse. The way we handle it is by blocking it out. There are now 50 percent more injection drug users in San Francisco than the number of students enrolled in the city's fifteen public high schools.[67]

As the population increases exponentially, the economic output of people increases exponentially. A chart at the *Economist* of a population-weighted history of the last two millennia demonstrated that 28 percent of the lives lived on planet Earth since the birth of Christ happened in the last one hundred years. There have been more years lived in the twenty-first century already than in all the seventeenth century.[68] (Maybe the "information explosion" is really just a "people explosion").

Some futurists predict we will reach 10 billion Earthlings in three generations. But the line is not pointing straight up. One hint about predicting the future is that it is never a straight-line extension of present trends. Another factor to consider is the fertility rate, or the rate at which the world grows. Currently, a rate of 2.1 keeps the population flat, where the number of births and the number of deaths is roughly equal. Of course, this is not fixed either, as advances in medicine and access to medical treatment increase life expectancy in First World and Third World nations. Thirty years ago, the world fertility rate was 6.0. Now it is 2.6.[69] What does that mean? According to conservative magazine the *Weekly Standard*, in an article on the economic problems of low fertility rates, "Populations increase even as fertility rates collapse, until the last above-replacement generation dies, after which the population begins contracting. The rate of contraction speeds up as each generation passes. No society has ever experienced prosperity in the wake of contracting population."[70]

In other words, nations get old. Of course, a country can reverse course and begin to have more babies, such as what happened in America's post-war baby boom, when the fertility rates jumped almost to an amazing 4.0. But there is a point of no return on low fertility rates from which demographers believe it is impossible to recover. China is already on an alarming aging pattern because of their one-child policy, which they now are feverishly trying to reverse. Why the urgency? Demographics. The nation currently has 5.4 workers to support every retiree in China. In forty years, because of its one-child policy, they will have only 1.6 workers to support every retiree, which is woefully economically insufficient.

It has been more than two hundred years since Malthus made his observation about the exponential rise of populations rubbing against the linear rise of resources, but it has held true. When a population has exponentially exceeded its resources, and then it begins to contract, two future options seem to emerge, neither of which look good. One future option is the continued exponential growth of the world population, with the incumbent growth of war and natural resource depletion. The other is a leveling and decline of the world population brought on by low fertility rates, which will result in a shrinking economy and an inability to sustain social programs. Threat of resource depletion leads to war, as well: "the likelihood of war is shaped by the paths of prices and quantities."[71]

Combine these grim economic realities with other factors, such as climate crisis and social inequity, and you begin to see what we're facing today on a global scale. We call it "decivilization." One engine of the decivilizing forces is a deeply schizophrenic culture marked by a raging apocalypticism combined with a rampaging utopianism.

Most apocalyptic literature makes astrology look respectable. Apocalypticism is evident not just in rape-and-death cults like ISIS but also in the environmental movement and its twelve-years-to-doom prophecies as embodied in "Extinction Rebellion" and the lifting up of Ebola and other environmental horsemen of the apocalypse as "the revenge of the rainforest." The dangers of utopian, millenarian movements, and the claims to moral certainty and cries of moral outrage have been well researched, even by those who were once participants in them.[72]

There is a constant in US history: a terrifying sense of a society on the brink of catastrophe and collapse, besieged by real or imagined enemies. Richard Hofstadter explored these sensibilities in his classic text, *The Paranoid Style of American Politics* (1964), a constant he called "the pornography of the Puritan." The greatest disasters in human history have been born of apocalypticism and utopianism. But when the two occur simultaneously, as we see today, it becomes a powder keg. All Western civilization, once the beacon of history and bulwark against barbarianism, now seems imperiled. All the world, for that matter.

In addition to the question of resources is the question of our current philosophical state. Jacques Derrida, in "On an Apocalyptic Tone Recently Adopted in Philosophy," one of his later essays, spoke to the theme of apocalyptic fervor in philosophy.[73] This apocalypticism has now become a more generalized phenomenon across the humanities and social studies areas. Theology (and specifically British theology) has become apocalypticism's latest purveyor in the form of the postmodern school of thought called Radical Orthodoxy.

The end seems present in the study and nature of knowledge, as well, as our academies bring deep skepticism to tradition and absolute truth claims, which have become pro forma. Semiotician Umberto Eco distinguished between two kinds of intellectuals. The "apocalyptic" intellectual is recognized by a Straussian hysteria in the face of contemporary culture—rap music, video games, Internet, and all like indicators of our interminable decline. Embattled and long-suffering, such intellectuals continue to trade in the debased coinage of what is known on college campuses as "Wes. Civ." Eco's other kind of intellectual is the "integrated" philosophe—in whose camp Eco proudly situates himself. "Integrated" public intellectuals are more willing to engage with the dynamic forces of trivialization at work in our culture, and would have no qualms about the comparison of, say, Milton's God with Optimus Prime.

You need some apocalyptic for its urgency and insurgency. "If way to the Better there be," wrote Thomas Hardy, "it exacts a full look at the 'Worst.'"[74] We seem unable to surmount our willful disregard for the potential impact of present actions on the welfare of future generations without the apocalyptic. We must scenario-think foretastes of apocalypse. But you need some millennial hope, though without the millennial hysteria and hype. We become human when we take the future seriously. Yet, this is a culture marinated in utopianism—"End injustice! End poverty! End racism!"—which leaves us in a miasma, fueling the apocalyptic and funding millennial delusions and disillusions.

Consider critical theorists. Once united in opposition to what they viewed as oppressive hegemonic systems of Western political power, they are now united by "negative dialectics," or the rhetoric of tearing down. Political scientist Stephen Eric Bonner writes about the rise of deconstructive critical theory:

> Deconstructive or poststructuralist approaches invaded the most prestigious journals and disciplines ranging from anthropology and film to religion, linguistics, and political science. They generated new insights on race and gender as well as the postcolonial world. In the process, however, critical theory lost its ability to offer an integrated critic of society, conceptualize a meaningful politics, and project new ideals of liberation. Textual exegesis, cultural preoccupations, and metaphysical disputations increasingly turned critical theory into a victim of its own success.[75]

The result has been a generations-long negation and deconstruction of Western culture. Twenty years ago, "postmodernism" was the darling of the intelligentsia. Now we see the results of this philosophical shift, even though the word "postmodern" is spent. Indeed, everything seems to be falling apart. Anarchism, nihilism, and even anti-natalism are rampant. Our dreams for a better future seem to be out of time. Apocalyptic fervor is high.

What happens next?

1.3 | A Brief History of Christian Apocalypticism

Anxiety about the decline and fall of civilization is not unique to our generation. Obsession with coming ruin has been around since antiquity and is a common feature of religious communities. After the fall of Jerusalem, some in the Jewish community looked for God to intervene in sudden and dramatic fashion. This view first appears in the book of Daniel and remains a consistent though minority view through the post-exilic period and into the life of Jesus. Some of his disciples were motivated by apocalyptic zeal, and it contributed to his arrest and capture.

Following Jesus' ascension, many of his first followers assumed Jesus would physically return from the heavens, as he had from the grave. Then he would embark on the overthrowing of Roman rule. This view held for forty years and in part motivated the Jewish War of AD 66–70. After the destruction of the Second Temple in AD 70, however, early Christians began to loosen their hold on and lose hope in a quick end to their struggles. Apocalypticism became less militaristic and more cosmic, a dramatic parting of the skies in which God intervenes in a dark world on behalf of a faithful minority. While Daniel's apocalyptic vision was linear and chronological—the end of time—John's was metaphorical and ahistorical—out of time.[76] In John's apocalyptic version of the story, the evil world will be destroyed and replaced by a new, righteous world.

Prophetic preaching is a critique of current realities in light of biblical ideals. But there are two types of prophetic discourse: (1) apocalyptic; and (2) jeremiad. Apocalyptic is revolutionary prophecy that seeks to undermine and overthrow establishment power. Jeremiad is political prophecy that seeks to change centralized structures by appealing to and challenging the establishment. Where apocalyptic dreams and visions challenge and attack the structures of power and clamor for new foundations, jeremiads appeal for change to those very same foundations.

Frederik Lodewijk Polak, a Dutch historian and sociologist, is the founder of future studies. His magnum opus, *The Image of the Future* (1973), demonstrates the degree to which human cultures have shaped their own destinies through the domain of the future. The primary driving force of history is one's image of the future. The roles of endisms such as apocalypticism, utopianism, millennialism, messianism, traditionalism, ahistoricism, and nihilism have been determinative but underappreciated. The African theologian Augustine, second only to Paul in terms of his influence on Christian thought, lived in a time of mounting crisis and social upheaval in the West but refused to succumb to any of these "endisms." He insisted that the church remain "in" the world—that is, not "leave" the world—but not become "of" the world. The world was not the arena of impending catastrophe. The world was the stage on which the divine drama of salvation played itself out.

The first person to break with Augustine and read the book of Revelation as a prophetic book by which to interpret the "signs of the times" was the twelfth-century Calabrian abbot Joachim of Fiore.[77] He has been called "the most important apocalyptic thinker in the history of Christianity."[78] His trinitarian theology of history, which divided history into three ages, had a profound impact on people as diverse as Dante, Christopher Columbus, and Adolf Hitler. In fact, Joachim of Fiore was the patron saint of Columbus's journey westward with three ships that made landfall in the Americas on October 12, 1492, ending the pre-Columbian era. The "founding" of America was an apocalyptic endeavor, as Columbus himself tried to prove in his Book of Prophecies, which he compiled and published from 1501 to 1505.

This apocalyptic understanding of history provided the cultural and intellectual underpinning for the USAmerican revolution. Would this new creation, a confederation of colonies brought together by the Great Awakening, become a "redeemer nation" that would fulfill its founding millennial mission of being a "city set on a hill" and a beacon of light to the benighted of the world? For a people steeped in apocalyptic thinking about the "mark of the beast," the 1765 Stamp Act's requirement that all commercial, personal, and legal documents and newspapers bear a stamp was a bridge too far. This apocalyptic thinking occupied such a cultural consensus that silversmith and engraver Paul Revere put this dragon-beast imagery into an engraving that he distributed far and wide to protest the Stamp Act.[79]

Apocalyptic sensitivities also fueled the millennial dreams of Manifest Destiny that shaped and steered nineteenth-century American life. But they took on a life of their own, less an "apocalypse" of unveiling the hidden and revealing the mysteries and more one of Armageddon anxieties. The original meaning of apocalyptic was not an end but a revelation. The modern idea of apocalypticism is a nineteenth-century construct, which perhaps reflects its position as a counter to notions of utopian progress.[80]

American religious history is littered with predictions of doom in both religious and secular contexts. Various groups have quibbled over the details, all based on a few passages from Revelation—does Christ come before the one-thousand-year reign? After? But what would happen in the void? The mythic tones of *Star Wars*, with the rebels representing the faithful and the Galactic Empire representing the evils of the world, has made for accessible cosmic storytelling. As a culture, it seems we have rejected any hope that we can achieve a good ending to society. When the zeitgeist turns on itself, we become obsessed with disaster. Where once the apocalyptic reading of signs sounded the alarm, it now is more likely to herald the apocalypse. Many of those who breached the US Capitol on January 6, 2021, were drugged on apocalyptic fumes. Some say similar dreams are behind the gleaming new city of Addis Ababa, the capital of Ethiopia, which is being restored and renovated by the evangelical prime minister Abiy Ahmed.[81]

1.4 |The Kingdom of God Is Not Birthed through Destruction

Apocalypticism is a false ending because it is self-defeating. In our fantasies about the future, disaster is a setup for scenes of hope and renewal. From the Revelation of John to Cormac McCarthy's *The Road*, stories of disaster end not with final destruction, but with the emergence of new societies built on better values. Yet even this is myth. Revolutionary history has proven that the end of the current age does not automatically begin a more beautiful age to come.

If you talk about the end of the age to many Christians today, or observers influenced by Christianity, you will likely find curiosity, fear, and the assumption that when Jesus comes again, there will be lots of explosions. Ruptures come with rapture. While such fear is not new, decivilization is not a sign of the impending reign of Jesus. At various points in history, civilization and even the planet itself has seemed to be on the edge of total destruction. In some cases, entire civilizations have indeed been destroyed.

The problem is that little thought is given to what happens after the explosions and ruptures. Although we remain obsessed with disaster, it is never the end of the story. This is the danger of apocalyptic fantasies. The desire to negate and destroy is so high that no thought is given to what comes next. In our generation, of course, neither Ebola nor COVID-19 are destroying the world. Life has a stubborn habit of carrying on, even in the cracks.

Perhaps the worst thing about being young is that the young have no experience of disaster survived (the phrase is E. M. Forster's) and the exhilaration that comes with it. The unexpected power of resilience has been documented by polymath Rebecca Solnit. In her study of disasters and their aftermath, Solnit was surprised to find the widespread presence of joy, both at having passed through the valley of the shadow but also amid misfortune. Disaster can bring out the best of what it means to be human and allow humans to showcase their heroic selves. It is not our preparedness or institutions that get us through a disaster. It is our ability to face catastrophe head-on and do so in collaboration with others. "Disasters are extraordinarily generative," Solnit concludes.[82] Or, as antagonist Solomon Lane says in the film *Mission Impossible: Fallout,* "The greater the suffering, the greater the peace."[83]

During the darkest days of the Nazi threat, C. S. Lewis gave a series of radio broadcasts to the people of Great Britain, which became his classic *Mere Christianity*. In them, he gave the same message that applies today: while we look for monsters on the horizon, the common enemy isn't some barbarian at the gate; it is the darkness of our own human hearts. The biggest evil lurks, not on the landscape of life, but on the inscape of the soul.

The idea that God will destroy the existing order to create a new one is poor theology, regardless of whether much of the USAmerican church lives here. Jesus describes de-civilizing forces in Matthew 24— "wars and rumors of wars" (v. 6). But he is clear that destruction is a not a sign of kingdom time or Jubilee. Jesus says the present age ends not with destruction but when everyone has heard the gospel (v. 14). After the flood in Genesis, God promised never again to destroy the world (8:21). Fear of the future is faithlessness. Any theology built on fear is faithless and false.

Fear is neither a feature nor a fulcrum of the future, and especially not of God's kingdom.

DOUBLE TIME: THE FALSE ENDING OF UTOPIANISM

*A map of the world which does not include utopia
is not worth even glancing at.*

—Oscar Wilde, The Soul of Man under Socialism

....

Are we capable of perfecting the world?

....

With the rise of the Enlightenment, Western civilization
seemed to find a purpose: to make the world we wish to see.

For a while, progress seemed to work. Our daily lives and
standards of living have risen dramatically in just a few
short generations and are the best evidence for the verac-
ity of Enlightenment values of scientifically based improvement. As modern experiments replaced ancient assumptions, society benefited to the point that scientific thinking
eventually took on metaphysical properties. The result was
a new creed of progress. With progress came the assumption that human knowledge and therefore culture is improving over time. If history is on the incline, then eventually we will achieve perfection. Human perfectibility is
possible, Rousseau and others chanted.

But progress has overpromised and underdelivered. Many
have benefited, yet many have suffered. Delight and danger
have risen in equal measure. Every age is equidistant from
eternity. Even though Thomas More didn't publish the original Latin edition of Utopia until 1516, culture has hung on to
utopian dreams despite great evidence to the contrary. We
now live split, residents of a schizophrenic world in which
the future is both great and terrible.

Progress has failed because we cannot define righteous-

ness through our own effort. Utopianism is a false ending: the promised future free of suffering never arrives. Putting faith in ourselves to achieve a better future takes us literally to utopia—"no place." The kingdom of God is not something we build or discover, because we do not have the ability to adequately chart our own destination.

2.1 | Bloodsucking Leeches

We find little more horrifying than the thought of a bloodsucking leech. When Len Wilson was young, his Army officer father would regale him with stories of wading through the deltas of south Vietnam, then having to strip off his Army uniform to search for and remove whatever leeches had attached themselves to him and begun sucking his blood.

Though loathsome to modern ears, the use of leeches was standard medical practice only a century ago. Leeching had been done since antiquity, despite its dubious success. Leeches were considered a best treatment for what Hippocrates had established as the four "humors" of the human body: blood, phlegm, black bile, and yellow bile (which correlated to the four core elements of nature—earth, air, fire, and water).[84] Like an auto mechanic who first checks the oil before diagnosing an automotive problem, the physician from antiquity to the Industrial Age would first "balance" a patient's humors by draining his or her "bad blood" via leeches.

The leech is a fairly pure animal, really: a simple parasite, ranging from a centimeter to a foot in length, whose most discernible feature is its dozens of teeth. Leeches attach to the surface of skin, bite, and suck blood until full, then fall off, gorged. Horrible though it seems, the leech was once considered a gentler, more civil version of the former barbaric practice of lancing a patient to let blood.

Leeches were once so ubiquitous that they ascended to industry and eventually to art in Victorian Europe. (Innovations often reach their peak in reputation and influence at the very moment better practices are emerging.) In the year 1832 alone, France imported almost sixty million leeches,[85] or about two for every living soul in the country. They were used for almost any sort of ailment, their popularity due in no small part to a physician known as "the vampire of medicine," Dr. François-Joseph-Victor Broussais.

Broussais would greet every new patient with a bloodletting of thirty leeches, regardless of his or her symptoms, and was known to drain 80 percent of a patient's blood.[86] A 1914 issue of the *British Medical Journal* praised the parasite as the "most beautiful of animals."[87] People wrote poems about them; apothecaries sold ornate jars for housing them.[88]

Of course, while we still like to talk about "bad blood," we know now that bloodletting is bad medicine. For example, the first American president, George Washington, died in 1799 at the age of only sixty-seven after catching a common cold, in no small part due to the estimated 40 percent blood loss administered by his physicians' use of leeches.[89] The "hideous regimen" of Washington's physicians would have met with approval from "a physician in Aristotle's Athens, or Nero's Rome, or medieval Paris, or Elizabethan London."[90]

The abandonment of bloodletting as a medical practice illustrates a much bigger shift that has occurred over the last several hundred years in our understanding of knowledge. To ask questions about The End and our relationship to it forces us to consider several fundamental questions: What is our basis for knowledge? What is our understanding of time and of history? And finally, based on these things, what—or whom—do we declare is authoritative? Let's begin with time.

2.2 | The Doctrine of Progress

For the last three hundred years of "enlightenment," Judeo-Christian Western civilization has lived with a dominant view of history known as *progress*. Progress doctrine is an ideology based on the incremental, inexorable improvement of the human condition through social, economic, and political advancement over linear time and achieved through science and technology. Better at being gods than the biblical God, science and technology are seen as having the answer to everything. The doctrine of progress tried to force the non-Western world into a mold of its making.

Progress arose with science. The emergence of science in the seventeenth century changed the basis of knowledge from tradition to experience. It challenged centuries-old practices, such as bloodletting via leech. Science regards the basis for all human knowledge not as a set of ancient, immutable laws, but as the cumulative result of human experience. The scientist does not assume and accept ancient practices as authoritative. Instead, she is a skeptic. She accepts no thesis a priori, but through a rigorous method of observation and questioning, seeks to establish better conclusions for the way things work. With science, knowledge is discovered, not kept.

For example, William Harvey's discovery of the circulation of blood overturned the ancient, assumed knowledge of the four humors. Scientific physicians replaced artisan physicians and overturned ancient orthodoxies such as bloodletting. Their experimentation led to several discoveries, which transformed medicine and dramatically improved both the quantity and the quality of life. The means by which Harvey discovered the circulation of blood was as significant as the theory itself—he drew his knowledge from his own experience and experiments, not from the past.

The success of science eventually elevated it to a philosophy. Gradually, authority shifted from the past to the future. This shift led to the rise of what came to be known as an "enlightenment" of the mind.

Harvard humanist and psychologist Stephen Pinker names reason, science, humanism, and progress as the four ideals of the Enlightenment era, which he identifies as a period spanning roughly the last two-thirds of the eighteenth century through the first half of the nineteenth century.[91] With the doctrine of progress, Western civilization seemed to find a purpose: to make the world we wish to see. The ideal of progress, or inexorable, incremental improvement to a utopian end is a direct result of the rapid improvements to society that emerged from the Enlightenment.

Counter to the later Romantic mysticism attached to progress, Pinker claims that Enlightenment progress is "prosaic, a combination of reason and humanism," and anti-spiritual.[92] True scientific progress is specific, tangible, and deliberate. It resulted in empiricism, the idea that truth may be tested and verified, which in turn can be tested.

Empiricism yielded incredible improvements to the human condition, in medicine and in other areas of life. Science promised to identify right answers, or more precisely to falsify wrong answers, through the systematic study of natural human experience. Science made people healthier, as doctors discovered that practices once thought to improve patients' health were actually harming them, even killing them. Leeches are a prime example: their use, along with many other ancient practices, was falsified through rigorous scientific study, and gradually fell from favor.[93] As shared knowledge gained through inquiry incrementally improved many facets of society, humans gradually avoided making the same mistakes over and over. Indeed, the recurring Ebola outbreaks of the 2010s would not have been so quickly minimized were it not for advances in medicine made possible by scientific practice.

Although initially limited to everyday concerns, as the benefits of science became increasingly self-evident, Enlightenment experiments took on metaphysical properties as well. What began with experimentation grew to a fundamental shift in authority, from the past to the future. Pinker's list is sequential and reflects his own belief in reason, then science, then humanism, then progress. The result is a new image of history as an upwardly sloping line, or an incline. The semiotics of the incline is prominent in nineteenth-century literature, particularly in the wake of Marx,[94] but is also the basis for a variety of assertions including the 1854 sermon on which Martin Luther King Jr. later based his famous "I Have a Dream" speech.

Progress was so seditious an ideology that it disrupted historic Christian doctrines, forcing foundation-shaking questions of human purpose (teleology) and human destiny (eschatology) on followers of Jesus. If it is truly possible to improve society over time, to change the world for the better, then how should Christians live? Progress implies that perfectibility, including the "kingdom of God," might be achievable on earth. Its influence has gradually oriented the Christian life toward work conducted for the sake of developing or, to use a term we often hear in church life, "advancing this kingdom."

Indeed, the English etymology of the word "progress" is tied to a king's journey through the kingdom. In Latin, it is literally to "take steps forward." In our lifetimes, practices once considered conventional are now brutish. We have taken great steps "forward" in a variety of fields and sectors and shudder and scoff at former sensibilities. This process is ongoing. What current practices will future generations shudder and scoff at? What are today's "leeches"? Physician Gerry Greenstone suggests, for example, our overuse of antibiotics, our tendency toward polypharmacy, and the bluntness of treatments such as radiation and chemotherapy.[95] The pursuit of scientific truth continues as medicine advances.

To be clear, some scientists, such as the late Stephen Hawking, argue that there is no such thing as a philosophy of science. Yet the benefits of science have been so powerful and self-evident that, increasingly, the entire Enlightenment experiment has taken on metaphysical properties: progress has become not just a result of empirical inquiry, or even an ideal, but an ideology, a belief in social, economic, and technological improvement that is incremental, inexorable—and increasingly immediate. Progress is the opposite of providence.

What was once radical and even revolutionary has now become commonplace. The influence of progress is normative and formative throughout culture. Everyone subscribes to its assumptions. The political theories of socialism versus capitalism have been merely questions of tactics. It has been said that while Democrats and Republicans engage in cultural death matches, an alien from another planet would see siblings arguing over nuance while ignoring deeper common bonds. To a stunning degree, progress has worked. We've seen great improvement through technological advancement, which has countered the Chicken Little Cassandra-ism of apocalypticism. The result is another "ism": rampant utopianism, or The End of the relentless incline of progress. To some, thanks to science and technology, society is on an inexorable stairway to heaven.

With this philosophical backdrop, let us consider our second false ending: utopianism. Utopianism believes in progress, not just as an ideal but as an ideology: a future world that we create. In this version of the grand story, history, though jagged, can be graphed as an incline. The major debate is only how steep is the incline. A common invocation today is the need to be on the "the right side of history"—the assumption being that change is overall an inherent good, and to be an advocate for change is to be an advocate for good. To use another phrase, "history will be written by the liberals"[96]—in other words, those who do the work of improving society over time shape the story of our lives.

Where apocalypticism sees current events through dark shades, utopianism sees massive societal change through rose-colored glasses. It interprets falling American statues as a sign of greater social consciousness. In this view, our current societal upheaval is a sign of the chaotic, messy emergence of a better future—whether that future is being orchestrated by science or God. Progress has been inexorably intertwined with Western visions of The End for over two centuries. We have sought to change the world ourselves through our own ingenuity and initiative.

To some degree, progress via technological and scientific advancement has worked wonders. For example, consider that the engine of Enlightenment progress has been mechanization, which began in the English textile

| Chapter 2 | Double Time: The False Ending of Utopianism

industry in the mid-eighteenth century and replaced ancient hand processes with efficient machinery. "Luddite" workers broke the machines, but the machines eventually broke the human backs of the "cottage industry." The Industrial Revolution was based on two simple, scientific concepts: every endeavor could be broken down into simple tasks, and those tasks could be accomplished on assembly lines. This thinking gave rise to machines that could replace human labor.[97]

Technology found a good fit in the United States. Founded at the height of Enlightenment intellectual hegemony, the United States began as an experiment in the power of progress. From the beginning its values have been Enlightenment values and technology its calling card. Empiricism led the American dream to the promised land of technological tomorrow. Time has been on our side. The human imagination seemed to be the only limit to what was possible. Belief in the ideal of progress now spans the political and religious spectrum. One recent popular work declared, "We do not know where an investment in creativity will take us. But if we could see the future, its flourishes would surely stagger us."[98] Rosy endorsements of empirically based improvements to Western culture indeed seem justifiable. The statistical evidence supporting progress is impressive. Massive technological changes across society resulted in improved standards of living around the world. Swedish liberal historian Johan Norberg notes that since 1820, the risk of living in poverty has been reduced from 94 percent to less than 11 percent.[99]

For the first time, poverty is not growing just because population is growing. Because of this reduction, the number of people in extreme poverty is now slightly less than it was in 1820. Then it was around 1 billion, while today it is 700 million. If this does not sound like progress, note that in 1820, the world only had around 60 million people who did not live in extreme poverty. Today more than 6.5 billion people do not live in extreme poverty.[100] Pinker notes that over the last twenty-five years, the rate of death due to cancer has fallen about a percentage point every year, saving millions of lives.[101] Proponents claim we have finally overcome Malthusianism.

Improvements are social and humane as well. Conservative author Eric Metaxas, in a survey of William Wilberforce's role in changing British policy on human slavery twenty years after Lord Byron's speech, describes Wilberforce's second named life goal, along with the abolition of slavery, as the "Reformation of Manners" of British society. The squalor of London society in the early 1800s is staggering. Poor children as young as five years old were assigned twelve–hour workdays in factories. Twenty-five percent of all young women in London were prostitutes, with an average age of sixteen. Alcoholism was more rampant by far than any substance abuse problem in First World societies today.[102]

There exists a mountain of evidence on the benefits to society that advancements in technology have provided in areas such as food, sanitation, life expectancy, the reduction of violence, and improvements in literacy, freedom, and equality. According to the progress doctrine, human ingenuity is working and will continue to work, if humans will only grapple with their fear of change and learn to adapt or even shed outdated beliefs, including Christian beliefs, which hold us back from benefiting from technological improvement. Advocates insist that as long as society adheres to Enlightenment ideals, the march forward is inexorable.

Another implication is the rise of the power of money. The American experiment and progress couple well with the capitalist economic theories of Keynes and Mill. As economic historian Joel Mokyr notes, "There are two models for economic history. One is the cycle and the other is a linear progression . . . The Protestant work ethic emerged with the shift from cycle to slope."[103] Indeed, modern corporate business cycles are dependent on shareholder return, which is not just an ever onward and upward progression of wealth, but one that returns profit every quarter. (The need to generate quarterly shareholder return may be the most dominant manifestation of progress in America today.[104])

To be sure, a bifurcated view of American society that divides everyone into a left or right bucket, with the left side aligned under an orthodoxy of progressive social ideals while the conservative side aligns under capitalistic economic ideals, is an overgeneralized view of America. But the persistence of this narrative is itself evidence of the power and influence of progress. Consider the labels for the two dominant political positions. The word "progressive" literally means to engage in an incremental forward motion, to change, to move forward, while the word "conservative" means to proceed with caution or stop altogether, to hold on to the status quo, to resist what is new. If movement is life and stasis is death, then the words themselves carry a bias. Our language itself is beholden to progress. That the nature of our language dictates the superiority of the ideology of progress reveals how deeply codified the metaphor is. America, and the West in general, loves progress. As both metaphor and ideal, progress is so deeply ingrained in culture that many do not even recognize its presence or influence.

The ideology of progress raised new questions of political control—namely, under whose agency does the end of history, whether initially characterized in Christian terms as God's kingdom or in more recent secular terms as a "great society,"[105] emerge? Does it emerge as the result of the work of a sovereign deity, a king given godlike power, or the result of human agency, also known as "the people"? As historian Victor Dias writes, "One of the differences between the idea of progress and Augustine's view of providence ultimately depends on whether or not the psychical and social elements of humanity are the sovereign factors in history."[106] Once the doctrine of progress becomes loosened from the doctrine of Providence, progress can be used to justify all sorts of both savory and unsavory enterprises and go off in surprising directions.

The Western churches have colluded so effectively with the split-level world of the Enlightenment that the cross is reduced to the celestial mechanism whereby we escape the wicked world of sin rather than the coming of God into the public world to establish His Kingdom.

—N. T. Wright, God in Public

As not only a method but a philosophy, the Enlightenment found its canon in the work of Charles Darwin, who in *The Origin of Species* provided a text worthy of offering a new metanarrative to replace the Christian Scriptures. One Pulitzer-winning historian credits Darwin for "'the proofs of the theory on which we today base the progress of the world" which is also notably a view that is "decidedly anthropocentric."[107]

Darwin claimed at least an intellectual commitment to orthodox Christian faith,[108] but his work was scientific and reasoned and ended with a naturalistic hope for the future. Darwin's theory of evolution formed a new image, as the philosophical conversation of nineteenth-century England expanded empirical analysis to life itself, formerly the exclusive realm of theology. While not directly assigning agency to humankind, Darwin's theories provided alternatives to theism, which apologists including Herbert Spencer and Richard Dawkins then used to position evolution as a secularization of the Christian eschaton. Spencer famously reshaped Darwin's work with the aphorism "survival of the fittest"—a phrase that never appeared in Darwin's work.[109] In this neo-Darwinian view, human agency replaced God's work and was achievable via innovation and its resultant technology. Darwin's work provided, for the first time, a secular alternative to a theological understanding of the historiographical variables of linearity, uniqueness, and finality.

The juxtaposition between Enlightenment ideals and classic Christian virtues is strong. Science offered a new basis for understanding the Scriptures, reason for faith, progress for hope, and secular humanism for love. Through industrialization, mechanization, and modern efficiency, a secularized version of the Judeo-Christian worldview emerged, fueled by mechanization, arranged by republicanism, funded by capitalism, resulting in technology, and given existential meaning by evolution.

Thus, nineteenth-century Europe gradually lost its religion, or rather, replaced metaphysical faith with faith in materialism, such that by the end of the century, G. K. Chesterton commented that atheism had become the "religion of the suburbs."[110] Neo-Darwinism became such a dominant metaphor of the age that for the first time, it became possible to be an "intellectually fulfilled atheist."[111] Neo-Darwinian evolutionary theory became a defining text for the seemingly irrefutable truth of progress and seemed to endorse the unlimited potential of human agency,[112] while Christianity and other established religions came to be seen as not only "groundless but culturally dangerous because they usually obstructed the progress of science."[113]

Perhaps given this epochal, epistemological shift, the emphasis on human agency in achieving the eschaton became obvious. America's philosophical founders not only wove progress into the fabric of the United States Constitution, but they imbued the culture with a mandate to make a better future. The dominant ideology of American political life, and the shaping force behind its current political iteration, became a "manifest destiny," an ideal future that demanded human agency.

The American ideology of progress even survived the First World War, which mortally wounded progress in Europe. The majority disagreement that has divided America in the postwar period has not been a fundamentally different view of the world as much as a difference in opinion over public policies regarding how best to achieve progress. In the 1960s, as US president Lyndon Baines Johnson audaciously promised a "great society," intellectuals debated the death of God.[114]

Scan any social media feed and you will find a sort of religion that puts its faith in science. One woman, a friend of Len Wilson's, posted about her brother, who was dying of COVID. A secular humanist (not a Christian), she sought prayer from her friends, and posted the reason why: scientific studies that showed the positive benefits of meditation.

Even today, as progress teeters under the weight of new challenges, many suggest that progress, along with the other three tenets of the Enlightenment, remains our only hope. People on each side of the political aisle agree that while, yes, bad things happen, we continue to get incrementally better and with each passing generation enjoy better standards of living. Societal advancement through science and technology has become an alternative religious system. We are a "runaway species,"[115] "makers,"[116] and "innovators"[117]—the self-help, self-making, "self-made man" syndrome streams along, driven by the pursuit of knowledge and "positive psychology."[118] We now live in a culture that has kept the concept of the eschaton but has replaced Christ with technology, and the rapture with the Singularity,[119] the prophesied moment when technological improvement develops beyond human control. Taken to a logical end, both sides of the political aisle might even agree that we are slowly moving toward cultural completion, a bloodless utopianism, free of human suffering, described by some in the language of technology, equality, and self-divination[120]—but that the utopian future is only possible if humankind makes it. We must merely draw the line ourselves or create the future we so desire.

The mockery of millennialism and rapture theology can be found in popular culture, including the founding of Apple computers and the 2007 introduction of the iPhone. Steve Jobs referred to the iPhone's development stage as the "Jesus phone" since it represented the second coming of technology and would rapture people into technological ecstasy.[121] The cultish following of the Jesus Phone prompted Apple to ask itself, "What would Jesus Phone do?" or W.W.J.P.D., which led to a series of products more friendly to the common people. The first Apple computer sold in July 1976 at a price of $666.66. The irony is that Apple's mockery of Christianity put a Bible in everyone's palm. The creativity of Life.Church's Bobby Gruenewald and his YouVersion Bible app (2008) was subvented by the sponsorship since 2012 of David Green of Hobby Lobby, who dreams of a Bible on every mobile phone.

Regardless of our preferred strategy, it seemed that most Americans have believed we are progressively marching toward a perfect future. One meta-study claims that "positivity" produces success as much as it reflects success.[122] Positivity researcher Barbara Ehrenreich writes that "perpetual growth, whether in a particular company or an entire economy, is of course an absurdity, but positive thinking makes it seem possible, if not ordained."[123] It can even be argued that in spite of the ferocity of the disagreements, the majority of social and political difference in postwar American culture was merely tactical, and even false in their assumed dichotomies.

Yet, as much as we assume progress, historically speaking, it is a new creed.[124] It is also dominant; its hegemony has made impugning it difficult—even sacrilegious. "To reject the very idea of progress must appear extreme, if not willfully perverse," philosopher John Gray writes. "Yet the idea is found in none of the world's religions and was unknown among the ancient philosophers."[125]

More important, despite its benefits, closer inspection reveals cracks in progress and in the larger closed dome of Enlightenment thought.

2.3 | Sin Devices

An American time traveler plucked from the early 1960s would be shocked at our cultural mood. In the mid-twentieth century, optimism about the future seemed as pure and as sure as baseball, to paraphrase *Field of Dreams'* Terrence Mann. Political parties on both the left and the right took the Enlightenment ideal of progress for granted.

Part of the power of progress has been that it is one of the rare ideals on which both the religious and the secular can agree. Progress found a comfortable synchronicity in Jewish and Christian theology, while Enlightenment philosophy provided a faithless alternative. The power of potential improvement was built into America's founding documents. But what began as an eighteenth-century ideal has "ramified and hardened into an ideology—a secular religion which, like the religions that progress has challenged, is blind to certain flaws in its credentials."[126] Now progress, along with Harvard humanist Stephen Pinker's other three pillars of Enlightenment philosophy—reason, science, and humanism—all seem to be in retreat. For example, even sacrosanct evolutionary theory is no longer a distinct ontology according to journalist A. W. Wilson, who suggests that Darwinism is "not in fact scientific at all, but expressions of opinion. Metaphysical opinion at that."[127]

The most obvious problem with progress is that not everyone has benefited. For many groups, the shape of history as an incline has not sufficiently alleviated suffering. Some scholars insist that what we call progress is merely justification for "cultural hegemony,"[128] a term for the dissemination of the dominant ideology of ruling nation(s). Millions of contemporary Americans, for example, because of race, gender, class, or simple ill fortune, do not participate in or benefit from the seemingly inexorable advancement of progress.

This is true historically, as well. In the last two hundred years of data cited by progress proponents, many groups have failed to enjoy the benefits of social-technological improvement. For example, as Lord Byron noted in his defense of the legendary Ned Ludd, an early-nineteenth-century weaver who was put out of work by mechanized production and who gave us the anti-technology axiom "luddite,"[129] with every technological advancement in society, jobs emerge and jobs fade away. Lives improve and lives suffer; some unwillingly sacrifice, that others would benefit. The data of societal advancement cited by progress advocates, such as the increase in literacy, life expectancy, and standard of living, are clean in aggregate but complicated in detail.

Progress had been a teleological force behind many of the waves of Enlightenment political revolution. Kant wrote that republican governments would bring about perpetual peace and progress humankind "toward the better."[130] Since war is the greatest obstacle to morality, political progress would thus lead to moral progress. But this view has proven problematic, to say the least, specifically, as Slaboch notes, "with regard to the 'cosmopolitan aim' of . . . universal history."[131] For example, consider the "evolution" of a philosophy of progress: while Kant championed that all people would eventually participate in progress, he saw European state powers as having a stronger role than other cultures and groups. Kant's Eurocentric view of progress had some effect on Fichte, who believed humankind is progressing through five epochs, from instinct to complete self-organization through the development of reason.[132] He saw the German people as leading these advancements. Fichte in turn influenced Hegel, for whom progress was not shared by all humanity but gave authority to certain superior groups, such as Nazi Germany. Slaboch writes, "Kant, Fichte, and Hegel each offered optimistic philosophies of history. Having provided visions of a better future, these philosophers—or their popularizers—naturally desired some entity to bring about that earthy Elysium; almost inevitably, the deity to which the worshippers of progress prostrated themselves to was the state."[133]

A state-driven ideal promised equality for all but was to be administered by a ruling party, according to a ruling party's rules. As Lenin famously summarized (and prophesied) regarding the progressive political ideal, "Who? Whom?"[134]—in other words, who overtakes whom to achieve "equality for all"?

Christians should be cautious about breezy support of authoritarian, utilitarian approaches to societal advancement, in which benefits to the majority outweigh losses to a sometimes-significant minority, or one in which we use the levers of politics to remove power from some and give to others in a zero-sum attempt to engineer a more humane, "kingdom" society. James C. Scott critiques "the imperialism of high-modernist, planned social order,"[135] which seeks to organize society according to scientific principles and ignores local, contextualized knowledge and relationships. Centrally managed social planning fails, Scott argues, when it imposes inadequate schematic visions that do violence to complex local and relational dependencies that cannot be fully understood.[136] The case studies of twentieth-century national politics have obviously demonstrated that the ability to engineer a more perfect solution, as we are still prone to do in society and in church, is vastly overstated.

The urge to save humanity is almost always a false-face for the urge to rule it.

—H. L. Mencken, Minority Report

Or just look at your mobile device and consider the state of education in America, both public and private. Mobile devices are easily one of the most invasive new technological innovations of twenty-first-century Western culture.[137] The predominant age when children receive a smartphone with a service plan is now age ten,[138] which is old news to anyone with school-age children. The result has been a battle in the classroom over use of devices, a battle the teachers are losing. This battle extends to the home, where Len Wilson has more than once told his children that their smartphones are sin devices.

While advocates may argue that mobile technology is improving society in the aggregate, what is it doing to those students for whom the additional distraction in the classroom is harming their ability to receive the education they will need later in life? The connected world is living out a real-time experiment, and the returns are not looking favorable, as a growing body of research suggests that "smartphones are causing real damage to our minds and relationships."[139]

Even the reams of statistics that defenders of Enlightenment philosophy employ are worth further examination. For example, while it is true that standards of living have dramatically increased since the beginning of the nineteenth century, any analysis of the past 150 years is remiss to ignore the introduction of "total war" with the Guns of August in 1914 a level of warfare unmatched in human history. As we noted earlier, in addition to the Black Death, the wars of the twentieth century, in aggregate, are the other deadliest catastrophe in human history. By the end of the Great War in 1918, so crushed was the nineteenth-century romantic ideal that an entire generation became known as "lost" for the profound epistemological disconnection between the ideals of their Enlightenment education and their firsthand experience of war. Further, it may be argued that the wars of the twentieth century ruined the progress ideal entirely where the scars of bombs are deepest, such as in western Europe, and that the version of progress that survived adopted American emphases on technology and material gain.

Cracks in the ideology of progress are even appearing in new histories, such as David Graeber's major new posthumous work, *The Dawn of Everything: A New History of Humanity*. Graeber takes another shot at the closed dome of Enlightenment thought with his grand attempt to rewrite the evolutionary history of humankind as thirty thousand years of ups and downs rather than succeeding stages of Darwinian progress and gradual improvement.[140]

Our planet is not even a speck of sand in a universe that is nearly 14 billion years old and at least 46.5 billion lightyears across—and somehow getting bigger. Our world is made up of subatomic

particles that don't exist in one definite place until we observe
them. It seems hard to imagine that, in our lifetimes, science will
offer satisfying answers to basic questions like: Why does anything
exist at all? or What is consciousness?

—David Gardner, "An Evangelical Icon Finds Salvation
in West Hollywood"

Considering war and other atrocities, what remains is both a love of technological progress and fear regarding a loss of control of technological progress. Since the early twentieth century, millions of people have flocked to epic displays of new technology and have appropriated them en masse into daily living, while at the same time artists imagine dystopian futures that ask deep, epistemic questions about the dangers of technology serving evil masters. Progress contains both good and evil. It is a paradox—just like human nature.

While the ideology of progress has helped some and has provided a shared purpose, we cannot define righteousness through our own effort. Utopianism is a false ending because the promised future free of suffering never arrives.

The benefits of Enlightenment thinking elevated progress from ideal to ideology. But while progress has helped some and has provided a shared purpose, it has also led to great suffering. Culture has hung on to utopian dreams despite great evidence to the contrary. We now seem to live in a schizophrenic world in which the future is both great and terrible. Progress is a myth. Putting faith in ourselves takes us literally to utopia—nowhere. The "self" is a false ending.

.

2.4 | The Kingdom of God Is Not a Location We Build or Discover

In 1985, plastic surgeon John Upton was having trouble saving a boy's ear. A dog had chewed the five-year-old's ear off in the suburbs of Boston, and the doctor could not seem to reattach it. The veins were not connecting.

After some thought, Upton hit upon an idea that seemed positively medieval. He contacted an online leech vendor (yes, you can buy leeches on the Internet). They ran about fifty dollars per pound, jumbo size. Once they arrived, he put two of the disgusting worms on the boy's ear. The leeches promptly ate through congested tissue, blood to begin to flow again, and the boy's ear was saved. Upton became the first plastic surgeon to successfully reattach a severed ear.

Upton's success encouraged the revival of the leech in modern medicine. It turns out that leeches are cheap, contain salivary chemicals that promote tissue regeneration, and automatically reproduce. In 2004 the Food and Drug Administration approved leeches as a "medical device," enabling new leech-farming companies from other countries to enter the market. Today leeches are frequently used as an aid for blood flow in "reattachment operations, skin grafts, and reconstructive plastic surgery."[141] Though the use of leeches wasn't conclusive, it had benefits, as Upton rediscovered. Leeches have made a comeback; what is old became new again.

History, as it turns out, has value for the present.

Upton's resurrection of ancient medicine was innovative in its restoration and illustrates the limitations of an ideology of progress. Utopianism is supersessive: it assumes that every age is better than the one that came before, and that humans are constantly "evolving" into new realms of consciousness. As such, it dismisses the past as primitive and glorifies the future. Yet reality belies such an easy, upward view of anthropology. Often, the answer to the future is indeed found in the past.

This means we need to rediscover the lost idea that the past has something to teach us.

For one, the past was often quite sophisticated—much more than we tend to give it credit for. The discovery of a twenty-three-hundred-year-old Scythian woman's boot in the receding ice of the Altai Mountains reveals an intricate, bedazzled pattern of beads and crystals that would rival any machine-produced artifact of the current age.[142] Ancient technology often rivals our best techniques. The walls at Machu Picchu were built without mortar yet still stand millennia later, so tightly fitted together that a knife blade cannot be slid between the stones.[143]

Utopianism is directly traceable to both Rosseau's noble savage and the sympathetic magic of anthropologist James George Frazer, whose comparisons of religious traditions highly influenced German theology and helped pave the way for the aforementioned deconstructionism of critical theory. Humanism now ascribes to a schizophrenic mixture of glory and dismissal of ancient culture.

Two, the future never seems to arrive. Humanism cannot achieve the end on its own. Critical theorist Ernst Bloch maintained an eschatological outlook yet suggested that the end would never come, but that time would forever march forward in dialectical fashion, with "each story open to interpretation and the interpretation to reinterpretation. Existence is always unfinished—its end is always 'not yet' in sight."[144] To the humanist, hope comes not in the morning but only in the mourning of what we have previously ignored.

As we write this, the "not yet" part of Bloch's humanist eschatology irritates, considering Geerhardus Vos's famous description of the kingdom as an already/not yet reality. The dualistic, "now and not yet" description of God's kingdom is ubiquitous. But by describing the end as a "not yet" reality, how much has the church conflated the end of the story with the need for human agency and thus blended our theology with humanism? Christ promises an end to the story that is final and definitive, not an ever-morphing dialectic of change. The humanist version of the future creates only an ever-present now.

Three, the supposed journey to "utopia" only accelerates with time. The boomer generation has been perhaps the penultimate utopian generation. But there is a darker side. We have hung on to these utopian dreams despite great evidence to the contrary and now seem to live in a schizophrenic world in which the future is both great and terrible. One of the consequences of utopian dreams has been great political and social chaos, which only seems to accelerate with time. Contrary to the four-hour workweek fantasy, technological advancement simply spins, and the hamster wheel goes faster and faster as we use technological advancement for selfish ends. The promised future free of suffering never arrives. All we have to show for it is exhaustion and alienation.

On the backside of COVID, some now predict an imminent new age of technological innovation.[145] While technological utopianism remains a big sell, the lived experience of current Western culture makes it clear that society is in fact regressing in many ways. Our technological society is on a road to nowhere, riding a lie. While some in the church want to remove language of blood from our hymnody and imagery, we cannot achieve a world free of suffering.

In his announcement of his ministry in Matthew 4, Jesus quotes Deuteronomy 6 to say the kingdom is present. Specifically, he says *eggizó*, which is in the Greek perfect tense and indicates an extreme closeness, even a presence, to God. Jesus said, "Repent, for the kingdom of heaven has come near" (Matthew 4:17). We perhaps hear images of the sky and clouds, but Jesus meant something else—in him, an entirely different reality has come. In Christ, we shift from *chronos* to *kairos*, or from *tempus* to temple. To realize this is a "time-out" experience. It stops us in our tracks, and we are forced to take a time-out from our work and our worry. It takes us out of the time in which we've been living, which is exactly what coronavirus has done to us.

> *Then they asked him, "What must we do to do the works*
> *God requires?"*
> *Jesus answered, "The work of God is this: to believe in the one he*
> *has sent."*
>
> **—Jesus, as quoted in John 6:28–29 (NIV)**

Contrary to what the utopian ideology of progress suggests, God's kingdom is not something we create, build, or advance. We don't make the kingdom. We receive it, just as we receive grace. We enter it. It has always been God's gift.

| CHAPTER 3 |
BACK IN TIME: THE FALSE ENDING OF TRADITIONALISM

Does the answer to the future lie in the past?

The role of high priest, the spiritual leader of the Jewish people, had been a flashpoint of much of protest in first-century Palestine. Some demanded the Roman overseers appoint someone favorable to the law, and of greater moral character, and not a politician in service to the empire. Governor Quirinius picked Annas, who along with his son-in-law, Caiaphas, gained favor with the people by appealing to tradition. Traditionalism seeks to make the past, not the present or future, authoritative. While tradition is remembrance and is a vital part of the relationship of God's people to the God of history, it tends to devolve into a form of religion devoid of life.

God doesn't appear in our rituals and customs. Jesus says that for the sake of your tradition, you make void the word of God (Mark 7:13).

3.1 | Annas and Caiaphas

In the generations leading up to the life of Jesus, young Jewish men tended to be a feisty bunch. The spirit of the Maccabee warriors lived on, and they dreamed of overthrowing pagan Roman oppression as an act of piety and provincialism. Dustups were common. A wise Roman overseer would not exacerbate his ethnic subjects, but Herod the Great, whose hubris was his name, legacy, and lineage, could not resist.

The incident began when Herod mounted a golden eagle over the entrance to the temple. According to the historian Flavius Josephus, two of the more eloquent Jews of the day, rabbinic masters Judas, son of Saripheus, and Matthias, the son of Margalothus, along with a group of protégés, could not stand for the blasphemy. They took axes to the eagle with courage in part derived from a rumor that Herod had died.[146]

A local king's captain heard about this brazen activity, and with his unit descended on the temple. Much of the mob dispersed, but the captain nabbed the two rabbis and forty of the young men and took the group to the palace.

Now Herod had a problem. Would he let the seditionists threaten his authority? Though in great abdominal pain, and with death imminent, Herod summoned the strength to convey his rage at the Jewish leaders for their ingratitude at his investment in them and their temple over the previous two decades. He then executed the rabbis and the group of captured seditionists.

This was Herod the Great's last act as ruler of the Jews. In short order, he died, and through a last-minute change in his will, left authority over Judea to his "hated" fourth son, Archelaus.[147]

Herod Archelaus promptly commissioned a very expensive, seven-day public festival in Jerusalem to honor his father and made attempts to appease the people through public declarations of lowering taxes and duties and by releasing a few captives who had been thrown in prison. This, however, was not sufficient for many of the people, who publicly mourned their lost rabbis and friends. Their cries in the temple were loud enough to be heard throughout the city.[148]

Archelaus, whose very name meant "authority," was an ethnarch, or someone who ruled over an ethnic group. It is safe to assume that Archelaus had little fondness or patience for his subjects, the Jewish people. Times were turbulent, and the Jews were a thorn in the side of Roman rule. He was expected in Rome but could not let the seditionists threaten him. So, he sent a general to the temple, then another group, both of whom were greeted and rejected with stones. Having had enough, Archelaus sent in a tribune of armed Roman centurions. When the dust settled, three thousand Jews lay dead on the temple floor. Archelaus published a memo to the region: Passover was canceled.

Little wonder Herod Archelaus became infamous in the Jewish community for his exceptional cruelty. News of Archelaus spread far and wide, including to the tradesman Joseph of Nazareth, whose young wife, Mary, had just given birth to a baby boy they named Jesus. Joseph was hiding in Egypt from the elder Herod. Having heard of Herod the Great's death, he had planned to return home, "but when he heard that Archelaus was reigning in Judea in place of his father Herod, he was afraid to go there. Having been warned in a dream, he withdrew to the district of Galilee, and he went and lived in a small village: Nazareth" (Matthew 2:22–23). The rumor of Archelaus's cruelty created the circumstance that led Joseph to settle in Nazareth.

With this decision, Joseph and his family were able to avoid attention over the next decade. As Jesus grew, Archelaus's cruelty only increased. Eventually the Roman palace tired of him and the entire Herodian dynasty. Caesar Augustus deposed him, and in his stead, changed how he handled governance over the region: Augustus declared the area a province of Rome called Judaea, putting its inhabitants under more direct Roman authority, to be led by a governor.

First up in this role was Quirinius, a career aristocrat who received the appointment as a political reward. To shore up the tax base, Quirinius called a census. It was the year 6 CE.[149]

The Jewish people hated the census because it violated Jewish law. In fact, its call led to the crystallization of a new Jewish political party, the Zealots. Josephus described them as the "fourth philosophy" of Judaism, along with the Pharisees, the Sadducees, and the Essenes. Much like the six "isms" described in this book, each party had its preferred solution for the political problems of the day.

In addition to the census, Quirinius also posted a new high priest: Annas, son of Seth. As a new governor, Quirinius was eager to understand and leverage the role of the high priest. The high priest was the religious leader of the Jewish people and the only person allowed near the presence of God in the Holy of Holies at Passover.

The role of high priest had been a flash point of much of Jewish protest. After Herod's death, the seditionists had demanded of Herod Archelaus that he appoint someone "more agreeable to the law, and of greater purity, to officiate as high priest."[150] While the position had begun with Aaron, brother of the patriarch Moses, and was traditionally seen as a representative of *YHWH*, in the Roman age it had often been used as a political tool. Through the appointment of Annas, Quirinius sought appeasement: he wanted to avoid the turmoil of the Herod years while keeping the Jews from establishing too much autonomy.

A twenty-six-year-old at his appointment,[151] Annas enjoyed a great career due to the political favor of the Roman governor. He had enough political savvy that he and his sons were to retain some measure of control over the post for the next fifty-seven years. The next decade was politically stable, at least according to the standards of the day. Annas served eleven years as high priest, though it is unclear how invested he was in the Jewish ideal or how much he fulfilled the people's desire for a "pious" priest worthy of the title. What is clear is that he enjoyed his position of authority and used his grown children to maintain power even after he was deposed in the shift of governorship to a new procurator, Valerius Gratus, in the year 15.

Annas had five sons and one daughter, but it was his daughter's husband who maintained the family stronghold position. The son-in-law's name was Joseph ben Caiaphas. That the son-in-law, rather than one of the five sons, should be appointed high priest says something about the charisma of Caiaphas. Caiaphas's name meant "comely," and it is not a stretch to imagine that he was afforded social favor and the privilege of beauty. Or, perhaps Annas chose him because his lack of bloodline left him more able to be managed. Or perhaps even both: to use the common tropes, a "beauty" managed by a "brain." Regardless, Annas maintained a hidden, unofficial power, and though Caiaphas was the appointee, Annas continued to be seen as high priest by the locals.[152]

If there was anything that Annas and Caiaphas cared about more than maintenance of their family's position, it was tradition. The high priest's role demanded it, for one. But beyond this, it was politically expedient. In their view, there was no benefit to them or to the Jewish people in challenging the Roman procurator and the rule he represented. Yet he had to deal with the fringe element of his own people, the Zealots, who were trigger-happy and ready for a fight. A strategic and political means to manage the tension was to uphold tradition as the value by which the people could maintain purity in a corrupt era—not because of a sincere belief in that tradition, but as a means of maintaining power.

After Annas's stewardship of the office of high priest, followed by a series of appointments in quick succession, Caiaphas settled into the role, with his father-in-law on his shoulder, in the year 18. He would maintain the position for the next twenty years, the longest tenure since Herod's family had been in power. During this time, the four philosophies of Judaism and their leaders formed themselves around Annas and Caiaphas as the power center of local Jewish life, with the Sadducees and Pharisees the power brokers and the Essenes and Zealots the resistance.

It was in this atmosphere of taut peace that John the Baptist began his ministry in the mid-20s, with Jesus following him. John the Baptist was likely one of the Essenes, a prophet from the foothills who began to draw humongous crowds. Now his cousin Jesus was doing likewise, which over time became a concern to Annas and Caiaphas. Too much attention to the fringe elements might result in an uprising.

This is the backstory of how tradition became an oppositional force to Jesus' ministry. As pastor and author Robert Glenn Johnson notes, by the end of his ministry, Jesus was unpopular with five primary groups: the Pharisees, the Sadducees, the Herodians, his own family, and disciples of his cousin, John the Baptist.[153] Of the five, a coalition of Pharisees, Sadducees, and Herodians became the force that brought Jesus to the Roman authorities.

As the leaders of this coalition, why were Annas and Caiaphas so concerned with preserving tradition, even at the cost of what their people considered a great teacher?

3.2 | Heritage and Heresy

The Prophet's task is to speak from the heart of the tradition, to criticize and warn those who, claiming to represent the tradition, are in fact abandoning it.

—N. T. Wright, What Saint Paul Really Said

It can seem at times that some in the church are more interested in the furtherance of a particular theological tradition than in the remembrance and radiance of Jesus.

No person is defined in terms of numbers, whether that number is a street address, social security number, IP address, or age. We love the Japanese tradition of saying something different to everyone you meet, since each person has distinct needs and distinct traits that require respect. But since one Len is older than the other, we thought it would be good for the eldest to give some examples of how traditionalism has reigned in the church and academy, and the silliness of such battles.

We both are "trads." We believe in tradition. We believe you cannot escape tradition, which is one of the failings of modernism, which Gabriel Josipovici calls "a tradition of those who have no tradition."[154] We believe that tradition is being a good ancestor to the future. We believe tradition is the act and art of passing on the baton to the future. We believe tradition is a verb. We believe each person should tradition the faith every day. We believe in intratraditionality, where you honor your own context and come to a deeper understanding of your own tradition out of conversations with another tradition. We believe, as Pablo Picasso said so scrumptiously, "Tradition means having a baby, not wearing your grandfather's hat."[155]

But both the church and the academy have been hard-core about wearing hats or confusing tradition with traditionalism. Len Sweet grew up in a hat-wearing tribe that defrocked his Pilgrim Holiness preacher mom (Mabel Boggs Sweet) for accepting a wedding ring from his Free Methodist father and for "bobbing" her hair for the wedding ceremony (cutting and curling it instead of wearing it in a bun). A few years later she was defrocked from his father's tribe and "banned" from the church because his father allowed entrance into the Sweet household of the "devil's blinking box" (television). It took a while for these tribes to take off their hats, but neither is wearing them today. In fact, both tribes recently have publicly apologized for wearing these hats to begin with. They even reinstated her credentials. But it took fifty years to do so, and by that time Mabel Boggs Sweet was no longer around to receive her reinstatement.

Another "tradition" that was really "traditionalism" was the hour of Sunday night worship: 7:00 or 7:30 p.m. About the same year, 1959–60, two shows made Sunday night television the campfire of the nation: *Bonanza* and *Walt Disney Presents*. In fact, one reason Len's father let a television into the house in the first place was to watch *Bonanza*. Both shows competed directly with Sunday night worship. Rather than change the worship time to 5:00 or 6:00 p.m. on Sunday nights, the church decided to keep its hat and go head-to-head with culture. When it comes to sacred texts and canonical traditions, we should go head-to-head with culture. But to take on culture over the hour of worship? How did that work out? How many churches today still have Sunday night worship?

There are so many other "hats" we might mention: putting screens in the sanctuary; substituting tables and chairs for pews; clearing up the confusion between faith religion and civil religion by taking the flag out of the sanctuary; even kids wearing hats into church, since many kids don't think they're properly dressed unless they're wearing a hat. Len Sweet was fired once in his life. He was both an organist and a youth minister at a Reformed Church in America (RCA) congregation in Rochester, New York. His kids were complaining about the music and how the three Bs (Bach, Beethoven, Buxtehude) didn't cut it for them. So, one Easter Sunday, Len decided to play as a postlude "Joy to the World," but not the Handel version, the Three Dog Night version. The kids loved it. Their parents didn't. That was the end of that job.

Thomas More (1478–1535) was beheaded because he refused to accept King Henry VIII as "Defender of the Faith and Supreme Governor of the Church of England," a title and position Queen Elizabeth II held until her death in 2022 and every monarch since Henry VIII has held. More is credited with saying, "Tradition is not the worship of ashes but the preservation of fire," a quote popularized by Gustav Mahler, who thought that much of what theater people called "tradition" was nothing more than "cosiness and laziness."[156]

Admittedly it is not always easy to distinguish between what is hat and what is hair, between being stuck and being rooted; between ashes and embers, between what is adiaphoric (things indifferent to salvation but not that without which Christianity would not be itself) and what is fatidic (prophetic of the future). But Jesus himself warned us that if we fail to make the distinction between "human traditions" and "the commands of God"; then "you nullify the word of God by your tradition that you have handed down." Then Jesus went for the jugular: "And you do many things like that" (Mark 7:13 NIV).

Sometimes when you discard received notions and take off hats, you aren't being "heretical," but being orthodox. You aren't embracing "heresy," but you are embracing heritage, a deeper and older heritage than the received notions express. We are called to be *depositum custodi,* or "custodians of tradition." That presupposes a *depositum fidei* or the "fullness of faith" deposited in Scripture and tradition, both of which find new ways of incarnating in all the cultures of the world.

There is an element of protectorship in the exercise of custodianship. But to "protect" is not to pull from behind but to push and move forward, careful of what lies behind. The very word *praesul* often rendered "protector," literally means "someone who leaps or dances in front," like David before the ark of the Lord (see 2 Samuel 6:14–16). To "protect" the faith is to make the faith fit and joyful to move forward. That's tradition as a verb.

In case we need a reminder of how movements (like "the Methodist Revolution") can become monuments on the way to mausoleums, think of a Hasidic figure today, dressed in clothes time-frozen from eighteenth-century eastern Europe. Yet when the Hasidic movement emerged, it was a protest against the Talmud-dominated, legalistic fundamentalism and entrenched traditionalism of the Jewish establishment. Hasidism began as a mystical form of Jewish faith that prized spontaneous religious devotion and defended the access of uneducated Jewish men and women to spiritual enlightenment and fulfilment. When we hand on the tradition as a "hermeneutic of reform" and not a "hermeneutic of rupture," as Pope Benedict XVI likes to say, then we do for our day what our ancestors did for their day but not in the way they did it.

3.3 | The Past Versus the Future

The appeal of tradition is a question of authority: On what basis do you determine what is definitive among competing epistemological claims? In changing cultural contexts such as first-century Palestine and twenty-first-century America, the concept of "truth" itself becomes open for debate. To make a claim for the truth of a once-assumed statement, groups must appeal to philosophical positions. Traditionalism is such a position. It submits that all moral and religious truth comes from divine revelation, which by nature occurred historically, in an immutable past, and that human reason is incapable of attaining it. In other words, traditionalism demands that the past, not the future, is authoritative.

Through much of common history, there was no alternative. But the rise of empiricism led to a philosophical shift in authority from an authoritative past to a to-be-discovered future. The split came into full form in a philosophical argument in the late seventeenth century that pitted two opposing worldviews.[157] A group of philosophers including Terrasson, Charles Perrault, the Abbé of Saint-Pierre, and Fontenelle,[158] building on ideas established by Descartes and his contemporary, the cleric and theologian Jacques-Bénigne Bossuet a generation earlier, [159] argued that the rise of new technologies, specifically, the printing press, firearms, and the nautical compass, had created a definitive split in history. This "quarrel of the Ancients and the Moderns," as it was called, challenged longstanding beliefs about authority and whether authority was best found in antiquarianism or experimental science.

The seminal quarrel of the Ancients and the Moderns identifies the core of the question of a philosophy of history: Which is authoritative, the past or the future? Arguments of authority in our current culture are best understood in the context of this question of authority. Authority is tied to time. Consider systems of authority, such as monarchy or oligarchy. These find their root in the Greek *arche*, a word that means "origin" or "beginning." The place we begin is the place we find our basis for authority. Our image of history determines our basis for authority, and from this, our thoughts and our actions ensue.

As noted, to the ancients time was immutable, eternity alone was real, and any progress was inevitably followed by decline, in a perpetual cycle. As such, authority was found in the past, not the future. Fueled by the new collision of ideas of nature and history, the Moderns argued for a new form of authority based on empiricism, which modeled itself after the scientific method and consisted of forming arguments and citing evidence in a step-by-step forward progression, from beginning to end. The Moderns combined "the early idea of *physis* as the necessary movement towards the fulfillment of any unit's intrinsic properties . . . into an idea of natural history that is to account for the unfolding of these constitutive properties over time."[160]

The new, modern view shifted away from orthodox Christian teaching with the notion that knowledge is discovered through trial and error or empiricism, as opposed to revealed by God. Opposing the long-held belief in immutable truth, in which all knowledge had been discovered in a previous age, the Moderns argued for a fundamental reorientation toward knowledge through discovery, which oriented the locus of knowledge toward the future, not the past. Moderns agreed with Christianity in the concept of a fundamental unity of humanity but suggested that all are called to improve or even transform in the same direction together. It was the responsibility of all humankind to do the work. Thus, moderns concluded that humankind must assert itself over nature.

Due to this future orientation or forward spiral notion of history, which began with the Hebraic understanding of God,[161] Greek concepts of *physis* and early Christian theology were replaced with a linear incline. Circular concepts of time and knowing continued a slow fade in human consciousness, and "circuitous" became a word of opprobrium.

The philosophy of progress began here.

Theologically, this new philosophy began to suggest that perfectibility, including the "kingdom of God," might be achievable. Its influence gradually oriented the Christian life toward work conducted for the sake of developing, or to use a term we often hear in church life, "advancing," the kingdom. The resulting culture shifted authority to the future—and increasingly without a need for religions of remembrance.

3.4 | The Kingdom of God Is Not Remembrance

The office of high priest that Annas and then Caiaphas occupied was the chief ecclesiastical authority of the world. It was the most important position of the Jewish people, barring the presence of a physical kingdom and a king. Only the high priest could open the intersection of heaven and earth, the veil of the temple, and enter the most sacred place on earth, the cube called the Holy of Holies. The high priestly office, as noted earlier, had begun with Aaron, who had been appointed by God (Exodus 28:1–2), and until the Herodian dynasty each priest had been a direct descendant of Zadok, the high priest of David and Solomon. As such, the position carried great responsibility. Though it had been diminished by Herod as a political tool, Quirinius's appointment of Annas was seen as restorative, and the people expected Annas and his family to uphold the traditions of their ancestors.

As part of the genealogical line of Levites that stretched to Aaron, and through Aaron directly to Abraham, Isaac, and Jacob, the high priest was understood by God's people to be the direct connection to and a living representative of God. Jacob had designated the first "house" (*beth'el*) to God by pouring oil over the rock that had served as his pillow the night God had appeared to him in a dream (see Genesis 28:10–19). The purpose of Jacob's rock altar? Remembrance. God had given the covenant to his grandfather Abraham, then his father, Isaac, but it was at this moment that God has appeared to Jacob and the family stories had become real. Jacob wanted to capture the electricity of the moment, bottle it up, and remember.

Tradition begins with remembrance. "Remember the rock from whence you were hewn" (Isaiah 51:1, authors' translation). To many in and out of the church today, Christian tradition is seen as an embarrassing narrative of the inability of Jesus' followers to live up to the calling of their Lord. Yet tradition is the natural consequence of an incarnate God. By taking on flesh within a specific culture, including its limitations and assumptions, God "necessitated continuing developments in how Christ would be appropriated in subsequent centuries."[162] This is made clear in relief to the religions of Islam and Orthodox Judaism, each of which requires its adherents to adopt specific cultural customs as religious commands. Christianity is the only major religion that does not require its followers to adhere to a specific set of social norms or cultural forms. We worship a person, Jesus Christ, who lived in a specific time and space yet incarnates in the time and space of every person who follows him. Jesus is beyond culture but within culture, and incarnation begets incarnation. Because of this, tradition is the record of revelation—the long, ongoing story and remembrance of God's incarnation to peoples in specific cultures and diverse contexts. God is a God of history. As the films say, "events depicted in this story are true." When events fade with our ancestors into the past, our memories are what tie us to them and to one another.

Memory is critical to the life of faith. Scientifically, the hippocampus is the basis of all knowledge. Contemporary research has rightly identified the human hippocampus as the holy grail and ultimate goal of data encoding.[163] But it is not just the brain where memory is located. Memory resides in the whole body–nerve connections, cells of immune system, all our senses (especially smell). Our stories and the remembrance of them are what keep us connected to God and one another. Stories are the binding tendons of the community of God; the religious traditions of remembrance are the ligaments of the body of the faithful. They even share the same root: *lig-*.

In the story of Jacob, it wasn't long after Jacob dedicated his rock as a memorial to God that God used it to help trigger his memory (Genesis 31:13). This rhythm—God appears, the people mark the moment, and then God uses their ritual to trigger the memory and experience the meaning of the moment later—describes the entire biblical narrative: "remember the Sabbath" (Exodus 20:8), "remember my covenant with Jacob" (Leviticus 26:42), "remember the wonders he has done" (1 Chronicles 16:12 NIV), "remember the deeds of the LORD" (Psalms 77:11 NIV), "then they remembered his words" (Luke 24:8). The focus on remembrance, clearly, is the result of our tendency to forget. The rituals of tradition help tie us to the story, help tie the story together, and keep us from forgetting or ceasing to care.

Yet, because of our inclination toward idol worship, the same rituals that help us remember can become the objects of our religion. The second commandment is evidence that in the hands of broken, hiding humans, tradition tends to devolve into traditionalism, which is the elevation of the story of God and the images of God above the God to whom they point. One of the common themes of Jewish and Christian religious history is the tendency for memory to take on sacred status. Because Christianity lays claim to events of history, and to a God of historical revelation, the temptation is to think that only events that happened in the past are true. When we elevate our memory of the past over our experience of the present, tradition ceases to serve as the connective tissue of God and the cloud of witnesses and becomes an object of worship.

In the case of Caiaphas and the chief priests of Israel, tradition was the remnant of what was considered the purest period in history, the kingdom of Israel, and Jesus threatened it. Something had to be done, and tradition provided the rationale to avoid political upheaval and any loss of autonomy: "If we let [Jesus] go on like this, everyone will believe in him, and then the

Romans will come and take away both our temple and our nation" (Caiaphas, in John 11:48 NIV).

Caiaphas and his council of leaders understood Jesus as a threat to the security of the Jewish identity. Their goal became to get rid of Jesus in order to maintain authority, preserve what remained of Jewish ethnic identity, and perhaps even begin a sequence of events that might restore what had been lost six hundred years earlier in the fall of Jerusalem to the Babylonians. Somewhere along the way, a good and vital tradition had become a destructive traditionalism.

The appeal of traditionalism is best understood with the axiom "Hindsight is always 20/20." The view of the present and future is overcast, and we perceive the past to be sunny and clear, though in reality the memories aren't as great as we think.

Twentieth-century novelist Thomas Wolfe wrote an autobiographical novel about growing up in Asheville, North Carolina. Its title, *You Can't Go Home Again*, is his enduring legacy. "You can't go back home to your family," he wrote, "back home to your childhood . . . back home to a young man's dreams of glory and of fame . . . back home to places in the country, back home to the old forms and systems of things which once seemed everlasting, but which are changing all the time—back home to the escapes of Time and Memory."

The year was 1940, and the previous three generations had been a time of change arguably more radical than our own: from a lamp-lit agrarian society to the modern, streamlined vision of the 1939 World's Fair. Wolfe had no idea that with world war looming once again, even greater change lay ahead.

Within the contemporary rise of political authoritarianism is a desire to fix culture by restoring it to its glorious past. But history has proven we cannot make the world better by defining righteousness according to culturally specific and provincial customs, clans, tribes, and nations. Indeed, the hero's journey is to return to home. But traditionalism is a false narrative because it is based on the premise that we can go backwards to the beginning, without having to go through the crucible of change that leads to a changed end.

The journey home is a journey forward. While some people focus on the past, which leads to a sincere desire to defend what has been handed down from the cloud of witnesses, it inevitably ends in the tragedy of tribalism and nationalism.

| CHAPTER 4 |
MARKING TIME: THE FALSE ENDING OF MILLENNIALISM

Can Jesus just come again and fix this mess?

There's an ongoing, morbid blockbuster mentality about the end of the world, and American religious history is full of doomsayers. One of the prime drivers of history has been the vision of a future millennium.

One of the least known but most influential figures in history was Joachim of Fiore, who developed a philosophy of history that was to dominate Europe until the advent of Marxism. His influence is still felt today. The ongoing passion that has driven millennialism is the desire to escape the crucible of change, which is the false narrative that we can somehow just skip the journey and slip through the chains of time. Millennialism has served as a divine Get Out of Jail Free card. Yet, eschatological fervor has precipitated some of the worst horrors of history.

Jesus is the eschatological temple. The laws are now written in the heart, and the stones are now living stones with Jesus as the Cornerstone. While we wait, what do we do? Love one another.

4.1 | Patriot Food

One recent gift-giving season netted the younger Len some interesting cultural artifacts from his extended family, including "Patriot Food" (supplies for emergencies from people who champion freedom and self-reliance, but who are "excited for what the future holds") and a generator. The gifts opened Len up to an entire industry designed to sell goods to people who assume the future holds some rough times. Is bunker-friendly mac and cheese a sign of opportunistic commodification of religious fears, or wise shopping for tribulations to come?

Political developments in American culture since the turn of the century have exposed significant differences in deeply held beliefs about what the future holds and what the kingdom of God is. These differences are more than academic; part of the motivation for this book for the younger Len has been a desire to help his family and the church address the topic of the future from a biblical perspective. Some of the younger Len's extended family, lifelong Christians, share a belief that the world is steadily worsening and that current events are signs of the "end times." They are far from alone; much of American Christianity is fascinated and even obsessed with the same two questions the disciples asked, as we recall in the introduction: When is the end, and What are the signs?

Any book about The End needs to address the common, conservative evangelical image of the end times. If you've read or seen the *Left Behind* franchise, you've been exposed to end-time theology. Tim LaHaye's franchise has been a Christian publishing juggernaut. Its sixteen books, which have sold a collective 65 million copies, outpace *Hunger Games* and George R. R. Martin's "A Song of Ice and Fire," on which *Game of Thrones* was based.[164] This is to say nothing of the four feature films. A recent study from Baptist Lifeway Research of pastors at evangelical and historically black churches found that 90 percent match current events to signs Jesus said would occur shortly before he returns to Earth. These "events" include a decline in traditional morality, a rise in wars and conflicts, an increase in natural disasters, and a rise in false teaching in the church.[165]

If you've been in the church for more than a couple of decades, this is not new: it seems every generation of churchgoers thinks the culture can get no worse.

On the eve of the 2002 invasion of Iraq, Aleksandr Dugin—the Moscow geopolitician and radio personality–published an essay entitled "The Road to Armageddon," in which he sought to explain the George W. Bush administration's war policy by referring to the Protestant theology of dispensationalism. Instead of a typical lament over the spread of ignorant conspiracy theology, it turned into a testimonial: "The most striking thing about Dispensationalism is the way its predictions have been fulfilled to the letter. However improbable it might seem the mythological Protestant fundamentalist interpretation of history turns out to be astoundingly close to the real state of affairs. In this strange, strange world, someone actually has gone mad."[166]

There's an ongoing, morbid blockbuster mentality about the end of the world, and American religious history is full of doomsayers. The younger Len remembers the book *The Late Great Planet Earth* by Hal Lindsey lying around the house when he was a child. Published by the Christian imprint Zondervan, Lindsey's premillennial dispensationalist prediction was the best-selling nonfiction work in America in the decade of the 1970s.[167] And on it goes. William Miller, the founder of the Adventists, was convinced the second coming of Jesus (parousia) would arrive in the 1840s.

People have been predicting the end since the beginning, and perhaps even taking matters into their own hands. So far, all predictions are batting 0.00%, even back to the church at Thessalonica. The earliest letter in the New Testament is an exhortation from the apostle Paul to the church to keep living and working while the faithful waited for Jesus to come back. Two thousand years later, Christians still wonder if the eschaton is happening, or has happened, or will happen soon. So, people buy "Patriot Food" and generators, and guns, and stock up the back room closet with supplies.

In the age of climate change, secularized equivalents have emerged as well, which view linear history through geological periods rather than the story of God as told through Judaism and Christianity. Movements such as Extinction Rebellion that predict the end of the current Anthropocene epoch are engaging in a form of political theology that shares the same form and many of the same chapters as end-time Christian theology.[168] Whether religious or secular, the common thread of these theories is the concept that at a predefined point in history, the end will begin. This is known as "the eschaton."

4.2 | Slipping the Chains of Time

L est we dismiss *Left Behind* readers as the lunatic fringe, consider that fascination with the end has a long history not just to conservative Christians, but in all of Western culture. The vision of a future millennium, inaugurated with the eschaton, especially as outlined in the Revelation of Saint John, has been a prime mover of history. Millennialism cannot be dismissed, as a respected historian tried to do, as "a certain hysteria, indicative of some mental unbalance."[169] Rather, a spirit of millennialism and concern for examining the future through the spectacles of the book of Revelation have signified not isolation from the mainstream of history, but total immersion in it.

> *But I and others who are right minded Christians on all points, are assured that there will be a resurrection of the dead, and a thousand years in Jerusalem which will then be built, adorned and enlarged, (as) the prophets Ezekiel and Isaiah and others declare.*
>
> **—Justin Martyr, Dialogue with Trypho**

Throughout history, millennial sentiment spread to exercise a formative sway over diverse social movements and over broad sections of society. One thinks of the year AD 1000; the crusades; the plague years, such as 1348, when even Petrarch was convinced that "the end of the world is at hand"; monastic movements inspired by Abbott Joachim of Fiore in the thirteenth and fourteenth centuries; the early periods of exploration and Franciscan colonization of the New World; Lollardy and the Radical Reformation (specifically Thomas Müntzer and Münster); Queen Elizabeth I's apocalyptic assessment (shared by many of her subjects, such as John Foxe) that her reign was set in "these last and worst days of the world"; the English, French, and American revolutions, and revolutionary periods in general; and nineteenth-century American reform movements.

One of the least known but most influential figures in history was the Calabrian abbot named Joachim of Fiore (ca. 1150–1202), who developed a philosophy of history that was to dominate Europe until the advent of Marxism. Even such modern philosophers of history as Comte, Lessing, Fichte, Hegel, Schelling, and Marx himself have been found to have Joachite underpinnings, and the secularized Joachite undertones in the phrase "the Third Reich" have not escaped attention. Joachim's predictions (based on Revelation) of an imminent third and final dispensation of the Holy Spirit were so influential that in 1215, when Frederick II was given the imperial crown of the Roman Empire, he was perceived (and perceived himself) as the predicted emperor of the last days, who would liberate the Holy Sepulchre and prepare the way for the second coming and the millennial reign of Christ.[170]

A similar mission largely motivated Christopher Columbus, a fact most historians have ignored. In his little-known Book of Prophecies, Columbus related his commission as a "Christ bearer" (Christoferens) to free Jerusalem from the Muslims and to diffuse the Gospel throughout the world to pave the way for the millennium. In addressing Prince John, Columbus revealed his role in this cosmic drama: "God made me the messenger of the new heaven and the new earth, of which He spoke in the Apocalypse by Saint John, after having spoken of it by the mouth of Isaiah; and He showed me the spot where to find it."[171] In a ship emblazoned with crosses on the sails and "in the name of Jesus," Columbus embarked on what was in many ways the last of the crusades, invoking Joachim of Fiore as his patron saint in the expected evangelization of the world and, inadvertently, in the discovery of the Americas. Joan of Arc had a similar dream as Christopher Columbus. Her life project was to expel the English from France, then to defeat the Hussite heretics in central Europe, and from there to liberate Jerusalem from the Turks and the Muslims and bring in the Age of the Spirit. As Mircea Eliade has admitted, it was in a "messianic and apocalyptic atmosphere" that "the transoceanic expeditions and the geographic discoveries that radically shook and transformed western Europe took place."[172]

To fully appreciate the influence that millennialism in general and Revelation in particular have exerted on history, we must turn to the sixteenth and seventeenth centuries. Within the past couple of decades, historians have mined an amazingly rich quarry of millennialism in the allegedly "communistic" ideal of Digger Gerrard Winstanley; in the poetry of the mystic William Blake, who was inspired by such millennialist movements as Joachism, seventeenth-century Muggletonianism, and Swedenborgianism; in the history of the struggle of women for emancipation from the shackles of Kinder, Küche, und Kirche, begun in earnest during this period; in the sophisticated thought of John Milton; in the political and historical writings of Thomas Hobbes; and in the ideological apologists and actors in the English Revolution, including the indomitable Oliver Cromwell and the New Model Army.

Equally fascinating is the fashionable attention given to Revelation during this period. Sir Isaac Newton, who spent more time ruminating on biblical prophecies than on scientific experiments, argued in his posthumously published commentary on Daniel and Revelation that to repudiate these prophecies was to reject the entire Christian religion and tradition. (The only conspicuous dissenters from Newton's observation would have been the early Martin Luther and John Calvin, who found the book of Revelation too elusive for intelligible exposition.[173]) Based on extensive studies of biblical texts, his private notes calculated a global "reset" in 2060, when "the kingdom of God" would prevail on the earth, "It may end later, but I see no reason for its ending sooner," Newton boldly proclaimed.[174]

This connection between science and Revelation was the norm for the seventeenth century. John Napier, whose commentary on Revelation went through at least twenty-three editions by 1700 and numerous translations, attempted to translate scriptural mathematics into scientific calculus. In so doing he invented logarithms, which he proceeded to use to compute the date of the parousia—between 1688 and 1700. Scientist and mathematician William Whitson, Newton's successor as professor of mathematics at Cambridge, was expelled in 1710 as a result of his Arian efforts to resurrect primitive Christianity, in his mind a necessary preparation for Christ's second coming. And William Oughtred, the inventor of the symbol x and "the greatest mathematician of his day," according to Christopher Hill, spent many hours hovering over the book of Revelation, trying to decipher the date of Christ's return. So did other mathematicians, such as John Pell and Robert Boyle.

But of all the English commentators on Revelation (King James I included), Joseph Mede—botanist, anatomist, mathematician, astronomer, precursor of Cambridge Platonism, and tutor of Milton—wielded the greatest influence through his *Clavis Apocalyptica* (1627). The relevance of this work so intrigued a committee of the British House of Commons during the English Civil Wars that they ordered it to be translated in 1643 under virtually official auspices. In fact, to Thomas Twisse, the Presbyterian divine and prolocutor of Parliament's Assembly of Divines, the merging of expanding scientific knowledge and an expanding world by means of navigation and commerce were harbingers of the millennium. And Roger Bacon's assertion that modern science contained the seeds for the eventual flowering of the millennium was shared by many Englishmen. They felt that both science and biblical prophecy were supplemental ways of getting to know God and his plans, purposes, and lessons for mankind.

In sum, millennialism, defined as a belief in and quest for an imminent period of total, ultimate, collective salvation and peace, has not been the preserve of fringe groups in history, but has pervaded the spirit of many ages and many leaders, both spiritual and secular. Although we do not share Friedrich Engels's estimation of the Revelation of Saint John as "worth more than all the rest of the New Testament put together," we ought at least to be aware of the immense historical importance attached to this supposedly least read book in the New Testament and to the entire subject of millennialism. We ought also to be aware of the phenomenon of what Michael Polanyi calls "moral inversion," where morally impassioned action (like the millennialism of Jim Jones) can be utterly disdainful and devoid of morality itself. [175]

The ongoing passion that has driven millennialism is the desire to escape the crucible of change, which is the false narrative that we can somehow just skip the journey and slip the chains of time. Millennialism has served as a divine Get Out of Jail Free card in the desire to jump straight to home while speaking all the way home in a higher register than is normal.

Eschatological excitement has been the source of some of the greatest horrors and holocausts in history. The greatest hells on earth have been created by the greatest hopes of heaven brought on by millennial dreams and utopian projects. This was the Bolshevik dream. Bolshevism was a millenarian movement, varying from earlier apocalyptic sects in its scale of power and territory.[176] The most murderous of the Bolsheviks' inhuman millenarian projects of remaking human society by exterminating class enemies (i.e., smallholding peasants) was Stalin's terror famine in the early 1930s. Mao's "Great Leap Forward" in the late '50s and early '60s is another example of millennialism as a political religion. In the words of Emilio Gentile, the world's premier cultural historian of fascist ideology:

> The sacralization of politics became an essential aspect of all the communist regimes that arose during the Cold War and copied the Soviet model . . . All communist regimes established a compulsory system of beliefs, myths, rituals, and symbols that exalted the primacy of the party as the sole and unchallenged depository of power. They all dogmatized their ideology as an absolute and unquestionable truth. They all glorified the socialist homeland and imposed a code of commandments that affected every aspect of existence. They all safeguarded their monopoly of power and truth through a police state and hard-line ideological orthodoxy backed by constant surveillance and persecution, which enormously increased the number of human lives sacrificed.[177]

There is faith religion and there is civil religion, which is a political religion. Communism is best seen as a political ("civil" or "secular") religion. Marxism is based on the idea that history has a purpose, which is being relentlessly worked out. It also boasts a powerful vision of future harmony producing accelerated development to contrast with present discord. The great historical theologian Jaroslav Pelikan even called Marxism-Leninism a "Christian heresy."[178] Marxism has an eschatological dimension that has religious roots. A conception of the world can have a religious origin without itself being religious.

Other millenarian movements have included Nazism, Mao's Cultural Revolution, Pol Pot's Cambodia, and the crusades, the last of which included, as we have argued, Christopher Columbus's journeys to the "new world." Much of twentieth-century politics has been the pursuit of millennial dreams and millenarian ends by political means and regimes. Jean-Paul Sartre justified his Marxist determinism because he said the ends justified the means, yet he argued philosophically that freedom was the only absolute moral value. As C. S. Lewis wrote in a letter to his friend Don Giovanni Calabria in 1953, "Almost all of the crimes which Christians have perpetrated against each other arise from this, that religion is confused with politics. For, above all other spheres of human life, the Devil claims politics for his own, as almost the citadel of his power."[179] Kenneth Collins' 2012 book, *Power, Politics and the Fragmentation of Evangelicalism*, showcases how a better perspective on teleology would diminish our fixation on and fetish of politics.

God did not say, "I will send you politicians to save you." Jesus did not say, "Your salvation is found in politics." Do we really think that a change of party, or a change of politics, or a change of economics will bring lasting change to our world? Only a schema change of heart, mind, body, and spirit—the power of Jesus working in us so that we can do abundantly above all we can imagine—will bring lasting change.

The church has been obsessed with this question of eschatology. Millennial dreams inspire the best and the worst. In this line of thinking, the future is something to skip or speed up or kick off to turn on a sequence of events. We either want to create it (social gospel), own it (theocracy), or escape from it (fundamentalism).

At funeral processions in the nineteenth century, drums were always muffled. At the same time much of the church is muffling its drummers and becoming a non-prophet organization, a prophecy industry grows outside of the church.

The millennial obsession with the eschaton turns God into a dispassionate, detached deity who created a Rube Goldberg world and is watching it unfold. It turns us into passive, impotent recipients of a grand design. The belief that the end is a mysterious grand plot leads to a sense of futility. When we believe that there is nothing we can do, we remove ourselves from the responsibility of doing anything.

Ironically, our willingness to become active agents of our understanding of God's future only perpetuates the very scenario many so fear. As we become agents of the grand scheme, we become willing to do harm to people. What many millennialists forget to ask is, to whom and to what am I responsible? In much of public life right now, there is little sense of personal responsibility for the things people say and do. It is as if it no longer matters to be faithful to the truth or to love one another because, to many, the world is ending, and it just doesn't matter anymore. At least Columbus and his peers saw some sense of agency in their theology of millennialism.

4.3 | Standing under the Arch

Have you ever wondered how a fringe religious subset of a persecuted people group in a backwater province of the great Roman Empire eventually took over the entire continent? The rise of Christianity is due in no small part to the innovative approach Christians took to health care.

When the pandemic of Cyprian struck in the year 250, the church had already developed a robust system of the latest in care. In the ancient world, "beneficence took the form of civic philanthropy on behalf of the community at large." But "the classic concept of *philanthropia* was not merely insufficient to provide the motivation for private charity, it actively discouraged it." Meanwhile, Christians "insisted that the love of God required the spontaneous manifestation of personal charity toward one's brothers: one could not claim to love God without loving his brother."[180] Jesus' brother James had reminded the church that pure and undefiled religion was caring for orphans and widows in their distress (James 1:27), and Jesus had redefined neighbor to include all people (see Luke 10:30–38). Thus, Christians in the Roman Empire, rather than seeking to escape their oppressors, saw the care of all people as part of the practice of faith.

Instead of buckling down and buying bunker food in response to the onset of the plague in 250, the church deployed their health-care system in the city. They became the only volunteer organization that cared for the dying and buried the dead. Without the benefit of our modern understanding of how to reduce contagion and spread, faithful members of the church exposed their own health to love their neighbor.

The worst kind of Christian theology toward creation and others is done in the name of millennialism, which promotes provincial thinking and nativism, ignoring the needs of people and creation. Millennialism can offer the false ending of escape. The church in Rome in the year 250 understood that you need the help of heaven to do healing on earth. You need the image and experience of the world to come to get the right image and experience of the earth that is here. You cannot be human without the divine. You cannot do earth without heaven.

"The end of the world as we know it," in the words of rock band R.E.M., is called "the eschaton." It comes from the Greek word *eschatos*, meaning "last" or "final." Eschaton is the final event of history that ushers in the world to come, the climax of the human story. Millennialism is the misguided "immanentization of the eschaton," in the memorable phrase of Eric Voegelin,[181] to create a sort of heaven on earth within history or to attain a premature climax for humanity and consummation of the kingdom.

Philosopher Timothy Morton occupies a chaired professorship of English at Rice University. Besides his celebrated theory of "hyperobjects," he is known for his argument that emotions are from the future and ideas are from the past. You go to a therapist to understand your emotions, your feelings, but once you get the idea of what is going on, you can now move on, because it's behind you and in the past. But Morton is most famous for his announcement that "the end of the world" has already taken place. We are already too late, living in a slow burn to burnout. Life is a matter of doing the best we can knowing that it doesn't matter because it's already too late.

In Morton's philosophy, the planet is burning and on fire: "Fire! Fire! Fire!" The house is on fire, and we should stop rubber-necking the damage and start acting according to the scale or level we are operating on at the moment, even if it's one of panic. The world's most famous climate alarmist is Greta Thunberg. "I don't want your hope, I don't want you to be hopeful," Thunberg declared in her coming-out speech in Davos in 2019. "I want you to panic. I want you to feel the fear I feel every day. And then I want you to act."[182] No wonder we live in a world of one moral panic after another. "Panic" comes from the word meaning "everything." The sense that "everything is happening all at once" is the real essence of panic. So, for Morton, it's okay to panic if we "panic cheerfully." We must not be happy in our panic, but we can be cheerful (which includes a sense of sadness) while we're in a panic. In fact, be an eco-dandy, advises Timothy Morton. The world is ending, so show up for the end of the world in the best dress or best outfit you can.

We believe Jesus is the eschatological temple, both Embodied Torah and Enfleshed Temple. The laws are now written in the heart, and the stones are now living stones, with Jesus as the Chief Cornerstone and the Keystone Arch. Jesus as the Genuine Eschaton changes everything.

A law in France once required anyone who manufactured fireworks to live on the premises with his family. The same principle applies to today's designers of roller coasters. They are the first to ride their creations. The ancient Romans were famous for their advanced engineering in roads (e.g., Appian Way), aqueducts, arches, and domes. Some of them are still in use today. In ancient Rome, when scaffolding was removed from a completed arch, the law required the engineer who had built the arch to stand beneath it. If the arch came crashing down, the engineer would take responsibility firsthand.

How different our world would be if we all had to stand under our own arches. If each one who is making eschatological claims of inside knowledge were forced to stand under the arch? Instead, every eschatological arch we build needs Jesus as its capstone and keystone. Time leans perfectly on him.

Signs of ending all around us darkness, death, and winter days,

Shroud our lives in fear and sadness, numbing mouths that long to praise.

Come, O Christ, and dwell among us! Hear our cries, come set us free.

Give us hope and faith and gladness. Show us what there yet can be.

Can it be that from our endings, new beginnings you create?

Life from death, and from our rendings, realms of wholeness generate?

Take our fears, then Lord, and turn them into hopes for life anew:

Fading light and dying season sing their Glorias to you.

Speak, O God, your Word among us. Barren lives your presence fill.

Swell our hearts with songs of gladness, terrors calm, forebodings still.

Let your promised realm of justice blossom now throughout the earth:

your dominion bring now near us; we await thy saving birth.

—Thomas John Williams (1869–1944)
"Signs of Ending Are All Around Us"

4.4 | The Kingdom of God Is Not an Escape Hatch

Two stories from the political arena highlight the multivalent meanings of millennialism, in all its various subdivisions. The first exemplifies postmillennialism; the second, premillennialism.

In 1912, the Progressive Party national convention met in Chicago to select former president Theodore Roosevelt as their candidate. Apocalyptic sensibilities ran high, and in his acceptance speech Roosevelt choose as his campaign motto the closing lines of his speech: "We Stand at Armageddon and Do Battle for the Lord." The theme song for the convention was "Onward, Christian Soldiers." They pledged to march forth from the convention to build the millennial kingdom of God in America. While the delegates snacked on "women's suffrage sandwiches," justice activist and social worker Jane Addams gave the seconding speech for Roosevelt's nomination.

In 1981 President Ronald Reagan appointed James G. Watt to serve as secretary of the interior. A proud Pentecostal, in his hearings Watt was asked how his premillennial eschatology would affect his conservation administration. Historically premillennialism has often given rise to a laissez-faire, insouciant attitude to the injustices of the world and especially the degradation of the environment. If Jesus is going to return to make everything right, why bother setting things right now?

When prodded about his concern for the care of creation, which would be his job as interior secretary, Watt's exact words were "I do not know how many future generations we can count on before the Lord returns; whatever it is, we have to manage with skill to leave the resources needed for future generations."[183]

Most of the world only heard his first sentence, "I do not know how many future generations we can count on before the Lord returns." PBS personality Bill Moyers, whose stint as a former Baptist pastor and graduate of Southwestern Baptist Theological Seminary heightened his sensitivities to the placidity of premillennialism, falsely revised Watt's statement. Moyers claimed Secretary Watt said, "After the last tree is fell, Christ will come back."[184] Watts never said that, and the caricature of Watt's position became even more severe in the press. But the legend of Watt's supposed antienvironmental attitudes became fixed in the public mind.

The truth is that the care for the environment in its current form is a Pentecostal legacy. The tradition of Earth Day was founded by a Pentecostal, John McConnell Jr., the son of a Pentecostal preacher, who coined the name "Earth Day" in 1968.

Millennialism is a wild card, but all forms of it exhibit the same ambition: the desire to skip or speed up history. It is a radicalization of history by the riotously righteous because it is built on impatience with this wanton, war-torn world. It is what happens when we try to force life and time. People lose the ability to empathize. The desire to skip to the end of the story has precipitated horrors throughout history.

What is the concept of the "end times," and why is it so perennially popular? There are four mainstream schools of eschatological thought: *postmillennialism, premillennialism, amillennialism,* and *ag-millennialism* (our coinage of our position). Each headwaters from a different understanding of when Christ will return and the kingdom of God will kick in. Each has been present in some form throughout all of church history. There is a fifth, small stream of preterism that was made respectable by Dutch lawyer and theologian Hugo Grotius (1582–1645). The full preterist position is that the prophecies of Scripture were fulfilled in the destruction of Jerusalem in AD 70. In other words, the kingdom of God is already here. In the partial preterist position, all prophecies have been fulfilled except those laid out in the last three chapters of Revelation: the visible, physical return of Christ in judgment, the final defeat of death and Satan, the resurrection of the living and the dead, and the coming of the new heaven, the new earth, and the new Jerusalem.

The most prevalent form of eschatological thinking in Christian thought has been postmillennialism, the notion that Christ will return after the thousand-year period of prosperity known as the *millennium*. In this line of thought, the millennium will come because of human initiative and industry, some of which fueled all sorts of reform and revival movements, including the First, Second, and Third Great Awakenings in American history, which abolished slavery, supported women's rights, endorsed workers' rights, and privileged those on the social margins.

By the late nineteenth century, premillennialism had become "the rage of the age," as Howard Snyder puts it.[185]

The form of premillennialism that dominated the twentieth century was a variant of classical premillennialism called *dispensational premillennialism,* which was formulated by Plymouth Brethren theologian and translator John Nelson Darby (1800–1882) and disseminated through the Scofield Reference Bible, published in 1909 by the prestigious Oxford University Press, which proceeded to make a fortune off its best-selling Bible for much of the twentieth century. Darby became a leading purveyor of a futurist reading of the Bible, which assumes the biblical text contains a set of mysterious codes, not unlike Dan Brown's *Da Vinci Code.* Unlocking this set of codes will reveal a sequence of events as outlined in Revelation that will lead to the vanquishment of all evil in the world and the establishment of God's final kingdom in victory.

Pursue these mystery codes and you fall into a deep rabbit hole where people debate the future fate of Christians on earth, based on literal readings of the books of Daniel and Revelation. Forty-one percent of USAmericans expect Jesus to definitely (23 percent) or probably (18 percent) return to Earth by 2050.[186]

Whereas human agency had a role to play in bringing about the kingdom in postmillennialism, in premillennialism Jesus will return first to inaugurate his kingdom, and the date of Jesus' return is unknown and uncertain. Dispensational premillennialism introduces the notion of a Rapture before the tribulation. Competing schools of tribulationists divided over when the church would be raptured, with pretribs arguing before the tribulation, posttribs arguing at the end of the tribulation, and midtribs contending that the church will not be completely spared the reign of the Beast but will not have to endure the whole seven years of suffering and persecution.

Amillennialism (literally "no millennium") focuses on the millennium as a symbol of a heavenly reality, not an earthly one. Ag-millennialism is our personal moniker and describes those who don't know and don't fuss about what happens when but instead concern themselves, by God's grace, with being faithful until he comes (see Luke 19:11–17).

Jesus never promises an escape from the world. Escapism isn't Christian; it's gnostic and based on Platonic Forms. Nazism was a malign Platonism that had no place for individuals, only a collective "we-ism." Its "Great Leader" or "der Führer," as he liked to call himself, was in Hitler's mind merely an emanation leader of the mass, its "drummer." Nazi race theory was based on a millennial idolization of the "perfect" society and the engineered collective. Secular millennial aspirations fueled some of the twentieth century's greatest suffering, as featured in Franco's concentration camps, Stalin's Gulag, Mao's Laogai system, Kim Il-Sung's labor and indoctrination camps, and the worst of all, Hitler's Germany.

Christian Gnostics reject Genesis 1 and the goodness of the created world altogether. The earliest church preached patience above all traits. Jesus says this present time is the birth pangs for the age to come (Matthew 24), and he came to not to rapture us from the world but to rapture us for this world and the world to come.

Hence, we are ag-millennial, meaning we are agnostic to the timing of the eschaton. What time is it? Only God knows. "It is not for you to know the times or periods that the Father has set by his own authority," Jesus said (Acts 1:7). Even when Jesus is four days late, he is "on time." In the words of Mabel Boggs Sweet, "God's clock keeps perfect time" and will keep ticking that perfect timing until the angel announces, "Time is no more" (see Revelation 10:6 KJV).

Postmillennialism reflects the hubris and effrontery of "we can bring in the kingdom by human effort, forgetting that Jesus IS the kingdom, and his presence is here with us now. Premillennialism reflects the capitulation and passivity of "we can only sit, watch, and wait for Jesus to bring in the kingdom," forgetting that Jesus calls us to love one another today. The church is called to prophetic witness today. This is the calling and obligation of every generation.

Consider again the opening questions of this book, when the disciples asked of Jesus, when is the end and what are the signs? Jesus spends two chapters of Matthew addressing these questions. An obsession with the future and the plot is the wrong focus. This doesn't mean the future won't come to pass; indeed, Jesus says, it will. And when it happens, we will know it; it will be unmistakable. Yet, we also know from Jesus' parabolic response to their questions (the parable of the ten virgins) that the parousia will be far enough down the road that we will be distracted.

We are still here in the world, making arches. There is no guarantee that the world is indeed ending. As we know with the Black Death and many other stories, there have been moments such as these before, when the end seemed nigh. One of the only guarantees of futurism is that the future will not be a straight-line extension of present circumstances. Things change; new variables emerge.

Jesus is clear: we cannot know the day or hour. While we wait, what do we do? Jesus is clear in both what he says and what he does not say: He never tells his disciples to stock up, to create bunkers of protection against invading forces, or to mark days off on a calendar. Instead, he says, "A new command I give you: Love one another. As I have loved you, so you must love one another. By this everyone will know that you are my disciples, if you love one another" (John 13:34–35 NIV). Love isn't an escape hatch; it is active and shaping, the single greatest force to turn negative forces to positive ones, and to make the future better, not worse.

We are ag-millennial because we believe we have a responsibility to do more than stock up on generators. It is not that the eschaton won't occur, but rather it is not to be our focus. Do we have a responsibility to our children? It is only when we return to having to stand under our creations that the world will start getting better. As we stated earlier, the darkest nights may turn into the most beautiful dawns. Indeed, Jesus gave us the thing on which we should focus: to love the Lord our God with all our hearts and with all our souls and with all our minds, and to love our neighbor as ourselves. To do this is to stay in the world, to stay responsible to those in our circles, and to continue to love and serve.

N O   T I M E :   T H E   F A L S E   E N D I N G   O F   A H I S T O R I C I S M

Is there even a purpose to history?

"Cancel culture" is a form of ideological shunning, now practiced by both the political left and right but common throughout history. It is a symptom of ahistoricism, which is the notion that history doesn't matter, or history can be judged based on the present, or we can cancel history as if it didn't happen. The cross is the ultimate symbol of cancellation: Jesus being canceled by the cancel culture of his day.

Some suggest there is no grand narrative at all, and life is purely circumstance. This material view of the world can only end in nihilism and in a struggle for power. Yet the kingdom of God is not mere metaphor, life is more than just survival, and history is more than a story written by the winners.

5.1 | Cancellations and Cancel Culture

We may try to be semioticians, then, but autobiography is always breaking in.

—Bharat Tandon

Cancel culture is not new. Every schoolchild learns of Puritan settlements banning and banishing dissidents such as Roger Williams and Anne Hutchinson. Seventeenth-century Puritanism could "banish" the dead even more graphically: the manuscript parchments of the thirteenth-century Franciscan friar and Scottish theologian Duns Scotus, and other proscribed authors, were used to make kites or were nailed up "in all common howses of easement"—as toilet paper.[187] More recently, the global darling of deconstructionist philosophy, Jacques Derrida, had his own brush with "cancel culture" in 1992 when the *Times* published a letter signed by nineteen academics (including Dallas Willard) objecting to his honorary doctorate from Cambridge.

"Canceling" people is a form of shunning and exercising the ban against those whose views offend the mainstream. One of us (Len S.) experienced this cancel culture as a child. The Sweet family was formally kicked out of a church, and Mabel Boggs Sweet was defrocked, as noted in chapter 3, because of the presence in the Sweet home of the Satan Box or "Satan's Tabernacle" (television). Sweet family members who remained in the church were pressured not to associate with *those* Sweets that the church had canceled.

Many of us admit that cancel culture is toxic, yet we practice it all the time. We block; we unfriend; we mute; we turn our backs; we don't show up; we in our own way "cancel" everyone and everything that challenges our sensibilities. One Twitterer even put on their profile: "If you aren't orthodox in your faith, don't follow me or just unfriend me." Whether you call it "fogging" or "shrouding," as the Chinese do, cancel culture is universal. It is more noticeable now because the liberals have become notoriously illiberal, especially on "progressive" college campuses. But conservatives were the first to perfect cancel culture. British philosopher Bertrand Russell was canceled by Trinity College, Cambridge University in 1916, not for his atheism and belief that all religions are based on fear, but for his "pacifism" and defense of conscientious objectors in the First World War.

The ultimate in ahistoricism is the notion that history doesn't matter, that it can be judged on the basis of the present, or that we can cancel history as if it didn't happen. We cancel the present like we cancel history. Or we make up history to fit our ideology.

Irish professor and media philosopher Gavan Titley, in his book titled *Is Free Speech Racist?* (2021), implies that the answer to the titular question in the book is yes. He even goes so far as to call rationality itself white privilege, or as he puts it, "the privileging of rationality."[188] So much for the United Nations' Universal Declaration of Human Rights (UDHR), which recognizes freedom of speech as a human right. And so much for the First Amendment to the US Constitution.

Both of us have been victims of cancel culture. Because of something we wrote, spoke, or due to a hate site that popped up, spewing nastiness and falsifications, we have been sometimes subject to a last-minute cancellation of a scheduled speaking event with a "Sorry, we can't honor our commitment to bring you." Then comes the imprimatur clause of cancellation: "We decided to go in another direction." Other times, it has come in the form of public heckling and jeers.

For example, after beginning a series of sermons at a certain annual convention, when the conventioneers found out that Len S. had baptized infants in the past, they mounted a campaign to cancel him during the event. They blocked every entrance with placards and shouts when he was scheduled to speak. Another tribe invited him to speak at their annual convention about the future but wanted him to sign an agreement that he would not pray or quote Scripture during his address. When he refused, the person who introduced him at the event went to great lengths to warn those in attendance to only take seriously what Sweet would say about culture and the future, but to ignore anything he might have to say about the Scriptures or Jesus. Len W. once could barely finish a workshop to hundreds of preachers because a few of them decided it was appropriate to heckle him and publicly question his legitimacy mid-speech. One of us (Len S.) was even canceled from speaking at a seminary, the invitation withdrawn, because some faculty objected, "When you get Sweet, all you get is Jesus."

The ultimate in cancellation, of course, is "No person, no problem," as allegedly formulated by Marxist revolutionary Joseph Stalin. It is based on the belief that if you remove the man, you remove the problem, or "Cancel the man and you cancel the problem." "No person, no problem" summarizes Stalin's approach to life as detailed in the novel *Children of the Arbat* by Anatoly Rybakov. In one episode, over the execution of army officers in Tsaritsyn, Rybakov formulated Stalin's attitude to problems with the short phrase "Death solves all problems. No man, no problem."[189] Stalin took the slogan seriously. His "Great Terror" took a toll on the lives of between six and seven million. And Stalin was Christian schooled and seminary trained (Tiflis Seminary) and sang in a church choir. In the 1920s, the Soviet Union was the only country in the world to recognize Yiddish as a language of national identity. Thirty years later, Stalin was busy exterminating the remaining Yiddish intellectuals to have survived his various purges. Thirteen prominent Soviet Jews, many of them writers, were arrested on vague charges of "bourgeois nationalism" and shot in Moscow's Lubyanka prison on August 12, 1952, in what became known as "the Night of the Murdered Poets."[190]

Ahistoricism is what enables a deepfake world that blurs the boundary between reality and ruse, between truth and illusion. Canceling things you don't like or that you disagree with is not Jesus. Canceling history, or the parts of history you don't like, is not Jesus. Besides, erasing history is like removing the best teacher of your life.

Jesus spent his life with canceled people—people canceled by the culture of their day: the poor, the marginalized, the outcast and outsiders. Jesus doesn't cancel people. Jesus cancels sin. "He breaks the power of canceled sin."[191] Charles Wesley did not write, "He cancels the guilt of conquered sin." There is no joy or song in that, since it means we have to conquer the power of sin and death ourselves. No, the cross cancels our sin, and Jesus frees us from condemnation and cancellation. "He sets the prisoner free."[192] As noted in the opening of this chapter, the cross is the ultimate symbol of cancellation: Jesus being cancelled by the cancel culture of his day.

Cancel culture is not kingdom culture, not jubilee culture. Jubilee culture is a Micah 6:8 culture, which calls for doing justice, but it also calls for loving mercy and walking in humility wherever we go and in whatever we do. Joachim of Fiore distinguished between the "reign of justice" or of "law" in an imperfect society, and the "reign of freedom" in a perfect, Jubilee society. To make injustice the fundamental reality of life is to give injustice a victory that it does not deserve and has not won.

We must risk delight. We can do without pleasure, but not delight . . . We must have the stubbornness to accept our gladness in the ruthless furnace of this world. To make injustice the only measure of our attention is to praise the devil.

—poet Jack Gilbert (1925–2012)

So how do Christians personate Jesus in a cancel culture?

First, Christians love our enemies, not cancel them. That means we don't join the mob. We love people who disagree with us, even those who hold us in contempt. That isn't easy because it involves loving our enemies.

It also involves asking questions of the mob and sometimes challenging them. When Jesus stood up for the woman accused of adultery, he asked the mob to go pick up a stone and start the stoning, but only to pick it up if they were without guilt themselves (see John 8:3–11). Besides, the law required that both the man and the women caught in adultery be killed (Deuteronomy 22:22). Where was the man? Jesus' targeted questioning and probing clarifications canceled the mob's canceling of the accused.

Jesus also listened to those who were offending and offensive. He listened to the woman without judging her or scolding her. He kept an open mind. We don't need to have such an open mind that our brains fall out. But we need to keep our minds bathed in and breathing fresh air.

Finally, Jesus responds with mercy and humility, as he restores justice to the situation. Justice, not judgment. So, when we see something that makes our blood boil and our heads roil, we don't cancel the offender but pray for that person and open our minds and hearts to him or her. Never cancel the person. Never cancel the relationship. Instead, cancel your anger and haughtiness.

The cross by definition is an offense. No person would have written a salvation story like the gospel story. Every part of it was an offense. The more Jesus disregarded the doctrines and dictates of the Law that worked to the detriment of the poor, the outcast, the stranger, the sinner, the more he fell afoul of the religious and political establishment. "Beware when all speak well of you," warned gospel writer Luke (Luke 6:26, paraphrased). Outraged anyone lately? If anyone should be able to handle offensiveness and those who offend, it is us. Søren Kierkegaard, the great Danish theologian writes, "Christianity has taken a giant stride into the absurd" and "Remove from Christianity its ability to shock . . . and it is altogether destroyed. It then becomes a tiny superficial thing, capable neither of inflicting deep wounds nor of healing them. When the absurd starts to sound reasonable, that's when we should begin to worry."[193]

5.2 | The Past Is Another Country

The fourth false ending, and to some, one of the most shocking current developments, is ahistoricism's resistance to historical consciousness and denial of a story altogether. We cannot afford to look backward, we are told. The past is toxic, filled with all sorts of "isms," and you should only take it in small doses. Especially repudiated is the existence of any "meta-narrative" (other than the self) that tells the whole story in one story.

Is there an app for it?

The story is legendary. About 370 BCE a student of the Greek philosopher Plato asked his mentor what was the use of the abstract conceptualizations and elaborate theorems he was being taught. Plato at once ordered his student be given a small coin, that he might not think he had gained knowledge for nothing. Then Plato sent him packing.

What is the use of math?

What is the use of philosophy?

What is the use of history?

Ahistoricism says "None." But history does some things:

It tells us about ourselves, and who we are as humans, giving us a sense of identity and helping us make better relationships.

It tells us about how humanity has treated one another, giving us a sense of morality and helping us make better judgments.

It tells us about how the past becomes the present, and how the present is becoming the future, helping us make a better future.

The present must not shrine the past but let the past shine wisdom and discernment upon the present.

Understood in the light of a denial of heroes and villains, or ideals of "good" and "bad," perhaps the ahistoricism we are witnessing is not so shocking. One of Kurt Vonnegut's story structures is a flat line. Much of our recent "golden age" of television has told such stories, such as *The Sopranos*, and *Seinfeld*, which was famously about nothing. *Seinfeld* is a perpetual act 2, with some subplots resolved and others carrying on. When nothing ever resolves, some conclude the only ethical alternative is to simply erase the momentary highs and lows that privilege some and disenfranchise others. Yet we flatten history at our peril.

British novelist L. P. Hartley (1875–1972) was the first to say that "the past is a foreign country: they do things differently there."[194] The refusal to acknowledge the past as deserving of being treated differently from the present, and the projection of the present into the past, the condescension of posterity, we call "presentism." The moral condescension of the present to the past, as if we would have done things differently or believed different things if we were in their shoes in their times, is to read history as versions of modern debates. History is an epistemological "dialogue" between the past and the present—neither "the past by itself" nor "the historian's thought about it by itself" but "by the two things in their mutual relations."[195] British historian E. H. Carr, in his classic text *What Is History?* (1960), called history "an unending dialogue between the present and the past."[196]

One day we'll be judged as we are judging. Our refusal to see the past within its context instead of the lens of the present brings with it a cheap superiority. Len Sweet has called his generation, the Boomers, the worst generation because of its presentist arrogance. Len Wilson has called his generation, the Xers, the worst generation because of its presentist nihilism. Yet if future generations look on our generations with dismay and disgust because of how far they've come from where we left off, our generations would have been a huge success story. Who else raised them to make life better and go where we weren't able to go? Who else raised them with the capacity to push back productively against the givens of their day and take new directions?

How can the church resist the ahistoricism and presentism of the culture and build a new historical understanding? It will not be easy for a culture steeped in self-esteem, self-help, self-care, self-realization, self-disclosure, and self-determination to hear the word "discipline," whether self-discipline or the discipline of historical context. But to exercise the discipline of historical context, to enter the quiddity of another human being or another cultural era, we will need to learn to do three things: Off, On, HI.

1. First, OFF the Auto.

Turn the autobiography OFF for a moment and stop looking at the present or the past through the lens of autobiography. This is the imperative of self-transcendence: the ability to get outside oneself, to come out from oneself, to come outside oneself to look at something without one's eyes of preference and preferment and politics, and to resist the culture-war reduction of religion to politics. To turn the auto OFF is to refrain from self-referential readings or analysis, as some try to do.

Charles Darwin once observed that human "moral sympathies" have evolved over time, from a primitive, exclusive regard for self, family, and tribe to a broader sense of responsibility for one's nation and all of humanity, and now to other living creatures.[197] Darwin advanced the idea that morality existed before religion, and speculated that our moral sympathies could evolve, as human society evolved:

> As man advances in civilization, and small tribes are united into larger communities, the simplest reason would tell each individual that he ought to extend his social instincts and sympathies to all the members of the same nation, though personally unknown to him. This point being once reached, there is only an artificial barrier to prevent his sympathies extending to the men of all nations and races.[198]

This is one of the hardest things anyone in semiotics, who seeks to study and understand the of signs of culture and therefore others, has to learn: to move from self-transparence to self-transcendence, to lay down what you like and think ("Well, I'm not like that;" or "But I don't think that") to get inside the skin of another person, culture, or historical era.

2. Turn ON the Attentiveness.

Pay attention to the point where you enter a state of allthereness. Attend and abide by finding the unique "tincture of time," or as we prefer to put it today, the terroir (from medieval Latin *territorium*), of the period you are looking at. Every age has a unique sense of place.

Duns Scotus was a medieval theologian who insisted on the vast importance and implication of the biblical "naming" of things into existence. God and Adam partnered in creation through the naming of every living thing, calling its essence into existence. This means that everything that lives has in some way the breath of God in it and is connected to the divine by the livingness of its name, by the livingness of its uniqueness, by its particularity. Scotus called a being's uniqueness its "isness" or haecceity ("haecceitas") and insisted on the intractable haecceity of history. W. H. Auden called this uniqueness a person's "eachness": each one is a one each, a one-off, an original.[199] C. S. Lewis called what makes you distinctively you your "quiddity" (our favorite),[200] rediscovering a medieval word that means "the inherent nature or essence of something or someone."[201] More simply put, a thing is the "whatness" of "what it is." (And no, J. K. Rowling didn't name the Hogwarts game after quiddity, though she has become one of the most famous culture cancellations.[202]) Each person has a quiddity. Every era of history has a unique taste, a unique smell, a unique vibe, a unique aura. Beauty comes from living in your quiddity. As a landscape architect friend of the younger Len's once told him, the answer to any landscape design question is found in the dirt. Just stare at a space long enough, and you will see the solution.

To follow Jesus is to bring out the quiddity in others and point to the quiddity in things and times. Trappist monk Thomas Merton loved Shaker furniture so much because he said the Shakers used wood to make furniture that revealed the "logos" or the "innermost principle" of its being.[203] To be able to "rub one's nose in" (as Lewis put it[204]) the quiddity of every person one meets, to kiss the quiddity of every place one encounters or every period of history one enters, no matter how beautiful or ugly the world deems the person, place, or thing, to enter into quiddity of each day, since we get no other one like it, is to get outside oneself and to enter the mystery of life and the divine.

3) Tune In and Turn HI the Aural. Develop a listening ear.

Our ears can hear what is behind us; our eyes can't see what is behind us. The focus on "visioning" in leadership literature doesn't address or even acknowledge the discipline of historical context. It is listening that turns information into intelligence, intelligence into wisdom, and wisdom into truth. Good hearing takes as much boldness and freedom as good speaking, and sometimes more. We must be careful not to speak before we first listen: "Speak, for your servant is listening," Samuel told the Lord (1 Samuel 3:10). When we listen to a historical context, like the time of the biblical patriarch Methuselah, we hear the reverberations of numerology, which was as big a deal in biblical times as it is largely meaningless now. Numbers told stories, and particular numbers were metaphors, not mere recitations and calculations. We may have lost the metaphorical significance of 969, but to say that Methuselah lived 969 years was to say that he lived to be a very, very, very old man. One day future historians writing about us will wonder about our hypocrisy in saying, "Just give me a minute," and fifteen minutes later we show up.

Can we hear the various meanings of the first-person pronoun? There is a semiotic distinction between the indexical and the anaphoric "I." There is the indexical "I" that a speaker uses to identity himself or herself. Then there is the anaphoric "I" by which texts incorporate recipients into a larger narrative. Can the indexical "I" recede and allow the anaphoric "I" of tradition and community to speak through the indexical?

To understand the present ahistoricism, we must not only recognize the past as another country but come to grips with what we mean by the "future." To do this, we will next look at shapes of history.

5.3 | The Shapes of History

We've been talking about history throughout this book, but what do we mean by history? As long as humankind has had a sense that time exists, and that we pass from one experience to the next, there has been with this understanding an awareness of a corresponding question of purpose. Is there a meaningful purpose to time? Is there a teleological structure to history? If so, what is it, and what is our role in it?

A philosophy of time can be broken down into an understanding of the past, present, and future. Our conceptions of the past and future have profound implications on actions in the present, particularly in Christian ministry. The question is, what is our understanding of history? If past is prologue, we need to go back to go forward.

Some would suggest history is irrelevant regarding questions of the soul. Yet at its most basic, history is the exploration of ultimate meaning. Boris Pasternak, the Russian poet and novelist who penned *Doctor Zhivago* in the aftermath of the Bolshevik revolution, wrote that history is "the setting in motion of centuries of work at the gradual unriddling of death and its eventual overcoming. Hence the discovery of mathematical infinity and electromagnetic waves, hence the writing of symphonies. It is impossible to move on in that direction without a certain uplift. These discoveries call for spiritual equipment."[205]

Consider this section to be spiritual equipment. The thinking Christian must develop both a philosophy and a theology of history. To be antihistorical is to accept the gnostic heresy. If we do not live in history, we are not a people of the God of history. To understand the end, we must adopt a philosophy of history, which takes us to views of history from antiquity. Ancient creation myths and the Greek concept of *physis* are indications that as long as humankind has had a sense that time passes from one experience to the next, there has been with this passing an awareness of a corresponding question of purpose.[206] Is there a meaningful structure to history? If so, what is it, and what is our role in it? Addressing questions of meaning in history, which we may consider a philosophy of history, is a prerequisite to addressing questions of the end. To understand what happens in the end, we need to step back to view the entire story, which necessitates an analysis of history. Our conceptions of the past and future have profound implications on our attitudes about knowledge itself and therefore our behavior. You cannot separate story from history.

Philosophies of history and therefore of the future are built on images of time. Does history have a narrative? If so, what is it? There are several mental images for the path of history. Accepting history as a (true) story is essential to our question. As with story itself, history has a plot or a map—a shape. Is it rising? Falling? This book explores not only the end of history, but its shape as well. What is the shape of history? The common shapes are the incline and the decline. As the doctrine of progress fades, fear of the future and of change leads some to adopt another false ending, which is to look to the past. And there is increasingly a return to circle thinking.

Let us consider several such images, each of which may be understood visually as shapes, by which we interpret the events of history.

The Circle

Before the rise of progress, history was understood to be circular. Any analysis of a philosophy of history has to begin with a circle. Indeed, the most well-worn axiom on a philosophy of history is that it repeats itself. American scholar Thomas Cahill writes, "All evidence points to there having been, in the earliest religious thought, a vision of the cosmos that was profoundly cyclical."[207] Because a circle ends where it begins, nothing was ever new; thus, meaning was found not in the future but in an immutable, eternal past. "No event is unique, nothing is enacted but once...; every event has been enacted, is enacted, and will be enacted perpetually; the same individuals have appeared, appear, and will appear at every turn of the circle."[208]

Because a circle ends where it begins, authority in antiquity was found in an immutable, eternal past. Various ancient, pagan cosmologies shared this common philosophy of history, with seasons to every year and life, and gods to oversee them. As the writer of Ecclesiastes observes, "Whatever has happened—that's what will happen again; whatever has occurred—that's what will occur again. There's nothing new under the sun" (Ecclesiastes 1:3 CEB). Journalist Frederick Raphael writes, "Progress was neither celebrated nor expected in the ancient world. Greeks were more likely to refer to their Golden Age and Jews to Eden (and later to lost Jerusalem). Romans set great store by the *mos maiorum*, the routine of aristocratic ancestors, who knew best."[209] Greek philosophy offered perhaps the most well-articulated enunciation, described by French political theorist Alain de Benoist:

> For the Greeks, eternity alone is real. Authentic being is immutable: circular motion, which ensures the eternal return of same in a series of successive cycles, is the most perfect expression of the divine. If there are rises and falls, progress and decline, it is within a cycle inevitably followed by another (Hesiod's theory of the succession of the ages, Virgil's return of the golden age). In addition, the major determining factor comes from the past, not the future.

Perhaps the premier progress scholar is historian J. B. Bury, who wrote that Aristotle believed "all arts, sciences, and institutions have been repeatedly, or rather an infinite number of times . . . discovered in the past and again lost."[210] Later, he wrote, "The theory of world-cycles was so widely current that it may almost be described as the orthodox theory of cosmic time among the Greeks, and it passed from them to the Romans."[211] Gray writes that "for Aristotle, history was a series of processes of growth and decline no more meaningful than those we observe in the lives of plants and animals."[212]

Although other shapes of history emerged over time, the circle has persisted, notably in the work of Giambattisa Vico, whom one scholar described as the "father of the concept of a philosophy of history."[213] Others have denied linearity in time as well, including Oswald Spengler, Henry Adams, Nikolay Danilevsky, Albert Schlesinger Jr., and Karl Marx, who famously wrote that history always repeats itself, "the first as tragedy, the second as farce."[214]

Like communism, socialism claims to liberate society from selfish profit and unequal gain by killing the individual and crowning the collective. A fundamental difference between socialism and communism, and one reason they should not be lumped together, concerns each philosophy's understanding of history. Marx denied linearity altogether, whereas socialist ideals of the Enlightenment are largely built on a philosophical foundation of political progress, as we will explore. Notably, socialist idealism and revolutionary experiments of the last two hundred years have largely failed to prevent the reassertion of longstanding cultural attitudes; for example, "in the Soviet Union, by the 1930s, most of the attributes of the Russian empire had reappeared."[215]

The circle is notably a core feature of story structure.[216] Anthropologist Mary Douglas observes the permeation of the image of the circle in ancient thought through an analysis of literature, in which she highlights the presence of what she describes as "ring composition." Ring composition "is based on parallelism in the straightforward sense that one section has to be read in connection with another that is parallel because it covers similar or antithetical situations . . . But the parallel sections are not juxtaposed in the texts. They must be placed opposite each other, one on each side of the ring. The structure is chiastic [mirrored]; it depends on the 'crossing over' or change of direction of the movement at the middle point."[217] In other words, to the one who sees history as a circle, the end of the story is the same as the beginning. Change is not assumed.

A great example of circle thinking is *Inside Llewyn Davis*, by the Coen brothers, a melancholy film about a folk singer who rejects the postwar American dream but can find no alternative direction to fulfill his life's purpose.

It is difficult to see the dominance of the circle worldview from our linear vantage point. Linear change is so baked in that we cannot grasp a worldview where authority lay in the past and everything eventually returns to the way it was before. In introducing the ubiquity of ring composition in ancient literature, Douglas highlights the deconstructionist prejudice of linear thinking, noting for example that "the structure of Jeremiah, and especially of its apparently chaotic chronology, has proved elusive to linear, critical investigators, many of whom have declared the text to be in disarray and have attempted a reconstruction of an 'original.'"[218]

The Straight Line

The Jewish people of the Old Testament were the first group to break out of the circle. What caused Jewish thinking to become distinctive from its contemporaries was their understanding of Yahweh's presence. According to anthropologist David Lempert, the Jewish people introduced four innovative philosophical concepts which influenced other cultures: "beliefs of individual free will, of a single 'God,' of a method of how societies would advance in parallel to the advance of technology, and the idea of historical processes moving linearly as a result of human action."[219]

One of the influences of the emergence of monotheism was a change in the orientation toward time. If God interacts with humankind, then history becomes driven by a series of unique events, and the past no longer defines the future. These concepts became signified as a "straight line" orientation toward history. Alain de Benoist writes, "Temporality . . . is directed towards the future, from Creation to the Second Coming, the Garden of Eden to the Last Judgment. The golden age no longer lies in the past, but at the end of times."[220]

Thus, the circle and the line became two distinct orientations toward history: the circle's orientation is toward the past and the straight line's orientation is toward the future. Eventually the Hebrew tradition's conception of linear time spread across multiple religious traditions.[221]

The shift from the circle to the straight-line view has been, to this point in history, absolute. The Hebrew understanding of history eventually became the predominant philosophy of history in the ancient world.[222] The circle as a philosophy of history and an epistemological structure is so lost in contemporary rhetoric that in her lecture on the presence of "rings" in ancient literature, Douglas treated them as a discovery akin to finding a textual fossil.[223]

Establishing the difference between the circle and line, however, does not satisfy any particular sense of meaning or purpose, because "if linearity and uniqueness are the sole features of history, it is consistent to argue that history is but a collection of unique events moving aimlessly forward."[224]

From its beginning, what made the Christian story distinct from its Jewish roots was not just that a line existed, but what happened at its end. Whereas a straight line at some point simply stops—indeed, the Sadducees, the ruling Jewish class of Jesus' day, did not believe in bodily resurrection (Mark 12:18)—the story of the resurrection of Jesus of Nazareth suggests a fundamental transfiguration, or changing of shape, at the end of the line. Because of the resurrection, the end of the line introduces a reality structurally different from the events of history that preceded it. Just as Aaron, the high priest, took off his clothes and left them behind after leaving the Holy of Holies in the tent of meeting (Leviticus 16:23), so Jesus, the new High Priest, left his graveclothes behind on the ark-like tomb to begin his post-resurrection life. The Christian understanding of time was circularity with a *telos*, the linear and the loop together moving in a spiral toward a *telos*.

Christian theologian Augustine explored a distinct philosophy of history through an emphasis on linearity coupled with change: "Time does not exist without some movement and transition, while in eternity there is no change."[225] The Christian story introduces a third variable, finality, to the structure of history.[226] It is not linearity and unique events, per se, but the resulting change in ontological state that characterizes the Christian story.[227] In other words, in the Christian story, the end of history is more than simply a line that stops. In *City of God*, Augustine expands on Jesus' metaphor of child development to codify a radical new Christian idea that the story of humanity ends, not with a boom and doom but with a bloom of blessings, both for the individual and for all of civilization.[228]

The basis for the future ideology of progress is evident in the combination of variables of linearity, uniqueness, and finality.[229] After Christianity became the dominant religion of the Western world under the Roman ruler Constantine, the Christian understanding of history as a line, coupled with some sort of transformed finality, emerged as the de facto cultural understanding of time. But this understanding was more eschatological than historical. While Christianity provided an end to history (eschatology) and from it a purpose to our place in history (teleology), events themselves were not necessarily understood as part of a grand sequence on a gradual, incremental incline to the end.

From the vantage point of millennia, this shift seems definitive and irresolute. Yet neither linearity, unique events, or even finality prescribe a concomitant inexorable increase or improvement in value or orientation. What caused the straight line to become a step-up line, or, to use the linguistic shorthand, an "incline"?

Incline

Due in part to the 2016 election of US president Donald Trump and the apparent cultural rejection of longstanding, positive attitudes toward

| Chapter 5 | No Time: The False Ending of Ahistoricism

science and technology, a set of books emerged defending the ideal of progress. A key justification of these apologetics is the rise of standards of living since the beginning of the Industrial Revolution in eighteenth-century England. The beginnings of progress however, go back much further.

In the 1600s, the philosopher Descartes created a research methodology that "revolutionized the developing field of science and changed the way mankind thinks in the world."[230] Descartes was a devout Catholic who was obsessed with certainty. His obsession culminated in *The Discourse on Method*, which ended with the simple observation that all might be doubted except one thing, namely, that he, the doubter, existed, because he doubted.

The story behind Descartes's discovery of selfhood is an interesting one. What became one of the mantras of modernity—"I think, therefore I am"—came to him as he fought off the cold in a secluded cabin of a small Bavarian village. The paradox of the self is there from the beginning. The modern self was born in separation from the world, in isolated rooms and secluded cabins, where a solitary scientist mixed doubts and certainties in the laboratory of his mind.

His famous dictum *cogito, ergo sum*, "I think, therefore I am," includes a lesser-known margin note that says, "We cannot doubt of our existence while we doubt."[231] This has been summarized as *dubito; ergo sum*, or "I doubt; therefore I am." The Cartesian raison d'être is doubt—not faith. In his obsession with knowledge, Descartes created a divide between science and religion that lasts to this day. The epistemological basis for religion is faith, but the epistemological basis for science is doubt.

Cartesian doubt provided a basis for scientific inquiry as philosophy. Empiricism, introduced by natural philosopher and Reformed Protestant Francis Bacon, promised to answer questions through the systematic use of experiment and experience—which Bacon championed not outside the church but as an "instauration" or restoration of humanity's dominion over creation lost in Adam's fall.[232]

Practical observation, rather than theological tradition, led to an "enlightenment" of the Western mind. Perhaps more than any other orientation, the fundamental shift of the Enlightenment epoch has been a move away from a backward-looking way of thinking, toward a future orientation defined by "principles of experiment and trial and error."[233]

The split came into full form in the aforementioned philosophical argument between the Ancients and the Moderns. The "moderns" won the debate because the application of scientific thinking and subsequent improvements to the human condition seemingly made its value self-evident. To the Christian, the discovery of powerful new technologies offered a natural explanation to Augustine's different ending of history with social improvement created by the scientific method. The image of history as an incline toward a perfect end, the ideology of progress, and the concept of a philosophy of history itself begin here.

Decline

History did not "finish" or "end" with the triumph of progress. Enlightenment ideals notwithstanding, a long look back belies any facile sense of onward and upward historical or deterministic development. The first and most obvious example is the history of the twentieth century, which, despite its utopian beginnings became the bloodiest century in human history.

Recounting the history of Christianity in Cambridge, Ian Cooper notes periods of rising and waning Christian influence over sixteen hundred years of British history, juxtaposed in varying degrees with periods of waxing and waning cultural flourishing.[234] Or consider the Silk Road, which carried both valuable trade and deadly bubonic plague.[235] It is hard to read any Christian or cultural history and retain confidence in a grand ascension to heaven. Indeed, the current pessimistic zeitgeist seems to be dragging down the ascendancy of progress, as well as the entire Enlightenment experiment.[236] Postcolonial scholar Margaret Majumdar writes, "Faith in progress as an unstoppable historical certainty has been shattered by real historical developments such as the growth of fascism and Nazism, the two world wars and the barbarity associated with them. There has been a recognition that history can go backwards as well as forwards, that there can be regressive as well as progressive phases."[237]

The curse of irresistible progress is irresistible regression.
—Theodor Adorno and Max Horkheimer

Of particular interest in understanding progress in relationship to the USAmerican church is Henry Adams, grandson of US president John Quincy Adams. Considering his social standing and intellectual heritage, if anyone should have believed in progress, it would have been such a figure. Yet the younger Adams had seen enough corruption form in Washington, DC, over the course of his lifetime to adopt a different view.[238] Whereas Alexis de Tocqueville and John Stuart Mill, two others who were acutely aware of democracy's shortcomings, thought these deficiencies fixable, Adams did not.

Late in his life, Adams wrote *A History of the United States*, a nine-volume study of early-nineteenth-century America commonly regarded as one of the great written histories. In it he drew from philosophers such as Hegel and Schopenhauer. And even when evidence showed the contrary and most published histories stressed an ideology of progress, "in the eyes of Henry Adams, immutable laws degraded every sphere of human existence, the political realm not excepted."[239] In an age when his contemporaries saw upward progress, Adams saw the downward turn of an epochal circle, a declining societal wheel, which must reach a bottom before an eventual rebirth could occur.

The Sine Wave

Considering the limitations of the circle, straight line, and upward slope, the one historiographical shape that seems most clear from the historical record is a sine wave, a repeating pattern of ups and downs, in which periods of rise are followed by periods of fall, with human events invariably triggering a societal regression toward the mean. Is a jagged sine wave the true shape of history—a synthesis of the circle with the straight line, a secularization of a meaningful understanding of history, coupled with a rejection of any sort of eschaton or transformative end? Cultural embrace of a sine wave—and, perhaps, our current spot on the downhill slope—may be contributing to the rhetoric of collapse, of a loss of teleology and even human agency in relationship to the future. This is not new. Even at the height of the Enlightenment, some struggled to reconcile belief in linear history with disbelief in a transcendent end.

In his study of select thinkers who rejected the Enlightenment ideal of progress, political philosopher Matthew W. Slaboch identified some who understood history as a downward slope to disintegration and collapse; others who saw some form of cycle, with hills and dales; and still others who saw nothing but chaos and randomness.[240] Philosophers and writers who viewed history as a "bumpy but straight road to nowhere" include Schopenhauer, Tolstoy, Adams, Solzhenitsyn, and Lasch. Schopenhauer argued that "constructive histories, guided by a shallow optimism, always ultimately end in a comfortable fat, substantial State" and that "almost inevitably, the deity to which the worshippers of progress prostrated themselves was the state."[241] In *War and Peace*, published more than four hundred years after the emergence of the printing press, Tolstoy writes that "the most powerful of ignorance's weapons" is "the dissemination of printed matter."[242] Addressing the virtues of progress, Solzhenitsyn said, "We all have lived through the twentieth century, a century of terror, the chilling culmination of that progress about which so many dreamed in the eighteenth century."[243] Lasch suggests that we have reached "the exhaustion of the progressive tradition," but carry it forward for lack of a better alternative.[244] Perhaps these philosophers were just grumpy. Yet, their positions seem prescient today.

Generational cultures theory is the closest pop culture gets to a philosophy of history. It is essentially a sine wave approach to history. Arthur Schlesinger Sr. first proposed a liberal-conservative sine wave to US history in his history classrooms at Harvard, where his son, Arthur Schlesinger Jr., sat as a child and listened to his father. Schelsinger Sr. put his cyclical theory of political history into essay form (*Yale Review*) in 1939 and called it "Tides of American Politics." Arthur M. Schlesinger Jr. popularized his father's theory about the relationship between these cycles of history and the influence of generational cohorts: "There is no mystery about the periodicity" of cycles of negative and affirmative government. They happen at roughly the span of a generation, and "the generational succession has been the mainspring of the cycle."[245]

The seminal work on a philosophy of history as seen through the lens of generational ecology and sociology comes from a 1923 Karl Mannheim essay on generations. Although he offers no evidence he knew this, Mannheim picked up on Augustine's metaphor of the development of a single human life to describe the course of history and writes that Positivists "all were anxious to find a general law to express the rhythm of historical development":

> The aim was to understand the changing patterns of intellectual and social currents directly in biological terms, to construct the curve of progress of the human species in terms of its vital substructure. In the process, everything, so far as possible, was simplified: a schematic psychology provided that the parents should always be the conservative force. Presented in this light, the history of ideas appears reduced to a chronological table.[246]

Despite praise for Mannheim's essay, the impact of autonomous generational cohorts on society remained largely underdeveloped for decades, "despite the notion of generation being widespread in everyday language as a way of understanding differences between age groups and as a means of locating individuals and groups within historical time."[247] Generational theory began to gain traction in the popular press by the 1990s, driven in part by corporate demographic studies. Strauss and Howe combine generational sociological theory with cyclical historical theory and claim that rather than a progressive upward slope, a better metaphor for history is that of a repeating cycle of "systole and diastole," with each cycle spanning roughly eighty years, or one human life.[248] The sine wave embraces Augustine's view of history as human development but includes the rest of the metaphor of a human life: decline and death.

In their 1991 book, *Generations*, demographic cartographers Strauss and Howe suggest a new Schlesinger thesis: that American culture and even all of Western culture can be understood as a series of repeating eighty-year cycles.[249] Their book became controversial for its appearance in the hands of President Donald Trump's adviser Steve Bannon shortly after Trump's election in 2016.[250] Between the book's publication and its popularity spike, Strauss and Howe established market credibility for their demographic analysis of audiences. They are credited with coining the term "Millennial" to refer to the cohort of people in the American market born between the early 1980s and the late 1990s.

Strauss and Howe advocate a circular view of history built around an eighty-year cycle, as well, which they describe using the term *saeculum* (Latin for a single, long human life, and a metaphysical term in early Christian thought for the secular, pre-kingdom age). They suggest, as already noted, that history repeats itself in definable eighty-year cycles, and that these may be broken down into twenty-year segments: a "High," an outer world period of peak structure and order, which is akin to spring; an "Awakening," a period of cultural flourishing, akin to summer; an "Unraveling," a period, akin to fall, in which we retreat from the outer world to the inner world; collapse, and finally a "Crisis," akin to winter, in which we collectively emerge from our inner worlds and rebuild a new outer world.[251] Howe claims we are currently living through a "crisis" period—which is of course good for book sales.

Scholars shy away from generations as a construct because it seems too broad and deterministic. Do demographics really win over psychographics? Yet it is undeniable that there is a zeitgeist at play in a cycle similar to what generational theorists describe. There is a period of reaching for the stars, which is external and focused on building society. When it does not materialize or achieve its aim, usually because of tension with the existing order, the zeitgeist changes to a mood of disillusionment. The external focus turns inward. If we cannot change the world, we will change ourselves. Periods of innovation are followed by periods of conservation, which are followed by periods of innovation, and then conservation.

Correlated to an inward focus is a degree of defeatism about systems and powers, which over time turns to apathy. The apathy leads to disengagement and a period of unraveling as the next generation eyes the landscape and follows the apathy and inward focus to the gradual extreme of focusing on themselves. Inattention to society turns to apathy and eventually, as society atrophies, to anger and antipathy. It leads to a type of nihilism. If external systems are beyond useless but in fact harmful, then the purest motive is to remove them altogether.

At each stage, the perception among cultural analysts is that current events will continue in a straight line forward. If society is growing, it will continue to improve and lead to a utopian end. If society is crumbling, it will continue to crumble and lead to a dystopian end.

Yet this never comes to pass because of generations. Each new generation that emerges brings fresh perspectives that lack historical context, and seeing the inadequacy of the present condition, wants to change it. Just as our existing generation wants to tear down institutions that don't serve the people, the next generation will rise, viewing the wreckage of society. Without a historical consciousness and lacking respect for why this came to be, they will make the obvious choice to rebuild a new society. This new generation's work will eventually create a new order, which will be followed by another new generation that will look at the imperfections of the new order and will seek to improve it. This too will fail to reach the stars, and the cycle will begin again. The actions of generations, reacting to what has come before, is why the notion of history repeating itself has merit.

Every society undergoes this. Consider this a boilerplate template. It plays out in different fashion and in different societies over time in different degrees. Of course, there are many variables to this template that make each new cycle both the same and unique. One strong variable and an accelerating factor is the primary means of large group communication.

Historically these cycles occurred in disconnected cultures and different moments. But as we have become a global culture, these forces have begun to happen in global concert. This began with the rise of the telegraph, which was the first communication system that allowed instant human communication across geographical and cultural boundaries. Since then, this cycle became part of the pan-Western experience, and post–World War II, part of the global experience. Every means of communication has made the cycles more extreme.

Others have employed scientific approaches to support claims of cyclical patterns in history. Data scientist Peter Turchin applied algorithms developed to track predator–prey cycles in forest ecosystems for the understanding of human history and came up with what he calls "cliodynamics," a pattern of cyclical patterns occurring every fifty years—which, as with Strauss and Howe, means the next ominous reset is imminent.[252]

Notably, each of the modern theorists listed has used a cyclical theory of history to call for a form of political nationalism to emerge to forestall inevitable decline and disintegration.[253] The question for us is, Do the recurring patterns of history indicate a lack of meaningful purpose, or is there something more?

5.4 | The Kingdom of God Is Not Solely Material

Our current cultural angst is partly the result of a nagging feeling that as a civilization, we have peaked. In this view, progress was our best shot at achieving utopia, and it did not achieve its aims. Decline eventually emerges, as it does with all civilizations: Pax Romana, the British Empire, the American Century. They all share a moment in time, a peace built on violence and power that cannot hold, and the inevitable decline emerges. We come to view our own history not as a glorious destiny but as a vile cycle of power. When we realize that our story is not the right one, and that our nation is not the kingdom of God after all, we reject our own history. We become ahistorical. If Western civilization is declining, what is authoritative? What recourse remains for the hopeful humanist in light of this decline?

The potentates of the world have conquered that "other" kingdom and its king, have satisfied themselves that God is power and that power is God.

—Alan Lewis, Between Cross and Resurrection

USAmerica still enjoys one common cultural shared value: money. Perhaps profit remains the one irresistible proof of progress in America. If you are not living your life for fame, fortune, and power, then in the eyes of this world you will be deemed a failure. The material desire and need to generate quarterly shareholder return may be the most dominant iteration of the ideology of progress in America today. "Progress is now often defined solely in terms of quantifiable economic growth, linked to the global extension of a particular economic system."[254] This is best captured by the image of the Dow Jones index, which rises and falls over time, but with an aggregate upward slope. It is hard to argue against the value of progress when standards of living increase and people continue to immigrate to the United States from around the world for the potential of economic betterment.

Frederick Winslow Taylor is one of the least recognized, most influential figures in American history. Known as the "Optimizer," he was the premier business consultant of the early twentieth century. His focus on corporate efficiency revolutionized American business.[255] Ironically, the obsession with efficiency, manifested by an increasing focus on quarterly shareholder return, has proven problematic. Immediate gain narrows the focus of "improvement" and leads to valuing efficiency over risk, much less over what is good, true, and beautiful. Efficiency paints a false picture of growth that can mask long-term atrophy and turns business into a game of survival, based on fear of loss over joy of gain.[256] Economist Daniel Kahneman won a Nobel Prize in 2002 for naming and drawing attention to this fear. He called it Prospect Theory, in which people tend to fear losses disproportionately more than they value equivalent gains.[257] When we are forced to return a profit every three months, there is no room for error.

As a society, we have waved our hands in goodbye blessings of "take care" than more than of "take risks." Quarterly profit models favor "failure prevention," yet "the more comfortable you are with looseness and uncertainty, the less fragile your environment is . . . complex systems are weakened, even killed, when deprived of stressors."[258] It is a myth to believe we can manage the error out of complex systems, whether in corporate settings or in personal relationships. When the highest value is failure prevention, one little problem can ruin everything. Malcolm Gladwell illustrated this in his celebrated story of the O-ring failure that caused the space shuttle *Challenger* to explode.[259]

The word *aftermath* was originally an agricultural word meaning "the new growth that comes after the harvest." There is an "aftermath" to everything that is creative and innovative. The lack of "aftermaths" is the consequence of our focus on efficiency and fear of failure. Risk is a prerequisite for creativity, which is a prerequisite for healthy growth. The creative life of "aftermaths" is a catalog of failures. Richard Branson is famous for "Try again. Fail again. Fail better."[260] "Economic growth and innovation rely on the emergence of new startups and entrepreneurs with disruptive ideas." Yet "when the gale of creative destruction stops blowing, industries stagnate."[261] In other words, our modern economic system's demand for growth without uncertainty is self-defeating.

Evidence bears this out. For the first time in sixty years of comparison, Americans younger than thirty-five now have less economic optimism for the future than Americans fifty-five and older.[262] People are less enamored with things and long for experiences.[263] The denizens of the metaverse are today's younger generations, who find enjoyment and fulfilment in both virtual and real worlds and are often more attracted to digital than physical objects. The lie is that economic gain is sustainable, as cultures around the world have known for generations. An old Scottish proverb states, "The father buys, the son builds, the grandson sells, and his son begs." Japanese culture's version is similar: "rice paddy to rice paddy in three generations." Modern American demographic data reveal that between 70 and 90 percent of rich families lose their wealth by the third generation.[264]

We are addicted to growth and need "economies that make us thrive whether or not they grow."[265] We apply a linear view of time to our economic models, but the reality is not perpetual upward progress. Data shows that it is more like a circle that draws back on itself, over and over. The focus on material gain through shared self-interest echoes the work of Ayn Rand. Material growth reframes progress as profit and minimizes human relationships at the expense of gain. We play nice in the shared sands of self-gain as long as we see quarterly shareholder returns. But the epistemologies of efficient production are weakening. People are awakening to the realization that relationships trump results.

The greater the realization that we cannot strip the planet of resources indefinitely, the louder the call to abandon ideals of economic and material growth,[266] or to redefine economic growth according to slower, more sustainable models.[267] Of course, the hard part is convincing all 195 nations to go along.

If material growth is no longer viable, what models are left? At each stage, meaning has been stripped from philosophies of history. Is it not possible to rise to heaven? In lieu of ultimate meaning, political purpose, or material gain, does history have any reason at all? Or is history a perpetual cycle of wandering in the wilderness, searching in vain for a lost land of milk and honey? While the rise of political extremism is in part a desire to fix culture by changing a sinful past, we cannot define what is right by ignoring, escaping, or rewriting our own history. "Progressive" ideology is ironically not progressive but rejects linear history altogether.

For some contemporary philosophers, the answer to the purpose of history is nothingness. In rejecting the philosophy of progress, John Gray reduces humankind to the state of animals.[268] Since progress is a delusion, humanity is actually "on a road to nowhere," to quote lyricist David Byrne.[269] Indeed, "no" + "place" is the original etymology of "utopia" (*outopos*), a word invented in 1516 by English humanist Sir Thomas More to describe a fictional account of the ideal society ("a little, true book, not less beneficial than enjoyable" declared the subtitle),[270] and the term used in much contemporary technology advertising to describe our shared future destination. The original Thomas More "Utopia" was an island—but no island, even the island (Orcas Island) on which one of us lives, is a utopia. It may be a eutopia—etymologically, "the good place"—but not a utopia.

The inadequacy of each shape of history has led some to reject the idea of an ending altogether and adopt an ahistorical view of culture. But this leads to a purely materialist view of the world, nihilism, and a politic of raw power, all of which are ultimately destructive. "Power in whatever hands is rarely guilty of too strict limitations on itself," insisted Edmund Burke in words that apply to the church as well as the state.[271]

To the biblically informed reader, such aimlessness may sound familiar. The book of Ecclesiastes is famous for its laments about meaning: "'Meaningless! Meaningless!' says the Teacher. 'Utterly meaningless! Everything is meaningless" (1:2 NIV). Or as it also says, "There is nothing new under the sun" (v. 9). The psalmist captures the seeming randomness of both gain and loss: "They sowed fields and planted vineyards that yielded a fruitful harvest; he blessed them, and their numbers greatly increased, and he did not let their herds diminish. Then their numbers decreased, and they were humbled by oppression, calamity and sorrow; he who pours contempt on nobles made them wander in a trackless waste" (Psalms 107:37–40 NIV).

Into this nihilistic vacuum steps human will to power. Power is the one immutable truth of George R. R. Martin's epic tale *Game of Thrones*, one of the dominant cultural phenomena of the 2010s, which presents a world in which there is no good or bad, only an ever-changing sequence of alliances and conquests. Without the common cause and purpose provided by science and progress, humankind devolves into an endless struggle for power.

Because of his rejection of an ontological historical structure, yet inability to completely reject a straight-line view of history, Schopenhauer reverted to the human will as the only guiding force of history. Despite all the upsets and upheavals that historians have recorded, he wrote, "We yet always have before us only the same, identical, unchangeable essence:"[272] the human will, which is the guiding force of the world (as opposed to the will of any sort of deity). He compared life's ups and downs to the thread of a needle running through an embroidery, guided by a proverbial single, human hand: "Life could be compared to an embroidery, of which we see the right side during the first side of life, but the back during the latter half. The backside is less scintillating but more instructive; it reveals the interpatterning of threads."[273] Ironically, though Schopenhauer distrusted the state, his orientation toward sole authority residing in the human will was a significant contributing factor in the late-nineteenth-century rise of nationalism through Europe,[274] which in turn motivated the consummate progress-denying event, World War I.

If we are not rising to heaven through political and social development, and material gain is not only meaningless but unsustainable, we are left with one end: that human will to power is the logical conclusion of the ideology of progress. As the philosopher and professor at the London School of Economics observes, at its best, "belief in progress has become a mechanism of self-deception that serves only to block perception of the evils that come with the growth of knowledge."[275]

The result of ahistoricism is nihilism and the loss of meaning altogether. With no future and no past, we are left with nihilism and the will to power. But nothingness is a false ending because life is more than just material survival. The story of the ironically named country of Liberia, the home of the Ebola outbreak we described in chapter 1, illustrates the conclusion of human will to power. Liberia was founded in the mid-nineteenth century by former African American slaves in a coming-home emigration. Tragically, rather than establishing an alternative republic based on the virtues to which the American experiment aspired, they instead established a plantation-style system of domination and subjugation of the native people of the region, based on the actual values they had experienced firsthand in America. Their life and worldview had been shaped by power, so when they acquired their own freedom, they used that power to in turn subjugate others.

Today, Liberia is one of the least-developed countries in the world. It was ground zero for the biggest global health scare to date of the twenty-first century, the Ebola virus. That such a virus would come from such a country is not a theological surprise. Liberia epitomizes the broken human condition and the zero-sum limitation of a worldview, no matter how well-intentioned, based in power.

Power is zero-sum because it assumes that there needs to be winners and losers. Of course, everyone is not deserving of a prize despite the Dodo's declaration "Everybody has won, and all must have prizes" in *Alice in Wonderland* when asked to judge the winner of a race. The dodo may be an extinct bird, but there are lots of dodoes of mediocrity still around who don't believe in competition or comparison or excellence. There are also lots of dodoes still around who believe that winning is everything. Richard Nixon once sent "We're-Winning-Winning-Winning" Donald Trump, in the 1980s, a note following a media appearance that had impressed Nixon's wife, Pat: "As you can imagine, [Mrs. Nixon] is an expert on politics and she predicts that whenever you decide to run for office you will be the winner."[276] For all the good that theologies of progress have done to draw awareness and improve social conditions of oppressed peoples, it has taught its adherents to consider human agency according to rules of power.

Like so many rulers (and philosophers) before and after him, the Roman governor of Judea Pontius Pilate asked Jesus with unexpected sobriety, "What is truth?" (John 18:38). There are those philosophers (e.g., Plato, Descartes, Leibniz, Husserl, Wittgenstein) for whom mathematics is the ultimate truth, the canonic code that surpasses verbal discourse. Then there are those philosophers (e.g., Aquinas, Hegel, Nietzsche, Heidegger, Sartre) for whom equations solve nothing of significance and instead plunge into the depths of being the mysteries of the transcendent, and the meanings of human existence. At least Pilate was honest in his questing and questioning. Did he suspect that the life of the mind is not the only meaningful life? A broken world knows no other answer than the drive for ever-increasing power as a ward for death, which in the end comes anyway.

The more we search for meaning, the more meaning we create and find. It's one of life's magic formulas. But as Dan Allender puts it, "Most people don't know how to read their life in a way that reveals their story. They miss the deeper meaning in their life, and they have little sense of how God has written their story to reveal himself and his own story."[277] Genesis, for example, tells us about the meaning of the world, not the making of the world.

The pawning of life's meaning for power, or the abandonment of any larger sense of historical meaning, what Camus called "the meaning of meaninglessness," issues in nihilism. Nihilistic tendencies may live for a period with hedonism ("Eat, drink, and be merry, for tomorrow we die"), which is perhaps the best way to understand the boomer generation's cynical switch in the 1980s from "Let's change the world" to "living in a material world." But parties weren't meant to last, as Prince sang in his chart-topping "1999." Numbness begets anger begets the sentence that if nothing good exists in the current social order, all must be destroyed. The Berlin of the 1930s was famous for its party scene. Nihilism is just a phase; it is never the end. New generations rise with contempt for the party and zeal to start over and do it right. Nihilism leads to revolution, which attempts to erase history, which leads us to our fifth false ending, ahistoricism.

From every destructive moment in history, life continues. While 80 percent of Americans see life out of control,[278] developing nations see signs of a more hopeful future emerging.[279] This is a phase. Unless 8 billion people somehow die, this is not the end. People rally. We've been through much worse, and we've made it.

The fall of statues in the wake of the George Floyd murder in June 2020 is a prime lesson in the dangerous crossroads of justice and ahistoricism. As the statues came down, first of Confederate generals and then of other historical figures with documented imperfections and sins, ahistorical sentiments appeared on social media. Consider this example from Austin geneticist Spencer Wells:

> Just a head's up: moving forward I will block anyone who defines themselves in their handles or comments by Bronze-age ideology: Christian, Jewish, Muslim, Hindu, I don't care. Grow up and engage beyond the bullshit you inherited from imaginary ancestors. They can't save you.[280]

Science can tell us what life is, even keep us alive. But only religion can address what life means, and why it is worth being alive. Science is good at solving the "soft" problems of life, but only religion can address the "hard" problems of existence. What happens when your worldview is built entirely on scientific discovery and truth can only be found in the future? The only natural consequence is ahistoricism. Someone remind the brassy Spencer Wells of the superior quality of bronze to brass. We arrogantly dismiss the past as barbaric and the future as just. But as Presbyterian pastor Scott Sauls correctly notes, and the story of Liberia, the home of Ebola, demonstrates, "social justice without Jesus can be more Darwinian than just, fighting against unjust power only to assume and assert unjust power."[281]

The problem with Wells's arrogant dismissal is that history is not a myth. Scripture says there are ages (*aei*), at least three: past, present, and future (see Luke 20:34–35). History is real. It is more than just a line that stops. The defining characteristic of the word "eternal" isn't the future, per se, but a qualitative word describing an age. As the statues fell, statesman and political observer Matt McNeil posted:

> One sentiment I've see over and over in the last few weeks is "learn your history." Couldn't agree more but we need some sort of vision for what we are willing to learn from history. One school of thought embodied by the statue smashers is a warts only history that is full of judgement and condemnation. Think Zinn's People's History. Another is the All Statues Matter school which gladly white-washes history, making it a video montage of highlights set to I'm Proud to Be An American. A third option [calls] us to repentance but not condemnation, love in spite of shortcomings and not treacly sentiment that ignores them, and appreciation for the past but a humble aspiration for a more just and loving present and future.[282]

In fact, our stale conventional wisdom about heaven—bored people sitting on clouds—is an ahistorical, pagan view derived from gods of ancient culture who exist outside of time. Yahweh is in time, yet not limited by time. God is the timeless becoming timely in the fullness of time. God is past, present, and future, all rolled up together.

The Christian view of history is this: God created. Creation is good. Evil entered into history. But then God entered history. The resurrection happened. Jesus redeems us—not only us but our collective history. God's kingdom doesn't negate the past. It turns what was meant for evil into good. The future is as real as the past and the present, not a vapor, but the home of our scarred, redeemed bodies. Jesus' resurrection proves that the history is real and material. As N. T. Wright says:

> Social gospel liberalism embrac[ed] modernist denials of God's action in history, when that action was just what they needed as their foundation. The heirs of that liberal theology are today keen to marginalize the Bible, declaring that it supports slavery and other wicked things, because they don't like what it says on other topics such as sexual ethics. But if you push the Bible off the table, you are merely colluding with pagan empire, denying yourself the sourcebook for your kingdom critique of oppression.[283]

We cannot erase parts of our own story just because we do not like them. Yes, history is unpleasant and rife with paradox. This is an inconvenient truth. Absolutely, the white hats aren't all white, and the black hats aren't all black. No one in the Bible gets it all right except Jesus. Some of the founders of the Constitution of the United States, the beacon of human rights, were themselves slaveholders. Moral absolutes are hard to find in the daily lives of lived experience. There are no simple human beings. Simple storytelling cannot capture the complexity of the soul. Nobody, ever, has gotten it all right except Jesus Christ. If you look long and hard enough, you will find the devil in everything.

Yet we cannot simply dismiss or "cancel" characters with stains, and we cannot pretend ages past do not matter. If we were to boycott anyone with a problematic past, we would be left with nothing. The only solution is to pursue true justice with Jesus, which seeks not to assert power, but to sacrificially use power to love neighbor as self.

Some things are wrong, and some things are worse than wrong. The founder of virtue ethics, Aristotle (384–322 BCE), not only condoned institutionalized slavery but provided an elaborate argument in favor of it, which today's virtue ethicists conveniently ignore. As if that weren't enough, Aristotle supposedly said man was "begotten" and woman "misbegotten."[284] Because a woman's reasoning was "without authority," he contended,[285] Aristotle accepted no female students. Aquinas (1225?—1274) followed in Aristotle's "misbegotten" wake, and in what some say is the greatest theological treatise of all time, *Summa Theologica*, he inserted these words about women: "As regards the individual nature, woman is defective and misbegotten . . . The production of woman comes from defect in the active force [in the male seed] or from some material indisposition, or even from some external influence; such as that of a south wind, which is moist . . . By . . . subjection woman is naturally subject to man because in man the discretion of reason predominates."[286]

Advocates of the Scottish Enlightenment philosopher David Hume gloss over his racism. Confucians excuse and excise their founder's misogyny. In pursuit of mindfulness, Buddha abandoned his wife and child. Gandhi was a racist, elitist, and supporter of the caste system. What he wrote about Africans would bring a smile to any KKK member's face. You don't want to examine Gandhi's patriarchal and parochial views of women or his relationship with his great-niece Manu, who slept with him naked when she was but a teenager to "test" the resolve of his vow of brahmacharya (literally "conduct consistent with Brahman") or abstinence as well as penance for his sins. "In my opinion," Gandhi asserted, "the Jews should disclaim any intention of realizing their aspiration of living in Palestine under the protection of arms and should rely wholly on the goodwill of Arabs."[287] Do such attitudes and prejudices disallow or disavow their teachings?

The problem with the fixation of "being on the right side of history" is that history is not always right. While attempting to escape the invading

Nazis in 1940 at the French-Spanish border, German Jewish philosopher Walter Benjamin committed suicide. Shortly before, he had written that "cultural treasures owe their existence not only to the efforts of the great minds and talents who have created them, but also to the anonymous oil of their contemporaries." Benjamin then continued in a broader vein:

> There is no document of civilization which is not at the same time a document of barbarism. And just as such a document is not free of barbarism, barbarism taints also the manner I which it was transmitted form one owner to another. A historical materialist therefore disassociates himself from it as far as possible. He regards as his task to brush against the grain.[288]

Korean American cultural critic and public intellectual Wesley Yang names the strand of politics aiming to supersede and abolish liberal thinking altogether a "successor ideology."[289] Others prefer the term "identitarian." Whereas liberalism is against all forms of racism and sexism, identitarians and "successor ideology" see white supremacy and white privilege as the center of structural oppression, coupled with misogyny and transphobia. Starting with university campuses and social media, identitarians unabashedly seek to demolish older liberal ideals of free inquiry and free speech in pursuit of ideological purity and political correctitude. As the English-born US-based writer Andrew Sullivan—a classic liberal and the pioneer campaigner for gay rights and same-sex marriage—puts it:

> In the successor ideology, there is no escape, no refuge, from the ongoing nightmare of oppression and violence—and you are either fighting this and "on the right side of history" or you are against it and abetting evil. There is no neutrality. No space for skepticism. No room for debate. No space even for staying silent. Silence, remember, is violence—perhaps the most profoundly anti-liberal slogan ever invented.[290]

The "successor ideology" is the Manicheanism of our day, committed to usurping liberalism just as the Manicheans sought to replace Christianity with a new cult.

To separate rights from duties is to vitiate the fragile concord of autonomy and self-restraint and violate the self-help that sustains a sense of identity and the shelf-help of strong civic institutions, social structures, and cultural ties that provide a healthy sense of belonging and security.

| CHAPTER 6 |
BIG TIME: THE FALSE ENDING OF MESSIANISM

....

Is there anyone with the power and authority to rescue us?

....

Our collective pop culture obsession with rebellion is a sign of the inescapability of the question of authority. The current political environment can be understood as the normalization of rebellion against the authority structures of society. Today, it seems that everyone's a nihilist. But it is not the diminishment of authority we are witnessing; it is a shift from vertical to horizontal authority, or the will of the public. The evil of this transaction is the lie of social morality, that virtue may arise from the public.

Authority is a vacuum that must be filled, and messianism is the three-way dynamic between the ruling powers, the people, and a third-party leader who comes to represent their political interests. It comes down to a question of authority: Who is the rightful power? Is it the ruling "few" or the promise of the "people"? The question of the authority of the few versus the authority of the many leaves out the deficiency of all: none are worthy, as Paul so eloquently describes in his letter to the Romans (3:10).

Throughout history, the deficiency of both models is what continues to lead people to look for a messianic figure to step in and provide political authority. The last gasp of society's search for authority is always to turn to the power of a single figure to rescue us from ourselves. But even the messianic figure, in the end, proves unworthy of leadership.

God's kingdom is not characterized by the exercise of human power, which is a zero-sum equation with some lording over others. Each of the six "isms" of part 1, taken to its logical conclusion, is furthest from the kingdom of heaven because each surrenders authority to something other than Jesus.

6.1 | Make Us a King

Starting in his late twenties, Len Sweet spent much of his life in theological administration as provost, president, chancellor, dean, and vice president of Graduate Studies. He still remembers as yesterday a conversation with one of his most feminist and "woke" faculty members, who assiduously kindled the flames of a "Great Awakening" among the faculty at the slightest presence of any feminist spark or gender ember.

One day she appeared at Len's door and complimented him sweetly on his leadership while complaining that he was on the road too much (the proverbial "warming the water before you drown the cat" routine). She and the seminary faculty needed him to "stay home" more, she intoned. She and the faculty needed him to be more available for drop bys, sit-downs, and show-ups without the protocols of appointments and scheduling. Len explained that he would love to "stay home" and "hang out" more, but his major job was to raise money for the school, and he couldn't do that sitting in his office, writing memos, or talking on the phone with prospects. He needed to "drop by" and "sit down" and "show up" with donors. Besides, there was a dean of faculty who was there to do some of that. Her response to his demurral is something he will never forget. "Don't you know, Len, that every faculty needs a father figure, a daddy, that we can run to, sound off in front of, and with whom we can pour out our frustrations and hurts? We need you to daddy us more. Please?"

Novelist, poet, and filmmaker Michel Houellebecq is a rock star in France. Yet he infuriates all sides of the political spectrum because he follows no party lines, expresses unconventional arguments in the most elegant ways, and does not have "authority issues" other than the advocacy of the need for authority and authority figures. He grew up in a hippie culture of utopian fantasies, was abandoned by his mother as a child, and critiques Western culture's confusion of consumer choice and self-actualization for existential freedom. He subscribes to the philosophy that people live better, and better people live, when they live under authority. Might the popularity of "strong-seeming men" like Putin and Trump be attributed to an unmet need for authoritative figures, especially father figures, in the wake of unmet utopian dreams?

The search for a savior is part of the argument of Gideon Rachman in his "The Age of the Strongman" (2022) as he charts the global rise of strongman rule:

in Asia (Do Xi Jinping [China], Narendra Modi [India], Rodrigo Duerte [Philippines], Min Aung Hlaing [Myanmar]) in the Middle East ("MBS" or Prince Muhammad bin Salman [Saudi Arabia], Recept Tayyip Erdogan [Turkey], Binyamin Netanyahu [Israel], Ali Khamenei [Iran], Bashar al-Assad [Syria])

in the Americas (Jair Bolsonaro [Brazil], Andres Manuel Lopez Obrador [Mexico], Nicolás Maduro [Venezuela], Donald Trump [USAmerica]),

in Europe (Boris Johnson [England], Viktor Orban [Hungary], Vladimir Putin [Russia])

in Africa Abiy Ahmed [Ethiopia], Paul Kagame [Rwanda], Yoweri Museveni [Uganda], Mohamed Abdullahi Mohamed [Somalia]), to name but a few.[291]

The threat of these "Men of the People" to liberal, cosmopolitan, humanitarian ideals puts the whole planet at risk, Rachman argues, as the peoples of the world yearn for messianic figures to save them from the clutches of bureaucratic cruelty, the chains of utopian dreams, the big (giga) and little (nano) threats that ambush around every corner, and the MAAMA powers of the MAAMAverse, which is ruled by Meta (M), Alphabet (A), Amazon (A), Microsoft (M) and Apple (A).

"The human is not the static center of the world as we thought . . . but the axis and arrow of evolution, which is much more beautiful," wrote Darwinian priest Teilhard de Chardin,[292] who may have been the first to envision the Internet, the first to posit a Singularity (Omega Point Theory [OPT]), and the first to advocate a kind of Christian transhumanism. Teilhard often speaks of a critical point in the evolution of human intelligence: "In our time Mankind seems to be approaching its critical point of social organization."[293] He refers to the critical point as "the entry into the super-human."[294] He says that intelligence will reach a critical point of intensity that "represents our passage, by translation or dematerialization, to another sphere of the Universe: not an ending of the Ultra-Human but its accession to some sort of Trans-Human at the ultimate heart of things."[295] Teilhard's "Ultra-Human" is what we would call the transhuman, and his "Trans-Human" is what we would call the posthuman.

Teilhard identifies the critical point with the Christian notion of the second coming of the Messiah known as the parousia: "the parousiac spark can, of physical and organic necessity, only be kindled between Heaven and a Mankind which has biologically reached a certain critical evolutionary point of collective maturity."[296] The parousia is the fulfillment of the mission of the Messiah. It is crudely portrayed in popular religion as the "second coming" of Christ or the "rapture." For Teilhard, it is a radical biological change in human life. When future human intelligence passes through the critical point, Teilhard argued, it "will penetrate for the first time into the environment which is biologically requisite for the wholeness of its task."[297] The critical point (identified with the parousia) is the Teilhardian Singularity.

Len S.'s experience in the academy, and Teilhard's image of the human as the "axis and arrow of evolution," beg the question: Who draws the bow, and who or what is the bulls-eye at which the arrow points? This is a question of authority.

One of the authorities of USAmerican colonial life was George Washington. For Washington's decision to return to his farm after the war rather than assume control of the nation, King George III called him "the greatest man in the world."[298] What made Washington uniquely significant to the story of the United States was not his military prowess or his statesmanship. It was his ultimate ambition for his own reputation as a man of virtue, a man of lofty ends, rather than a man of means. We need more concern for character over means, what David Brooks calls eulogy virtues over résumé virtues.[299]

It is uncommon for a human to decline the opportunity to acquire more power. The systems of checks and balances built into the "mixed-government" design of the USAmerican republic is proof: its framers assumed the nation's future leaders would seek empire. Indeed, fear of the American presidency gaining too much power has been a recurring theme. Harvard historian Arthur M. Schlesinger Jr. made this argument in *The Imperial Presidency* in 1973, and it comes up again every four years. Although the haunting role that public opinion plays in constraining presidents' ability to act unilaterally, according to historians Douglas Kriner and Dino P. Christenson, makes valid their corrective title *The Myth of the Imperial Presidency* (2020).

The tendency of power to consolidate around a single individual is more than the reflection of leadership ambition, though. It is often the will of the public. Public opinion can constrain and crescendo power. From modern Russia's failure to embrace democracy to the ancient demand of the Israelites for a king, the illusion of safety supersedes the benefit of liberty. When the future is uncertain, we seek security in the arms of charismatic figures, like a shopkeeper who approaches the local mafioso for "protection."

In the story of God's people, this demand occurred at the end of the life of Samuel, the last judge and first prophet of Israel. Samuel was old, and he had appointed his sons to be judges. But they were corrupt, and the people became worried about their leadership situation. They went to the prophet Samuel and said, "Make us a king" (1 Samuel 8:5 KJV).

Just to be clear, it is never a good idea to demand anything of God.

Does God have a right to be upset with the people for such a slap in the face? God says, "Okay, is that what you really want?" He then grants their request in the same way a parent allows a child to gorge on Halloween candy until he vomits and learns the hard way that rules actually help to keep us from our worst tendencies. The Lord told Samuel, "Listen to all that the people are saying to you; it is not you they have rejected, but they have rejected me as their king" (v. 7 NIV).

God then granted them their wish, with a warning: Kings take.

Kings will take some of your sons as warriors to stand at the front line, in harm's way.

Kings will take other sons as servants to forge their instruments of power.

Kings will take your daughters to serve in their courts, just as David later took Bathsheba (even the "good" king was not good).

Kings will take your property and your assets and give them to his cronies.

God had tried to avoid this eventuality because he knew what would happen. And why? Simply, sin. The nineteenth-century English politician Lord John Dalberg-Acton is famous for his remark that power corrupts. Whether this is causal (the acquisition of power is a corrupting influence) or correlational (power and corruption tend to go hand in hand) is irrelevant. Perhaps corruption is even a prerequisite for power. Evidence is plentiful that if you give a person power over other people, that person tends to make the maintenance of power his or her number one priority. This is known as "looking out for number one."

One of our favorite films is Michael Mann's *The Insider*, the retelling of the whistleblower Jeffrey Wigand's testimony that took down Big Tobacco. The film's protagonist is not Wigand, however; it is Lowell Bergman, the *60 Minutes* producer who stood up not only to the tobacco industry but to his own corporate overseers to speak truth to power on behalf of those who could not speak for themselves. In the film, Bergman represents the highest and best of American journalism. What is noble about journalism—and yes, journalism is prone to corruption—is the realization that truth is imperiled by power, and the calling of the journalist is to continually opt for truth, even in the presence of money.

This does not mean that we favor revolt, like the Zealots of Jesus' day and so many since, who have taken up arms in the name of Jesus to overthrow compromised authority. What is the end result of political revolution? "Meet the new boss, same as the old boss."[300]

Jesus knew the true source of the problem and thus did not speak against pagan power; he in fact encouraged his disciples to pay their due taxes to Caesar. Instead, Jesus reserved his harshest words for the Pharisees and Sadducees, those who manipulated God's words in the pursuit of power. He called them a "brood of vipers" (Matthew 3:7).

Power corrupts because it reflects our own fear and desire to be in control. The Pharisees and Sadducees sought signs of the consummation of their vision of a new kingdom, but Jesus rejected their idea of power (Matthew 16:4), and then warned his people to beware of their leaven, their glutenous vision of human authority, which slowly grows and takes over (v. 16). Jesus is clear: the kingdom of God is not found in the formation of political systems and in the exercise of human power, no matter how noble the intent; the kingdom of God is only found in the presence of God and is only built by Jesus (v. 18). Jesus is the only good, true, and beautiful source of authority. He is the magnet that, when dragged over the scattered, razor-sharp iron filings of our lives, puts them all into patterns of transcendence, as life's dissipated, chaotic, scrambled dregs are turned into coherent, compelling, authoritative lines of force and meaning.

The young man who became the first king of Israel was Saul. He was tall, handsome, and charismatic. Photogenic leaders are not just a modern phenomenon. Saul had "the look." People are seduced by the appearance of power in the same way we break the first commandment; we want to see our gods. This is the cycle of human power that perpetuates human suffering. Messianism is an extension of the same problem that began when the Israelites, who out of fear for Samuel's old age and his sons' weakness, did not wait on the Lord but jumped the gun and demanded a king.

To humankind, seeing is believing. But Jesus says believing is seeing. As human kings take, God gives—to the point of giving even his own Son. Our hunger for power causes us to ignore and disrespect acts of giving. We think this to be weak. But God's way of self-giving love is actually strength, while human power is weakness.

The desire of the public for a strongman to lead them is a form of idolatry, an exchange of trust in an invisible Lord for the illusion of security in a visible leader. This tragic choice repeats throughout history and continues to this day and manifests whenever we put our faith in a lowercase "messiah" to save us.

Such signs of messianism are prevalent today, as we will see next.

6.2 | I Fight Authority . . .

One of the important books in the first years of the twenty-first century has been *Hold on to Your Kids: Why Parents Need to Matter More Than Peers* (2004). Developmental psychologist Gordon Neufeld and physician Gabor Maté name what any visit to a 1990s mall made obvious: that in postwar twentieth-century Western culture, teenagers have come to raise one another. A vertical, authoritative orientation of parent to child, which traditionally has helped each new generation establish values, identity, and codes of behavior, has been replaced with a horizontal "peer orientation," and a desire above all to be cool. With weak parental influence and strong peer attachments, the results have been tragic: adolescents have struggled with conformism, alienation, a lack of identity, and destructive behavior: what we call schoolyard socialization.

Schoolyard socialization found its roots in postwar youth culture. The film *Rebel Without a Cause* came out in 1955 and catapulted the angst-filled, blue-jeaned James Dean to a short-lived stardom that ended in his death by car crash from high-speed driving on a California highway.[301] In his death, Dean embodied and codified a set of signs that has since proven impervious to cultural change. The image of disaffected young man searching for truth in a culture of conformity and falsehood has become a defining image of USAmerican life. Why?

Perhaps because at its inception, the image of the rebellious young man captured a deep-seated image of life that symbolized a group of people who did not share the values of their authorities. To those who resonated with the solitary, leather-bound biker, the rebel is the one who holds on to what is true, fights the "man," stands up against lies, and speaks truth to power and authority. The Star Wars brand is built on this metaphor (and some embrace it to the point of religion). Swiss-born political philosopher Jean-Jacques Rousseau exhorted rebels and romantics everywhere to seize "The Power of Now" 250 years ago.[302]

The value of rebellion is quite USAmerican. It can be found in Robespierre, the anti-English colonials, and throughout revolutionary political movements.[303] The rebel is the one who knows the "truth" and shares it with others who will join in the fight against the entrenched establishment. The rebel exercises this knowledge via sheer will and autonomy and in fact holds on to individual autonomy—what we call "rights"—as the sacrosanct value of life. The Latin root of "rebel" is the same word that gives us the word "bellicose." It describes a human physical stance, an act of "bowing up" one's back against a person or standing in a fighting position.

Whereas the World War II generation thought of rebels as activists fighting for a political cause, such as in the global 1930s, the teenager in

Rebel Without a Cause expanded the image to fighting unseen domestic oppressors—the unspoken hypocrisy of false order. In a postwar era of conformity, to be rebellious became "cool"—a sign of the times, or a similitude for the *zeitgeist*. The image was first articulated to a nationwide audience by Marlon Brando in the 1953 *The Wild Ones*. Brando's film character established a visual archetype for a kind of person, usually a young white male, who rejects the social mores of American society, even if he is incapable of articulating why. At one point in the film, another character asks Johnny what he is rebelling against. Johnny replies, "Whaddya got?"

It is difficult now to contextualize the original sonic boom of Brando's characterization because it has been so widely copied and parodied. James Dean clearly drew on Brando's characterization in his own portrayal of a disaffected young man. Elvis Presley used the archetype as the basis for his song "Jailhouse Rock" and his film of the same name. These characterizations helped establish a visual and musical identity. Rock and roll became both a musical genre and an entire lifestyle. Iconic films such as *Grease* suggested that graduating from conformity to rebellion was a form of liberation. The theme of the American rebel became codified.

The rebel biker metastasized into baby boomer rebellion in the 1960s—"Don't trust anyone over thirty"—and became entrenched with latchkey Generation X kids coming home from school alone in the 1980s while Silent Generation and baby boomer parents pursued careers and interests. Popular teen movies of the 1980s, such as *Back to the Future, St. Elmo's Fire,* and the filmography of 1980s film director John Hughes show a world largely devoid of healthy parental hierarchies. Parental figures are mostly absent or, like Homer and Marge Simpson, are largely sweet hearted but ill-equipped to help navigate the quandaries and questions of life.

To some degree, Gen X has quietly attempted to address the problem of authority while parenting Gen Z children. Yet the broader cultural message has stayed the same: parents and other authority figures are not to be trusted. We only have "friends" to help us figure life out. (We put *friends* in quotes because the word *friend* no longer aspires to the greater love of laying down your life,[304] but now merely means someone you had a conversation with at a conference ten years ago or a social media connection.) The problem, as we say, is systemic—the belief that authority is bad.

Consider the archetypal 1990s icon, rebellious Bart Simpson. When *The Simpsons* appeared in 1990, cultural observers in and out of the church wrung their hands at his potty mouth and disrespect for his elders. But he was a ten-year-old boy, albeit an animated one. The real question is, where were the authority figures guiding Bart's decisions and behaviors? In Bart's world, adults were either incompetent, weak, or corrupt. Bart had only himself and his peers to guide him. *The Simpsons* is pop art for a peer age, both mirroring and manifesting the loss of authority in culture.

In rebel culture, Christianity—the practice of the faith and its institutions—is a symbol of the oppressor. Some make a distinction between Christianity and Jesus, saying Jesus was a rebel (therefore good, true, and beautiful) but the religion that came after him is bad, bigoted, and ugly.[305] Jesus and his disciples, like the Essenes, were perceived in their culture and day as something of a "protest group" of rebellious, obedient Jews looking to purify a corrupt Jewish establishment. Some of Jesus' followers (like the master of the house who hosted Jesus and his disciples for Passover) may well have been rebel converts to Jesus' messianic movement from the Essene movement. When Christian leaders get tattoos, wear leather, curse, drink, and ride bikes, they are mirroring the images and habits of the rebel, presumably in an attempt to minister in a culture of rebellion—perhaps because they, too, wish to overthrow "the old man"—but also to mirror the Master Rebel named Jesus.

The result of the rebel fetish in the culture has been a *Lord of the Flies* schoolyard step-up in the social dynamics and destructive formations of peer pressure. From an early age, kids lead kids, which they are not set up to do. Charismatic leaders emerge, form cliques and in some cases gangs, and strong-arm their peers into submission. (As *Mean Girls* showed us, when it comes to the dynamics of peer orientation, the only difference between a clique and a gang is the status of its leader.) The very thing that children so desperately need—meaning and mission, to be known and know their identity in community—becomes impossible in rootless social environments. Elementary anti-bullying campaigns of the last decade are signs of an attempt to reverse the effects of backward, schoolyard peer socialization.

In such a vacuous system of values, children have no choice but to cling to those around them. As Claire Standish, the popular girl played by Molly Ringwald in *The Breakfast Club*, confides, "I hate it. I hate having to go along with everything my friends say!"[306] We have had generations of rebellion against parents, leaders, and other authority figures.

As children of the age have become adults, they have led one another with the same schoolyard rules. Rebellion has become a normalized project for a "mature" adult in USAmerica. To "rebel" is a feat not just for a Che or a Marx or someone fighting political power but for a person in any realm of society, from entertainment to politics to religion. Western culture celebrates the person who overthrows authority and discovers his or her own individual, autonomous will, which had previously been suppressed by unseen forces.

Images of the rebellion theme, such as jeans, leather, tattoos, motorcycles, and more, became so mainstreamed that they are still visible sixty-five years later in shopping malls and commercial centers around the United States. One can go to the grocery store and see grandmothers with spiky blue hair, black T-shirts, and torn jeans, still appropriating the image of the rebel, many clueless about what they are rebelling against. Support and voice are sacrosanct to any individual who claims an identity counter to any sort of authoritative influence from another.

While the shift to peer orientation and schoolyard socialization sheds light on very adult problems (such as mass shootings to "drain the swamp"), this is not a new phenomenon. It was expected that any messiahship, including Jesus' messiahship, would seize political power from the Romans and establish Israel as a political reality. This was at the heart of the desert duel with Satan. Jesus was tempted to betray his mission and to abandon his vocation by the devil's taunting and tempting him to him to "be his own man," to inaugurate the king not by suffering and death but by politics and economics.[307]

6.3. | . . . But Authority Always Wins

Throughout history, we have looked for a political solution: revolutionary figures to violently overthrow the present age. It is into this void of purpose that strong men (and women) step in to assume power. Far from Francis Fukuyama's famous "end of history," which claimed the victory of liberal humanism post-1989, Vladimir Putin's invasion of Ukraine in early 2022 demonstrated that old ideas and allegiances have not only not faded; they haven't even abated. The why of the invasion may seem politically and economically illogical, and the West has watched developments with shock and confusion.

One clue comes from Russian Orthodox Patriarch Kirill's support. Why would a leader of Christ's church support such a war? No less than messianic vision. German Reformed theologian Jürgen Moltmann presciently predicted this moment twenty-five years ago when he quoted Russian political scientist Emanuel Sarkisyanz, summarizing the destruction of the twentieth century:

> What mobilized millions in the USA as the American dream of "the New World" became in Tsarist Russia the Russian dream of the world's End-time redemption. Moscow was "the third Rome" and there was to be no fourth. The messianism of the Byzantine empire became the matrix for Orthodox eschatology. This forged the Russian idea that, after the fall of Constantinople, Moscow had taken over leadership of the one Christian-Orthodox empire, and with it had inherited the Byzantine claim to world hegemony too.[308]

The politicizing of Christianity by the Moscow patriarchate has allowed Vladimir Putin to pursue his "Russian world" (*Russkiy mir*) dreams and to plunge Europe into its biggest land war since 1945. Putin even admitted in 2010 that Eastern Orthodoxy was closer to Islam, a political religion, than it was to Catholicism.[309] One can only imagine how red-faced old Bolsheviks would be at the close relationship between Putin's Russia and the Orthodox Church, since they thought they had smashed religion for good.

Messianism has nothing to do with a messiah, per se. It is about the three-way dynamic between the ruling powers, the people, and a third-party leader who comes to represent their political interests. As noted in the introduction to this chapter, it comes down to a question of authority: Who is the rightful power: the ruling "few" or the "people"? The story of politics throughout history has been the struggle between these two groups. Even the American experiment is an argument between a true democracy and a representative republic, which is why the framers of the US Constitution were so brilliant to create three branches. But even in this governing structure . . . there remains a fundamental problem: whether part of the few or part of the many, no one does what's right, according to the apostle Paul (Romans 3:10).

Throughout history, the deficiency of both models is what continues to lead people to look for a messianic figure to step in and provide political authority. But of course, this doesn't work, because even the messianic figure, in the end, proves unworthy of leadership.

Acknowledging the deficiency of political models begs the question, what do people seek? Peace and prosperity, as the saying goes. But when has that ever worked? Consider the story of the Israelite slaves. They had neither peace nor prosperity. Look at the exodus story. Moses was Israel's leader, who followed the pillar and cloud to lead them to safety from Egyptian harm. How many days after having crossed the Red Sea and safely fled from the army were they satisfied? Three, according to Scripture, until they decided they were hungry and needed better accommodations. The people complained about the bitter water (Exodus 15:23–24). Then they complained about being hungry (16:1–3). Then they complained about not having enough water (17:1–4). Then they complained about Moses being gone so long on the mountain (32:1). Then they complained about the quality and quantity of food (Numbers 11:1–6). Then they complained about Moses himself (12:1–3). Then they complained about their disappointment in the land flowing with milk and honey (Numbers 14:1–4). Then they threatened to kill Moses and Aaron (14:10), and then complained some more about their leadership style (16:1–3). Then they complained some more about the food, the land, and not having enough water (20:1–5), Ultimately, they complained against God (21:5). One wonders how long it took the Israelites to complain about the Promised Land after having entered it?

It is not just the Israelites who were never satisfied and couldn't turn off the "complaint" button. To paraphrase Kierkegaard, humans are either anxious or bored, to which we would add proud, which is symptomatic of our basic problem: sin. The psychology of the human mind goes to great lengths to overcome the consequences of this fundamental problem, including overthrowing our own political freedoms for the sake of perceived threats and opportunities.

God of course knew of this problem of the human heart, which is why he warned the Israelites, through Moses, not to begin to think that Canaan was the result of their own initiative and industry (Deuteronomy 8:17). Often, people don't know what they want. Though Henry Ford was falsely credited with saying, "If I had asked people what they wanted, they would have said faster horses,"[310] the notion itself is still likely true. Malcolm Gladwell says,

"Focus groups suck" and "should be abolished."[311] Steve Jobs bluntly said, "People don't know what they want": "Some people say, 'Give the customers what they want.' But that's not my approach. Our job is to figure out what they're going to want before they do . . . People don't know what they want until you show it to them. That's why I never rely on market research. Our task is to read things that are not yet on the page."[312]

They are authoritative figures, all of them, though we don't mind so much when we like their business products and services. Authoritative figures, all of them, who when they adopt the same attitude to justify their political power, become something altogether different, as the history of the twentieth century alone testifies.

Political experiments throughout history show us that giving authority to the "people" inevitably leads to giving authority to a single representative of the people. Plato observed that democracies are more susceptible to becoming dictatorships than other forms of governance, such as oligarchies and aristocracies. As Andrew Sullivan writes:

> Freedom's excesses, and the refusal of many in a democracy to accept any limits on what they can get or buy or conquer eventually hit reality. And when the reality hits, the frustration and insolence at finding that money does not grow on trees or that the world cannot be hammered into the shape our ideology demands easily gives way to a new form of government. That new government promises to remove all the perils and difficulties of self-government in favor of the certainty and security of raw executive power.[313]

What happens when the need to give voice to the individual fighting power against authority becomes itself authoritative? What happens after you win the fight? It is difficult to assume a position of authority if your reason for being is to fight authority. When a person or a society rejects all authority, the result is a never-ending cycle of schoolyard violence. Recognized or not, protesters are trying to create new modes of authority. If authority is corrupt, the voice of the oppressed is vital and necessary to overthrow the oppressor and create a more balanced, more equitable reality. But if authority is good, then this attempt to overthrow is seen as corrupting, evil, and "communist." Your opinion on this question—and everyone has one—is largely a reflection of your access to authority and ignores the fact that we can never be free of the question of authority.

To understand what is happening, we must understand authority. We are on the precipice of open conflict because Western culture no longer shares a common basis of authority. This has happened before in history, and it leads to an old question, once thought solved, that must be asked anew: What can we trust? What is authoritative—reliable, right, and real?

The question of who is worthy of the authority of the people has haunted philosophers for millennia. At a weekly gathering of ideas, Greek philosophers asked the apostle Paul, "May we know what this new teaching is that you are presenting? You are bringing some strange ideas to our ears, and we would like to know what they mean" (Acts 17:19–20 NIV). What was Paul's "new teaching" that so piqued the curiosity of the philosophers at the Areopagus? Is it the same teaching we offer today in the church? Or has the curriculum of the church become confused?

The key question of this book—What happens in the end?—is a question of authority.

Liberal democracy is a form of politics that advocates individual rights, freedom of speech, tolerance of difference, free press, equality under the law, and free elections. Liberal democracy is historically inconceivable without the Christian gospel. But liberal democracy is not "thy kingdom come," nor the "end of history," only a major source for human good in history and often used by the Holy Spirit to move humanity away from the dream of theopolitical harmony. As nihilism wins and the old structures are torn down, then what? Whether giving voice to the public results in a free state or a mob depends on one's perspective, perhaps. It has become a truism that the oldest continuous democracy in the world remains the US. But that is true only if you ignore the participatory democracy of the Native American Six Nations Confederacy (Iroquois), and you skip over the fact that the US wasn't a true "pure" democracy until 1965, when the Voting Rights Act became law. Even if a pure democracy is possible, do we want it? Lest we think majoritarianism is a panacea, remember that Hitler came to power in 1933 by majority rule.

Soren Kierkegaard, the nineteenth century Swiss theologian, philosopher, social critic, and cultural sign reader, warned about going with the crowds and majorities:

> There is a view of life which conceives that where the crowd is, there also is the truth, and that in truth itself there is need of having the crowd on its side. There is another view of life which conceives that wherever there is a crowd there is untruth, so that (to consider for a moment the extreme case), even if every individual, each for himself in private, were to be in possession of the truth, yet in case they were all to get together in a crowd—a crowd to which any sort of *decisive* significance is attributed, a voting, noisy, audible crowd—untruth would at once be evidence.[314]

An old saying goes, "Put it to a vote, and they'll always vote to go back to Egypt." There is something about the anonymity of crowd decisions, the headlong, headstrong energy of "the pack," that makes wrong decisions seem so right, bad choices seem so flawless, and cruel actions seem so sensible. The word "crowd" comes from the Latin *turba*, from which we get the words "disturb" and "perturb." The word "mob" comes from *mobile*, which means volatile and ever-changing. This is truer of an Internet culture. Crowd assessments, majority judgments, and crowd conclusions are often wrong, very wrong.

Time and again in scripture, in story after story, when the crowd spoke and its majority vote was taken, it was a big mistake. Here are some examples.

12. Adam and Eve—they were a majority—disobeyed God in the garden.

11. The tower of Babel was built by a crowd.

10. The whole world chose wickedness except Noah—and they were destroyed in the flood.

9. The 9–1 vote of Joseph's older brothers resulted in his enslavement in Egypt (although Genesis 50:20 puts an interesting slant on that).

8. The golden calf debacle happened when the Israelites put Aaron in the position as leader while Moses was on the mountain.

7. Ten of the twelve spies outvoted Joshua and Caleb's minority.

6. The whole town, worshippers of Baal, came against Gideon in Judges 6.

5. All of Israel wanted a king, even though Samuel and God thought it a bad idea.

4. "The hearts of [all] the people" were stolen by wicked Absalom (2 Samuel 15:6).

3. The people supported the prophets of Baal—not the prophet Elijah—in the contest on Carmel.

2. All the disciples fled and left the one man, Jesus.

And possibly the most inexplicable and worst crowd decision ever made?

1. The crowd responded to the choice Pilate offered them, "Give us Barabbas!" (John 18:40 NIV).

Jesus was crucified by majority vote, by a crowd mentality. In fact, can you find a single majority vote in Scripture in which the majority voted right? If you want to elevate the language from "majority rules" to "community standards," then we've got to talk about witch trials, kangaroo courts, strange fruit, censorship. The biblical model of decision-making is not consensus but critical mass. If you want to see how tedious lawmaking can be, and how feeble the end compromises, ask Indonesians about their consensus-based parliamentary system. Only a small amount of leaven is needed to make a loaf of bread (Galatians 5:9). "Where two or three are gathered together...," Jesus said (Matthew 18:20 KJV). An official gathering required to form a synagogue was at least seven; a special number for prayer is ten; Jesus says, "Forget that." Only two or three are needed for him to be present, challenging the whole system.

A more fundamental reason a true democracy is more historical myth than model? Authority. Everyone has one.[315] Are Trump and others like him around the world, such as Duterte, Tsiprs, and Boris Johnson, the arbiters of a free state or a state governed by dictate? Or is Trump the sledgehammer who will clear the way for other authoritarian figures to emerge?

Every revolution produces new authorities. The question comes down to the character of these individuals. To a public used to monarchial rule, George Washington focused on unifying the new American nation rather than seeking power.[316] Without this leadership by the hero of the American revolution, the American experiment as it has been known may never have come to pass. On the other hand, Lenin embraced sole authority as the hero of the Bolshevik revolution, which led to a starkly different outcome of human suffering. History shows that, as John Mellencamp sings, "I fight authority [but] authority always wins."[317] Society cannot function without authority; in the absence of authority, authoritarian figures will emerge, and more and more people will choose the authoritarian option.

In a Western political environment that glorifies diversity, or the fragmentation of a national ethos into tribalist groups with disparate agendas, who has authority to lead the coalition? We live in a "secessionist age,"[318] but at the end of every revolution, someone emerges, on whose character the future rests. Neither Trump nor Biden, as much as Biden represents the elite class, nor the unnamed leaders of the Left or Right, have yet appeared, ready to lead the public into a new promised land.

This realization that no authority is worthy, and the subsequent rejection of authority, forms the basis for our last false ending: messianism. Messianism is the false narrative that a hero will rise up from somewhere and carry us through the harrowing crucible, which lets us avoid the difficult work of changing our own hearts. Messianism is the last gasp of every society that searches for authority away from God. This is the endgame when the question of what happens becomes the practice of politics and the exercise of power. It is also the endgame of the obsession with leadership.

At the core, each of the six false endings revolves around rebellion against authority.

6.4 The Kingdom of God Is Not Hierarchical

And the chief priests and the teachers of the law were looking for some way to get rid of Jesus, for they were afraid of the people.

—Luke 22:2 (NIV)

As we have noted, the current American cultural crisis is not new. For at least some of Jesus' disciples, the ending they were counting on was messianic. Messianism had already enjoyed a long history among the Jewish people. The question behind the question, as it were, was Roman rule. To varying degrees the band of twelve saw Jesus as a revolutionary leader who would finally finish what Judas Maccabeus had begun two lifetimes earlier, overthrow oppression, and begin a new age of independence and justice. Such imagined endings are always both spiritual and material. Even the religious wars of the seventeenth century, ironically waged against the church and catalyzed initially by the revolt of a knight who had banded up with one of the first religious humanists, was a question of both spirit and material.[319] Throughout history, we have looked for a "big time" political solution: revolutionary figures to violently overthrow the present age.

In the story of the Israelites, the last judge was Samuel. As he became old and unable to travel the circuit of Israel, judging disputes and ruling in local towns, he tried to pass down authority to his sons, Joel and Abijah. But like Samuel's mentor, Eli, the sons proved unable to rise to the demands of their office, instead opting for dishonest gain, accepting bribes, and perverting justice. Hereditary monarchy was once found wanting, but Israel's organizational culture survived, and the elders came to Samuel to make a change. They said, "You are old, and your sons do not follow your ways; now appoint a king to lead us, such as all the other nations have" (1 Samuel 8:5 NIV).

Their rationale is a hinge point in the tragic story of Israel. They wanted a king, "as all the other nations have." Forgetting that they were a people set apart, led by YHWH, they saw a solution to their urgent problem in the "best practices" of rival nationals and clans. Samuel knew their inclination was wrong but no longer had the strength to resist. He prayed, and God said:

> Listen to all that the people are saying to you; it is not you they have rejected, but they have rejected me as their king. As they have done from the day I brought them up out of Egypt until this day, forsaking me and serving other

gods, so they are doing to you. Now listen to them; but warn them solemnly and let them know what the king who will reign over them will claim as his rights. (1 Samuel 8:7–9 NIV)

As from the beginning, God's design was to be the people's King. There is no other solution; no other authority is worthy. All other leaders fall short of the glory of God. But the Israelites rejected God's leadership and insisted on an earthly king. The entire story of the Israelites is summed up in this single moment: the people rejected God as their king and authority and sought a visible monarch, to their own tragic end. Like a father who cannot control a young adult child's insistence on a poor choice, a loving God acquiesced to the stubborn insistence of the people. But with the king came a warning: unlike God, a human ruler will claim rights. Each of these are false endings because demagogues ultimately focus on their own glory and the maintenance of their own power. They end up turning the people on one another.

From this hinge point in the narrative, the rest of the Old Testament story is predictably bad. Human kings sinned, and from their sin came suffering. The people turned away from God, the effects compounded, and eventually their society collapsed.

Yet God is faithful and promised redemption. In exile, the Israelites learned of a prophet who will come, a messianic figure who would

proclaim good news to the poor.
He has sent me to bind up the brokenhearted,
to proclaim freedom for the captives
and release from darkness for the prisoners
to proclaim the year of the LORD's favor. (Isaiah 61:1–2 NIV)

The oppressed people clung to the promise of a Messiah who would release them from captivity and establish freedom and self-rule. The bewildered disciples expected no less of Jesus, right up until the moment he was arrested. But the Israelites' understanding of a Messiah only solved the revolution. What happened after the dust settles? As we have learned, how do we solve the question of authority? A revolution focused on extrinsic circumstance is bound to fail, because as we have learned, authority is a vacuum which must be filled.

Why would this redemptive force be a human king, when God never wanted His people to be led by a human king to begin with? The prophets were clear: God doesn't just want to manage us like constituents, but desires no less than to know each of us. He promised in Ezekiel 37:27, "My dwelling place shall be with them, and I will be their God, and they shall be my people," which is no less than a summary of God's covenant in Exodus—

"I will dwell among the people of Israel and will be their God" (29:45–46 ESV)—which is no less than a reclaimed vision of the garden of Eden.

When Jesus resisted the opportunity to become the people's version of a ruler, his disciple Judas sold him out. Thus, the Easter story is the same story of rebellion against God's authority that has played out through the story of God's people: the impatient need to know rather than trust, the self-reliance on ourselves and one another, and the strident need to fix the problem. The most sympathetic view of Judas's decision to sell Jesus' life for money is that he wanted the same thing as Jesus—for the world to be free of suffering—but he tragically trusted only his own intelligence to make it happen.

As the true Messiah, Jesus was not interested in people's politics, but Luke 22:2 reveals much about the other two parties' thinking: the ruling powers wanted to get rid of the leader who threatened their authority, because they were afraid of the power of the people.

And so it goes and has gone throughout history—a dynamic of power between the people and those in authority. Visions of messianic endings continue today. Absent God as sovereign, the cycle of history repeats itself. If one takes a long perspective, the view is clear: the problem isn't in our systems or our structures or our politics. The problem is in us. On our own, humans cannot escape our fatal attraction to naked self-interest. The one story that is common over and over in scripture is that we put authority in our own hands to tragic ends. The great Russian philosopher Fyodor Dostoevsky said that the triumph of any "ism" would be "the furthest point of removal from the Kingdom of Heaven."[320] Or, as the great British philosopher Sting sang, "there is no political solution."[321]

The story of the end comes down to a question of authority. When the Israelites demanded a king, they rejected God as king (1 Samuel 8:1–9). This same pattern culminated with the people rejecting Jesus as sovereign and savior. Rejection of authority crops up in the most unlikely of places. Recent studies of sleeplessness reveal that this problem that affects between a third and a half of US adults (at some point in their lives) is due in part to a rejection of their own inner authority.[322] We don't like to be told what to do, so our "revenge bedtime procrastination" is our rebellion against our own inner authority. Our sleeplessness can be an "I'll show you" declaration of independence from ourselves and a rebellion at the assumptive naughtiness of our oughtiness.

On the contrary, Jesus' rule is characterized by surrender and sacrifice. This submission to authority is easier than it sounds. We keep hearing and singing about "sweet surrender." But the truth is, there's nothing "sweet" about surrender, whether to a lover or to the "Greatest Lover Who Ever Lived." Surrendering is sundering from the self. It's one of the hardest things anyone can do in life.

At the end of book 2 of Virgil's *Aeneid* (19 BCE), Troy has been defeated and Aeneas has lost everything. As he leaves the city, two options stretch out before him. One is to remain in place and end his life in weeping and sorrow. The other is to follow that path that leads up the mountain, a path that lures him into the unknown but a path that would leave the war behind. Here is what he decides: "*Cessi, et sublato montem genitore petivi*," or "I surrendered to destiny [authority], and, bearing my father on my shoulders, made for the mountain."[323]

The one thing that unites each of the six isms of part 1 of this book is that it places authority in something other than Jesus, in whom the church lives, moves, and has its being. Each of these "isms," taken to its logical conclusion, is furthest from the kingdom of heaven because it surrenders authority to something other than Jesus.

The 2009 U2 song "Moment of Surrender" was crowned by *Rolling Stone* as "the best song of 2009." It was written and produced by British composer and visual artist Brian Eno, who played keyboard and confessed at the conclusion of the taping that it was "the most magical experience [he'd] ever had in a studio."[324] "Moment of Surrender" was the peak moment when the U2 band supposedly came the closest to realizing their original dream of writing "future hymns" (as Eno put it) for the *No Line on the Horizon* album.[325] The seven-minute song features gospel-like vocals in the chorus, along with a predominantly organ- and piano-based musical accompaniment, as it tells the story lyrically of a drug addict who is undergoing a crisis of faith. To surrender life to God is to surrender to life and to encounter God.

The impossible is made possible through "these three": faith, hope, and love (1 Corinthians 13:13 NIV). This is human hope. This present time is but birth pangs of faith, hope, and love for the age to come (Matthew 24:8). The only way to solve the cycle of history is to form a new understanding of the end. We cannot save ourselves; we can only be saved from ourselves by the cross. When we surrender not to one another or unseen political forces but to Jesus as the authority, Jesus will rewrite our life story.

To get past these false endings we keep repeating, we need to turn to our own understanding of what we define as truth. From this we can establish what is authoritative, recover the right story, and discover what really happens in the end.

TRUTH IS NOT A PROPOSITION

The conclusion of each false ending is the furthest point from the kingdom of God. Each is the ideological consequence of human-formed propositions regarding ultimate meaning. Truth is not an idea over which we may argue. Truth is the person of Jesus, who invites us into relationship.

What Is Truth?

Pilate met Truth on Good Friday, stared Truth in the face, and asked Truth, "What is truth?" (John 18:38).

Pontius Pilate was an emperor-worshipping Roman prefect with a reputation for cruelty. He was notorious for insults and could not resist jabbing at Jesus, thus giving us—to his credit—the Gospels' most obvious jest: "What is truth?" One of many jests in the Gospels, Pilate's "What is truth?" is a question less to laugh at than to live by. Pilate sent the Son of God to die a lowlife's death on a stake and crossbeam, atop a hill called Skull. And yet his name, beside those of Jesus and Mary, is an *articulus fidei.* So, what is Pilate doing with his named appearance alongside Mary in the core profession of Christian belief called the Apostles' Creed?

To further complicate the issue, when it was time for Jesus to speak truth to power, his response to Pilate's interrogation was silence (Matthew 27:14). "The Gospel According to Silence"—someone needs to write the story of Jesus' life from the perspective of his silences. When words will only lead to more words and less comprehension, more heat and less light, silence may be the best response. Jesus was crucified, not for claiming to be the Messiah (lots of people did that), but for offenses against public order and for being a goad and gadfly to the religious bureaucracy and power establishment.

Could the answer to why Pilate made it into the Apostles' Creed have something to do with his ultimate answer to his own question "What is truth?" Did Pilate preach his answer in what turned out to be the first Christian sermon? Maybe we need to take another look at the sign ("titulus") Pilate placed above Jesus' head on the cross, a sign mostly missing from images of the cross. All four gospels mention the titulus:

Mark 15:26: "The King of the Judaeans"

Matt.27:37: "This is Jesus, the King of the Judeans"

Luke 23:38: "This is the King of the Judaeans"

John 19:19: "Jesus of Nazareth, the King of the Judaeans" (from which we get INRI, the Latin acronym of Jesus, literally *Iesus Nazarenus Rex Iudaeorum*)

Only John tells us that Pilate actually wrote the inscription and affixed it to the cross in Latin (the language of Roman law), in Greek (the lingua franca of the empire) and Aramaic (the convict's mother tongue). The titulus was a sign with the words setting out the crime for which a man is dying. That Pilate dictated Jesus' titulus can only mean that Pilate himself declared the crime for which Jesus would die. You also know that Pilate authored the titulus himself because some of the religious authorities wanted him to change it from a statement "Jesus, King of the Jews" to a quote from Jesus, touting himself, "I am King of the Jews." But Pilate dismisses them with "What I have written I have written" (John 19:22).

Just as English is known as the "universal language" around the world today, during the first century Greek was the dominant lingua franca, especially in Roman Palestine. Pilate's base language was Latin. Jesus' base language was Aramaic. Most likely it was Greek that Pilate and Jesus used when they spoke to each other.[326] Could this have been the first "Christian sermon" ever preached? Pilate, the one who, like us, asked, "What is truth?" trusted the silent Jesus enough to speak for him and utter Christianity's first sermon: "This is Jesus, the King of the Jews," Messiah and Lord. Pilate delivered this preachment in all the global languages of his day, a truly global sermon for a global Messiah. Greek to the culture, Latin to the politicians, Hebrew to the religious, a global sermon that spoke to the world, announcing that Truth is a person.

Philosophically we are still bound by the values and assumptions of the Enlightenment, which lead to some endarkened conclusions: One, *truth*, is confined by reason. Reason reveals truth, but reason is not truth. David Hume, in proof of his position that "reason is and ought only to be the slave of the passions," argued that "'Tis not contrary to reason to prefer the destruction of the whole world to the scratching of my finger."[327] The Welsh poet and Christian pacifist Waldo Williams (1904–71) names the birth of Jesus "the great music beyond reason and reckoning."[328]

> *The madman is not someone who has lost his reason.*
> *The madman is someone who has lost everything except his reason.*
>
> **—G. K. Chesterton, Orthodoxy**

Two, *meaning*, is confined by empiricism and results in critical inquiry. Criticism breaks incorrect beliefs, but not every belief should be broken. All of us went to a school where, if a teacher asked, "What do you think?" you were being asked to be a critic, to be a voice "against." To be critical about critical thinking, to be against "against," is itself to be critical. We are instructed to study to "show ourselves approved," to celebrate before we cerebrate, and that divine approval does not come from "quarreling about words," which "only ruins those who listen," but from "rightly dividing the word of truth," which has a positive not negative impact on people. (See 2 Timothy 2:14–17 NIV.)

Three, *agency*, is confined by humanism. The future is shaped by what we do, but what we do is not the sole factor in forming the future. Creativity and imagination are drivers of the future. The Romantic poet and theologian Samuel Taylor Coleridge called the imagination "the recapitulation of the 'Great I Am' in the human soul," as the late Thomas H. Troeger liked to point out. Being is as authoritative as doing.

Four, the *future*, is confined by progress. The future can improve or decline, but the kingdom of God is not the end point of the line of history. German philosopher Ludwig Feuerbach professed atheism, not because he disputed the teachings of Christianity, but because he wanted to reclaim Christ's kingdom from the transcendent and supernatural as the only way humanity could progress to the place of "thy kingdom come" on earth.

"Critical race theory," as it is known, has become a cultural flash point. Few know what it means, which makes it a convenient bogeyman. Yet many understand the vague and threatening forces it conjures up. James A. Lindsay, Peter Boghossian, and Helen Pluckrose created a storm in 2018 with the publication of an essay outlining a project that successfully published a series of hoax articles in academic journals. They did this to expose what they identified as the authoritarian takeover of "grievance studies," or "fields of scholarship loosely known as 'cultural studies' or 'identity studies' (for example, gender studies) or 'critical theory' because it is rooted in that postmodern brand of 'theory' which arose in the late sixties."[329]

These fields of scholarship have since become widely referred to, and poorly understood, by mass media as "critical race theory" (CRT). Lindsay, Boghossian, and Pluckrose, who identify as atheists and liberals, created the project as a way of identifying destructive scholarly trends in academe. The coruscating clarity of their bare-knuckled argument is worth quoting at length:

> Because of critical constructivism, which sees knowledge as a product of unjust power balances, and because of this brand of radical skepticism, which rejects objective truth, these scholars are like snake-oil salespeople who diagnose our society as being riddled with a disease only they can cure. That disease, as they see it, is endemic to any society that forwards the agency of the individual and the existence of objective (or scientifically knowable) truths...
>
> The problem is epistemological, political, ideological, and ethical and it is profoundly corrupting scholarship in the social sciences and humanities...
>
> Underlying these alleged "social constructions" is the most deeply concerning of them all. This is the belief that in urgent need of "disrupting" is the simple truth that science itself—along with our best methods of data-gather-

ing, statistical analysis, hypothesis testing, falsifying, and replicating results—is generally a better way of determining information about the objective reality of any observable phenomenon than are non-scientific, traditional, cultural, religious, ideological, or magical approaches. That is, for grievance studies scholars, science itself and the scientific method are deeply problematic, if not outright racist and sexist, and need to be remade to forward grievance-based identitarian politics over the impartial pursuit of truth. These same issues are also extended to the "Western" philosophical tradition which they find problematic because it favors reason to emotion, rigor to solipsism, and logic to revelation.

As a result, radical constructivists tend to believe science and reason must be dismantled to let "other ways of knowing" have equal validation as knowledge-producing enterprises. These, depending on the branch of "theory" being invoked, are allegedly owned by women and racial, cultural, religious, and sexual minorities.

The project, which was of course widely criticized by those whom it sought to discredit, used parody to identify and articulate the core problem, which they name as

an overarching (almost or fully sacralized) belief that many common features of experience and society are socially constructed. These constructions are seen as being nearly entirely dependent upon power dynamics between groups of people, often dictated by sex, race, or sexual or gender identification. All kinds of things accepted as having a basis in reality due to evidence are instead believed to have been created by the intentional and unintentional machinations of powerful groups in order to maintain power over marginalized ones. This worldview produces a moral imperative to dismantle these constructions.[330]

The worldview has made its way into the church, not least through the influence of the bestseller *White Fragility* (2018) by Robin DiAngelo. The CRT worldview is basically a competing religion based on the sovereignty of invisible forces (privilege and oppression) that can only be assumed, not disproved, and are impossible to measure but must be taken on faith. Basic tenets of CRT religion include the social construction of all reality, the absence of absolute truth beyond "lived religion," and the inherent violence of speech, which is untethered from facts and only accountable to political ends. It is a religion without redemption, only reparations. CRT religion depicts the USA (without expanding its scope to the rest of the world) as irredeemably racist with an insurmountable legacy of slavery. Racist, yes. Irredeemably, no. Legacy of slavery, yes. Insurmountable, no.

CRT is an Enlightenment religion in that repentance and forgiveness are the only ways forward but are impossible to get to from an Enlightenment mindset. You can only get to repentance and forgiveness from a Christian perspective. Christianity is where we get such things as human freedom, dignity, and equality of all persons, distrust of the mob, exercise of tolerance, love of mercy, practice of forgiveness, solidarity with the downtrodden, and spotlighting and repair for injustice.

What does this mean for the central questions of this book? In the prologue, we ask three core questions: First, what happens at the end of our present age? Second, since for Christians this is so closely tied to our understanding of "the kingdom of God," what exactly is the kingdom of God? Third, like the disciples, we ask, what are the signs? Part 1 of this book outlined six false endings to the present age, each socially constructed, and each based on a flawed understanding of authority.

Our three questions are philosophical and yet deeply practical. The volcanic cultural events of our age have proven that philosophy is not merely an ivory tower activity but affects real lives and can cause or alleviate real suffering. These questions address who we are and how we understand truth, ourselves, and our relationship to truth.

To understand what happens in the end, we must agree on the journey we are taking. In essence, the emergence of "critical race theory" in the public consciousness is a label for the philosophical elevation of experience over reason as the basis for truth. Today's argument between liberals and critical constructivists is no less earth-shattering than the argument we described earlier, made three hundred years ago, between the Ancients and the Moderns, between Aquinas and Hume. Whereas that argument positioned tradition against reason, this argument positions reason against experience.

They beg the question, what is truth? From truth we decide what is authoritative, or what we decide will author or determine our lives.

Here is a quick summary of each position, with our summary statement and a note about its limitation.

> **Truth as tradition.** The recurring position of religious establishment—but truth is not limited to our tribe or clan.

> **Truth as reason.** The classic Enlightenment position and liberal tradition that has shaped the church of the last three hundred years—but truth is not limited to our ability to understand it

but is an objective proposition that may be discovered through research.

Truth as experience. The "woke" position—but truth is not limited to our ability to experience it.

Truth as scripture. The fundamental/evangelical position—but truth is not limited to the laws of Torah or the stories of Jesus on earth.

Each of these is true but not *the* Truth, a profound partial truth. Each is a stained glass, a filmy (but never flimsy) lens through which to view the whole as window, mirror, and artistry. The church is in the whole-truth business. When we parrot one of these authorities, we diminish our witness. The church does not tell "half-truths."

We have looked for authoritative answers in the past and in the future, in ourselves and in others. None satisfy. In the height of Enlightenment hegemony, evangelical theologian Carl F. H. Henry, who wrote a monumental six-volume set defending an epistemology based on the revealed knowledge of God over the empirically acquired knowledge of reason and experience, says the "sinful human spirit slants its perspectives in a manner that does violence to the truth of revelation."[331]

We are losing a shared cultural definition of truth. It was at best a useful myth anyway, right? Contemporary scholarship scorns any attempts at truth that deny cultural construction, except its own explorations of truth, which of course defy cultural construction. In this climate, is it even possible to have a shared definition of what is true? We love to hate "death-of-God" Nietzsche because we love what he hates. The moral order of our world has been based on a belief in God. But as Nietzsche saw so clearly, without God that moral order comes crashing down, and "good" is no longer good but only good in one's own eyes. The same goes for evil. There is nothing timeless or true, only "my taste" and "my truth" and "my feelings" and "my way."

Reason was predicated on empirical thinking, the idea that we could achieve a universal knowledge. Yet we learned that the language on which we base our shared knowledge is not "pure" but is contextual and a product of the storyteller, storyreceiver, and the codes, channels, and contexts of our messages. This realization has led to the concept of "particular knowledge" and eventually to an abandonment of the very notion of objective truth.

How are we to move forward considering this philosophical impasse in this post-truth world? When there is no tarmac of truth to land on, what is to happen to a church that is called to traffic in truth, not facts or correctness? Correctness is not the same as truth. To say that Sherlock Holmes lived at 221B Baker Street is correct, but it is not true. Are we to become like the Greek philosophers of Areopagus, never committing to any idea? What happens to truth claims when personal experience is seen as the same as truth, when #mytruth becomes #TheTruth?

Searching for Truth

In a podcast episode, rambunctious raconteur Malcolm Gladwell investigated the backstory of perhaps the most iconic photograph in the history of the civil rights movement. The photograph, taken at a march in 1963, became a sculpture in 1995 called *The Foot Soldier of Birmingham.* Use of a key photograph was one of Martin Luther King's strategic goals with his marches. He used mass media to turn the tide of American public opinion.[332] Gladwell notes that the image that emerged from the march that day in Birmingham was wildly successful. It appeared on the front page of papers around the world. A year later, Congress passed the Civil Rights Act, which according to Gladwell's recounting was "written in Birmingham."[333]

Yet, the events of the day the photograph was taken were more complicated than the sculpture suggests. For instance, "foot soldier" is a term for each of the people who marched in King's army. The sculpture shows a foot soldier being accosted by a racist cop and his attack dog. But the man being attacked—Walter Gadsden—was not actually a foot soldier. As Gladwell discovered, Gadsden was a bystander, a student who was skipping school that day. He was in fact trying to avoid the protestors, and neither supported the civil rights movement nor believed he benefited from the movement.

Second, the sculpture shows the police officer releasing a vicious dog upon the young man. But the actual officer in the photograph, Dick Middleton, was trying to restrain the dog and did not want it to attack the young man. In the podcast, Middleton's widow tells Gladwell that her husband was vilified on account of the photograph. It was not the truth, she said. But the hate mail came just the same from all over the world.

Third, the positions of the two men in the sculpture are entirely different than the photograph indicates. Both the photo and the witnesses to the event describe a sudden accidental bumping together of two people incidentally connected to the march. The sculpture captures an entirely different narrative, a core visual of what was happening during that time, with a vulnerable boy whose hands are behind him in nonviolent resistance. The artistic framing of the sculpture was not a mistake. It was intentional.

Gladwell interviewed the artist, Ronald S. McDowell. McDowell knew that the sculpture was an interpretation. He had no interest in being "objective." He wanted to tell a story. He made the boy in the sculpture smaller than the young man in the photograph, and the officer larger. There are plenty of other events surrounding King's marches that captured actual moments of vicious dogs and oppressive police. Some 8 mm footage as shown in the PBS documentary film *Eyes on the Prize,* for example, shows imagery that is strikingly similar to McDowell's sculpture.[334]

The question now is: Which one is the truth? Are the events surrounding the publication of the photograph and its impact on the course of history the truth? Does Gladwell's investigation uncover the "real" truth, the truth behind the reframing? Is McDowell's sculpture the truth?

What if all three are the truth? The photograph documented a moment. It happened. It is by definition nonfiction. But sometimes photographs can represent things in ways that seem different from what happened. That is what happens here, as Gladwell observes. While perhaps misleading in terms of the characters involved, the "spirit" of the image captures a spirit of resistance and a moment of historical change. While not necessarily factual, it is still truthful.

The sculpture is clearly not factual at all in the sense that it does not reproduce the photo but actively reimagines the photo. What it does do is reproduce the story behind the photograph, better perhaps than the photograph itself. As Gladwell notes, the sculpture is a work of imagination. It is not literal. It is art. Yet, the statue is understood as having historical authority.

All three interpretations—the photo, the story behind the photo, and the artistic reimagining of the photo—are truth, each in its own way. These three perspectives on truth belie the conventional wisdom that there is a single perspective on truth. According to Gladwell's investigation, truth lives separate from the sender's intent; it is a function of message, medium, context, and code. Truth is dependent on the receiver's knowledge and perspective.

Philosopher-scientist Michael Polanyi acknowledges the impossibility of achieving the stated purpose of science to establish complete, empirically verified control over experience, because of the necessity of extrapolating the probable to the certain. He uses the example of a bunch of white balls in a sack. If you add a few black balls, and then happen to draw one out, you still believe it is mostly full of white balls: "Now suppose that we had ourselves placed the balls, 95 percent of them white and 5 percent of them black, into the sack, and then having shaken them up, we drew out a black ball. We should be very surprised yet remain unshaken in our belief that the bag contained the balls we had put into it."[335]

In other words, scientific knowledge is always probable knowledge. Since we cannot do experiments forever, we must eventually conclude with a high degree of probability that our answer is correct. We start succumbing to a form of confirmation bias and verify only what we believe is probably true. Continued experiments amount to an infinity rule in mathematics. We can get close but can never know with complete certainty. Polanyi writes, "All truth is but the external pole of belief, and to destroy all belief would be to deny all truth." He later adds, "Objectivism has totally falsified our conception of truth, by exalting what we can know and prove, while covering up with ambiguous utterances all that we know and cannot prove, even though the latter knowledge underlies, and must ultimately set its seal to, all that we can prove."[336]

This is not to say that there is no such thing as truth, as some have concluded. Rather, our personal perspective is both limited and inextricably intertwined with a full understanding of truth. Our ability to see a final answer is limited to our view of the problem. In the words of the apostle Paul, who understood the importance of context, "There are doubtless many different languages in the world, and none is without meaning, but if I do not know the meaning of the language, I will be a foreigner to the speaker and the speaker a foreigner to me" (1 Corinthians 14:10–11 ESV).

It is time to increase our truth intake by diving deeper into the three types of truth presented in Gladwell's investigation. The first are the events surrounding the publication of the photograph, or what we may call *rational* (or *absolute*) *truth*. These events are nonfiction. Indisputable. Immutable. They happened. Therefore, they are true. The second is Gladwell's investigation into the "story behind the story." What he finds is the immediate, firsthand, sensory experience of the characters in the story, and of course the revelation that in this backstory belies a "different" truth. We may call this *relative truth*. The third is McDowell's sculpture, which captures not the photograph and the events surrounding it, but the larger narrative at play during the story of the civil rights movement as a whole. We may call this *relational truth*. Let us look at all three in more detail.

Truth from Varying Perspectives

What we think: rational truth

Theologically speaking, rational truth is absolute truth or time-full truth. Truth that is timeless and absolute is akin to truth that comes from God the Creator, who is timeless and absolute. Rational truth is often the position of the positivist, who according to theologian N. T. Wright, claims that "there are some things that are simply 'objectively' true… which can be tested empirically."[337]

Positivism holds that there is a definable, rational, usually single explanation for every phenomenon we can discover through empirical methodologies of criticism. This understanding of truth emerged from and alongside the scientific study of the material world. Beginning in the mid-nineteenth century, the pursuit of rational truth extended into the study of the spiritual world.

Culture has benefited greatly from empirical thought and the idea that there is a rational answer to every situation. But despite the realization of its limitations among the scientific and philosophy communities,[338] positivist thinking remains pervasive such that many in the Western world now assume there is only a rational, usually single explanation for everything material. Many also now assume that actions and behaviors follow rational convictions. While this view has largely been abandoned by philosophers, it is still common in a variety of spheres within Christendom, including both fundamentalist and progressive camps. Wright calls this view "naive realism."[339]

The classic Western apologetic is to present truth as a set of claims with supporting argumentation, just as this work seeks to do. If we cannot articulate and defend it, we cannot stake a claim to it or justify its truthfulness. This kind of truth is private, analytical, and detached—as studies have shown that detached silent reading is private, analytical, and detached.[340]

Western Christianity is so ingrained in a positivist approach to truth that to see through a different lens is more than many can grasp. This is particularly true in the church, where many are wedded to positivist thinking not only as an epistemic worldview but as an expression of righteousness and efficiency as we shift into McKinsey (management consultants) mode with our strategic planning and leadership corporate strategies. In this rational view, the goal for the apologist, or the one defending the church, is to simply persuade another of the rightness of a position, and having done so, it is assumed that right action will follow. Of course, this does not always happen, and in our current era of "fake news," increasingly less so.

Rational superiority often has little to no bearing on individual behavior. Albert Einstein confessed that the main reason he went to his office at Princeton was to walk home with logician-mathematician Kurt Gödel.[341] Brilliant, but a hypochondriac and delusional, Gödel was known for submitting all on the altar of logic and rationality. What doomed Gödel, however, was his rationalization of irrational thinking to the point that he insisted on a permanent catheter to control his bowels even though he didn't need one. Often joined with Aristotle as the greatest logician in all of history, he died in 1978 of malnutrition in one of the wealthiest townships in US-America (Princeton, New Jersey). As Pascal was not the first to remind us, one of the purposes of rationality is to understand and showcase the limits of rationality. We are all dual-process thinkers.[342]

What we feel: relative truth

If rational truth is objective, relative truth is subjective. Absolute truth is timeless truth; relative truth is timely truth. It occurs in contextual space and time (which is also the etymological basis for the word "contemporary"). Relative truth is rooted in the human experience of the five-plus senses of sight, sound, hearing, taste, and touch. We can only know absolute truth subjectively. The absolute exists independent of us, but that absolute is unknown and unknowable apart from our subjective experience.

To some, relative truth is relativist truth, or the opposite of positivist truth. As N. T. Wright notes, "The much-discussed contemporary phenomenon of cultural and theological relativism is itself in this case simply the dark side of positivism."[343] Postmodern thought positioned relativism as the opposite of rationalism.

But relative truth is not solely subjective or purely phenomenological truth. Wright rejects the dichotomy and suggests a third way of "critical realism," which is "the process of 'knowing' that acknowledges the reality of the thing known, as something other than the knower (hence 'realism'), while also fully acknowledging that the only access we have to this reality lies along the spiraling path of appropriate dialogue or conversation between the knower and the thing known (hence 'critical')."[344] In other words, truth is indeed something objective and "pure" that exists outside of our personal experience, yet it unknowable apart from our personal experience, which inevitably introduces bias.

Novelist Cormac McCarthy places this relative view on the protagonist in his critically acclaimed novel, *Blood Meridian*: "In this world more things exist without our knowledge than with it and the order in creation which you see is that which you have put there, like a string in a maze, so that you shall not lose your way. For existence has its own order and that no man's mind can compass, that mind itself being but a fact among others."[345]

At some level, truth is relative. It is timely, or "of the time" (contemporary), and experienced through the five (or more) human senses. However, while by appearance, relational truth opposes rational truth, relative truth does not necessarily negate rational truth. Rather, the two forms can live in paradoxical tension, similar to different hemispheres of the mind. To use brain researcher Iain McGilchrist's categories, relative truth is the right hemisphere of the five senses and of experience, while rational truth is the left hemisphere of reference and rationality. The human mind experiences first, through the five-plus senses, and then rationalizes by making references, premises and syllogisms based on human experience. McGilchrist says:

> The right hemisphere [of the brain] needs the left hemisphere in order to be able to unpack experience. Without its distance and structure, certainly, there could be, for example, no art, only experience—Wordsworth's description of poetry as "emotion recollected in tranquility" is just one famous reflection of this. But, just as importantly, if the process ends with the left hemisphere, one only has concepts—abstractions and conceptions, not art at all. Similarly, the immediate pre-conceptual sense of awe can evolve into religion only with the help of the left hemisphere: though, if the process stops here, all one has is theology, or sociology, or empty ritual: something else. It seems that, the work of division having been done by the left hemisphere, a new union must be sought, and for this to happen the process needs to be returned to the right hemisphere, so it can live.[346]

All language forms in this fashion, as references to human experience. Because of its relationship to human experience, rational thinking is not incorrect, but it is incomplete. To be critical is to begin by saying "No." But God's first word to humankind is not no; it is "Yes."[347] While the fundamental stance of the Enlightenment philosopher is doubt, the fundamental stance of the Christian is faith. God begins not with criticism but with celebration, which is a sensory experience. Relative truth builds on rational truth by returning rational truth back to the world of human experience.

Rational truth is truth that is immutable and from God the Creator. Relative truth is truth of the time and from God the Son, incarnate in Jesus. In this way relative truth is best understood in the specific time and space in which it is experienced. All ontology collapses because it is isolating and not relational. An ontological quest for definitions is the desire for some stable, unbending statement that is universal. Modern philosophy got stranded here and stuck by logical positivism and existentialism. The "suckiness" of postmodern philosophy is a symptom of its stuckness.

The experience of relative truth requires full body involvement, not merely our detached, mind involvement. More complete knowing requires not only detached intellectual acknowledgment but a full commitment of faith and the passion of one's personal presence and creativity. In the novel and film *Jurassic Park* by surgeon and storyteller Michael Crichton, doctor Alan Grant has studied dinosaurs his whole life, but when he encounters a living dinosaur, he realizes that there is so much more than he could ever have known by looking at bones in his lab. Based on his lab work, Grant thought he understood the meaning of various concepts and abstract categories. However, when he experienced dinosaurs firsthand, many of his preconceived definitions changed. Author Michael Crichton writes, "They knew so little about dinosaurs, Grant thought. After 150 years of research and excavation all around the world, they still knew almost nothing about what the dinosaurs had really been like."[348] In the film, actor Sam Neill portrays Dr. Grant as a child, beside himself with joy as he leans on a prone stegosaur, experiencing firsthand things he has merely imagined his whole life, correcting false notions.

This kind of dynamic meaning-making falsifies facile perceptions of "objectivity." One of us has written elsewhere that "to be modern meant to trust in objectivity and to learn to be objective. In fact, to say someone is objective is a high compliment. But does anyone want to be treated like an object? When you treat something like an object, when you get objective, you bring under your control what you are studying and make it submit to your authority."[349] The metaphor of a bird in a pan versus a bird in the bush is instructive. Modern scientists learned much about nature by pinning down dead specimens and dissecting them. But their perspective was incomplete. A living bird is out of our objective control. We cannot pin a live bird to a lab pan on a table to study it. We must stand under the subject's nest to study its habits. A subject dictates the terms by which you study it. "There is no understanding without standing under."[350]

What we share: relational truth

Finally, truth is also found in what we share. Truth that is time-full, or understood in the fullness of time, is relational. While at one level we may "know" something to be true in a rational sense, we only "know" it at a deeper level through our relative proximity to it. Students of Hebrew will recognize this sort of relative knowledge, as there is a deeper sort of knowing that aligns with proximity. To the Hebrew, knowing is intimacy, as is captured in the verse, "Adam knew Eve" (Genesis 4:1 KJV). To the Christian, truth is not a proposition at all, but a person: Jesus. Our perspective on truth changes depending on our proximity to Jesus. William of Baskerville, the titular character of Umberto Eco's classic *The Name of the Rose*, describes his deductive ability to his novice according to his proximity to the object in question, a horse:

> If you see something from a distance, and you do not understand what it is, you will be content with defining it as a body of some dimension. When you come closer, you will then define it as an animal, even if you do not know whether it is a horse or an ass. And finally, when it is still closer, you will be able to say it is a horse even if you do not know whether it is Brunellus or Niger. And only when you are at the proper distance will you see that it is Brunellus (or, rather, that horse and not another, however you decide to call it.) And that will be full knowledge, the learning of the singular.[351]

William teaches his disciple that truth is fully understood according to the observer's proximate relationship to the object. We cannot fully know from a distance, but only when we are intimately close to it. Thus, truth is relational, and therefore understood in community. Verbs are the bearers of actions and feelings. Nouns are the bearers of things and propositions. Prepositions are the bearers of relationships.

Theologically speaking, this means that to some degree, truth is revealed. Truth is apocalyptic. It comes to us not as knowledge acquired by human inquiry, which can be discovered as a detached observer, but as wisdom acquired by revelation of God's Spirit, which occurs in relationship with the observed.

Luke's Gospel tells a story about Jesus being baptized: "And the Holy Spirit came down on him in bodily form like a dove. And there was a voice from heaven: 'You are my Son, whom I dearly love; in you I find happiness'" (Luke 3:22 CEB). An alternative reading is: "You are my beloved Son, who brings me great pleasure."

To the Christian, this is surely one of the most beautiful verses in the Bible. You could see the Holy Spirit. You could hear God's voice. You could touch Jesus. In that moment, you could physically experience the entire Trinity. All three persons of the Trinity were present. The whole divine family was there. This passage is an example of the inner relationship of the Trinity, which may be understood as *kenosis*—a word that captures the emptying of self simultaneously present in all three persons of the Trinity. The three persons of the Trinity, Father, Son, and Holy Spirit, model kenosis. Each empties the self out for the others. Each person of the Trinity is focused not on self but the others. Through perfected love, each is in turn filled up (*plerosis*) even in the act of emptying (*kenosis*). The Father, the Son, and the Holy Spirit love one another—they are truly love itself. In this beautiful scripture passage, we get to witness the Trinity engaged in the kenosis-plerosis dance (the perichoresis) that is the essence of the Trinity: happy in the mystery of an inner-connected relationship of love. Relational truth is understood in community.

> *You know from experience that self-will does not cause you to flourish. Follow instead the path of obedience. I guarantee it will take you where you want to go.*
>
> **—Rule of St. Benedict**

"If you want to discover the secrets of the universe, think in terms of energy, frequency, and vibration" said Nikola Tesla (1846–1953),[352] whose father was a priest in the Serbian Orthodox Church. We would only add relationships. Truth is a person, not an idea or a proposition or a doctrine. Jesus did not give us a list of rules and regulations to check off, or principles to placard, but a matrix of relationships to make and keep, with God, with each other, with ourselves, and with creation.

The word *sharia* in Arabic means "Way." It refers not to a body of laws per se but to a set of ethical principles and moral practices drawn from the Quran and sayings (hadith) of the Prophet Muhammad. "Sharia law" establishes the way of truth as the way of precepts and practices. Jesus said, "I am the way" (John 14:6) For Christians the Way is a Person. Not sharia. Yeshua.

The rehabilitation of truth as a category of meaning is one of the great tasks of the twenty-first century. Truth is just as important to religion as to science. The convention is to define "orthodoxy" of truth in terms of beliefs, and "orthopraxy" of truth in terms of practices. It is time to define truth as "orthodoxy" and "orthopraxy" in terms of healthy relationships and connections.

Truth Is a Person

Revelation describes heaven as a city. The Greek word for city is *polis*. Simply, politics is the ongoing discussion among humans about how to achieve heaven on earth and do "on earth as it is in heaven" (Matthew 16:10). The more recent phenomenon of "politicomorphism" reverses "on earth as it is in heaven" to "in heaven as it is on earth" as God and the dictates of the divine are changed to suit changing political contexts and congealing political correctitudes.

We have been trying to figure out the secret of "politics" for centuries. What is it? How should we do it? First up is a shared understanding about the terms of the discussion. This may be understood as the epistemological question: Is there a shared basis for knowledge?

When you look at the broad scope of history, the scope of the politic has slowly expanded—from family to tribe and clan to village to county and region to nation to the entire globe. In fact, the current political crisis in USAmerica may be understood as the struggle between a future orientation toward a new form of "global village" or a past orientation toward a smaller entity in the devolution revolution—either country, clan, or family. Critical race theory, though it seems progressive, has taken on the same question when it defines individual identity according to race. This is how we end up with the oddball situation in which a "progressive" Presbyterian King University race training event in Bristol, Tennessee, can assign restrooms signs according to white and "people of color" in a full-frontal return to the restroom signs of the Jim Crow South.

The racist throwback of a restroom sign is a tell of the larger epistemological question: What is our basis for truth? To understand our basis for truth, we must cup our ears to hear about authority. What is authoritative? We begin with what we know to be unassailable.

When the politic shifts, the question of authority raises its head. Each new generation must answer it for themselves. When people riot the Capitol, they are making a violent, forceful claim that their basis for authority is their understanding of a national identity, a civil religion, or a Christian nationalism. When people claim, "I am spiritual but not religious," they are unmindfully declaring that their religion is private, self-determined, and free of authority, tradition, and communal constraints.

So, what is the basis for our authority? How do we arrive at the city?

All the false endings outlined in this book commit the sin of the Greek philosophers of the Areopagus, who were always eager to explore new ideas but never actually committing their lives to anything. They pretended to be above it all, deconstructing each worldview according to its merits, just like the deconstructionists of the twentieth century.

Each false "ending" contains shards of truth. For example, you need some apocalyptic in life, in both the unveiling/dystopian senses of the term. Good preparedness for the future requires scenario-think foretastes of apocalypse. To shape the future, you also need some millennial dreams that take the future seriously. But when a culture is marinated in utopian visions such as "End Injustice," "End Poverty," or "End Racism!" it leaves us in a miasma of millennialism that fuels the apocalyptic in tense and terse ways. The elements of truth in each of these endings make them seductive and attractive. But none are the full truth. So how do we know the full truth?

Robert Caro has spent a lifetime writing biographies, not of people, although it looks that way, but biographies of power. At the age of eighty-three Caro had come to this conclusion:

> While I am aware that there is not Truth, no objective truth, no single truth, no truth simple or unsimple, either: no verity, eternal or otherwise, no Truth about anything, there ARE Facts, objective facts, discernible and verifiable. And the more facts you accumulate, the closer you come to whatever truth there is. And finding facts--through reading documents or through interviewing and re-interviewing--can't be rushed; it takes time. Truth takes time.[353]

So, there is truth, after all. But for Caro, like much of this culture, truth is just facts, no meaning. Benjamin Franklin liked to say that one of life's greatest tragedies is watching a beautiful theory being killed by a gang of brute facts.[354] So brute facticity is truth. Yet Polanyi (and others) insist that "facts" are not ever the most important part of knowing, much less wisdom. In a culture where there is at best "facts" and no "truth," or when truth is put on hold to soothe ruffled feathers, life becomes a matter of finding out what works for you and what doesn't.

"Truth or Consequences" is a teleological ultimatum. The only cure for illness is truth. We must cure evil with truth. The cure for the treadmill suicide machine we are "on" is truth. To "mean well" is not enough. Human actions may be well intended, even based on "facts," but they are never undertaken with full or real understanding of their consequences.

The crisis of authority in USAmerican culture is the loss of a shared basis of truth. The crisis of authority in the Western church is the failure to see the true basis of authority, which is the person of Jesus. Truth comes into the world, not abstract pure and antiseptic clean, but cradled in dirt and mangered in mystery.[355]

Jesus told the truth about the Truth: "I am the truth" (see John 14:6). The world of philosophy has positioned Jesus as one of many teachings or paths to truth. But as Paul taught the philosophers at the meeting of the Areopagus, Jesus is not a teaching, or a teacher, but the "Author and Finisher" of a Story, the Fullness and Fulfilment of a Metanarrative that has existed since the beginning of time and will complete the end of time.

A focus on linear time leads us to think eschatologically, but the story of Jesus invites us to reorient ourselves teleologically. When we define truth according to Jesus, everything becomes clear. The key is to put the person of Jesus, not a philosophical proposition or theological doctrine, on the throne. This is the goal of part 2 of this book.

When love becomes a principle, a person becomes an object. The centerpiece of every wedding ceremony is vows. But vows are made to a person, not to a proposition. Love is more about the constraints of vows than views. Views end up nailed on doors and posted to blogs. Vows end up nailed on crosses, taking out bedpans, and chained to deathbeds.

5   1   5   6   9   6   8   9   8   4   7   3   5

2   8   7   8   7   1   5   4   4   3

2   9   3   6   7   5   8   1   8   3   9   5   6   2   3

3   6   7   8   8   1   1   8   5   1   6   8   2   4   5

5   2   3   1   8   8   7   8   5   1   5   5   1   5   2   4

1   9   8   3   3   6   3   1   2   7   9   8   2   8   8   9   8   6   9

1   1   7   1   4   8   1   2   8   9   6   8   7   1   1   8   8

9   2   9   3   9   6   2   8   1   4   4   6   8

6   1   7   5   3   7   1   4   4   9   4   5   4   9   3   7   9

9   5   6   7   8   8   9   7   7   9   8   7   8   1

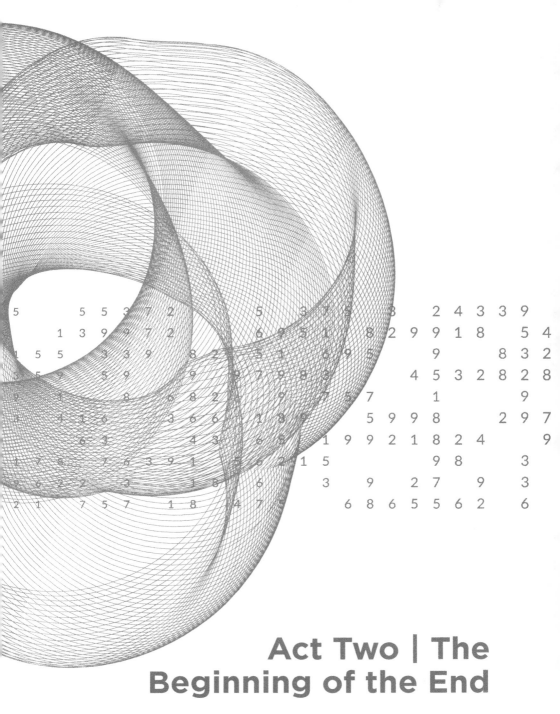

Act Two | The Beginning of the End

The Age To Come

| CHAPTER 7 |
REAL TIME: AUTHORITY

....

In the end, Jesus has all authority on heaven and earth.

....

Each chapter in part 2 mirrors the questions raised in part 1. In this chapter, we address the question raised by messianism: is there anyone with the power and authority to rescue us?

As institutions and individuals get torn down, the old question of authority has again emerged. What does it mean to have authority? It is to have power over something—the power to create or author. From our understanding of truth, we determine what is authoritative, what has moral influence, and what has power.

The world and Christ's church have tried to give authority to everything imaginable, but all fall short. The desire for an authoritative figure to save us is only fulfilled in Jesus, who has been given all authority over heaven and earth.

7.1 | A Crisis of Authority

One of the more sympathetic expressions of incredulity at coronavirus deniers comes from Australian journalist Claire Lehmann, founding editor of the online magazine *Quillette*:

> I understand why people are skeptical of experts. I just feel really sorry for people who don't have the intellectual tools to be selective in their skepticism. I don't know what the answer is—and I doubt blanket deference to "experts" and "the science" is it.
>
> It would be helpful if more people understood how robust randomised clinical controlled trials are. And how risk-averse regulatory agencies are.
>
> It's quite possible that many more lives have been lost to the precautionary principle than saved.
>
> But again it is "experts" that impose the precautionary principle. And it's other "experts" who oppose it. The trick is working out which experts to trust. I get that this is a hard task.[356]

Not too long ago it was septic to be skeptic. Now, skepticism is the order of the day. Both Left and Right are rife for self-deception: it seems the Left cannot tolerate any kind of universal truths, which are seen as strident, because all it can embrace are ambivalence, ambiguity, skepticism, and uncertainty; the Right cannot tolerate any intellectual ideas other than populism and the lowest common denominator, and issues declarations not to affirm but to pander prejudices, inflame hostilities, and arouse passions.

Pandemics, political strongmen, and race paradigms are new expressions of power in a world in which formerly binding principles have fractured, frayed, and faded. For the past three centuries Western civilization has been governed not only by congressional bodies and democratic principles but by an assumed and commonly shared philosophical worldview and glue loosely called "classic liberalism." The core values of classic liberalism include generosity, fair play, fairness, protection of free speech, and tolerance. You can find this smattering of values scattered in the past, but what brought them all together into a force for the future was the Christian belief in the dignity of every human being, which comes from the origins story of humanity in Genesis 1 and 2. Acknowledged or not, Enlightenment values of reason, science, humanism, and progress are built on this foundation, a foundation of shared values that is now cracking and crumbling.

What we are witnessing today are the first throes of the new anti-foundationalist era. If this sounds frightening to you, it should. It is every bit as earthshaking as the shift from the church to science that rocked Europe and led to wars in the sixteenth and seventeenth century. Our crisis is ultimately one of authority.

As we write this, massive protests against racially motivated police acts of brutality are shaking the Western world. Political revolution seems to be taking place. But of what sort? What is the ideology the protestors espouse, and to what end do the protesters march? Is there a leader pointing the way, or is this purely a movement of the people? Is it possible to have a movement purely of the people? While these questions may have clearer answers shortly, one thing is already clear. We are witnessing the results of forty years of postmodernist deconstruction. Universities are now filled not with teachers but with activists and nihilists. Political analyst Martin Gurri writes, "Today, everyone's a nihilist. President Trump is a nihilist, many times over . . . But Trump's predecessor in the White House, Barack Obama, turns out to be a nihilist too—and at least one bewildered commentator has proclaimed, 'we are all political nihilists now.'"[357] The Left and the Right each have shared a desire to tear down the institutions of Western society. The desire to destroy as the only pure motive remaining is the definition of nihilism. Gurri writes, "The US public, like the public everywhere, is engaged in a long migration away from the structures of representative democracy to more sectarian arrangements. The public craves meaning and identity. From his perspective, late modern society, including government, exists to frustrate this desire."[358]

Why has this happened?

One filter for understanding the clashes of authority roiling the globe today is the rise of social media, which has given voice to the public square. A generation ago, the public was largely passive, receiving information by broadcast media controlled by a small group of curators—as Gurri describes, a class of elites. Getting published was, for most, a dream. Many scholars of media worried about the dehumanizing effects of passive consumption. Think about the future couch potato in the film *Wall-E*, whose body had slowly melted into the shape of his seat. Already in the pre-Internet era, media scholars such as John Fiske recognized the rise of media platforms as agents of a slow migration to more active empowerment, participation, and meaning making.[359] Fiske dubbed this "semiotic democracy" in his seminal work *Television Culture*: rather than be handed meaning from an authority figure, each person is now free to create his or her own meaning.

The advent of digital platforms accelerated this more active vision of the future. Since the dawn of the new century, digital media have given voice to anyone who steps on a platform and speaks. For the first time, we were hearing directly from one another. And the transformation has been, historically speaking, immediate: "Almost immediately, great institutions in every domain of human activity began to bleed authority."[360] While some saw the Internet through utopian-colored lenses, others noted the dangers in what has become a much more fractured information landscape. Whether the voices are controlled by a few elites (a vertical orientation) or the general public (a horizontal orientation), the question of authority is inescapable. All social media did was further shift authority to a horizontal, peer direction.

While it is true that anyone can create a Twitter account, getting people to listen is an entirely different question. The problem is a platform is best built by getting noticed. Some do this work the long, hard way, by building trust. But most do it by expressing extreme opinions, by outrage, by outlandishness. Enragement increases engagement. In the months leading up to the 2016 US presidential election, Donald Trump, a longtime veteran of media who had fronted his own reality television program, understood this better than any other candidate. He thrived not on advertising (paying for exposure) but on the free kind—also known as "public relations." Using his favored channel for direct communication, Twitter, Trump developed a direct relationship with the public through constant, unfiltered commentary. Every other candidate had social accounts too, but approached them carefully using handlers and "experts," more scared of saying the wrong thing, preferring the more traditional strategy of angling for favorable treatment among established journalists and channels.

Meanwhile, Trump tweeted with shock-and-awe abandon and seemed to get away with everything. Controversies that had downed previous campaigns (see Gary Hart) had no effect on Trump. The result was that he won traditional media too. Trump received far more coverage from traditional media than his Democratic or Republican competitors, even though he spent far less money on advertising. As Gurri writes, "Donald Trump is a peacock among the dull buzzards of American politics."[361]

Why did traditional media participate? Because of the power of the public. "Media people pumped the helium that elevated Donald Trump's balloon, and they did so from naked self-interest. He represented high ratings and improved subscription numbers."[362] Trump made for an easy villain. Even in traditional media environments, controlled by a small group of people Gurri simply calls the "elites," public opinion reigned. In early 2020, he broke his own record for tweets and retweets in a single day with 142.[363] His strategy—constant, direct, unfiltered conversation with the public—worked. One study estimated he was tagged more than a thousand times a minute on Twitter.[364] In the spirit of "nothing fails like success," Twitter permanently banned its most successful user from the platform in January 2021 during the final days of his term.

Correlated with the rise in social media and the shift from vertical to horizontal authority, public trustworthiness of traditional broadcast media plummeted. Traditional broadcast channels shifted from curiosity to revulsion and attacked Trump. Many openly abandoned traditional journalistic values of restraint and objectivity, reveling in their advocacy, a fundamental departure from their longstanding ethos of "fairness" and "even-handedness." Rather than governing their coverage of Trump, traditional broadcast media ratcheted up the outrage, going so far as to—justifiably, in their minds—advocate deposing a man they perceived to be a tyrant.

Claiming that a journalist's core value should be "truth, not the pretense of objectivity," staff at the *New York Times* canceled not only a conservative op-ed but managed to get the editor who approved it fired.[365] Whether this shift in mainstream media from "objectivity" and "even-handedness" to "advocacy" and activism is irreversible or not is unclear. The paradox, of course, is by doing this, broadcast media only solidified its position as a tool of the elites, thus benefiting Trump's connection with a public sick and skeptical of the elites even more. With every attempt to control, elite institutions paradoxically accelerate nihilistic glee and the destruction of their institutions. Gurri calls this the "revolt of the public." Elites declare the result to be the "death of democracy and the dissent into authoritarian darkness." While "the connection between political turmoil and the new information landscape is now broadly understood . . . the issue is often framed in terms of social media opening the gates to destructive or undesirable opinions."[366] Of course, many in the public say the exact opposite is happening—we are now seeing true democracy emerge, finally and for the first time. It is difficult to determine: Are we witnessing the death of democracy or the full flowering of democracy, not in the form of a representative republic, à la the American structure, but a participatory democracy that is truly public, or of the people, in which every person may speak?

Media in a democratic society is market driven. It publishes what the market buys. The evil of this transaction is what Danish theologian Søren Kierkegaard calls the lie of social morality, that virtue may arise from the public. British broadcaster-turned-Jesus-follower Malcolm Muggeridge once observed that public opinion, as mediated through the press, doesn't lead to greater faith or greater virtue, because it is only concerned with the now. Muggeridge quoting Kierkegaard: "On the whole the evil in the daily press consists in its being calculated to make, if possible, the passing moment a thousand or ten thousand times more inflated and important than it really is. But all moral elevation consists first and foremost in being weaned from the momentary."[367]

The transactional nature of the contemporary mediated relationship between people and their informational channels assures that people only receive information they wish, ergo information that reinforces their existing worldview—or at the very best, elevates the ideal that a group of sinners can somehow discover a moral framework that exceeds the framework of a single sinner. Muggeridge quotes Kierkegaard, again:

> Day in and day out the daily press does nothing but delude the masses with the supreme axiom of this lie, that numbers are decisive. Christianity, on the other hand, is based on the thought that the truth lies in the single individual. If someone adopts the opinion of the public today and tomorrow is hissed and booed, he is hissed and booed by the public. A nation, an assembly, a human being can change in such a way that they seem to be no longer the same; but the public can become the very opposite and is still the same, the public. It is very doubtful, then, that the age will be saved through the notion of social organization, of association.[368]

At their core, protests are about authority.

Thus, all this activity begs the question, what—or who—is authoritative?

To answer, first, let us define authoritarianism. One definition may be the opposite of tolerance or civility, or the enforced obedience to specific beliefs at the expense of personal freedom. Elites declare Trump to be authoritarian. But as Gurri notes, true authoritarian regimes are founded on state-sponsored violence. According to this definition, America and the other Western democratic societies, incidents of police brutality notwithstanding, are if anything moving in the opposite direction. When we can count "bad cops" in the hundreds and protestors in the millions, it is clear we are not suffering as a people under the oppression of a tyrant. Ask an elderly Italian what it is like to live under a true tyrant in Mussolini. Trump is not an authoritarian as much as he is a tool of a right-leaning public, which is at war against a left-leaning public. Trump was the "style of the moment: a man from nowhere, with no stake in the system, ignorant of history, and curious about our political habits and traditions, but happy to bash and to break old and precious things in exchange for a little attention."[369]

The categories today are less defined on a simple horizontal axis from left to right and more on a scattered plot graph including a vertical axis from authoritarian to libertarian. Most activity seems to be happening on the edges of the graph. At every plot point, nihilists seek to destroy the center.[370] The Left and the Right are more aligned than each realizes. Trump wants to drain the swamp and spent years defunding programs and putting populists in charge. Antifa on the left and the Boogaloo Bois on the right, both of whom boast chaplains, want to tear down the patriarchy and start a revolution.

Together, this disparate group of warring factions forms the public with a single common enemy: the elite class. In response, elite behavior in America "is the opposite of authoritarian. It is a drift to dysfunction: to paralysis."[371] Witness governmental authorities being publicly humiliated or prostrating themselves in public to win favor with the public.[372] Elites don't know what to do, but neither do the protestors, who turn to Oprah to figure out what to do next. A current business axiom states that leaders get the organizations they deserve. Trump was not an anomaly but a mirror of a people who have rejected authority, and in so doing, leave themselves open to schoolyard socialization.

The political mood we are witnessing may be understood as a transition in the American experiment away from its history as a representative republic not to an authoritarian regime but to a "pure" democracy of majoritarianism. The question is now, Is a pure democracy even possible? Writing two years before the death of George Floyd, Gurri worried about the rise of what he described as the myriad of sectarian groups, who at the time of his writing had committed very little in the way of violence. Yet he observed, "Democracy seems to be negating itself."[373] Since the time of Gurri's observation, of course, we have seen these groups pick up clubs, and recoiled at the stark footage of burned-out city centers across the United States.

As we outlined in chapter 6, messianism is the desire for a strongman to come save us. But as nihilism wins and the old structures are torn down, then what happens? Today we witness a barbaric savagery, a prehistoric predatory violence, that is frightening. Urban predators stab people randomly, shoot people casually, kick and knee the disabled on the head with new reinvented forms of random violence called "knockout punching." Along with this, we see "wilding," "flash mobbing," carjacking, drive-by shootings, gangs, and societal collapse. Psychiatrist Robert Lindner (1914–1956) predicted in his classic text a future when "it is the psychopath who rises in great numbers within any society when that society is in the stage of collapse and dissolution."[374]

Whether giving voice to the public results in a free state or a mob depends on one's perspective, perhaps. But there is a reason true democracy is more historical myth than model. That reason is authority. Everyone has one. Current culture attempts several authorities, each of which is found lacking, and no single authority is respected. George Floyd was sent by his pastor in Houston to Minneapolis to minister to youth in the inner city. His murder at the hands of a police officer prompted peaceful protests in sixty countries on all seven continents. Those protests quickly turned to riots, and in cities like Atlanta, Dallas, and DC, stores were ransacked. Downtown Seattle was gutted.

7.2 | The Question of Authority Is Inescapable

"**T**ake thou authority . . ." These words are spoken by a bishop at the ordination of every elder into Methodist pastoral ministry. What does it mean to have authority? What does it mean to give authority? What does it mean to take authority?

Authority is power: power over something, power in something, power to do something. We live in a world where people are overpowered by fear, high-powered by false Powerball dreams, or disempowered by institutions and economics. We are desperate to be empowered by the Spirit.

Authority is the power to create or author. Whomever you let author your life, your story, your life story, is your authority.

In John's story of Jesus, Pilate claimed he had authority over Jesus to crucify or release him. This was the one falsehood from Pilate to which Jesus responded. Of the 183 questions posed to Jesus in the Gospels, he answered only three directly: one concerning his authority, another about being a king, and the third about how to pray.[375] While he did not feel compelled to solve problems and answer riddles, there were a few things about which he was very clear, and at the top of the list was authority and kingship.

In answer to Pilate's question, Jesus was not defending himself but rather his Father. Jesus said to Pilate, "You have no power over me except that which has been given to you" (see John 19:11). In other words, "Pilate, you think you are powerful, but you're just a tool." Jesus schooled the ruling power of the day in the lie of his life: Pilate thought he was in charge of his own life. This is the same lie we hear today.

We cannot solve the question of the end of the story until we understand the story itself. The question of authority is a question of authorship—who authors our lives. The born-again Bob Dylan famously sang, "You're gonna have to serve somebody," to which the humanist John Lennon replied, "You gotta serve yourself."[376] The six false narratives of the future we sketched in part 1 are a by-product of allegiance to a variety of authorities. Let us review our false endings through the lens of authority:

Authority in the past or future. Earlier we wrote about the role of authority in the question of history. The Quarrel of the Ancients versus the Moderns debated whether authority is rooted in the past or the future. The question of time is a useful philosophical entry into the question of authority, but it doesn't offer answers.

Authority in empirical thought. One of our mentors, an influential theologian named Kenneth Cauthen, researched the intersection of science and theology and published twenty books on these subjects. He believed that scientific method was authoritative for all life and thought, including faith. The elder Len loved the way Cauthen's mind worked, took every course he could from him, and shamelessly pursued him into his office for further conversations whenever he could.

Len asked this brilliant mind one day what he would do as a theologian if reason pushed him all the way back to the Big Bang, and the only thing that existed were two hydrogen atoms. What would he do then? Would he push back further and ask what had brought them together? Would he probe who made these hydrogen atoms? Cauthen's answer was cursory and certain. No, no—as a theologian who trusts the scientific method as the surest guide to truth, you have to stick with science."

"Even if it comes to the fact that the God of the universe is two hydrogen atoms? What then?"

Cauthen replied, "Then I will kneel and worship those atoms as my god and give them my devotion." At that point, one life changed forever. As Len walked away from the office, he said to himself, "I'm not giving my entire life, turning over my whole being, to two hydrogen atoms. I'm not singing praises and dedicating my life to two hydrogen atoms." Len will ever be grateful to the John Price Crozer Griffith Professor of Theology for proving to him that everybody worships somebody. Everybody submits to an authority. If the scientific method is allowed to author your story, then it is your authority and is authorized to take you where it will.

The scientific method has largely authored the story of the modern church, to the church's detriment. The Enlightenment provided a shared philosophical basis for authority, which provided the basis for the founding of the United States and dominated Western thought for centuries. Recent revisionism on the Enlightenment has moved scholars from seeing it not simply as a great philosophical movement, but a style of reasoning, a set of shifting public habits and habitudes. During this so-called Age of Reason, between 1700 and 1808, two-thirds of the enslavement of 12.5 million Africans took place, the most horrifying act of history, along with the Jewish holocaust.[377] As we have noted, we are increasingly dismissing the Enlightenment, and the decline of the authority of scientific voices in our culture is a prime reason for the rise of fighting in our streets and in the halls of Congress.

Authority in the mob. It used to be the upper classes feared the mobs. The mobs are back. This time it's not economic differentiation that is birthing them, but ideological differentiation. In place of scientific thinking, which is dictated to the public by a small group of highly educated "elites," we have witnessed the true rise of a democratic society, in which everyone has an equal voice—the educated and uneducated alike. As Clay Shirky wrote, "Here comes everybody."[378] Yet the "voice of the people" is not always, or even usually, the voice of God. Descartes's famous premise that "good sense is of all things the most equally distributed" has been rebuffed and refuted by Nietzsche, Marx, Freud, and a host of others.[379] In Jesus' day there was a familiar rabbinic "Quiet, please" hand motion after which the crowd grew silent. That rabbinic gift for crowd control has gone, and even the sign they used is no longer known.

> *One beginning and one ending for a book*
> *was a thing I did not agree with.*

—narrator of the novel At Swim-Two-Birds (1939) by Flann O'Brien

Authority in tradition. The traffic between the past and the future, between tradition and innovation, has been a staple and stable one until recently. Now the church sends students out of seminary to travel the world with a light suitcase in tradition. Now the past is a paste that we scatter and spread, distort, and reimagine, to suit current agendas. Scientist/philosopher/photographer John W. Draper (1811–1992), who took the first detailed photograph of the moon in 1840, was convinced that Christianity's epistemological basis in tradition was so strong that it would always be an obstacle rather than an aid to progress, which he defined as the advance of science and technology.[380] There is a difference between rooted and stuck. Today we are stuck in blame-laden finger-pointings of what's wrong rather than being rooted in the common ends and commonsense strategies that can lead us forward.

Authority in the community. One of the most controversial ideas about authority comes from a Catholic priest and theologian named David Tracy. In *The Analogical Imagination* (1981), Tracy says the best metaphor for authority as it relates to the Christian Scriptures is a "classic."[381] To Tracy, when something gains the status of a classic, it is given authority. But it only gains the status of a classic when it has been deemed of high value by the community. To Tracy, it is the community that authorizes and credentials a document or a text to be a classic, so that it has a force on the community. In other words, the Scriptures are authoritative because they are classics, and they got to this point because of history and tradition. Tracy's understanding of the Scriptures is that they are only authoritative because they have been given authority by the community.

In many ways, you cannot have a higher view of community. In Tracy's view, regardless of the intrinsic value of any text or document, or whether it is inspired or not, what de facto authorizes the text is the community itself. What makes the Scriptures authoritative? According to Tracy, they aren't authoritative in and of themselves, but only by virtue of the authority the community gives them.

These six false authorities play out again and again, and the cycle of history repeats itself. For the Christian this news may be equally as depressing as for the non-Christian, but with a twist. While the humanist has no recourse in a post-humanist world, the Christian knows another story. In the Christian story, authority is not found in principles but in a person—the risen and rising Jesus, under whom all authority on heaven and earth has been given. If one takes a biblical perspective, the view is clear. The problem isn't in our systems, or our politics, but in us. Recent political events in America have proven once again that on our own, we cannot escape our human predilection toward naked self-interest. We cannot save ourselves; we can only be saved from ourselves by the cross.

Our salvation does not lie in politics. Our problems are not solved in political solutions. Our highest political commitment as followers of Christ is to the church of Jesus Christ, which makes party politics as we know it an idolatrous distraction. The church is to hold all governmental feet to the fire, no matter what that government or party is. The church is not called to play footsies with politicians or be foot warmers for any state or party. It is important to be a good citizen of whatever state we are in: to vote, to pay taxes, to serve in office. All the while we pledge allegiance to our true citizenship, which is in the kingdom of God.

7.3 | In the Kingdom, All Authority Has Been Given to Jesus

> Then the eleven disciples went to Galilee, to the mountain where Jesus had told them to go. When they saw him, they worshiped him; but some doubted. Then Jesus came to them and said, "All authority in heaven and on earth has been given to me. Therefore, go and make disciples of all nations, baptizing them in the name of the Father and of the Son and of the Holy Spirit, and teaching them to obey everything I have commanded you. And surely, I am with you always, to the very end of the age." (Matthew 28:16–20 NIV)

Above all semiotics, hermeneutics, or Wesleyan "quadrilaterals" is this fundamental reality: Jesus is Lord. Jesus is a singular noun but a plural experience—

> of verbs (the bearers of actions and feelings)

> of adjectives (that modify and describe the noun to flesh out Jesus so we can experience him better)

> of propositions (the bearers of relationships, the witness of witness)

Matthew's gospel was written to a group of people who had come to place authority in the law. At best, they had elevated the story—its plotlines and bylines—not the Author of the story. The law is just the guardrail to keep us from flying off into the ditch. There is no power in a guardrail. The power to move, the engine of life, this is *exousia* (authority). Exousia is found in Jesus our Christ.

The biblical story may be understood through the lens of authority. Satan exerts *exousia* in Luke 4 when he tempts Jesus. Ephesians 2 describes the ruler of the kingdom of the air. The word is sometimes described as "dominion." But the battle is already won, for in Ephesians 1:18–23, Paul affirms that Jesus has already been given all authority. Colossians 1–2 says the same. In Revelation 11–13, authority is given to the beast before ultimately being taken back by God.

Consider the plot of Matthew's story of Jesus. In his narrative, Matthew gradually introduces a radical new idea: authority is found not in commandments, but in a commanding person, one who lived, was killed, buried, rose again, and will return again. Matthew gradually introduces this radical idea to his Jewish listeners and readers:

First, Matthew 7 offers a first glimpse of Jesus teaching "as one who had authority" (v. 29 NIV). Matthew doesn't make the full claim just yet but introduces the idea and foreshadows the story to come.

A second glimpse appears in Matthew 9, where we learn of the story of a Gentile who acknowledged Jesus and submitted to his authority. The first person to recognize Jesus' authority wasn't an Israelite, but a Gentile. Why a Gentile? Because the Pharisees had confused the law with the author of the law.

The idea of authority continues to build throughout the gospel. In Matthew 21, Jesus' authority becomes obvious and uncomfortable to the Pharisees. Eventually, Jesus responds directly to their question of his authority.

Finally, at the end of Matthew 28, comes the coup de grace. All authority on heaven and earth, Matthew confesses, has been given to Jesus. The implications of giving all authority to Jesus are radical. They shake the foundations on which we have built much of the modern church. An Episcopalian Facebook follower recently argued for the theology of the humanist John Spong, saying he was trying to help the church "evolve" from "modernist" to "postmodernist" thinking. Spong's naturalist thinking is the natural consequence of the conclusions forced upon the church by a linear philosophy of history that reduces time to a single dimension. When you see history as past, present, or future, not as a Maranatha moment of three tenses of time at once (was, is, is to come), you become forced to choose one over the other, and you lock yourself into conclusions that become unacceptable.

With his resurrection, all authority on heaven and earth is given to Jesus. Jesus is king and has all authority on heaven and earth to save us. No one is worthy to rule the world except Jesus. The kingdom is ruled by Jesus.

Christians keep looking for a ruler, but we already have one, whom we ignore. Only one Person has authority, the power, and strength to hold all things together (Colossians 1:17). Jesus' politics did not end in election to high office, but elevation on a high cross. The campaign to victory was not the rule of the majority and the lifting up of a platform. The campaign to victory was the love that suffered and died for the lifting up of those on the margins and making them centers. On March 16, 2022, the pope held a Zoom conference with Russian Orthodox Patriarch Kirill. After Kirill read him a document detailing all the reasons supporting Putin's invasion of Ukraine, Pope Francis said simply, "Brother, we are not state clerics. [W]e shouldn't speak the language of politics, but rather the language of Jesus."[382]

Politics has become a religion. In fact, politics is the golden-calf religion of our day, and it is destroying the neighborhood. Politics has replaced religion as a religion. "Do not be swept up by the crowd into waywardness and wickedness," Scripture says. The Psalmist prayed to be hidden from the noisy crowds and nasty politics that shoot at the innocent: "Hide me from the . . . mob . . . who sharpen their tongues like swords and aim their bitter words like arrows, shooting from ambush at the blameless, shooting at him suddenly and without fear." (Psalm 64:2–4, ESV).

This refusal to let politics become a religion is really what got Socrates killed. Socrates was celebrated as the wisest person in Athens. But he refused to engage in politics, which had reached a religious fervor in his lifetime. He was accused of not speaking up, and thereby endorsing all sorts of nefarious things, such as totalitarianism, anti-democratic sensibilities, and authoritarianism. When he was brought to trial, Socrates professed a deep love for Athens and an abiding concern for its welfare. Yet he refused to enter the fray on its own terms. He stood back, asking people to look at what was going on from different angles and urging them to find more lasting solutions to their problems. Paul Cartledge, a British expert on ancient democracy, says that "Socrates was not a quietist." But he disagreed with some of his fellow-citizens who "saw politics like religion, as something to be done in public if it was done at all."

The call to social justice is not a call to start another social program or to make the kingdom into a social program. It is the call to live teleologically, to live life in a human dimension that is truly divine, one that expects that we all see through a glass dimly, that we now only "know in part" (1 Corinthians 13:12) and that we all are wrong about some things and stand equally at the foot of the cross, which judges us all.

According to Isaiah, the nations are like a drop in a bucket to Him, and He counts the Isles as a very small thing (Isaiah 40:15). God doesn't limit God's self to working through nation-states, which in their present form (along with denominations) are creations of the modern era and the 1640s. In our grand story God works through individuals, families, tribes, fiefdoms, cities, cultures, kingdoms, and nations. We belong to a "kingdom" different from the "stated" one we're in: a "stateless" kingdom. To have a bit of fun with Paul's way of putting it, although in a different context, "in whatsoever state I am, therewith to be content" (Philippians 4:11 KJV).

Luke calls Jesus "the Author of Life" (Acts 3:15). Hebrews' author calls Jesus "the author and finisher of our faith" (Hebrews 12:2 KJV). We can indeed have a better future. It does not come through our own efforts, through a strong man, or through any of the six false endings we have mentioned so far. It only comes when we authorize Jesus to author our life story. Authorization is key. In Revelation 22:14, only those to whom Jesus has given authority have the right to come to the tree of life.

No authorization, no entrance to life.

CHAPTER 8

END TIME: TELOS

....

The end is the completion of the story.

....

In chapter 5, on ahistoricism, we asked, "Is there a purpose to history?" The answer has been in the Scriptures all along. The Greek word for "The End" is telos, *a word largely lost to the modern imagination. Telos is a word with multiple meanings, and we can only understand the core questions of this book by recovering it. Telos is the heart of this book, and we spend the bulk of the rest of our time exploring it.*

To begin, telos *means the end of history, which is chronological plus much more. It is distinct from* teleute, *which is simply the chronological end, such as the end of life. Telos also means the completion of history, the purpose of history, and a command to a right ordering of our lives. Above each of these implications is the ultimate* telos: *God's presence.*

8.1 | The End Means Telos

We live in a culture that discusses means but not ends. We love proximate arguments and not ultimate ones, such as "What is the best way of life?"[383] Means sell, which is why we love them so much and why we absolutize means. Faith commitment is not the same as political commitments, which take sides and take over. Faith commitment is all about relationships and ends. Political commitments are all about principles, propositions, doctrines, ideologies, and means, which is a sign of our elevation of efficiency and production to end and purpose. This is why arguably the most important modern philosopher Immanuel Kant condemned espionage as an "infernal art." We are not morally permitted to treat fellow humans beings as mere means to our ends. One of our goals in this writing is to reorient our perspective from means to ends.

The entire New Testament is about ends. The word "end" is a powerful password. The Greeks describe the end in many ways—some as just the cessation of a sequence of events, some as the completion of a larger and more purposeful historical narrative. In the New Testament, the English phrase "the end" is a translation of a Greek word we have largely lost: *telos*. *Telos* means not just termination but the completion, fulfillment, and raison d'etre for which something exists. The core purpose of this book is to reclaim this word *telos* in all its forms.

Consider the variations of the word "end" in the New Testament:

Telos

Christ is the *telos* of history: the purpose, fulfillment, and object of all time. There is no higher understanding of Christ than the "image of the invisible God" (Colossians 1:15). *Telos* is simultaneously about the end of time and the fulfillment and completion of time. Marry ends, date means.

Runners don't get runner's high on a treadmill. They know the difference between the joy of an outdoor route, with a purposeful beginning, middle, and end to a journey, and the wretchedness of an indoor treadmill, which goes on endlessly, a road to nowhere. *Treadmill*, by the way, is a terrible word. It literally means to grind steps. It reduces walking, the movement of life, to a machine's work, exercised solely as a means, not an end. Treadmill companies even add videos of outdoor paths to help their users experience a sense of purpose to their steps.

Telos is the difference between the treadmill, a linear philosophy of history that just ends when you press the stop button, and the outdoor route, the end of which completes, unifies, and explains all that has come before. *Telos* signifies that history doesn't just happen, but that we live according to a larger purpose. *Telos* is both the goal of our story and the activating agent of our story.

And what is our *telos*? Romans 10:4 says, "The end of the law is Christ" (our translation). The early church and Reformers understood *telos* as completion of purpose in a "prophetic as well as a purposive signification."[384] Christ is both the means and the end of our religion, though in the modern church we focus on means and miss the end. The importance of *telos* to the story of God cannot be overstated. In all its forms, the word appears almost two hundred times in the New Testament.

Teleute

To further understand the distinct meaning and importance of the concept of the end as fulfillment or completion, the Scriptures offer a separate word that simply refers to the treadmill vision of life. This word is used in Matthew 2:15 ("the death of Herod") to signify the end of a life outside of the new creation. This variation of the term refers to an ending without purpose. The word is translated into English as simply "death." *Teleutao*, the verb form of *teleute*, denotes to come to an end, to die an earthly or "first" death, apart from being born a second time or being given a "second life." *Teleutao* is the end for the ahistoricist or the person who does not believe life contains any greater purpose or meaning.

Other forms of Telos

More versions of the word appear throughout the New Testament with the same denotation. *Teleiótés* is a noun that describes one who finishes or completes. This term appears in Hebrews to describe Jesus, the author and finisher of our faith. *Telesphoreó* means "to bring to completion" and appears only once, in Luke, to describe mature seeds in the parable of the sower, implying the parts of us that, matured in faith, carry over from this life to the next. *Teleios* means to be mature and perfect, which is an affirmative way to understand the seemingly demoralizing command from Jesus in his Sermon on the Mount to become "perfect."

Entole

Last, *entole* is a command that intensifies *telos*. In Matthew, the repeated word the writer uses to his Jewish audience is to explain the commandment as a way to intensify *telos*—the completion and presence of God.

While *telos* has been the end vision and calling of the church through most of Christian history, in the nineteenth century the primary theological interpretation changed and became eschatological—terminal and temporal, a linear end of history.[385] We began to elevate means above ends. This is incorrect and misleading. History has meaning. The passage of time is teleological in nature, not simply chronological. Christ does not just supersede or repeal the law; he completes it. Romans 10 reveals Paul's teleological view of scripture. While *teleute* simply refers to the chronological end, *telos* simultaneously refers to both the end and the completion of its mission. There is an end that is simply a conclusion to a sequence of events on a linear time line, and then there is an end that is the completion and fulfillment of something greater, a purpose to history.

The six false endings of part 1 agitate and depress because they seem to suggest there is no end to the struggle. What they all share, though, is the absolutism of means, with little thought to the end. To get past the seemingly never-ending struggle of these false endings, we need to reestablish the end. We must recover the *telos* of time.

8.2 | The End Is the Purpose of History

Our obsession with the eschaton, and its concomitant focus on means, empties much of the meaning of *telos*. Time doesn't simply end. Time has a purpose, which is God's kingdom. *Telos* is the end. But it is more than the simple conclusion or termination of an activity. It refers both to the fulfillment or completion of a thing and the completion of whatever the thing is aimed at and designed to do. *Telos* is not just the terminal stop on the random subway line of time. It is the perfection and completion of something according to its own course and destiny. In Christ, we shift from chronos time to kairos time, from tempus to temple. *Telos* is the end of the story. It is a conclusion of completion.

While shifting our understanding of *telos* from the end of time or the end of space to the end of the story is a start, we cannot end there. *Telos* also means the fulfillment or completion of something. This purpose is the restoration of humankind to the presence of God, the return of the divine that makes the human. It is the completion of the present age and the beginning of the age to come. Indeed, the end of Matthew's gospel captures Jesus' last words before his ascension: "Surely I am with you always, to the very end of the age" (28:20 NIV). The end of the age that Jesus describes is *synteleias*, not a physical space but a shared purpose. The root Greek word of *synteleias* is *telos*. To understand The End, we must understand *telos*.

There is a potential problem with the story view, however. Stories can still be understood as linear. In the Christian tradition, God's *telos* is three-fold: creation, reconciliation, and eschatological fulfillment. You might argue for all three, of course. But to see these as linear or sequential and existing in a singularly ordered and consecutive time line creates problems. The logical next step is to favor one over another, which becomes theologically problematic. If the purpose is creation, did God create humankind with tools for future reconciliation? If the purpose is reconciliation, is eschatological consummation just a bonus? If the purpose is eschatological transformation, this places God's purpose in the future and negates both the past, creation, and the present, reconciliation.[386]

Thinking in terms of linear time, as a story with a single beginning, middle, and end, leads to the sort of false endings we described in part 1. While we are indeed living a story, the story is all-encompassing, and the end is full time—a full-court-press congruence of past, present, and future into a single existence. God does not just have one purpose, understood as the consummation of an ongoing narrative, but a fullness described by German scholar and translator Claus Westermann (1909–2000) as a "steady-state active relationship" that includes creation, reconciliation, and fulfillment.[387] To be in the kingdom is not to be in the future, or in the past, or in the present. It is to be in all three at the same time. In other words, it is to be in the presence of a God who exists beyond time.

One of the favorite kingdom descriptions of the earliest church is the new creation. The word "new" here is critical. We tend to hear "new" as innovative, inventive, or "new and improved." But the new creation is not *neos* new, or a replacement of what is old, but *kainos* new, a qualitatively different reality. *Kainos* literally means "out of time." The new creation isn't a new version of the old, broken first creation, or a vacuous utopia. It is the fullness of time, which exists simultaneously in the past, present, and future.

Perhaps you are wondering, how can three distinct temporal states be one? We should be used to such mind-bending realities. In the mystery of the Trinity, we see a single God in three persons. In God the Creator, Jesus the Redeemer, and the Holy Spirit the Purifier, we see all three purposes playing out simultaneously—creation, redemption, and sanctification, not modally, or with one role assigned to each Person of the Godhead, but with all purposes in all Persons. All of these may be combined under a single banner of transcendence, or what we call the "three transcendentals of being": the good, the true, and the beautiful. Theologian David Kelsey writes, "There is no difference in reality between God's existence and God's goodness. There is a conceptual but not an ontological distinction between the two. God simply is the Good itself. Creatures are good in their kinds only as their being reflects the good Being who creates and sustains them. So too in God 'to know' is identical with 'to be.'"[388]

As "godfather of soul" James Brown was fond of exclaiming, "Good God!" The terms are synonymous and redundant—to know God is to know good, and to know good is to know God. The same applies regarding truth and beauty. Desire is built into *telos*. The end is the satisfaction of completion. T. S. Eliot writes:

> Every phrase and every sentence is an end and a beginning.
>
> Every poem is an epitaph. And any action
>
> Is a step to the block, to the fire, down the sea's throat
>
> Or to an illegible stone: and that is where we start . . .
>
> But to apprehend
>
> The point of intersection of the timeless
>
> With time, is an occupation for the saint . . .[389]

The only true, beautiful, and good "rapture" of being alive is in Christ. As the Westminster Catechism reminds us, the Christian's *telos*, the ultimate end or purpose of life, is to glorify God and enjoy God forever. How do we do this? It may start with a sandwich or sushi, a cup of coffee or tea, and conversation with family, friends, and strangers. This is the teleology of the kingdom. In Christ, we shift from *chronos* to *kairos*, from tempus to temple. To realize this and to actualize this is a "time-out" experience. It stops us in our tracks. We are forced to take a time-out from our work and our worry. It also takes us out of the time in which we've been living, which is exactly what coronavirus has done.

This is Jesus' answer to the disciples' first question, recounted at the beginning of this book: "When is the end of the age?" The purpose of the Christian life is *telos*, not *eschaton*. When we are in the presence of God, we are in the end of the age.

8.3 | The End Is the Completion of History

If The End is *telos*, not *eschaton*, then what does that mean for our understanding of time and space? Jesus' use of *telos* is not an end of "time" as we tend to think of it, nor an end of space. Each of these ends had different words and uses.

As we showed, the end of time is not *telos* but *teleut*. These are distinct terms. This use of the root *tel* is common in Greek writings but appears only once in the New Testament, when Matthew describes the death of Herod during the Jesus birth story: "So he got up, took the child and his mother during the night and left for Egypt, where he stayed until the death [*teleutē*] of Herod" (2:14–15 NIV). The clear meaning of this is a word describing an end to time without any accompanying purpose—a life that just ends. In other words, a wasted life. In our previous look at a philosophy of history, this was the most common linear understanding of time in the ancient world. It just ended, with no larger purpose.

Nor is *telos* the end of space, which is *péras*. This word means "to the edge or boundary or limit of space," as in "to the end of the world." This meaning of end has a violent connotation as well in the ancient Greek, as in to "pierce" or "run through" as with a sword. Christian mission, conceived during the age of progress, has often been understood as something that happens "to the ends of the world." But Jesus never uses this word in the context of his teaching to his disciples. This word only appears once in the Gospels, when Jesus describes the queen of the South appearing from the ends of the earth to condemn the current generation (Matthew 12:42). The connotation of mission fulfillment, even if it takes violent means, has proven all too true in Christian history, from the Crusades to Manifest Destiny. Just as the "end of time" is insufficient to satisfy purpose, so is the end of space. Some eschatological theories emphasize the inauguration of the kingdom based on the 100 percent missional coverage of the earth, but it is possible to reach the ends of the earth and still not find God.

In the Old Testament, discussions of the "end" are often oblique and enshrouded in language. When God asks Amos, "What do you see?" Amos answers "A basket of summer fruit" (8:1). The Hebrew word for "ripe" or "summer fruit" sounds almost exactly like the Hebrew word for "end." This sets up God's pun to Amos: "Then end has come upon my people, Israel." Miss the pun, you miss the point. The most common use of *telos* in the New Testament is when Jesus describes the end of the age, or when Paul describes the purpose of Christian faith as a result or completion of righteousness (Romans 6:21–22). Later in his same letter, Paul describes Christ as the *telos* of the law, or the culmination of it: "Christ has brought the law to all *telos*." This use also appears repeatedly in Hebrews, James, and 1 Peter.

John's gospel reveals what is perhaps the best and most beautiful understanding of *telos* as the apostle opens the scene of the Last Supper on that Thursday night: "Before the Festival of Passover, Jesus knew that his time had come to leave this world and go to the Father. Having loved his own who were in the world, he loved them fully [*telos*]" (13:1 CEB).

In John's gospel, we get to the heart of the matter. *Telos* is a state of complete love, or fullness and fulfillment of the larger story of healing and restoration that occurs throughout the Bible. It's all there in the small space of the upper room on that night, in the relationship Jesus has with his disciples. His love for them was full and complete.

A video game called *The Sims* portrays a virtual society. With its predecessor, *SimCity*, you as user had God-like powers. You could build roads and towns and construct an entire megapolis. Several iterations and updates of the game offered increasingly powerful tools for city building and progressively impressive graphics. Yet the city building was ultimately unsatisfying. Eventually the makers of the game added destruction as a variable as well. Having built it up, and having gotten bored, you could send a meteor or an alien invasion and blow it all up, suggesting of course that the building itself is insufficient—and also offering a chance to do it all again in a never-ending cycle of destruction and construction.

Later, the makers of the game introduced a new version of the same Sim concept in which you could manage an individual household. In this game, *The Sims*, the goal was "happiness," as measured by a set of variables represented through a bar chart that always floated over an avatar's body. If you created the right environment, two people would come together and their relationship would make each person's bar rise to the top, which was a green color. If you failed in this effort—or if you deviously sought the avatars' harm—their bars would decrease to a low, red state. One of the authors (not saying which one) began to use the Sims bars image to joke about relationships with each other and with family and friends. Over time this turned into a shorthand signal: *Honey, my bar is low.* Or, *wow my bar is so full right now.*

This image of bars, low and high, hints at what Jesus refers to in his full relationship with his disciples. The last dinner together in the upper room became a time of fullness and completion. Jesus loved his followers completely, and they loved him back, as much as they were able to love him. In that moment they experienced firsthand everything Jesus had been saying about "the kingdom." In the upper room, the *telos* the disciples experienced wasn't only a completion of time or space, but a state of full love.

The first thing Jesus does, as he loves them "fully"? He washes their feet. He serves them. The *telos*, the end of the story, is a state of agape love in which we sacrificially and selflessly serve one another. This is what the Eastern fathers understood as *kenosis*, or a pure state of mutual love for one another in community. This is the purpose, the end, the completion, the *plerosis* and the *telos* of the entire biblical story.

To say something is "finite" is to say it has a beginning and an end. *Fin* means "end." The infinite God created a finite universe. The universe had a beginning ("In the beginning," Genesis 1:1) and it will have an end.

8.4 | The End Is a Command

*T*elos brings purpose. The Greek word for "command" is *enteli* (*telos*). As a reference to God's intention for our lives, it is an activating agent.

Much of our religious behavior is *enteli*, commandments, commands, or obligations to honor moments when God appeared in the story of human-kind. We keep them because they have proven in the past to have "worked" as a means for us to be drawn into God's presence. In this view, commands are instruments to achieve a good end, similar to house rules that keep the patriarchs and matriarchs happy: put the silverware out because that is how Mom wants it or edge the grass because that is how Dad wants it.

Some commands are understood as mores or obligations, a means to achieve harmony. In this view, rules do not exist for personal benefit but as relational obligations to avoid bad outcomes. This understanding of a commandment is negative, in that its primary purpose is to avoid conflict, and it is extrinsic. We obey such commands not out of desire but because of the expectations of others.

This is not the purpose of God's commands. God's *enteli* are not propositions based on the past but ingrained trajectories or what semiotic theologian Tim Valentino calls "implanted intentions" of God. The "commands" of God are God's desired ends and our desirable future. There is a whole school of philosophy around the word *entelechy/entelechies*: the realization of potential. Paul described this to the church at Corinth: "Circumcision is nothing, and uncircumcision is nothing; but obeying the commandments of God is everything" (1 Corinthians 7:19).

The Greek for "commandments" here is *entolé*, or injunctions or things we are called to do to intensify our desired end. "Commandments" are the fulfillment of the end for which we were created. *Telos* is the life-giving gyroscope that guides the development and functioning of an organism, other system, or organization. We are teleologically ordered to an end that we cannot attain without God. In other words, the more we obey God's commands, the more we realize the end or potential of the life God designed for us.

In our rebellion, we view God's law as restrictive and punitive, but to reject God's commands separates us from God and diminishes our potential. The psalmist understood the purpose of commands when he wrote:

> The law of the LORD is perfect,
> reviving the soul;
> the decrees of the LORD are sure,
> making wise the simple;
> the precepts of the LORD are right,
> rejoicing the heart;

the commandment of the LORD is clear,
enlightening the eyes;
the fear of the LORD is pure,
enduring forever;
the ordinances of the LORD are true
and righteous altogether.
More to be desired are they than gold,
even much fine gold;
sweeter also than honey,
and drippings of the honeycomb. (Psalms 19:7–10)

We obey God's commands not merely because God tells us to, but because God's commands are sweet like honey and revive the soul.

Of course, the problem with God's commands is that they are too hard; we cannot keep them on our own. Even if we know the path of righteousness, we neglect to take it. In this context we can see Jesus' intent when he declared in the Sermon on the Mount:

> Do not think that I have come to abolish the Law or the Prophets; I have come not to abolish but to fulfill. For truly I tell you, until heaven and earth pass away, not one letter, not one stroke of a letter, will pass from the law until all is accomplished. Therefore, whoever breaks one of the least of these commandments [*entolon*] and teaches others to do the same will be called least in the kingdom of heaven; but whoever does them and teaches them will be called great in the kingdom of heaven. For I tell you, unless your righteousness exceeds that of the scribes and Pharisees, you will never enter the kingdom of heaven. (Matthew 5:17–20)

When the law is seen as a set of extrinsic obligations to satisfy God the Patriarch and keep the house happy, Jesus' words are impossible to fulfill. They contradict the concept of a grace-filled God who loves us despite our inability to do the right thing. When the law is seen as how we experience the full life God designed for us, then Jesus' words make sense. God's laws are the set of guidelines by which the kingdom of heaven is realized.

The Sefer Torah is the Torah Scroll containing the Five Books of Moses, handwritten on animal-skin parchment. It is the holiest of all books of Tanach. A Sefer Torah is kept in the Ark in the Shul [Synagogue], and portions are read from it publicly on Shabbat, Yom Tov (holidays), fast days, Mondays, and Thursdays during prayers, and only in the presence of a minyan (quorum of ten Jewish males above the age of thirteen). According to ancient tradition, this verse constitutes the last of the precepts of the Torah: "Now write down this song and teach it to the Israelites and have them sing it, so that it may be a witness for me against them" (Deuteronomy 31:19 NIV). Here the Torah is called "this song" and has been interpreted as the command for Jews to write a Sefer Torah based on their own integration of the commands into their own lives. Maimonides did so, as did other medieval commentators.

Ultimately, *telos* is a song.

8.5 | The End Is God's Presence Now

As a young seminary student, the younger Len was once perplexed at the end of class by Matthew 5:47, a summary line in Jesus' Sermon on the Mount when Jesus told his listeners to be perfect, as God is perfect. After class, he walked to the front of the room and asked the professor what it meant. The professor gave a semiotic answer that both helped and hurt. He said that the word Jesus used was the same word that appears in other texts (presumably Colossians 4) to describe someone as having the rights and privileges of full Roman citizenship. His interpretation pointed to someone who is mature in his or her faith, a full believer.

While the comparison isn't totally invalid—we are not slaves but indeed heirs, sons and daughters of God—it also missed the mark, because the image leads to the social and political implications of following Jesus. It focuses on behavior.

Jesus' exhortation to be perfect alludes to something higher than behavior. The ultimate goal of being human is not that we behave or believe rightly. The fulfillment and completion of our purpose as people is not to be the best employee for God, but to be one with God, to be in God's presence. To emphasize the social is to make the same mistake that utopians made with social gospel, which is to focus on our actions as the arbiter of God's grace. We cannot achieve perfection on our own. No human is mature enough in his or her faith to be perfect. To translate it according to what we do is to miss the point entirely. It is to reduce Jesus to means and miss the end.

Doing the right things is not the passcode to unlock God's grace, but the outcome of a life lived in *telos*—the completion and fulfillment of our purpose as humans, to be in communion with God, as in the garden. When we are in the fullness of God's presence, we can do no wrong. We are perfect, not because we have achieved perfection but because God has made us so.

A thousand years before Jesus, Solomon ordered God's chest brought into the newly completed temple. The chest didn't even contain God, but the two tablets God had touched. Yet it wielded such power that when the priests, including Zadok the high priest, had deposited the chest in the inner sanctuary and left, a cloud filled the temple such that "the priests were unable to carry out their duties due to the cloud because the LORD's glory filled the LORD's temple" (1 Kings 8:11 CEB).

The appearance of the glory of the Lord was an unusual and significant moment. The priests would have known this. So why were the priests trying to carry out duties at this point? The purpose of our customs and rituals is to remember and honor God, which is in turn motivated by a desire to see and know God, who is the source of all goodness, truth, and beauty. The priests in the temple had become so caught up in the ongoing rituals and acts of remembrance that they had forgotten the reason for their tradition. When God showed up, their first instinct was not to drop everything and worship God, to savor God's presence, but to continue to care for their signs and carry out their duties. For the sake of religious tradition, the priests missed the purpose of religion entirely.

As we said earlier, God's kingdom is not remembrance. God is not found in our rituals and customs, although these may help us be more aware of God's presence. The purpose of our religion isn't to honor the memory of God, but to be in God's presence. The highest thing we can do is to seek God's presence. All good things—all justice, all mercy, all love—can only be made real and made complete through God's holy and powerful hand on the earth. The most important thing we can do is to come out of hiding and seek (look for) God, and when the glory of God's presence appears, then drop everything and worship and pray for the presence of the Holy Spirit to be known, to fill every space and blow through every human heart. Only then will this world be made right.

The gospels record an exchange that happened between Jesus and the Pharisees shortly after Jesus had fed thousands of people on the hillside—by far his most public and semiotic miracle to date. The Pharisees, the keepers of the tradition, questioned Jesus about his disciples because his disciples had broken tradition by not ceremonially washing their hands before they ate. Jesus replied:

> Why do you break the commandment [*entolen*] of God for the sake of your tradition? For God said, "Honor your father and your mother," and, "Whoever speaks evil of father or mother must surely die." But you say that whoever tells father or mother, "Whatever support you might have had from me is given to God," then that person need not honor the father. So, for the sake of your tradition, you make void the word of God. You hypocrites! Isaiah prophesied rightly about you when he said: "This people honors me with their lips, but their hearts are far from me; in vain do they worship me, teaching human precepts as doctrines." (Matthew 15:3–9)

When the Pharisees complained to Jesus that his disciples ignored tradition, Jesus corrected their thinking. He asked them, "Why do you cut yourself off from the *telos* of God? Why are you choosing your tradition over God's presence?" He wanted to help them see that tradition is not the purpose of religion. As we discussed earlier, the temptation of tradition is always that it devolves into traditionalism. Traditionalism has attracted people for millennia perhaps for psychological reasons. Because Christianity lays claim to events of history and to a God of historical revelation, the temptation is to elevate only events that happened in the past as true. The past feels more certain than the present. Fear of the uncertain leads to a preference for memory of the past, which over time devolves into nostalgia, or the illusion that the "glory days" of the past were somehow better than the troubles of the present. Memory becomes mythology. Witness the Russian nostalgia for empire, which led to Putin's 2022 territorial and geopolitical conflict with Ukraine.

In the church, the nostalgic desire to recover a better, purer expression of faith has led to several movements. Primitivism, a philosophical movement of the seventeenth century, sought to counter the emerging modernism by reestablishing authority in the past. Primitivism and its offshoots had many adherents in the church, including John Wesley, the founder of Methodism, and hung around for centuries as a counter to encroaching modernism. While Walter Rauschenbusch's social gospel sought to build the kingdom of God through human ingenuity and initiative, others were pointing to the "primitive eschatology" of the early church to understand the signs of the times and the coming future.[390] These arguments were, and are, social and psychological as much as they are theological. Another form of Christian primitivism is the Restoration movement of the nineteenth century. Parallels exist today in the church and in social communities.

Some continue to prefer to look for the story's end in the past. Having rejected the classic options for the end of the story, which Shakespeare defines as either comedy (a good ending) or tragedy (a bad ending), some want to return to the beginning. Indeed, the hero's journey is to return to home. Apocatastasis is a branch of Christian universalism that suggests that in the end, the world and everything in it will be restored to its original state. But the reason traditionalism is a false ending is that it is based on the premise that we can go backwards to the beginning, like the mythical bird found in Akan art (Ghana) called the Sankofa, which looks backward as it flies forward. It is true that you can't drive forward without a rearview mirror, but that mirror is less flat glass than a metal crucible of hot change that leads to a transformed and transfigured end.

Traditionalism happens all too often in both religious communities and in the larger political atmospheres that surround them. Tradition became the pretense under which Jesus was arrested. According to John's gospel, Caiaphas would have agreed with the theological idea that Jesus' purpose was to be a sacrifice for the sins of the world, to save the Jewish people. But Caiaphas, like many faithful Jews of that moment, saw Jesus' sacrifice as serving a different purpose: a catalyst for the physical restoration of the nation of Israel. Caiaphas interpreted Jesus' teaching on the kingdom of

God as a description of a glorious past in which King David presided over a sovereign nation of God's people. Caiaphas wanted to restore the Israelite nation and saw Jesus as the long-awaited means to activate this politics. "He did not say this on his own," John tells us, "but as high priest that year he prophesied that Jesus would die for the Jewish nation, and not only for that nation but also for the scattered children of God, to bring them together and make them one" (John 11:51–52 NIV).

Caiaphas thought killing Jesus was a form of righteousness. Of course, Caiaphas was tragically mistaken. Not only is traditionalism a false ending, but as the story of Caiaphas illustrates, a desire to look backward blinds us to the present and how God desires to create "a new thing" (see Isaiah 43:19, Hebrews 8:13).

In every story, we do come home, but we arrive by forging the crucible of change, not by retreating to whence we came. The story of the Israelites is a tale of what happens when we elevate tradition to traditionalism. The past offers no paean, and traditionalism ends in tragedy.

In the best sense of the word, tradition is an activity, not an entity. To "tradition" is to do more than curate. To tradition is to make anew the old, to redeem and renew tradition. Pope Benedict XVI, as we noted earlier, liked to distinguish between handing on the tradition as a "hermeneutic of reform" and handing it on as a "hermeneutic of rupture" and discontinuity. When we focus on the past exclusively or even primarily, we hold on to a desire to defend what has been handed down from the cloud of witnesses. This inevitably ends in the sicknesses of tribalism and nationalism, two tape-worms of tradition. When we look to the past to solve our problems, we end up making history into a god instead of worshiping the God of history. Because God is a God of history, and history continues, God necessarily is a God of today and tomorrow as well as yesterday.

| C H A P T E R   9 |
FULL TIME KINGDOM

....

The end is the kingdom of God.

....

In chapter 4, we looked at millennialism, and echoed the common lament, Can Jesus just come again and fix this mess?

The answer to this question lies in a proper understanding of God's kingdom. The kingdom of God is not symbolic, but real, the new creation, and the completion and purpose of history. In the "age to come," the heavenly realm envelops the earthly realm. For the follower of Jesus, this is not a future destination or even an incomplete construction project but a present, all-time reality that for the follower of Jesus is in the present time, wherever Jesus is. The kingdom is Jesus.

9.1 | The Kingdom of God Is Where Jesus Is

Once, on being asked by the Pharisees when the kingdom of God would come, Jesus replied, "The coming of the kingdom of God is not something that can be observed, nor will people say, 'Here it is,' or 'There it is,' because the kingdom of God is in your midst."

—Luke 17:20–21 (NIV)

The End is the kingdom, according to Jesus (Matthew 24:14). This is the age to come, a mirror image of the world's view of the future. Any question of The End is a question about God's kingdom. What do we mean by "kingdom"?

Discovering Jesus' meaning to this word "kingdom" is an archaeological dig worthy of burying this book alive. The church's conception of the word "kingdom" is positively medieval, obsessed with office, policy, economics, and war. While any image of The End brings limitations, none bring more than the overused word "kingdom." There is so much baggage, so much cargo, that the temptation is to shut down further thought, abandon the grueling question, and slide back into cliché and convention.

The first task is to define what The End is not: a nation-state. God doesn't limit God's self to working through nation-states. In our story God works through individuals (even "We Three Kings," who were pagan Persians kings, like Cyrus, Darius, and Artaxerxes[391]), families, tribes, fiefdoms, cities, cultures, kingdoms, and nations. But we don't belong to the kingdoms of the world; we belong to a different kingdom, a "stateless" kingdom.

If you're still hung up on land, then check out the opening to Acts. The disciples, who were hung up on land too, asked Jesus again, "Lord, *now* are you going to restore Israel?" (Acts 1:6, paraphrased). Jesus then redirected them like toddlers to two realities: one, they were about to receive the Holy Spirit, and two, their job was not to worry about the times and dates, but to focus on being witnesses of Jesus. Ag-millennial.

One day, as Jesus was teaching, the Pharisees questioned him about the "when" of the kingdom of God. When would it come? Jesus answered with two very interesting statements.

In his first response, Jesus countered with something the kingdom of God is *not*: it is not something that can be discovered with observation, no matter how careful or clinical. As both cognitive and communication studies have discovered, the set of assumptions and contexts a party brings to a conversation color what they perceive. What philosopher Henri Bergson allegedly intuited in 1896—that in truth, all sensation is already memory—

has recently been proven by cognitive scientists. As Dutch psychologist and brain expert Douwe Draaisma puts it, "For every neural connection transporting information from the eyes to the primary visual cortex in the back of our brain, there are ten connections in the reverse direction. What we see is, in large part, what earlier experience leads us to expect."[392]

When the Pharisees asked Jesus when the kingdom of God would come, they brought to their question a set of assumptions:

1. that the kingdom of God is geographical and political,

2. that it is set against other simultaneous kingdoms and rules, and

3. that Inauguration Day begins on a specific future date at a specific place.

In their context, the kingdom of God and Jewish sovereignty were one and the same. They were basing their question on the assumption that a new, material, and political Israel would someday reemerge and reestablish Jewish national authority. Since the days of Babylon, the Jewish people had been living under the authority of a foreign king. Some days were good, but most were not. Their tradition had been very patient, waiting for hundreds of years since the times when the prophets had predicted the coming of a new kingdom, which would overturn the present kingdom of Rome and reestablish Davidian rule. As keepers of Jewish national traditions, they were looking for clues for the glorious comeback. Making predictions about the future date when God would fix it all had become a parlor game in which people would encode and decode various *Da Vinci Code*-style schemes and puzzles to figure out the great puzzle of The End.

In one spine-chilling, heart-rending, mind-bending, soul-stirring, mic-dropping sentence, Jesus challenged this entire worldview. The kingdom of God, he said, is more than something you can see. Jesus' answer meant that everything the Pharisees had been thinking about, investigating, predicting, and teaching for generations was moot. It was null and void. If what Jesus said was true, it meant that the kingdom of God wasn't geographical or political at all. It could not be a new Israel. You are not going to find the kingdom of God by trying to investigate it like scientific phenomena. It is not something you can see. Because what Jesus was describing wasn't a kingdom in any traditional sense, it could not be geographical or political. It could not begin at some future date, and thus it could not exist next to other kingdoms in the conventional understanding of the word "kingdom."

We do not learn of the Pharisees' reactions to his single sentence bombshell, but we can only imagine how befuddled, dismayed, or angered they may have been. In one sentence, Jesus blew away an entire history of assumptions about the kingdom of God. For many of them, it was their life's work.

Perhaps this news was too much to process for the poor Pharisees. Their assumptions apparently did not change in the days, years, and centuries following this conversation. In some aspects of the Christian tradition, as we established in part 1, the understanding of the kingdom of God has kept the Pharisees' set of assumptions but expanded it from Jewish national sovereignty to cosmic rule, and from the rule of a small band of people in the Middle East to the rule of a much larger group of people over the whole universe. The base set of assumptions have remained. What the Pharisees brought to their conversation with Jesus colored their ability to hear what he was saying.

To be clear, in his conversation with the Pharisees, Jesus was not necessarily countering the cosmic question of The End or claiming that there is no physical ending to our current reality. Later in the same conversation, Jesus talked about the last day, saying, "It will be just like this on the day the Son of Man is revealed" (Luke 17:30 NIV). Elsewhere, Jesus clarified that there is indeed an actual ending to the world. He described it as a time in which "heaven and earth" will pass away (Matthew 24:35; Luke 21:33). The ancients understood earth as everything below the horizon—terra firma, the soil of the world around them, including dirt, rocks, trees, and water. The heavens were everything above the horizon—the sky, the stars and moon, and space. Jesus was saying that one day, this physical arrangement would cease to exist. He used his listeners' understanding of the story of Noah as reference, a story about the destruction of the world. "As it was in the days of Noah, so it will be at the coming of the Son of Man" (Matthew 24:37 NIV). So there is indeed an end of days. But no one knows this future date—not even King Jesus himself, but only the Father and Creator of all (v. 36).

Jesus was not necessarily countering the cosmic question of The End. He was responding to the Pharisees' specific interest in Jewish national sovereignty with a clarifying statement about the nature of the kingdom of God—that it is not something you can find or discover with careful observation. Coupled with his first statement, Jesus' reference to the future shows that the kingdom of God and the future revelation of the Son of Man are two different things.

Much of the bad theology we counter in part 1 is based on poor interpretations of the physicality of the kingdom and the conflation of kingdom with the future revelation of the Son of Man. The kingdom of God is indeed real and physical, but not in the sense of the location of Canaan, as the Israelites assumed.

Jesus answered with a statement about what the kingdom of God is. He said, "It is in your midst" (Luke 17:21 NIV). In the conversation as recorded in Luke 17, what was in the midst of the Pharisees? Clearly, there was a scene the details of which we do not know. Presumably, it was nondescript. Jesus was teaching among the many small towns and villages in the countryside outside of Jerusalem. Nothing special stood in their midst, with one exception: Jesus himself. With his answer, Jesus was saying that the kingdom of God is found wherever there is the presence of Jesus. Jesus IS the kingdom. Period. He could not have been clearer.

One way the image of "kingdom" is helpful is through a metaphor underemphasized in the modern church. As a state ruled by a single sovereign monarch (literally, "one authority"), a kingdom is the place where the king resides. Monarchies are a foreign concept to citizens of a republic such as the United States. In the United Kingdom, a constitutional monarchy, the Royal Standard heraldic flag moves with the king. If he travels, it goes with him. The kingdom is defined by his sovereign presence. In any kingdom, the monarch is sovereign. As Pilate questioned Jesus about the nature of his kingship, Jesus' first response was to declare "my kingdom" (John 18:36). We have already established that Jesus has been given all authority on heaven and earth. As Jesus is the king of God's kingdom, to be in God's kingdom is first to be in the presence of its sovereign King, Jesus.

The same answer emerged when the Pharisees and then John's disciples questioned Jesus for hanging out with Matthew and his sinner friends. Jesus was breaking norms, and they questioned him for it. His response? Association with the unclean, and the lack of fasting, are manifests of God's desire for mercy, not sacrifice. The norms keep us oriented toward righteousness, but they will not achieve the kingdom. Then, the very next thing Jesus said is one of his most important statements on the kingdom, in the parable of the wineskins: Jesus, the new wine, is found in new (*kainos*) wineskins—wineskins that are qualitatively different from the old means and norms of kingdom seeking. Jesus was saying, "The kingdom is not a place that emerges in the future, or through our acts of piety; it is present, in my midst, yet qualitatively different from our present reality."

The kingdom of God is a physical realm, invisible to us, except in moments of God's grace; past, present, and future together. What does it mean that the kingdom of God is found wherever the presence of Jesus is? It is to this we turn next.

9.2 | The Kingdom of God Is Maranatha

One problem with the image of a "kingdom" is our material view of the world. We are bound by space and time. In space, we are like the Israelites in Canaan. Like the disciples, we conflate God's presence with God's property, a physical location, on earth or off it, where we are to live. In time, we cannot help but think of the kingdom as a future destination. Jesus taught his disciples to pray by saying, "Your kingdom come, your will be done, on earth, as it is in heaven" (Matthew 6:10 NIV).[393] Yet the way we translate these verses is poor and, in some ways, totally misses the mark. The English translation is limited by tense: the kingdom is to be described as past, present, or future—one of the three. Indeed, much of the copious theological debate about the kingdom argues which tense is better: future or present.

Perhaps the most common understanding of God's kingdom comes from a definition provided by theologian Geerhardus Vos. Vos split the difference at the height of the age of progress (1904) as a "now/not yet" reality. Vos was likely countering the views of fellow scholars such as Walter Rauschenbusch that the kingdom is a purely future place to which we are evolving.[394] But both Vos and Rauschenbusch were bound by a linear philosophy of history and the Enlightenment view of progress, which shaped the lens by which they viewed apocalyptic literature in Scripture. These constraints on our understanding of time as a linear progression of events has tainted our reading of the kingdom as a physical place that exists in the future.

To define the kingdom according to a single dimension of time and space is to reduce its scope. On space, it is the same limitation as the Israelites' view of the Promised Land, and the temple as the confines of God's presence. At Jesus' crucifixion, the curtain to the Holy of Holies ripped in two. God is not confined by human boundaries. King Solomon understood this: "But who is able to build a temple for him, since the heavens, even the highest heavens, cannot contain him? Who then am I to build a temple for him, except as a place to burn sacrifices before him?" (2 Chronicles 2:6 NIV). The semiotics of a physical space, a "house of God," limits our view of God. Regarding time, our conventional, purely future orientation reduces biblical time and tense, makes Jesus' promises that he is coming soon, and that the kingdom is here a falsehood, and turns the Second Coming into a carrot on a stick.

One of the most underreported facets of the passion narrative are the other resurrected people. Jesus wasn't the only one: "And the tombs broke open. The bodies of many holy people who had died were raised to life. They came out of the tombs after Jesus' resurrection and went into the holy city and appeared to many people" (Matthew 27:52–53 NIV). This little verse in Matthew's gospel is freaky science fiction stuff. People came out of their tombs and appeared to people throughout Jerusalem in the days after the resurrection! Who were they? What did they look like? Even more fascinating, what happened to them? If the kingdom were a future place, this testimony wouldn't make sense. They would have to die a second time to wake up in heaven.

Thus, the first task is to separate the future from the kingdom. The kingdom is at hand. The kingdom has already arrived. It is not in the future, nor is it a "not yet" suspension of time. It is our present reality.

Imagine a straight-line on a piece of paper. The line is time. The paper is God himself. Time is in God just as the line is in the paper. Consequently, he is at the beginning and the end at the same time.

—C. S. Lewis

Jesus minced no words in Mark 12:26–27 correcting the poor theology of the Sadducees on this topic: "He is not the God of the dead, but of the living. You are badly mistaken!" This isn't just a nice sentiment for a funeral. The great I AM is present tense. Jesus rebuked the Sadducee, who did not believe in the resurrection, and confirmed that God is a God of the living, the present. Indeed, he foretold his own bodily resurrection in this conversation.

According to Jesus' statement, the story of Abraham's deity, and the deity of his offspring, isn't just a story of remembrance, but a living story that is still active today. Jesus was referring to the physiological state of people, not of God. In the sentence "God of the living," the living is a reference to the people, not to God. Abraham, Isaac, and Jacob are in fact not dead and gone but alive and well.

Plot twists and temporal distortions pepper the end narrative, as biblical scholar David Barr observes.[395] Hebrews 13:8 tells us, "Jesus Christ is the same yesterday and today and forever." Jesus was there at the beginning ("in the beginning was the Word," John 1:1), and in the end, he is there. At the cross, Jesus announced, "It is finished" (John 19:30), speaking at the same time and with the same words that the high priest used when he brought Passover to a close with the sacrifice of the Pascal lamb. The kingdom is another realm containing all time, or the fullness of time, meaning the past, present, and future. The kingdom has come, is here now, and is coming soon. This is how Jesus could say, "Your father Abraham rejoiced to see my day" (John 8:56 KJV).

To understand the kingdom as an all-time reality in our present time requires some time bending. German theologian Jürgen Moltmann says, "We arrive at the completion not by traversing the longitudinal lines of history to their end, but by erecting everywhere in history the perpendicular line. Just as every time is equally close to the primordial state and the Fall, so every time is also equally immediate to the completion."[396] Every age is equidistant from eternity.

We are neither creating the future nor escaping the future but receiving the present reality. It is the exact opposite of the millennialistic desire to remove ourselves from time or escape the limitations of time. On the contrary, the kingdom of God is the consummation of time: it is full time. One of Mabel Boggs Sweet's favorite sayings, "God's clock keeps perfect time," was truer than she may have realized. God's clock is a teleological clock. God keeps teleological time.

""You are not yet fifty years old," they said to him, "and you have seen Abraham!"
"Very truly I tell you," Jesus answered, "before Abraham was born, I am!""

— John 8:57-58

The time-bending nature of this chapter may seem weird, but no weirder than the conjecture of some quantum physicists that there are minimal distances ("hodons") and minimal time ("chronos") in nature. Consider the story of Exodus, which is the story of God revealing the divine self to a specific person in Moses over time. Over the course of the story, Moses learns that God is steadfast, slow to anger, and abounding in love. But the biggest thing Moses learns? Simply, God is, in time.

If we are rushed for time, sow time & we will reap time. Go to church & spend a quiet hour in prayer. You will have more time than ever & your work will get done. Sow time with the poor. Sit, listen to them, give them your time lavishly.

—Catholic activist Dorothy Day (1897–1980),
offering a kingdom view of "time management"

While other gods of ancient culture live outside of time, Yahweh is in time—yet not limited by time. God isn't timeless; God isn't timely; God is the fullness of time, which includes timelessness and timeliness. God is past, present, and future, all rolled up together. Time in Torah thinking, a sense of time in Judaism, is not linear but cyclic in a spiral design. When you remember you "re-member": you experience it again; you enter it one way and leave it changed. Every cycle of time empowers us and changes us and makes us experience the whole of time until we become fresh and new again. Therefore, to be in God's presence means that we are by necessity in the fullness of time—past, presence, and future, all at once.

The kingdom is the presence of God, and God is the fullness of time. Thus, the kingdom is the fullness of time. Or to paraphrase John 10:10, full life, full time, lifetime. We still call the middle of a sports match "half-time," but we've lost the rest of the story. Historically, in English soccer matches, the end of the game wasn't "zero" on the clock but "full time." The end whistle marked the culmination of the time spent together in sport and camaraderie. It was *koinonia*, also known as the time of your life.

Defining the kingdom as a past-present-future perfect reality is hard to comprehend. People tend to respond with jokes about time-bending, mind-blowing science-fiction movies. Reading Einstein's theory of relativity may help, or a viewing of the Spider-Man multiverse. Another closer-to-home metaphor is our own human experience. Consider how our understanding of time changes over the course of our lives. In infancy and early childhood, there is only the present. We are helpless, with no conception of time, obsessed with food, sleep, comfort, and play. As we grow into young women and men, we become obsessed with the future. What will our lives become? Whom will we meet and marry? What great things might happen? As we age and make choices that have life consequences, we come to terms with the one life we have been given. We try to become "mindful" of the present and accept things as they are. Then, as we become old, we think of the past. We remember our ancestors and reflect on the stories our lives have told. Each view of time is true, yet each is a glimpse of a larger narrative, experienced in sequence but in some ways also experienced simultaneously (e.g., Jesus' "become like children," Matthew 18:3). Perhaps this one life is preparation for the life to come, the Great Convergence, when future, present, and past come together as one.

Paul's closing declaration in his first letter to the church in Corinth is a simple phrase: *"Maranatha,"* or "Come, Lord!" (16:22 KJV). In Greek form it is the closing declaration of the Bible: Maranatha (Rev. 22:10). *Maranatha* is a word that exists in three tenses simultaneously. Jesus has come; Jesus is come; Jesus is coming. This is the kingdom: Jesus has come; Jesus is here now; Jesus is coming soon. Too much of the Christian community lives in one tense only, not three at once, which is a tragedy. Paul's encouragement gives us a glimpse into the alternate reality, the fullness of time of the *kairos* kingdom.

At one point in Jesus' ministry, he gave three of his disciples a glimpse of this reality up on the mountaintop. Jesus shape-shifted into something so brilliant, so dazzling, so beautiful the disciples were literally knocked over (Matthew 17:1–6). Paul later described this state as a vision of glory: "And we all, who with unveiled faces contemplate the Lord's glory, are being transformed into his image with ever-increasing glory, which comes from the Lord, who is the Spirit" (2 Corinthians 3:18 NIV).

Notably, this revelation of glory brings together the Old and New Testaments with a returning cameo of the same two people who had previously seen God on a mountaintop.[397] The Mount of Transfiguration story also brings to the fore another, contrasting mount: the Mount of Temptation. Satan led Jesus to high mountain and tempted him with power and glory. Jesus led his disciples to a high mountain and showed them the meaning of power and glory. Satan's version of power and glory is self-glorification and self-aggrandizement. Jesus' version of power and glory is sacrificial love and self-emptying. If the moment were merely a hall-of-fame preview of saints, many people could have appeared and spoken with Jesus. Since it was the same two people, what if, in some strange twisting of time, the transfiguration was the exact same moment experienced in three moments of time?

> *Your kingdom come,*
> *your will be done,*
> *on earth as it is in heaven.*

> **—Jesus**

The result of a kingdom found in all three tenses—past, present, and future—is that the age to come is not something we're progressing toward. It is our present reality as followers of Jesus. A better translation of Jesus' prayer is this: "Let it show up, this realm of yours. Let it happen, that desire of yours, as in skies, also on earth." What we translate as "kingdom" literally means "realm in the skies," where *realm* is defined as "God's desire, God's dream, God's will."

The resurrected bodies rose with Jesus to become citizens in a present reality, defined not by time or space but by the presence of Jesus. To be a citizen in God's kingdom is not to live in the future or in a specific space, but to be in the presence of a God who exists beyond time. This is one of the reasons corporate worship is so important. We align with other believers, including the cloud of witnesses, in the presence of God. This even includes the other resurrected people from the biblical story, who, having been resurrected, remain alive with Jesus, with others who have passed over.

Even the thief at the cross experienced this present reality. This convict was Jesus' last disciple and first convert in heaven. Having bade Jesus, "Remember me when you come in your kingdom," Jesus promises him a garden paradise that very day (Luke 23:42–43). The scandal of this story is that unlike the resurrected bodies, the thief wasn't even a holy man. A criminal sentenced to death, he too entered Jesus' alternate reality.

> *When the time is right, I, the LORD will make it happen.*

> **—Isaiah 60:22**

| Chapter 9 | Full Time Kingdom

Matthew's preferred term for this new reality is the *kingdom of heaven,* singular, different from the "heavens" as a synonym for the skies. Many scholars assume Matthew's term is synonymous with "kingdom of God" with deference for mentioning the name of God to his Jewish audience. Yet, as theologian Robert Foster observes, Matthew was not afraid of the phrase "kingdom of God." He uses it four times. Foster claims that the kingdom of God is what his Jewish audience was expecting, but the kingdom of heaven is what Jesus inaugurated.[398]

In Christ, the kingdom is come. The age to come isn't something we're progressing toward. It is a present reality in the person of Jesus. In this new kingdom, good food and drink and table talk are time stoppers, where whole evenings go by unnoticed. Time in the kingdom is a different realm, where we are both in time and above time.

While historiographers debate a linear time line of history, which we outline in part 1, Jesus offers nonlinear reality. *Maranatha!* Paul's farewell at the end of his letter to the church in Corinth exists in three tenses simultaneously: Jesus has come; Jesus is come; Jesus is coming. The kingdom has come, is here now, and is coming soon. The kingdom is the fullness of time, and Jesus invites us to be full of it now and to experience the full life in the here and now (see John 10:10).

9.3 | The Kingdom of God Is Purpose, Not Project

So go ahead. Eat your food with joy,
and drink your wine with a happy heart,
for God approves of this!

—Ecclesiastes 9:7 (NLT)

Considering this new way of thinking about the future, how do we return to today's tsunami of troubles? How do we live? Clearly, Christ's kingdom is not yet fully realized. The entire biblical story, from the original garden forward to the garden city at the end, is the story of a state of flux, what Jesus calls "birth pangs" (Matthew 24:8). No wonder the current age can be so painful—imagine a birth that takes thousands of years! In an age in which little seems to work as it ought, and we are caught in the painful in-between, what does Jesus call us to come together to do?

The life-changing answer is found in our understanding of authority, and our surrender to the full authority of the King. The question of authority is the question of the relationship of the one governing to the governed. God provided a model for living under authority, which we know as the Sabbath. But the people would not live the Sabbath life. Enter Jesus, who declared that the story is finished by inaugurating Jubilee. After the resurrection he couldn't be clearer: "All authority in heaven and on earth has been given to me" (Matthew 28:20). More than just a state of mind, Jesus is the completion of the story. His new and true free state is a state of grace, both national and personal, of people and of personage, a community organized under a single authority. "Thine is the kingdom, and the power, and the glory" (Matthew 6:13 KJV) is to say, "Jesus is the kingdom, Jesus is the power, and Jesus is the glory."

Stories of the struggle for power have been told since the beginning of time. They are present through the biblical story and through the sagas of our entire present age. Human will to power powers the sameness of the story. The only way to stop the cycle of bad advice and false endings is to assign authority to Jesus, who both lived in time and lives out of time and let him author our lives. In Christ—not in the work of our own hands—we find our hope. Thus, the goal of this work is prophetic. In the middle of the turmoil of our age, we hope to call church and culture forth to a new age of *telos* and a new way of living. When we assign Jesus authority, we discover our shared purpose.

Understanding these forces empowers humans to see God in the tweets and trends of today, identify people's deep hungers and groanings, respond well, and be the church. With Jesus as the Author of our lives, what new story emerges? Living into Jesus' authorship means living into the times and out of the times simultaneously. The end of the story is an eschatology of teleology.

When we see the kingdom as shared purpose, our understanding of mission changes because our understanding of time changes. Instead of embracing social and technological change as intrinsic good, as we have done in the age of progress, we are free to consider the good, true, and beautiful of every age. For example, as our story on the use of leeches demonstrates, while medicine improves, letting go of the old has proven to be shortsighted. The third leading cause of death today is iatrogenic disease,[399] or when "he lay at death's door," and doctors pulled him through it. Sometimes the treatment is worse than the problem, and sometimes the future is not necessarily better than the past. Change can be for good or ill. Ironically, the promised technological future of tomorrow may result in joylessness today. Because the perfect future never comes, we are always left striving for more. Utopia literally means "no place."

We the people are not capable of making a perfect society. Jesus says to worship God and God alone. In other words, stop putting trust in your own ingenuity and genius. As it turns out, we cannot define righteousness through our own effort. The idea that we can build our own kingdom is hubris and sin. Much of old-line Protestant liberalism lives here. For left-and-right types, kingdom is king. For Jesus disciples, king is kingdom.

The previous chapter and this one argue against a bifurcation of transcendence and immanence. When we accept only the divine Jesus or only the human Jesus, we miss half the story. If destruction isn't the answer, and yet the future does not offer a technological utopia, then where does that leave us? Jesus says, "Very truly I tell you, whoever hears my word and believes him who sent me has eternal life and will not be judged but has crossed over from death to life" (John 5:24 NIV). The kingdom is life, not only eternally in the future, but earthily here and now, in the present. A full life, eternal and yet earthen, infinite and yet intimate, is the promise of the infinite, infant God.

Now this is eternal life: that they know you,
the only true God, and Jesus Christ, whom you have sent.

—John 17:3 (NIV)

Life as citizens of the now kingdom begins with understanding what we mean by the kingdom of God and learning to recognize it when it appears. The practical question is, how do we recognize the kingdom of God?

As the kingdom of God is life, it is reasonable to conclude that wherever there is life, there is the kingdom. This has been the approach of the

Christian liberal tradition, which has used the oft-cited Matthew 25 as proof that the goal of the Christian is to make life more abundant and fully realized. From this increase in life, we may achieve an increase in the kingdom. For example, if someone is the victim of oppression, then to liberate that person is to give him life, and therefore it is to give him the kingdom of God.

But this bottom-up building project approach has proven inadequate to understanding the full nature of the kingdom. Physicist and artificial intelligence expert Jeremy England elegantly argues that the origin of life may be found in the laws of thermodynamics, but we cannot solve the problem using purely mathematical approaches. Typically, in an equation, one may solve a large problem by reducing it to several smaller, known rules, applying the rules, then expanding it back out to answer the bigger problem. While this approach has yielded some benefits, it underestimates the unknown. England writes, "The smallest inaccuracies in the simulated properties of individual pieces in a system can lead to dramatic qualitative differences in how the collective will behave."[400]

As England points out, boiling water at 215 degrees Fahrenheit is less than 1 percent different from water at 208 degrees, yet liquid and gas states are qualitatively different. While the reductionist approach assumes we can solve big questions using small answers,[401] it is a fallacy to determine the whole from the simple rules played by its parts. Yet we do this all the time. Given a small piece of information, we try to predict the whole, and given one property, we think we can change the behavior of the whole. But the whole is always greater than the sum of its parts. The kingdom is such a mystery that the Quaker artist Edward Hicks painted one biblical passage more sixty times because there was so much in it: Isaiah 11:1–10, which answers the question "What does the kingdom look like?"

> The wolf will live with the lamb,
>   the leopard will lie down with the goat,
> the calf and the lion and the yearling together;
>   and a little child will lead them.
> The cow will feed with the bear,
>   their young will lie down together,
>   and the lion will eat straw like the ox.
> The infant will play near the cobra's den,
>   and the young child will put its hand into the viper's nest.
> They will neither harm nor destroy

on all my holy mountain,

for the earth will be filled with the knowledge of the
Lord as the waters cover the sea.

Isaiah 11:6-9 (NIV)

This is how it is with the kingdom of God. A living organism is more
than an exact combination of raw material. To use England's example, what
is the difference between Moses' staff and the snake it becomes? Once we
realize that "the lens of physics reduces every living thing to looking like
a specially configured pile of inanimate sticks, we confront the vast ex-
panse of gray area stretching between the obviously alive and the obviously
inanimate."[402]

Liberating people from oppression and giving people a better life is
good and may be understood in Jesus' ministry as healing, but it is not the
same thing as giving people the kingdom. We cannot achieve the whole
from its constituent parts. While the kingdom is life, life is not the kingdom. Life is more than an exact mathematical configuration of material
behaviors.

Likewise, God is love, but love is not God. We cannot see the fullness of
the presence of God, and the fullness of God's realm, merely from piecing
together a whole picture out of constituent parts. Thinking that we can is a
sign of the arrogance of the modern, scientific mind, and the absence of a
biblical mind. We can have all the pieces and still not see the whole of the
kingdom come.

Yet we act as if life is something over which we have command and control. We are given glimpses of shards and sparks and think we understand
the whole. We are given will and intellect and think we can achieve the
whole. These fallacies of human agency undermine and deceive us. The
kingdom is not something we can fully grasp, nor is it some point in the
future we can gain and attain. The state of water at 211 degrees Fahrenheit
gives no indication of what the state of water at 212 degrees Fahrenheit will
become.

We cannot make life, nor even understand life, using known rules. In
the same way, we cannot achieve the kingdom, nor even fully understand
the kingdom, using our linear mindset, limited properties, and conflicted
behaviors. Thus, the first rule of the kingdom is that we cannot recognize
it using observed experience. It is more than the sum of its parts. The kingdom is more than simply life as we know it, even fully lived and righteously
ramped. Like vaporization, the kingdom is the same life we have already
known, yet it is a transfiguration to a different state. We prefer the language
of transfiguration over transformation. A caterpillar is transformed into a

chrysalis; but a chrysalis is transfigured into a butterfly. The kingdom is *kainos*: new, yet not improved, but qualitatively different.

Surely, if Jesus had wanted us to "build" his kingdom he would have told us how to do it. His thirty years of construction, masonry, and carpentry would have led to some blueprints of Jubilee and how-to manuals for kingdom-building. If the kingdom of God (kog) is not something under our construction, the question rises of agency. Do we have any role other than receiving and reciprocating?

We believe our role as cogs in the kog is akin to a life of Easter egg hunts. *Easter eggs* is the name given to unexpected messages or playful features hidden somewhere in a product that produce grins, giggles, nods, and winks. As jazz hands or jazz fingers, easter eggs issue in joy and pleasure. Much like misericords in the medieval construction of cathedrals, easter eggs showcase their creators' humor and humanity. For example, search the word "askew' on Google. You land on a page defining "askew" that tilts downward, looks off-kilter. Or take the logo for UK's National Lottery. The two fingers that aren't part of the hand's crossed fingers produce a smile, signifying the joy that comes from winning the lottery. Not everyone likes Easter eggs. The humorless Bill Gates had Microsoft get rid of easter eggs in its software in 2002. But Elon Musk has brought them to the fore again, with the number 420 (4/20 being the annual marijuana festival) hidden in a recent price offer for Twitter, or the fart sounds and whoopie cushions hidden in Tesla switches and seats.

In the life of faith, Easter eggs are everywhere . . . tokens of Jesus' presence, signs of the risen and rising Christ that we must learn to recognize. Once we pick out what Jesus is doing, we pick up and prod ("nudge") further his presence. We egg on the Easter eggs.

The "kingdom of heaven" is a gift, a presence, a transfiguration, a Jesus reign in which we receive and then gift others with its blessings. While the future is an eschatology that starts now and builds to an end of our making, Christ's kingdom is a teleology that starts at the end and plays backward from an end of God's making. Eschatology is not a story of endings but of unendings. Teleology is the story of endings.

The best way to change the present is not railing and flailing against the status quo or dismantling its decaying structures but to showcase and body forth a mesmerizing and enchanting alternative future that makes the current realities outdated, outlandish and outrageous. Like Jesus did. Like Jesus is.

Followers of Jesus receive and then gift the kingdom, and create the future, both at the same time. This may be the greatest shift in mentality to touch Christianity in nineteen hundred years, at least according to one scholar: "The paradigm shift in the theological view of 'power,' in the context of the twentieth-century reappraisal of soteriology, represents what may be the most radical shift in mentality to touch Christianity in eighteen hundred years."[403] The solution is to change our thinking from *eschaton*, or the end of time, to *telos*, or purpose for which we exist.

Let us turn to this next.

T I M E   O U T :   P R E S E N C E

....

The end is the presence of God.

....

In chapter 3, we looked at traditionalism and wondered, Does the answer to the future lay in the past?

As we have described, in Christ is the kingdom and the power, to quote the Didache. This means that to be part of the kingdom is to be empowered with the authority of Jesus. The end is like it was in the beginning, when God dwelled with us in the cool of the garden. God's presence is a fire in us that sustains us: a Holy Spirit fire, not to destroy but to sustain and grow. The end is the relationship—not just a destination but the purpose of life now and the raison d'etre of our pilgrimage. This power is what enables us to love others— but like any fire, it must be nurtured.

To "come home" is to come home to the future, our true home. Jesus is not calling us to a diminished life of problems, plagues, and purges but to a distinguished, richer life of deepening relationships and increasing Divine Presence.

10.1 | Hiding from God's Presence

The greatest temptations are not money, sex, and power, but self-rejection—because self-rejection contradicts the sacred voice that calls us beloved.

—Henri Nouwen

Money, sex, and power are downstream activities. The source of the problem is the sense of identity that we can only find when we are in the presence of God. By God we mean the triune God—God the Father, God the Son, God the Holy Spirit—the source of life. If we think of God as being like the sun, then to be near God is to be near life, and to be far away is to be away from life. The issue of life, the ultimate question, is about our proximity to the presence of God.

What happened after the fall? The very next thing after Adam and Eve gained the knowledge of the world because the "eyes of both were opened" in Genesis 3:7) was that they hid from God. Verse 8 says, "They heard the sound of the Lord God walking in the garden at the time of the evening breeze, and the man and his wife hid themselves from the presence of the Lᴏʀᴅ God among the trees of the garden."

Why did they hide from God? Well, we say, they were naked. But that's a modern answer. They were naked before, and that wasn't a problem. So, what happened? Adam and Eve flat-out fled from the presence of God. What does it mean to hide from the presence of God? They didn't want to be seen. They didn't want to be known. We are hiders, not seekers. We don't want to be known. We fear intimacy because we think if someone really sees us, he or she will find us unworthy, and we'll be unwanted.

Humanity's fundamental rebellion against God has been a rebellion of autonomy.

—Alan Noble, You Are Not Your Own

Our rebellious desire to "find ourselves" apart from God leads to the very thing we seek to avoid—a loss of self. Apart from the Creator, we do not know how to be human, and in fact become inhuman. Sin creates four breaks: a break from God, a break from one another, a break from creation, and a break from ourselves. We believe a loss of autonomy will lead to a loss of happiness, so we reject authority. But in the end of this alternative story, we only get tragedy: distance from God, one another, and ourselves.

A break from ourselves . . . what does this mean? Money, sex, and power, to return to Nouwen's quote, are just cover-ups for the fear of being found unworthy. If you were to ask a group of people if they've ever feared being found unworthy, and they were to answer with honesty, every hand would go up. Knowledge of our own sin means we no longer think we are worthy, so we reject the ultimate worth of the voice that says, "*I made you; you are in my image; you are loved.*"

We just don't believe it. Instead, we turn to downstream vices to fill the void that is left in our souls. Some of us, once we know the emptiness of money, sex, and power, just settle into a form of ongoing sadness. We reject one another, and we reject ourselves. For each of us to truly know ourselves, and to believe that we are beloved, it is necessary for us to be able to love others, and to sacrifice fully, to love fully. When we fundamentally, in our core, think that we are unworthy, that is a very difficult place indeed.

God is looking for us in the cool of the garden, and we hide, because in our sin, we understand the depth of our own brokenness—both the broken things done to us, that wound us, and the broken things that we have done to others. Part of us wants to come out from behind the bush, to run to God, and to return to the joy of full acceptance in God's presence. Yet we hide. We remain in our hiddenness. Why? Because we are wound up in our woundedness. Because we think we're not worthy.

The consequences of hiddenness are tragic. We have seen relationships suffer, shrivel up, and die because of the inability of two people to overcome the gaping wound of unworthy and unwanted that taints every conversation and every connection. We have seen people create terrible self-fulfilling prophecies, in which the very suffering that exists in the ongoing videos of unworthiness playing in their own minds comes to life, just because they're unable to reach out beyond their own pain.

We are stuck in the bushes, scared of being seen, cringing from our vulnerabilities, unable to cry out. Meanwhile God is searching for us in our hiding places, calling us out, summoning us to come out, and saying, "Where are you? I love you."

This is the radical story of grace. God knows our waywardness and loves us anyway. God forgives us our wrongs and wants us to forgive one another. When through grace we come out of hiding and come into God's presence, we rediscover our worth. This gives us the authority we have sought and have been unable to find through the means of the world.

10.2 | God's Presence Frees Us to Love

But what if the old videotapes playing in our heads are too loud? The story of the Bible is the story of God seeking us over and over, and us rejecting the invitation because we're too busy watching the same bad videos over and over, the ones that tell us we are not worthy, we are not loved, we are not wanted, we are not capable.

Since then, at an uncertain hour,
That agony returns,
And till my ghastly tale is told
This heart within me burns.

—Samuel Taylor Coleridge, The Rime of the Ancient Mariner (1798)

The only way to overcome these attack videos is to cry out to Jesus, over and again, every day. Jesus leads us out from the bushes and turns hiding bushes into burning bushes of God's presence. He returns us to the garden, to the joy and peace of God's presence. Jesus says, "Very truly I tell you, whoever hears my word and believes him who sent me has eternal life and will not be judged but has crossed over from death to life" (John 5:24 NIV).

What does this mean? This bears repeating: the kingdom is life, not only eternally in the future, but here and now, in the present. A full life, eternal and yet present, infinite, and yet intimate, is the promise of the infinite, infant God.

Jesus introduced a revolutionary turn of thought: "Now this is eternal life: that they know you, the only true God, and Jesus Christ, whom you have sent" (John 17:3 NIV). The kingdom isn't some future reward or destination site or building project. It is our present reality freely given, Jesus says, to whomever hears and "believes him who sent me." It's not just "believe in Jesus," whatever that means. It means, believe that the God who calls us out from behind the bushes loves us, seeks our good, and wants to be with us so much that God sent Jesus to prove it. Instead of merely calling us out of the bushes, God sent Jesus into the bushes to find us.

God seeks us. God is the Seeker. We are the hiders. When we come out of hiding and seek the Seeker, we are ready to overcome the divide that exists between us and restore the garden relationship. This garden relationship is about the pleasure of presence.

What does this mean for us personally, in our relationships and sense of well-being?

We experience glimpses of it in our everyday relationships. When we reject ourselves, and reject one another, we rebuff God's healing and restoring presence. The purpose of all time and the true end of the story is that we shall once again live in the pleasure of God's presence. Indeed, the end of Matthew's gospel captures Jesus' last words before his ascension: "Surely I am with you always, to the very end of the age" (Matthew 28:20 NIV). The end of the age that Jesus describes here is *synteleias*, not a physical space but a shared purpose. The root Greek word of *synteleias* is *telos*.

Thus, to be in the kingdom is not to be in the future, or the past or the present, but all three at the same time. In other words, it is to be in the presence of a God who exists beyond time. *Telos* is the end. It is full time, and the purpose of all time. When we begin to see the purpose of life, the meaning of life, as teleology—not its alternate worldview, eschatology—it changes everything.

One way to understand a teleological view of the world and vision for God's kingdom is to understand the nature of human relationships in general. The teleological relationship is one in which each party is fully present to one another.

Is it possible to have a fully present relationship with another human? What do we mean by fully present? Well, let's describe it in relief. A completely hidden relationship is one in which things are purely transactional. It is the way the world sees relationships. It is the "quid pro quo" of the world's view. *Quid pro quo* is the Latin legal phrase that has come to mean "I did something, and now you are obligated to do something in return for me."[404] It's a phrase that has taken on a lot of life in recent years. It is used in a relationship based on reciprocity, with the assumption that a person only wants to engage in relationships with other people if they are due to receive equal or greater benefit than effort.

Reciprocity is the basis for all human relationships, sociologists say. But love is giving without reciprocal expectation. God's primary characteristic, according to the book of Exodus, is *chesed* love. The word *chesed* has a reciprocal root, but what makes it surprising and different is that with God, we constantly, consistently fail to return the love God gives to us. We hide. Yet, instead of withdrawing himself as all human do, God continues to seek us out, to give, to love, even though our ability to love back is limited.

We are broken people. We fail to love as we are loved. We see life, and all human relationships, through the lens of power and glory, not love and service. We calculate relationships as net neutral or net positive power arrangements. In the world's view, things that reduce our power make us "suckers" and "losers." The goal is to increase our panjandrum of power (our personal authority).

The panjandrum is a conundrum. The way you overcome this panjandrum conundrum is to give and to love. To give life is to find life. The world encourages us to take what is ours. But Jesus says a life of seeking our own happiness never works. What works is the counterintuitive approach of giving ourselves away. This means that Jesus calls us to the constant, unending work of loving others without quid pro quo—with no reciprocal obligation of return favors. When we give to others in love, others' perceptions of the world and of people heal just a bit each time. Over time both they and we respond by assuming the best, not the worst.

The Jesus *telos* is challenging. Every time someone has a bad day, he or she can set a relationship back. But Jesus would have us "assume the best" of one another. When someone snaps at you, assume that person doesn't mean you ill will. Sometimes, people do. But most of the time, if an interaction is less than edifying, it's because that person is coming from a place of his or her own hurt and cannot see past it. Assume the best on your friend's behest.

Because the *telos* life is so challenging, sometimes we just give up trying. Many people, even many Christians, have given up on the idea that it is possible to have a pure relationship with another human. We have reduced human relationships to mutually beneficial transactions. We have a word for this, even: *consent*. The result is a transactional culture in which our highest aspiration is lack of harm, or a set of relationships composed of mutually beneficial transactions. Willie James Jennings calls this the "diseased social imagination" of Western culture.[405] Having given up on the pure vision of full presence with God and one another, the best we can do is to create negotiated transactions that do no harm to one another.

But avoiding harm is nowhere near as high a bar as love. This is nowhere more obvious than in sexual consent. Sex, the act signed by God to be the purest expression of intimate love between two people covenanted together through the sacrament of marriage, is reduced to a contract, if not on paper, then at least verbally arranged. The lie, of course, is that there is mutuality between people, when this is never the case. Arrangements based on a worldview of power always create various levels of power, and with various levels of power we find imbalances. Imbalanced power in relationships of sexual consent ends up with coercion, assault, abuse, and other, more degrading forms of violence—usually to women and children, who typically have less power.

The *telos* way of living is to be filled with the authority of Jesus, and with the power of Christ in us, to find the power to love others fully, regardless of their ability to return the favor.

10.3 | God's Presence Is a Consuming Fire

There's a scene in the film *Cast Away* (2000) in which Chuck Noland, played by Tom Hanks, needs to light a fire. He has begun to recover from the shock of waking up on a deserted island and realizes he needs to make camp. Using a rounded piece of deadwood as a flint and a split piece as a trough, he rubs sticks together, first slowly, then vigorously. But the kinetic energy of his rubbing doesn't work. He rubs faster and faster, until finally the flint stick pops out of the trough stick, and he cuts his hand. He yells in frustration and quits.

Later, he returns to the project, this time with some dead flora shoved in the split of the trough stick as kindling. He rubs again and after a moment glimpses a bit of smoke. He picks up the trough stick, stares, then turns to Wilson the volleyball and exclaims, "The air got to it!"

Excited, he tries again. He places the kindling back in the split and lays it on the ground. This time he digs out a gap in the sand below the kindling to allow air to flow under and around it. He rubs the sticks together again. At first, nothing happens. Then a little spark catches, unseen to Chuck and the viewer. Smoke rises out of the kindling. Chuck drops the stick, leans in, and blows on his smoky concoction. Then, a little explosion—the spark becomes a fire. Overjoyed, he exclaims, "I made fire!"

Cut to dusk, same location. Chuck is dancing around a roaring bonfire, singing, proud that as a modern office worker, he has achieved something so essential. Beyond his pride, he knows that fire is step one to his ability to survive alone on an island. Nothing else can happen without it.

Fire is a paradox. Fire keeps us warm. It prepares our food. Controlled burns eliminate garbage and chaff. Forest fires lead to regeneration. Rangers use controlled fires as pruning to clear away excess brush and overgrowth. But if we touch it, fire scalds and scars us. Out of control, it is a punishing symbol of hell. Jesus' reference to the fire of hell in Matthew 10:28 is *gehenna*, a name for the valley southwest of Jerusalem outside the city walls, where citizens took their trash for burning. Fires there burned ceaselessly, out of control. Some people actually lived amid the fires—the outcasts and lepers of society. You can imagine their miserable existence. They are Jesus' metaphor for those in hell, who weep and gnash their teeth.

The old spiritual goes, "No more water, the fire next time." But what sort of fire? Some see the end as a punitive fire. After the flood, God made an everlasting promise that never again would waters destroy all life, even though "every inclination of the human heart is evil from childhood" (Genesis 8:21 NIV). Many people think there is another half to this promise—that God will next destroy the world with fire. But God made no such promise to

Noah. Instead, God intervened a second time, using power made perfect in weakness, with the cross.

The idea that God will come again via fire comes not from Genesis but much later. Writing to congregations in Asia Minor, the apostle Peter said that the same Word that made the heavens and the earth through water and used that very water to destroy the world that then existed, now exists by fire (2 Peter 3:5–7). It is a different world; it now exists for fire. Fire is the end purpose of the world—its *telos*.

Some understand this fire in future, eschatological terms and look for a fiery explosion to signify the end. Yet God has already promised that God will never again destroy all life, so this cannot be true. Fire isn't a weapon, a flamethrower used by a vengeful God to one day wipe out the bad people like a scene in *Left Behind*.

Fire is God's Spirit, which appeared to Moses in a bush and comes upon every disciple. Listen again to the famous biblical story of fire: "They were all together in one place. Suddenly a sound like the blowing of a violent wind came from heaven and filled the whole house where they were sitting. They saw what seemed to be tongues of fire that separated and came to rest on each of them" (Acts 2:1–3 NIV).

As Chuck Noland discovered, wind precedes fire. The breath of God, violent in its intensity and purity, blew on the community of Jesus follow-ers. The wind activated the kinetic energy in the room and lit up the whole house. Like the kindling in Chuck's deadwood, the room came alive with the fire of the Holy Spirit. In the first believers, and in you and me, the breath of God converts our kinetic energy into fire.

When Scripture says God will come instead via fire, it is not the fires of destruction, but the tongues of fire dancing around the community of *koinonia* in Acts 2. The sequel to the flood already happened. The "fire next time" is not a promise of a dreadful future judgment day but a promise of hope for our present reality. When we surrender to faith, it is the next dawn of our present reality. This fire is not just for our consumption. As Peter said, the world exists for the fire of God's Spirit, which sustains us, but also burns away every impurity. Only controlled fire leads to regeneration.

Neither of us has never experienced frozen tundra–level cold, but both of us have had experiences with power outages and cold interiors. One of us lives on an island called Orcas Island with a cooperative power com-pany called Orcas Power and Light but nicknamed "Occasional Power and Light" because the power goes out so often, sometimes for days on end. The other has lived through a freak Texas snowstorm and power outage in February 2021 that crippled the state. The jet stream had dropped into Mexico, which allowed a rare polar vortex to bring Arctic air down through the American plains. Electricity use spiked, and the state grid could not handle the load. To avoid total and catastrophic electrical failure, the state's

/ Chapter 10 / Time Out: Presence

energy agency began controlled, rolling electrical blackouts. With temperatures in the teens and electricity in the house randomly shutting on and off for days, the younger Len's family had to become strategic about something they had previously taken for granted.

On the coldest night, it bottomed out at –2 degrees Fahrenheit. Len awoke to a dark house with an internal temperature in the mid-forties, cold but thankful that home builders had insulated the house well enough to keep it fifty degrees warmer than the outside. Many were not so lucky; pipes burst, homes were lost, and souls perished.

As the Wilson family shivered together, they used every bit of available wood to keep a fire burning in the front room fireplace. At one point, while poking charred logs, Len thought, *what it would be like to try to light a fire in the frozen northern plains on a winter night?* What did pioneers do in the open plains with only purple moonlight and a few trees lining the horizon? Fire is not self-sustaining. It must be stoked and cared for to continue burning.

"The soul's safety is in its heat. Truth without enthusiasm, morality without emotion, ritual without soul, make for a Church without power. *Destitute of the Fire of God, nothing else counts; possessing Fire, nothing else matters.*"[406] These are the words of Samuel Chadwick (1860–1932), who served a term as president of the Wesleyan Methodist Conference and whose writings on theology continue to be reprinted even to this day. Chadwick once said that there were two men in church history who "never knew the word retreat": John Wesley and William Booth. For both the Wesleyan and the Salvationist movements, the symbol of "fire" was central.

The fires of our lives likewise need constant care, for the cold winds of the human heart threaten to extinguish them. The presence of sin is real. It leads us into places of hiding, where we flee the warmth of God's presence. Fires don't keep burning on their own. They use up their sources of fuel and need new sources. Without attention, fire turns to embers and embers turn to ash. In Jesus' prediction of the end, he said, "Because of the increase of wickedness, the love of most will grow cold" (Matthew 24:12 NIV). But then Jesus made a promise: while wickedness is a constant threat, those who *endure* to the end will be saved (v. 13).

"Endure" is what most English versions of the Bible use, but it is a poor translation of the Greek (*hupoménō*). It connotes an apocalyptic view of the future. If we understand "the end" as a future reality, and fire as a tool of judgment that either inaugurates, finishes, or perpetuates that reality (whether premillennial, postmillennial, amillennial, ag-millennial), then what do we do as we wait through the trials and tribulations? A future-end theology forces us to "endure," like a trip to the dentist, or like sitting on our couch in a cold, dark house, waiting for the heat to come on again.

Is this what Jesus is asking us to do? Passively wait on the couch for the heat to come on? No, Jesus is asking us to do something active, not passive.

A truer translation for *hupomēnō* is "abide under." Disciples of Jesus do not practice acquiescence or avoidance but abidance. Despite the constant suffering, blows, and wounds, other-afflicted and self-afflicted, Jesus says that those who abide under the presence of Christ will be healed. What Jesus is saying is not that the one who waits for a future day of happiness will be saved (we've established that the "future" is a modern concept anyway). Rather, the one who remains or abides in *telos*, in the presence of Jesus, trusting in the Spirit, will be saved.

In other words, Jesus' prediction for the end is not "left behind," but "stay behind." Not escape the trial or even "hang in there," but "stay in there," "pray in there," "run in there," and "sing in there." Getting left behind sounds horrific, as does a trial by suffering, but choosing to stay behind is something entirely different. In staying behind, we choose to remain by the fire, even when it seems the fire is going to die. In a cold, dark house, when it is −2 Fahrenheit outside and only one fire burns, where do you stay?

Some days the fire of the presence of God's Spirit will thunder and lighten all who come near. Other days the fire will seem weak and small compared to the cold around it. When the fire seems weak and others have grown cold and lethargic or left entirely, do you stay and keep adding wood, stoking the fire, blowing on the embers? Though everyone else had turned away to a life of cold brutality, Noah stayed near the fire and let the warmth of God's Spirit protect his family. Jesus says to be like Noah. Those who stay by the fire, who abide under the fire, will be saved. We think of hell as the fiery place, but as Dallas Willard says, "the fires of heaven, I suspect, are hotter than the fires of hell."[407]

So, the question is, how do you keep the fires burning? To answer this question, we tell you a story.

10.4 | God's Presence Is an Active State Relationship

A one-inch white scar above the younger Len's left eyebrow is the only remaining evidence of a wound that for over a year would not go away. It started simply as a cut, self-inflicted, from scratching his forehead. We all can remember times in life when we scratched our heads a lot in confusion and frustration, unable to solve serious problems in life. In Len's first-person recollection:

> The problem was the poor trajectory of my life. I was nearing forty, and through relentless pursuit of a calling had achieved a level of professional platform few attain. In the niche world of professional church people, in the sub niche world of professional church people who are interested in communications, technology, and worship, I was as known as anybody. I was a two-bit celebrity, as I joked with my family.

Being one of the best at something is what the self-help gurus say is a key to happiness and success. But all it had gotten Len was exhaustion, alienation, an empty bank account, and an uncertain future. After fifteen years of hard work, several books, hundreds of conferences, and a high degree of name recognition, he said:

> I was miserable—so much so that I was contemplating leaving all of it. I had tried "platforming" and discovered it didn't bring life.
>
> And I kept nicking the same dang scab on my forehead.

It would seem to heal, and then Len would get out of the shower and notice it was bleeding again. He had no idea how he kept wounding his own face. The trouble spot kept recurring for the better part of a year, and each time, it somehow reopened. Each time it reopened, it seemed to get a little bit bigger.

> I began to get concerned that it was going to be permanent or that I would need some kind of cosmetic procedure, that I'd be the church guy with forehead Botox or whatever it is that people do with plastics on their faces. My forehead was a bad metaphor for the brokenness of my own certainty, a show of bleeding strength.

One day, soon after my fortieth birthday, the same day I'd scraped my scab open again in the shower, I was faced with two choices. With one option, I had an attractive opportunity that would require abandoning what had seemed to become an ashen world of calling, work, and family. By the grace of God, though, I recognized the opportunity not a sign of God's Spirit. So, I took the second option. The only problem was that the second option was in Tennessee, and my family and I lived in Texas. So, I got in my pickup, said a temporary goodbye to my family, and drove. But as I drove away, I couldn't run from my scab, which was visible every time I looked in the rearview mirror. I had turned a different direction, and my future held hope, but the underlying problem remained—I had been doing faith wrong. Without seeing it, I had been living like the Israelites in the Promised Land, thinking my power and the strength of my own hands have produced the good things in my life.[408] I needed to turn in another direction.

My new job opportunity was in Nashville, and because of the power of the Christian community, I had been told about a friend of a friend named Greg, who had also recently moved to the city and was leasing a townhome with an empty second floor. I arrived at the home of a man I'd never met at 1:30 in the morning on January 17, 2011.

As I settled into my new job and what was hopefully short-term housing, I began to contemplate my journey in spiritual terms. If my own strength was insufficient to improve my life, how then should I live?

One night, I prayed in deep earnestness, as sincerely as I had ever prayed. The prayer was simple. I just said, *God, fix it. I don't know what to do, and I need you to fix it.* The response was immediate. Two words appeared in my head: "seek first." I was confused at first, and thought my neurons were randomly popping off. But in subsequent days, the phrase wouldn't go away. I became a little annoyed—God, I'm asking you for help and you're telling me to "seek first"? My needs were urgent! My family was in another state, my bank account was empty, I had stuck a knife into my professional platform, and you're telling me to do more devotional time? Faced with a clear choice to leave the church gig behind or go all in on faith, I had chosen to go all in, but my issues hadn't magically disappeared. I was praying—no joke, no half-baked nod, but a full commitment to this thing called faith—and God's only answer was to "seek first."

I researched "seek first." The phrase in my mind was coming from Jesus' Sermon on the Mount, when he summarizes a section by concluding, "But seek first his kingdom and his righteousness, and all these things will be given to you as well" [Matthew 6:33]. Seek the kingdom? I protested. That's what I've been doing all this time and look where it got me. Then it hit me: maybe I was thinking about the word "kingdom" incorrectly.

My entire life, I had heard in church that the kingdom was something you "build" or "advance." I had heard preachers say that as good Methodists interested in social holiness, we were working to build God's kingdom together. I hear this still today and fear it is the dominant message people in our congregations receive: that if we are good Christians, we will do stuff—work, give, serve. The message I had always heard, more than any other, was that God's kingdom was something we work on, together with other believers, and that being a Christian is akin to being a good employee or an obedient child. But what if this is missing the mark?

As I studied the Scriptures, I began to realize the prevalence of God's simple directive.

Consider:

Moses tells the Israelites, "But if from there you seek the LORD your God, you will find him if you seek him with all your heart and with all your soul" [Deuteronomy 4:29 NIV].

"Hezekiah prayed for them, saying, 'May the LORD, who is good, pardon everyone who sets their heart on seeking God—the LORD, the God of their ancestors—even if they are not clean according to the rules of the sanctuary.' And the LORD heard Hezekiah and healed the people" [2 Chronicles 30:18–20 NIV].

David writes, "The LORD looks down from heaven on all mankind to see if there are any who understand, any who seek God" [Psalm 14:2 NIV].

Jeremiah says, "You will seek me and find me when you seek me with all your heart" [Jeremiah 29:13 NIV].

Isaiah says, "Seek the LORD while he may be found; call upon him while he is near" [Isaiah 55:6].

Seeking is the main thing! It is the core directive Moses gives God's people. It is David's secret. It is the answer the prophets bring to the scattered remnants. It is the summary of Jesus' teaching to the crowds and the disciples alike. It is a statement of presence that precedes a statement of purpose. It comes before anything we do. But what are we seeking? If the Kingdom isn't a place we are building together, a big work project, then what is it? Without the presence of God leading the way, our understanding of God's kingdom has too often turned into something we fight for. Rather than "seek first," we "seek fist."

As I studied the Scriptures, the difference became obvious. The answer is in the rest of Jesus' phrase: ". . . and his righteousness." Jesus explains "righteousness" in his Sermon on the Mount when he tells his listeners, "Blessed are those who hunger and thirst after righteousness, for they will be filled" [Matthew 5:6].

Biblical scholar Kenneth Bailey reminds us that Jesus does not say blessed are those who live righteously or blessed are those who are upright and maintain a righteous lifestyle. Rather, he says, blessed are those who hunger and thirst after righteousness. Righteousness isn't a goal but a purpose. It's *telos*. Those who uphold a relentless drive for righteousness will be blessed.[409]

Jesus offers a parable to flesh this out when he compares the kingdom to a merchant who is looking for precious pearls (Matthew 13:45). Jesus doesn't compare the kingdom to fine pearls, but to the merchant's search for them. The kingdom is in the searching, not the arrival; the kingdom is in the pilgrimage, not the possession. The end is the relationship. The joy is the journey. Bailey observes:

> Popularly understood, righteousness is no more than adherence to an ethical norm . . . But if righteousness describes a relationship granted as a gift of God that brings peace, then only God can satisfy the longing . . . Each day, prompted by hunger and thirst, all people seek food and water, hoping to be satisfied. But for how long? A few hours later, the cravings return. This Beatitude makes it clear that the blessed are those whose drive for righteousness is as pervasive, all-consuming, and recurring as the daily yearning to satisfy hunger and thirst.[410]

| Chapter 10 | Time Out: Presence

The first understanding of righteousness—adherence to a set of norms and values—had been the younger Len's unrealized approach to faith in the first stage of his life. The second has been his approach ever since. The difference has been the shift from work toward a goal (adherence to a set of norms) to a relationship. Len concludes:

> In the aftermath of the "seek first" moment, I realized that I had been angry with God but not admitting it. I felt resentful, like I had been a good employee and wasn't getting compensated fairly. Those six months in Greg's townhouse were the most introspective and educational of my life. I had been hiding behind my work, thinking I was a good employee for God. While I had shown up every day to work the previous twenty years, and God has used me, I had been missing something critical to the life of faith. Faithfulness and desire are different things entirely. I learned the difference between hiding behind my works and coming out into the open and fully receiving God's love.

A surprising result of this discovery is that disciples become emboldened to speak honestly to God. Like the widow who harasses the judge in Jesus' parable, we become persistent and insistent with God because we understand our relationship to God differently (see Luke 18:1–8). The widow wouldn't give up! She kept approaching the judge's bench, praying, and seeking answers.

Contrast that with the story Jesus tells after the story of the persevering widow. It features two men, one a lowlife tax collector and the other a Pharisee who was "confident of [his] own righteousness" (v. 9 NIV). While the Pharisee humble-bragged his prayer, the tax collector said, "God, have mercy on me, a sinner" (v. 13 NIV). Jesus concludes by saying, "For all those who exalt themselves will be humbled, and those who humble themselves will be exalted" (v. 14 NIV). A humble spirit is the thumbprint of righteousness. True humility is not groveling, but gratitude.

Why did the Delphic oracle tell Plato that "Socrates is wisest"? Because Socrates admitted, "I know I know nothing." When you begin to truly know, you discover that there is so much more to know that you "know you know nothing," since the universe is so unfathomable and ungraspable. You become grateful for those who mentor your learning and keep you in service.

Perhaps the number one piece of advice in marriage seminars is that you should never stop courting your spouse. Just because you are married doesn't mean you should lie around the house and scratch away the mystery. Open the door on her side of the car after dinner at the restaurant. Go to the seminar she's teaching. Read his white paper for work. Buy surprise gifts. In good relationships, both parties never stop seeking one another. Constant courtship keeps the relationship fresh.

In the beginning, humans walked with God. But after the fruit and the fall, what happened? God sought Adam and Eve, but they hid. They didn't want to be found (see Genesis 3:8–10). Sin happens in the hiding. We don't want to be found. If we want to make our lives better, the first thing to do is to step out from behind the bushes. Stop hiding.[411] Seek God, as God seeks us. Let God see us and know us. Marvel at the ways God desires to be with us.

In the Scriptures, some of the parables talk about us seeking, as we've noted. But in the three "lost" stories of Luke's gospel (Luke 15), it is important to recognize the prime Seeker. In the first one, about the sheep, the shepherd finds the lost sheep. In the second one, the old woman finds the lost coin. In the third one, the lost younger son decides to turn home, and the father runs to him. In all three stories, God is doing most of the seeking.

This isn't a theological statement about soteriology as much as it is a simple statement of God's character. God loves us so much that God will hunt us down, run after us, turn over the entire house for us, and give us the very best to celebrate when we are found. Amid the cold and darkness of sin, God seeks us and desires that we come out of hiding and be found by the Seeker. Seeking the Seeker isn't a theological discussion about who's doing the most searching (which sounds like a zero-sum power equation), but the realization that a relationship is most alive when both are chasing each other. God never stops seeking us. Are we seeking God?

Jesus has a simple description for experiencing the kingdom: Seek it. Jesus uses *telos* to describe the widow and the judge in his story. In describing the widow's behavior, the powerful judge says, "Yet because this widow keeps bothering me, I will grant her justice, so that she may not wear me out by continually coming" (Luke 18:5). That last phrase, "continually coming," is best understood as persistence and perseverance. *Telos* is in this case an active state in which we continually seek to place ourselves in God's presence and posture ourselves to receive God's presence.

As we seek, though, we must be careful. Even our seeking can become a source of pride. And why does the fire die in the first place? What happens to Chuck Noland? After he has made fire, he jumps up, literally beats his chest, and yells, "Fire! I made fire!" Of course, Chuck didn't invent fire. Instead, through some mysterious chemical combination of elements and activity, he was able to rediscover it. Inventing and discovering are two very different things, and all creative work is *ex materia*, a derivative of existing elements.[412] Convinced he is safe, Chuck jumps and dances and sings, eats and sleeps. Once the fire is going, we get distracted by other interests and needs. Fires die because we stop tending to them.

Seeking God means we do not and cannot create the fire, but we can strive to keep lit the lamp of the Lamb. We can pass the torch, not the ash pan. Most of us become more a people of sackcloth and ashes than of Pentecostal fire and feast. Our love grows cold and calculating. Jesus promises that those who keep seeking God's presence will be saved. It is a lifetime discipline. When we let the fire die out, hypothermia sets in, and faith grows frigid. But when we persistently seek the living fire of the presence of Christ in and among us, the fire will not just ember but blaze. Living fire. Saved and secure, we flourish in the warmth of its glow. Lord, give us fire.

CHAPTER 11

PARTY TIME: JUBILEE

In chapter 2, we looked at the optimism of the modern age and asked, "Are we capable of perfecting the world?" The world seeks happiness through new technologies and the gadgets of our works, but these fade. The Jesus story begins and enjoys something that does not fade, regardless of the state of the world: joy, which so impressed J. R. R. Tolkien that he wrote about it: "The end is good and joyous. There is a wonderful epiphany at the end. The happy ending we all desire is indeed the end of our story. In life under the king, we have jubilee."[413]

*Wisdom is to know the harmony of things
and joy is to dance to its rhythm.*

—Gerard W. Hughes, God in All Things

11.1 | The End Is Jubilee

*The universe is organically resting on . . .
the future as its sole support.*

**— French Jesuit priest Pierre Teilhard de Chardin,
Activation of Energy**

The good news is that we get to witness how it all ends. We will be there for the finale of the last act of God's story. As Moses and Elijah appeared on the mountaintop with Jesus, and the resurrected bodies walked around Jerusalem, we live in The End. Longing for "the life of the world to come" is what inspires us to live for "the life of the world."

Jesus illumines us from the future. The most mind-bending and life-changing reality of *telos* is the shift of our viewpoint from the present, looking to the future, to the future, looking at the past and present. God constructs from before us, which construes what's behind us: "Your kingdom come, your will be done on earth, *as it is in heaven.*" Christianity begins with the end in heart and hand. The end blows up the world "as is" in light of the "as it is" world to come, a world where what is to come has already come in the coming of the Promised One.

And what is that future? Jesus is clear—the gospel invitation is addressed to the individual being introduced and welcomed into a community whose fulcrum and fulfillment is an End called Jubilee. Jubilee is the hope of heaven today. It is the purpose of Jesus' redemptive work and the promised party—the moment when freedom comes for all, when we finally come home, debts canceled, and suffering ceased. The kingdom is Jubilee. Jubilee is the goal and end of history, its *telos.*

If Jubilee is the goal and end of history, the Bible still insists that Jubilee, the kingdom of God, is present with us now, has been prophesied in the past, and is here now . . .was, is, is to come. God has planted the future in the present. God has embedded the End in the Beginning and the Now. That is the most teleological statement you will ever hear.

Rightly understood, the essence of Christianity is teleology. In the resurrection of Jesus, the end is not just near, but now. The end is among us, within us, around us, through us. Jubilee is an event, and Jesus is the presence of that event, the completion of all events, even of history itself. The follower of Jesus begins with the end, the invasion of earth by heaven, a kingdom of the future ("as it is in heaven"), planted into the present ("your kingdom come on earth").[414] Faith is not the working toward some "end" from the practices and premises of the "present." Faith begins with the End, an arrival that determines the practices and premises of the present.

Jesus is Jubilee, and the church is the presence of Jesus as Jubilee joy in the here and now. Jesus began his mission with a teleological declaration and a teleological meal. The five-point declaration came when

> the scroll of the prophet Isaiah was handed to Him. Unrolling it, he found the place where it was written:
>
> The Spirit of the Lord is on Me,
>
>> because He has anointed Me
>
>> to preach good news to the poor.
>
> He has sent Me to proclaim deliverance to the captives
>
>> and recovery of sight to the blind,
>
> to release the oppressed,
>
>> to proclaim the year of the Lord's favor. (Luke 4:17–19)

That final phrase, "to proclaim the year of the Lord's favor," was a teleological moniker pointing to The End reign of God.

British New Testament scholar James D. G. Dunn sees Jesus' use of the term "Son of Man" as a teleological one, an implicit referring to the powerful figure in the vision of Daniel 7:13: "there before me was one like a son of man, coming with the clouds of heaven" (NIV).

Numbers in the Bible have semiotic and theological significance. Beginning in Genesis we learn that the number seven conveyed a sense of "fullness/completeness" and is even spelled with the same consonants as the word "complete/full." The Second Testament continues this identification of seven with perfection and adds to it the symbolism of the unity of the four corners of the earth with the holy Trinity. The number seven is also featured in the book of Revelation (seven churches, seven angels, seven seals, seven trumpets, and seven stars).[415]

Fifty was the year of Jubilee because when perfection is squared (7×7) you get 49. Just as the eighth day of creation is a symbol of a new creation (which is why Christians worship not on the seventh or sabbath day but on the seventh plus one, or eighth day), so 49 + 1 is the symbol of a new beginning for the whole earth. Even though Jubilee was never actually celebrated as a festival in Hebrew history (as far as we know, there was no set jubilee date on which slaves were set free, debts were canceled, fields lay fallow, prisons were emptied, sick were healed, and relationships restored), it was kept alive as a hope and dream for God's people. The expectation of an anointed one who would come and inaugurate jubilee was especially strong in the post-exilic period.[416] The year of Jubilee was also pregnant with meaning because few people lived beyond their fiftieth birthdays. The cultural hysteria of New Year's Day, an arbitrary date and an arbitrary time set on a man-made calendar system, was nothing compared to a "New Age" day of Jubilee, when the ram's horn is blown (hence "Jubal") and every iota of the whole universe would witness and celebrate ontological change.

In other words, Jubilee is the fulfillment of Jesus' five-point mission, which he outlined in his first sermon. The beginning of Jesus' mission declared the ending of Jesus' mission, the Year of Jubilee.

As we noted in the prologue. Jesus also began his ministry with a teleological meal. His mission with the Twelve was framed with such meals. Jesus began his mission with the Twelve by conducting his first miracle, a hospitality of a feast. In Cana of Galilee, in one act and one word, Jesus removed the ceremonial legal washing water with the wine of Jubilee.

Jesus ended his mission with the Twelve by presiding at the Last Supper and offering the hospitality of a feast. During that dinner, Jesus took a loaf and said, "This is my body," then after supper took the cup and said, "This is my blood" (Luke 22:19–20). In the sobremesa part of the Last Supper, he passed on the mantle to his disciples: "I confer on you a kingdom . . . so that you may eat and drink at my table in my kingdom" (vv. 29–30 NIV). Then there was singing and dancing and, ultimately, they proceeded out to the Garden of Gethsemane.

Borrowing again from the prologue, Jubilee is a time of feasting and drinking at heaven's banquet table (see again Isaiah 25:6–8 and Revelation 19:9). Every meal is a festivity of the future and an incorporation of The End into the Here and Now. Meals are a symbol of belonging, and Jesus' meals are a teleological symbol of a life of Jubilee.

The first miracle and the Last Supper are earnests of The End. The marriage banquet at the start and the marriage of the Passover Lamb at the end, are foretastes of the future, when Jesus returns to the Table. "For whenever you eat this bread and drink this cup, you proclaim the Lord's death until he comes" (1 Corinthians 11:26 NIV). The Greek basis for "until" is unusual: "*achri bou*" means grammatically keeping an end in mind. At the moment of the church's highest "remembrance" of the past is also its moment of greatest focus on the future. This is why the Aramaic prayer "*Maran atha*" was connected to the eucharist by the church's earliest believers.[417] It may also be why Paul's first letter to the church at Corinth ends with "Maranatha." It was, as we discussed at the beginning of this book, a segue to the fellowship meal that would have followed the oral reading of Paul's letter.[418]

11.2 | The End Is Rapturous Joy

Jubilee may be interpreted through a lens of equity. But its scope is bigger. The end game of all economic systems is increased inequality and ultimate destruction of everyone, both the haves and the have nots. Inequality isn't just bad for the powerless, but for everyone. This gets lost in the current focus on grievance. Jubilee isn't an individualistic practice to grant appropriate rights to individuals, as is often positioned in social justice hermeneutics, which retains a power paradigm, but a system of redemption necessary for the flourishing of humanity and to counter the destructive effects of a transactional view of relationships. The jubilee end isn't just fair distribution of wealth; it is joy.

A few years ago, a well-intentioned book came out with the title *Unraptured: How End Times Theology Gets It Wrong* (2019). Our mission is not to "Unrapture" the church but to truly "Rapture" the world with the love of Jesus. Not rapture us *out of* the world, but rapture us *into* the world. People are not hungry for beliefs or things, but for the rapture of ravishment, or more precisely, the rapture of being alive in Christ. Both Joseph Campbell and Abraham Maslow talked about "moments of rapture" as the end of human yearnings, which cannot be quenched until "visions of rapture now burst on my sight."[419]

The only true, beautiful, and good "rapture" of being alive is in Jubilee Jesus. Without this teleological focus, Dallas Willard was right when he said that the gospel of Christ as commonly understood does not fill the emptiness of the human soul, does not meet the need. When the rhythm of our relationship with God gets surprisingly ramped up and raptured, that's called joy. That ramping can either be an acceleration or a deceleration, an "all in" or a "time-out."

> *Sing, ye islands of the sea,*
> *echo back, ye ocean's caves;*
> *earth shall keep her Jubilee:*
> *Jesus saves! Jesus saves!*
>
> **—Priscilla Jane Owens (1829–1907),**
> **"We Have Heard the Joyful Sound"**

One of the common complaints against the church is hypocrisy, the persistence of brokenness and sin amid the gospel promise of healing and wholeness. Didn't Jesus consistently call out as hypocrites those teachers of Mosaic law who didn't practice what they preached?[420] In fact, Jesus, in whom there was not a hint or glint of hypocrisy or guile, may just have coined the term "hypocrite." Jesus seems to be the first to take the Greek actors who performed at outdoor theaters, wearing a variety of faces, and use them to describe people who pretend to be something they are not, or who put on faces to make a good impression: sinners masquerading as saints.

> *Hypocrisy is the most difficult and nerve-racking vicar any man can pursue: it needs an unceasing vigilance and a rare detachment of spirit. It cannot, like adultery, or gluttony, be practiced at spare moments; it is a full-time job.*
>
> **—English novelist Somerset Maugham (1874–1965)**

If *telos* is a state of being in which we experience the fullness of Christ's love with one another in community, why does it seem to come and go, at best? How then are we to understand our current state of incompletion?

Paul acknowledges the imperfections of the world and the faith community at the end of his first letter to the church at Corinth:

> For as in Adam all die, so in Christ all will be made alive. But each in turn: Christ, the firstfruits; then, when he comes, those who belong to him. Then the end [*telos*] will come, when he hands over the kingdom to God the Father after he has destroyed all dominion, authority, and power. For he must reign until he has put all his enemies under his feet. The last enemy to be destroyed is death. For "he has put everything under his feet." (1 Corinthians 15:22–27 NIV)

In his teaching moment on Tuesday of his end week, Jesus returned to this idea: "You will hear of wars and rumors of wars but see to it that you are not alarmed. Such things must happen, but [*telos*] is still to come" (Matthew 24:6 NIV).

Then, "because of the increase of wickedness, the love of most will grow cold, but the one who stands firm to [*telos*] will be saved" (vv. 12–13 NIV).

Finally, "this gospel of the kingdom will be preached in the whole world as a testimony to all nations, and then [*telos*] will come" (v. 14 NIV).

This isn't easy, Jesus says. But *telos* will prevail. In other words, the story is unresolved. Jesus is still destroying death, and new life is being born. The word Jesus uses is "renewal", or *paliggenesia*: *palig* (again) plus *genesis* (birth or beginning). A new birth; another beginning.

Jesus' image of birth helps us to understand how the kingdom can co-exist with sin today. A birth isn't a singular event, but the culmination of a long period of gestation, which ends with an intense period of transition from one reality (the womb) to another (open air). As newborn babies, we must literally learn how to breathe and live in an entirely different world.

We await the future as we live with Jesus in the present and Jesus finishes the job for which he came. Teleology says we get to see how it all ends; the reality not just the promise. We will be there! We get to be a part of the end of God's story. We will be there for the finale of the last act, a last act which in some sense has already been accomplished through Jesus' death and resurrection.

While this love story remains unresolved, we have opportunities for *telos* now, through something quite simple: joy. As Jesus taught his disciples, "No one will take your joy from you" (John 16:22). Let no one take your joy from you. Christianity is divided between the conservatives (longing for a bygone religion of law and recompense) and the progressives (serving bespoke ambitions and untethered dreams on earth). Both groups seem to despise nothing so much as a call to joy, as the reminding of a great joy announced and given at the beginning of the gospel, which is the life of faith.

As the apostle Paul puts it in his "Letter of Joy": "Rejoice in the Lord always: and again I say, Rejoice" (Philippians 4:4 KJV). Or in the words of Orthodox theologian Alexander Schmemann (1921–83), "Some say, 'How can one rejoice when millions are suffering? One must serve the world.' Others say, 'How can one rejoice in a world lying in evil?' If only they could understand for just one minute (that lasts secretly and hidden in the saints) the fact that the Church has overcome the world, the victory was won through Joy and Happiness."[421]

God has planted the future in the present. God has embedded the End in the Beginning and the Now. It is not the prophet's task to get the future right. It is the prophet's task to right the present by calling forth the future, which God has planted as plumblines in the present. Jesus comes to us from the future and pulls us forward. Jesus is the real inventor of futurology, even though the German political scientist Ossip K. Flechtheim (1909–1998) coined the term. Jesus is always ahead of his disciples. He pulls us toward him more than pushes us from behind. To study Jesus is to study the future.

A truly biblical, truly Christ-centered view of the end times can be the very thing that rescues Christianity and helps us rediscover our first love. After all, Christianity itself was born in the fires of apocalyptic fervor. The early church and the writers of the New Testament believed fervently that they were living in the last days. If we see the last days not as a dark moment of fear and dread but as a moment of hope that was inaugurated with the resurrection of Jesus, then the end times become what the church originally understood them to be: a time of radical transfiguration, when the promises of God are made manifest in the here and now as the kingdom of God comes to earth as it is in heaven.

We live in the last days because on Easter morning, Jesus walked out of the tomb as the firstfruits, or beginning of a new way of life. With Christ's resurrection, the old order of things began to pass away as all things are being made new, not just in some distant future, but here. Now.[422]

Joy is not one feature of the life of faith. It is the totality and tonality of faith. Joy is the bona fide sign of the Spirit, the mark of the Christ. Without joy, there is no presence of the divine. Where there is no joy, there is no Jesus, and the church becomes torment and dejection. The mark of the beast (Revelation 3:16) is the sign of the Antichrist, symbol of opposition to Christ. Might there be a contrasting symbol, an opposite sign of the presence of Christ, and a teleological marker of being Jesus follower? The contrasting mark of the beast is the Mark of the Feast: The Mark of the Feast of the Kingdom of God, the Messianic Banquet of Heaven, the Jubilee.

When will the church recover its joy? "Rejoice," a chained Paul insisted from the pits of a prison, "and again I say, Rejoice!" It is a joy that Jesus said no one can take away from you (John 16:22).

Christianity is itself so jolly a thing that it fills the possessor of it with a certain silly exuberance, which sad and high-minded Rationalists might reasonably mistake for mere buffoonery and blasphemy; just as their prototypes, the sad and high-minded Stoics of old Rome, did mistake the Christian joyousness for buffoonery and blasphemy.

—English theologian and "Prince of Paradox" G. K. Chesterton (1874–1936), "Christianity and Rationality"

The Ezra principle is fundamental: "The joy of the LORD is your strength" (Nehemiah 8:10). How can you be in a relationship with God and not be joyful? How can Jesus be present and not evoke a transcendental joy? How can you experience the Spirit in your life and not rejoice? To be joyless is to be graceless and powerless. The power of life is in joy. When faith becomes joyless, it is without grace or power. It is weak and whitened. This is the kind of sickly religion that makes one sick. Inability to rejoice is a heart disease, a "hardening of the heart" ("their hearts were hardened," Mark 6:52). Even after the miracle of the loaves and fishes, the disciples didn't get it. When stuck in a storm, they let their joy be stolen from them. Their "hearts were hardened."

Music is what can kiss the whole world, and when the music is about Joy, it's a smacker that shakes the world. As the chorus sings in Beethoven's final (Ninth) Symphony (1824), "This kiss [is] for the whole world." This is widely conceived to be one of the greatest musical compositions in the history of the world, including the famous "Ode to Joy."[423]

"Be embraced, ye millions!
This kiss is for the whole world!
Brothers, above the arch of stars
A loving Father surely dwells."[424]

"Ode to Joy" is the symphony of Jubilee! A hallmark and homiletic of joy is born into the very word Jubilee.

11.3 | The End Is Our Beginning

The distinction between the past, present, and future is only a stubbornly persistent illusion.

—Albert Einstein

The End is our Beginning. That is the paradox of the Christian life. Christianity is a faith in which you can't find yourself unless you lose yourself. You find your life by losing your self-centeredness and seeing yourself in the light and life of the Christ who saves and heals. The world believes that you save and heal yourself, first by putting yourself number one, then by searching yourself, understanding yourself, and esteeming yourself.

Where there is no paradox, there is no true Christianity. There are always two poles for the Christian universe: "For God so loved the world . . ." (John 3:16) and "Love not the world, nor what is in the world" (see 1 John 2:15–17). One pole without the other is a dead-end defection from the faith. "Love of this world" without "leave the world behind" is apostasy. "Hate the world" without "God so loved the world" is apostasy. Heresy is a cross uncrossed.

This is why labels are so libelous and hurtful in Christian circles. They tamp down living with contradictions; they deny the holding of opposites together; they make it difficult to comprehend than no one is only one thing. They deny the cognitive dissonance of opposites.

The teleological heart of the Christian faith is its union of the transcendent and the immanent, the otherworldly and the this-worldly. Any rift between them, any loss of telic dimension, and Christianity self-destructs. The paradox is that when Christianity ceases being teleological, the world steps in to become teleological.

Now you know the title of the book that will be a follow-up to this one: The Beginning.

| CHAPTER 12 |
TIME BEING:
AUTHORSHIP

What do we do for the time being?

In our first chapter, we asked, Given the state of affairs today, is the world going to be destroyed? As we discussed, this ultimate question is a question of story, which is more than a matter of curiosity. Our story is our guide: where we think we are going in life determines the actions we take today.

In Jesus, we have confidence that the answer lies in the end, and that the end is good—it is comedy, not tragedy—because Jesus has been given all authority on heaven and on earth.

We cannot make the kingdom any more than we can dictate the future. Rather, we await the future, living with Jesus in the present while Jesus finishes the job for which he came. In the time being, we look to Jesus as author and finisher of our faith. In God's kingdom, when we submit to the authority of the risen Lord, we allow Jesus to author our life story. The result is the release of all of us held in captivity and the renewal of all creation.

12.1 | Release and Renewal

Much of the conventional teaching about the end of the world comes from the last book of the Bible: The Revelation of St. John the Divine. Before the book of Revelation, however, there was Jesus' response to questions from the disciples about the end of the age. In his answer, he predicted the destruction of the temple: "Then he asked them, "You see all these, do you not? Truly I tell you, not one stone will be left here upon another; all will be thrown down" (Matthew 24:2).[425]

It is hard to fathom the magnitude of his statement or perhaps the satisfaction of some of his listeners. The temple, which was actually the rebuilt temple, was the largest building most of Jesus' listeners had ever seen. King Herod had commissioned a massive expansion, which doubled its size. It had been completed when Jesus and his contemporaries were children. Though Roman residential apartment buildings stood several stories tall in the city, nothing else that large existed within the province of Judea.[426] It was over 1.5 million square feet, or about the size of an average American pro football stadium today.

The prediction from their teacher that the temple would be "thrown down" was disturbing to say the least. The key to Jesus' statement lies in understanding what sort of destruction he was predicting. Conventional Christian wisdom regarding apocalyptic destruction is perhaps most strongly associated with *apollumi*, meaning total destruction, annihilation, and ruin. In John's gospel, Jesus describes the work of Satan as *apollumi*, a "thief who comes to kill and destroy." It means to perish utterly and completely, to die with an expectation of complete ruin, to come to a miserable end—to be canceled.

In reference to the temple being "thrown down," though, Jesus used a different word—*kataluó*, a compound word with both literal and metaphorical meaning. *Kata* is a reference to motion, of something coming from a high place to a lower place. *Luó* is a reference to release or unbinding. It could mean to overthrow something, a form of catastrophe, but a form with a different ending—akin to loosening or unyoking an animal, releasing it from its cage. Elsewhere, including the announcement of his ministry in Luke 4 (which we already addressed), Jesus spoke of loosening what is bound on earth, suggesting that the end he was referring to is not an age of destruction but an age of power previously bound, a catharsis of release that precipitates renewal. Jesus said, "Do not think that I have come to abolish [*kataluó*] the Law or the Prophets; I have not come to abolish them but to fulfill them" (Matthew 5:17 NIV).

While *apollumi* is frequently used to describe the literal killing of people, *kataluó* is more akin to deconstruction than destruction. Think the iconoclasm of the Reformers here—a loosening and release of old restrictive systems that precipitates renewal. It is the same word used as testimony against Jesus as he stood before the Sanhedrin (Matthew 26:61). Like so much of Jesus' teaching, his word choice is a metaphor, inviting comparison between a physical destruction of the building and a metaphorical release of its bound contents. Jesus was saying that the temple contains something valuable and good, which has been held back and is about to be released.

The word *apocalypse* refers to a revelation, or an unveiling. A scholarly definition of the word *apocalypse* is that it is "a genre of revelatory literature with a narrative framework, in which a revelation is mediated by an otherworldly being to a human recipient, disclosing a transcendent reality which is both temporal, insofar as it envisages eschatological salvation, and spatial insofar as it involves another, supernatural world."[427] In other words, the apocalypse is the moment when God reveals a new transcendent reality (a "kingdom") that exists in both time and space. (This is distinct from *eschatology*, the study of the narrative end of the world, and a forecast of rewards and punishments.)

Instead of a literal prediction about the future destruction of the temple, Jesus was making a statement about the release and renewal of a bound-up relationship between God and humankind, a tearing of the curtain to come. He distinguished between destruction and deconstruction. Destruction is the result of our own hubris, but in God's good hands, apocalypticism means revelation, not destruction, and periods of human suffering open windows of God's kingdom.

Thus "the end of days," as it is commonly understood, is not about explosions, but about the release of God's power on the world and the renewal of all creation. Whether or not Jesus' disciples understood him is unclear. But, being guys, talk about explosions piqued their interest. They asked, "When will this happen, and what will be the sign of your coming and of the end of the age?" (Matthew 24:3). In response, Jesus gives a heavy speech on wars, wickedness, persecution, and death—an apocalypse lover's dream scene. He concludes with a promise: those who endure to the end will be saved (v. 13). Throughout, Jesus is clear that destruction is a not a sign of God's kingdom. While forces of de-civilization are real, they are not signs of the impending reign of Jesus. Rather, in God's creative hands they become means by which God's kingdom is revealed.

Further, periods of suffering may feel like the work of a wrathful God, but in response to a question in a separate conversation about a regional disaster, the collapse of the Tower of Siloam, Jesus was clear that suffering is a consequence of human sin, not punishment of sin by a wrathful God (Luke 13:1–5).

The best answer is the simplest. Human populations increase and societies flourish. Resources can't keep up, and humans sin against themselves, against one another, against creation, and against God. Another way of understanding the Malthusian premise is that when resources become too consolidated and inaccessible, corrections inexorably occur. The worst of human nature emerges. Rather than tend and till and make greater things, people hunt and hoard and fight over a scarcity of resources. Societies suffer as the story of Babel is played out over and over in the hearts of human beings. We become prisoners of our prosperity, occupants on a revolutionary road, having believed our own press clippings and ignored the imperfections of the tiny empires and kiddie kingdoms we have wrought.

Yet, though tough times are the inevitable result of human activity, in every case, life carries on. After the flood, God promised to never again destroy the world. Jesus says the present age ends not with destruction but when everyone has heard the gospel (Matthew 24:14). The idea that God will destroy the existed order to create a new one is poor theology. Satan destroys, but Jesus saves (see John 10:10). When apocalyptic conditions emerge and reemerge in overwrought societies throughout history, God intervenes to save our perpetual tendency to destroy ourselves.

In God's good hands, periods of human suffering serve as a new unveiling of God's kingdom. As the saying goes, it is when the chips are down that you know who your friends are. When things fall apart, the kingdom of God is revealed, as God saves us from the iniquity of the world. Apocalyptic, revelatory moments relieve the tension and stress of human sin.

Rather than authoring destruction, Jesus authors release and renewal. The invitation for us is to let him do this work in our hearts, lives, and communities.

12.2 | Letting Jesus Author Our Lives

"**A**uthority" is a derivation of the word "author." Each one of us is a story, wrapped in skin. And the question for each person is, who is going to author our story? When we surrender not to one another or unseen political forces but to Jesus as our authority, Jesus will rewrite our life story. The challenge for the Christian will be to rediscover the authority of Jesus buried under the ruins of centuries of syncretized Christian theology. The core of this book is not about what happens in the future, but about rediscovering the authority of Jesus. Only when we know the one true authority of our lives are we ready to let the future be authored.

Two of the most famous phrases and metaphors in English literature— "for whom the bell tolls" and "no man is an island"—come from the same sermon, "Meditation 17" by John Donne (1572–1631).[428] But the climax of the very first paragraph is a metaphor that is worthy of being equally as well known as the "bell" and "island" metaphors: "All mankind is of one author, and is one volume; when one man dies, one chapter is not torn out of the book, but translated into a better language; and every chapter must be so translated."[429] Donne's metaphor of "author" and of our need to live every day as a page-turner in the Book of Life, with no page or story ("chapter") ever ripped out, is one we have taken to heart and developed in this book.

The future begins when we cease our rebellion and surrender to the authority of Jesus. Whoever you choose to author your life story is your authority for life. The person that we let author our story is our authority. Some of us say, "I am going to author my own story." Okay. Then you must realize you are choosing to be your own authority. Some of us elect to have brands author our story. In a celebrity culture, this often translates to entertainers, moguls, and magnates, or to corporations who can craft the most compelling commercial. Self-authority leads us in wayward directions. Jesus' authority leads us into the presence of God.

The question, who authors my life story? is a question of identity. The messages the culture sends us today are mixed and confusing:

You are who you are—you're born that way!

You are never going to be what you want to be—you're hopeless!

You are whomever you want to be—you're a blank slate!

No wonder so many of us are in therapy. We sometimes hear people change the basis of their own story in the same sentence.

In claiming, "I am the way, the truth, and the life," Jesus was saying that the only person anyone should authorize to author your story is the Alpha and Omega. Luke calls Jesus the Author of life (3:15); Hebrews calls him the author and finisher of our faith (12:2). Along with titles like King of kings, Lord of lords, Light of the World, and Bread of Life, another title for Jesus is Author of Life. There is only one source we trust to "author" our story—not Nike, not Netflix, not Rihanna, not the Rock, not science, not politics, and not politicians . . . only Jesus. Every story has an author. The only authority you can trust enough to author your life story is Jesus. Jesus is our true and ultimate authority.

Our identity is neither a blank slate on which we compose our feelings of the day, nor fixed by the sins of our past. Our identity is found not in race or gender or politics or class but in Christ. It is written by Jesus when we become part of the new creation: "If any man be in Christ, he is a new creature: old things are passed away; behold, all things are become new" (2 Corinthians 5:17 KJV). Authority is found only in the Jesus revealed in the Scriptures and in-spirited in us by the Holy Spirit. Not found in the community, economics, science. Nor in the past or the future. Nor in politics or philosophy. Nor in the self. Nor in power, celebrity, or brand. God can be found in all these things—in the past, the future, economics, self, even in politics. But the authority for meaning is only found in Jesus. Anamorphosis is a word that describes how an image or picture is distorted and warped until that one vantage point is found from which all relations fall into place and the image becomes meaningful. The moment that point of view is found, the significance of the projection is apparent. Jesus must be for us that one vantage point and pivotal position. Meaning in life is found in the Lord of Life: Jubilee Jesus.

Matthew 28:18 is one of the most pivotal passages in all of Scripture: All authority has been given on heaven and earth to me. This is the authority under which we go as followers of Jesus. The question of authority is also a question of agency. In Matthew 10, Jesus gives authority to the disciples. No one knows God except Jesus and those to whom Jesus reveals God. Our authority is a commissioning authority from Jesus. When we allow Jesus to author our lives, we are sent into the world to personate Jesus.

The Latin root of authority is *augeo*, which means, to increase or grow. Any authority in your life that doesn't help you to increase, or grow, or become more of who you are, is a false idol and a false authority. The authorship of your story belongs to the one who created you, who loves you into being, and who stays with you in your becoming. That is God. The more your Creator authors your creation, the more original, unique, and exciting your life story becomes.

Identity requires narrative form, but our stories are losing their narrative significance and becoming commodified and commercialized. Indeed, in a world where every commercial is inviting us to trust our lives to this story or that story, the only story worth trusting your life to and turning your life into is the Jesus Story. Our deepest and truest identity comes, not from what we buy, or what we feel, or where we come from, but from whom we love.

Behind the issue of authority is the question of power. Columnist Natasha Lennard's first collection of essays, *Being Numerous: Essays on the Non-Fascist Life* (2019) argues that "fascistic desire" which "craves authority" and wants to "dominate, oppress and obliterate" difference is widespread across society and exists, to a greater or lesser extent, in everyone. It crops up among conservatives and liberals alike and needs to be checked and called into question. We will do everything in our power to get more power and bring down everyone who has more power than we do. We must reframe this innate human quest for power in terms of gospel power. When you think of divine power and omnipotence, what are you thinking of? You better be thinking about the power and powerlessness of love. Suffering love, sacrificial love. The cross does not define God in terms of power but in terms of love. And a specific kind of love at that: "No greater love . . ." (John 15:13 NLT).

We must give each other permission to be powerful—but not wielding the power of the world that is found in success, but the power that is found in service, the power of forgiveness, grace, and love. Look for the uniforms of the powerful, not the medals and trophies, Teslas, and Tiffany's, but look for the towels and trowels, aprons, and shawls.

Identity is the wellspring of well-being. We have made identity one of the most taxing tasks conceivable by expecting our children to invent their own identities, to make them up from scratch, out of random cloth. The "Jesus human" finds his or her identity in Jesus our Christ, our authority for life and author of our story for life.

"But what about you?" Jesus asked. "Who do you say that I am?" (Matthew 16:15).

How each of us answers that question— "Whom do you pronounce me to be?"—determines who we are. Who you are is not what you do. Who you are is not what you say or even what you believe. Who you are is whose you are. We each get to decide what kind of man or woman we are. Or as Ray Charles would put it, "What kind of man are you?"[430] Some of us are company men, or family men, or sports men, or Mustang men, or a twelfth man—all these identities are available and popular. Whose man or woman are you? We are Jesus men and women. We are Jesus humans.

A few years ago, British American writer Simon Sinek took over the corporate world with his simple observation that the very best companies have a clear vision driving their daily decisions and activities. He called it "The Why."[431] It was nothing more than a reframing and popularizing of the concept of a brand statement in clear, layman's terms. The brand statement, or "The Why," is the statement of purpose and being for a company. Another way of understanding it is that it is the decision-making statement. When two executives are at odds over the direction of a company or a frontline manager needs help in supervising a new employee, the "Why" statement clarifies values and provides direction for the next chapter or activity in the company's story. "The Why" became such a popular idea that it captured the zeitgeist for a hot minute before COVID-19.

In Auschwitz, the largest of the Nazi extermination centers, a *kapo* was a Jewish prisoner forced by the SS to act as a guard, supervising forced labor on behalf of the Nazis. Primo Levi recalled that the first thing a *kapo* said to him when he was put into the concentration camp at Auschwitz was "*Hier ist kein warum.*" In English, "There is no why here."[432]

For us, The Why is The Way. If you allow Jesus to be the author and finisher of your faith, the why is found in Golgotha, the what is found on the mount of beatitudes, the when is found in the garden tomb, the where is found in the temple in Jerusalem at Pentecost, and the Who is found in Bethlehem, the same Who, who wants to be born again in you, so that you can bring others into the Why of Christ.

Even at our best, our being best and or best being, each one of us has a lot of room to *augero*, to grow and mature. Each of us is a bundle of has-beens, not quites, never wases, wannabes. The great I AM judges us not as "I am who I was" or "I am who I want to be" but "I am who I will be under the authority and authorship of Jesus the Christ." When you allow Jesus to author your life, you will become a new creation. Consider the transfigurations that happen through Scripture when people submit to the authority of the Lord.

Moses said when God called him, "No way, Yahweh! Send someone else." But No-Way Yahweh became Moses the lawgiver, one of the greatest leaders in the history of the world.

Gideon said, "Forget it, unless you send me better brothers, I'm not doing anything!" But Gideon the Timid became the Gideon the greatest judge of all of Israel.

Jonah said, "I'm out of here!" But Jonah the Runaway, who got angry when God did what God said he would do, became Jonah the Dove, the prophet of resurrection.

Isaiah said, "I can't do it because I have a swearing problem," but Isaiah the crude and uncouth became the Isaiah the writer, who used epigrams, metaphors, hyperboles, paradoxes, stories, and dialogue to compose arguably the greatest masterpiece in Hebrew literature.

Jeremiah said, "I can't do it because I'm too young and immature," but Jeremiah the Weeper became Jeremiah the Deeper prophet who inspired us to issue jeremiads, warnings, and calls to repentance.

Ezekiel just hid. He fell on his face in silence until God said, "Stand up and act like a man!" Then Ezekiel the Hider became Ezekiel the Comforter

| Chapter 12 | Time Being: Authorship

and Consoler of his people, who lifted high the promise of an end to exile and a return to the homeland.

Zechariah said, "I hear ya, God, but what you're saying you're going to do with me and Elizabeth is biologically impossible." But Zechariah the Impotent became Zechariah the father of the most important biblical figure outside of Jesus, John the Baptist.

Peter said, "I'm too unsanctified to do what you're calling me to do." But Peter the Leaden and Artless became Petra the Lead Apostle, the very rock on which the church was founded.

Thomas said, "Seeing is believing." But Doubting Thomas the Skeptic became Thomas the True Believer and Evangelist of India, where there's a thriving community today, the Malankara Church, which arose from the mission of doubting Thomas.

Ananias said, "You've got to be kidding! You want me to help the very person sent here to kill me and kill other Jews?" But Ananias the Hesitant became the Ananias the healer of Saul and the baptizer of Paul, the greatest missionary in the history of the church.

Timothy said, "I'm not smart enough," but Timothy the Obtuse became Timothy the apprentice of Paul, the church's greatest theologian, and eventually the bishop of Ephesus.

What happens when you allow the author of your life to be Jesus, and let him be the authority for your living? "All authority in heaven and on earth has been given to me" (Matthew 28:18). That's more than enough authority for us to go and invite others to let their stories be authored by the true author and finisher of life, of faith, of all of existence. Life is not an end in itself. Life is an end in Himself.

Life is not a means to an end, or an end in itself. Life is an end in Himself.

12.3 | The End of the Story

There is one word that takes you on a magic carpet ride throughout the whole galaxy of the gospel. It is the word that lies behind, opens up, and takes forward every other word of the Bible, all 783,137 of them as contained in 1,189 chapters. What is the word that is so deep it would take every other word in the Bible to explain it? A word so profound you can't get over it and you can't get around it? A word that stands as the greatest word Jesus ever spoke.

It is the shortest word spoken on the cross, but also the longest word in meaning and message. It was the last word Jesus spoke, but at its utterance the earth shook, the heavens thundered, the veil of the temple was sundered, and the seraphim lay down their flaming swords, the very cherubim that had guarded the garden and kept humans away from the breathings of the Tree of Life. We know it as "finished." It is actually

Tetelestai.

> *The greatest word from the greatest man on the greatest day in all eternity! One word, but no word ever uttered has so changed the history and destiny of mankind.*
>
> **—Gahanian biblical scholars Jonathan E. T. Kuwormu-Adjaottor and Patrick Yankyera**[433]

Tetelestai is the perfect tense of the verb *teleo*, which comes from the Greek noun *telos*. The aorist tense means that something has been "dead and buried," as we like to say. It is done and gone and will never rear its face again. The perfect tense is used to describe something that has been done but is not gone. It is still doing and will keep going on doing. There is a consummation, but the consummate culmination is a continuation that is ongoing without anything more needing to be added.

The kingdom is not unfinished. God sent Jesus to "finish the works" (John 5:36), and he did. Jesus cried from the cross not "*I* am finished" but "It is finished" (John 19:30). The government is on *his* shoulders, not our own, and not even us as his representatives. Either of these interpretations convince us that it's up to us, and we put ourselves in the driver's seat. We start making decisions based on our understanding of what we think Jesus would do. This has never ended well. Without Jesus, we remain in one time and one reality only, unaware of the kainos space and the kairos time of God's kingdom. The only other understanding is one that requires us to have a multi-dimensional understanding of time. It is one in which Jesus says, "it is finished."

Tetelestai was also the word the high priest used to announce that "the sacrifice is accomplished." Every Jewish person there at Golgatha would have instantly recognized this word as the equivalent of a Hebrew phrase used in the Old Testament sacrificial system. Jesus transfigured the rich heritage of the Jewish people with new meaning.

> Out of *tetelestai* we can celebrate the joy of knowing that Jesus has overcome the world.

> Out of *tetelestai* we can release our obsessions with distant diatribes and partisan polemics and relax in the rhythms of local relationships.

> Out of *tetelestai* we can give grace and encouragement and be set free from the temptation to offer opinions on every issue du jour.

> Out of *tetelestai* we can live abundantly in the present and courageously and cheerfully face the future.

> Out of *tetelestai* we can enjoy the surest evidence of lived faith with one another, which is not philosophical fashion but fruits of the Spirit.

The cry of "*Tetelestai*" was as much a victory cry as the word *euangelion* was a battle cry announcing the "good news" of a victory won. Early Christians picked up the word *euangelion* from the culture to describe the "good news" of *tetelestai*.

Much like the Aramaic word *maranatha*, *Tetelestai* celebrates a completed past that is never past but comes to pass in the present and passes through every present that has a future. "It is finished" means it was finished, stands finished, but is still finishing its finis. In that finish we rest and take our confidence.

In Jesus, we know the end, and the end is good.

OVERTIME: SIGNS OF THE TIMES

What are the signs of the end and how do we see them?

We close with the question of how to read the signs of the future. The future is obvious for those who have ears to ear: for those who can read the signs. Pentecost is as much about the "gift of ears" as the "gift of tongues."

As we consider the end, we return to the disciples' question, posed at the outset of this book: What signs of the end exist today, and how do we learn to hear and see them? Signs are communication, not prediction. Though they may offer clues about the future, they are primarily about an emerging present. To understand the end, we need to understand signs for what they are.

As we've established, "the end" is *telos*. What, then, are signs of *telos*?

Two of the most ignored holy days of the church, Holy Saturday and Ascension Day, are some of the most teleologically trenchant and tense in the liturgical calendar. Jesus did not rocket to heaven from the launchpad of a cloud, escaping earth's orbit. On the cloud of a prospective future, he is entering the Father's glory, after prepping the earth to receive the glory of eternity: "All the earth shall be filled with the glory of the LORD" (Numbers 14:21).

For the early church, Ascension was an orienting summons to turn around and face the future. The word *orientation* means something different today from what it meant in the early church. To prepare for the nativity of Jesus, beginning on December 17 and concluding Christmas Eve, a series of seven "O" antiphons have been sung by the church since the eighth century. Each is based on an image from the prophet Isaiah that prepares us for the nativity of Christ. The "O" antiphons were originally sung before and after the Magnificat at Vespers. The fifth "O" antiphon was "O Oriens," which invokes Christ as the "Oriens," the Morning Star, the Dayspring that comes in the East.

The early Christians expected his second coming, too, from the East. This is why churches architecturally turned their churches to face the East and why Christians in prayer turned their bodies to face the East. The Ascension orients us properly to the purpose and end of history, the fulfillment of the universe in the coming of Christ and the direction of creation toward its Creator. Instead of pointing fingers at each other, the Ascension reminds us to point our fingers heavenward with a teleological imperative that sets our hearts on fire, inspiring them to perceive Christ's Ascension, not as a barrier, but as an opened door by which eternity and time meet in a burning, infinitely desirable embrace.

Most often Jesus ascends with his right hand in blessing, an erect posture as he presides over the cosmos. In the Rabbula Evangeliary, a rare sixth-century Syriac manuscript known for its depiction of the Ascension, Jesus is blessing with his right hand, but his left hand is propping up the unhinged door of hell. This symbolic gesture of Jesus is pointing to the harrowing of hell, the second half of what the Apostles' Creed refers to when it says, "He descended into hell . . . He ascended into heaven."[434]

Holy Saturday is a day when everything is going on *in* the earth, the harrowing of hell, while on an unknowing, unwitting, mind-blown earth, it seems nothing is going on. At the gates of hell, Jesus prophesied the founding of his church with Peter (Matthew 16:17–18) and dedicates the church to busting hell's gates. The first place the risen body of Christ goes is to bust the gates of hell and liberate its captives.

Harrowing means to "break up the clods, smooth out the soil, clean out the weeds, cover the seeds." The harrowing of hell is a teleological hallowing of heaven, as the very earth is being sown and seeded with the future, those resurrection energies that constitute the coming Eden that mirrors heaven, a "new heaven and new earth." Whether you have a triumphant or non-triumphant version of Holy Saturday (did Jesus go there in Good Friday or Easter morning mode?), there is only one person who can lead us out of our hells: Jesus our Christ.

If you stand outside the city at night, away from light pollution, you can see the band of the Milky Way across the sky. It is shocking to modern urbanites to see the nightly view before the age of electricity. Ancient cultures used to view the Milky Way as the staircase from earth to heaven, trodden by the souls of the departed. The Swedes called it "winter street, where we all must someday pass"; Norsemen called it "path of the ghosts"; Hebrides Islanders, "pathway of the secret people"; North American Indians, the "trail to Ponemah"; African Bushmen, "the ashen path"; Patagonians, "the White Pampas where ghosts hunt rheas." The real staircase from earth to heaven is the shuttle that started at a mount called Calvary, descended into a pit called Sheol, and then led an exodus from hell to heaven that continues to this day. No matter how harrowing (or hollowing) the moment you are in, Jesus can hallow it heavenward. Just come to Christ and follow Christ forward. Jesus is not where heaven is. Heaven is where Jesus is. Those magic moments when heaven and earth mirror each other are possible in the here and now. Heaven begins now. Now or never.

For those whose ideal of heaven is spending their lives between spreadsheets or bedsheets, heaven will be a disappointment. Heaven is living in the presence of Christ. But to come to Jesus there are some come-to-Jesus meetings involved. One of the biggest come-to-Jesus meetings for the church today? To remind Christ's church, that it's not "come to church" but "come to Christ." The church is not about the church. The church is about Christ, the body and blood of Christ. The church is more than a bridge between heaven and earth or a bridge over troubled waters. The church is the bride. It's not just a bridge to those in need, which it should be, but the bridge is a bride, the bride of Christ, the very body and blood of Christ. Teleology is all about Christ.

> Christ harrows hell, and nowhere are we
> beyond the hand that holds that harrow.

—Marilyn Chandler McEntyre, "Holy Saturday in a Harrowing Time"

What Are Signs of the Kingdom of God?

When Jesus responded to his fellow rabbis about signs, he didn't let his adversaries dictate the terms of the conversation. Instead, he re-interpreted their meaning to point not to evidence of God but to the context for their communication. This story is particularly helpful because it is meta. It is both about the definition of signs and a demonstration of how signs work: the former a discussion about what the Pharisees were exactly looking for with their request for a sign, and the latter a demonstration by Jesus on how to (re)sign meaning from one understanding to another.

This was not the first time the Pharisees and Sadducees had demanded a sign. Four chapters earlier in Matthew's gospel, they had asked the same question, presumably with less belligerence. The first time, he had replied:

> A wicked and adulterous generation asks for a sign! But none will be given it except the sign of the prophet Jonah. For as Jonah was three days and three nights in the belly of a huge fish, so the Son of Man will be three days and three nights in the heart of the earth. The men of Nineveh will stand up at the judgment with this generation and condemn it; for they repented at the preaching of Jonah, and now something greater than Jonah is here. (Matthew 12:39–41 NIV)

Jesus used the story of Jonah, which they knew well, as a sign to point not to a coming future Messiah but to a present reality: himself. Jonah is the prime Israelite understanding of repentance, expressed as a story. As the sign of Jonah, Jesus was both declaring himself the present embodiment of repentance and also pointing to a future narrative juxtaposition: as Jonah was swallowed up, buried, and spit up after three days, so Jesus would be crucified, buried, and resurrected in three days. Then, for a little extra flair just to clarify and reiterate, Jesus ended by using the word "greater," which is his shorthand for the "kingdom of God."[435]

Jesus was telling the teachers of the law that the sign they sought was not an obscure reference to a future event, but an obvious and present reality that stood right in front of them, and to rely on signs as proof of life is misguided. The teachers of the law were looking to the future, but Jesus was oriented to the present. The future restoration of the kingdom of Israel they dreamt of was manifested through his presence, and they did not see it. While they went to Jesus seeking answers and indications about the coming future, Jesus responded by pointing to evidence of what God was already doing in the present.

So, the question is, not what signs can we find that will tell us about the future? Instead, let us ask, where do we see Jesus in the present? Look for truth, not tragedy. To look for Jesus in the signs of the times also means we need to be willing to let go of our preconceived notions, because we cannot know or control where God's Spirit moves (see John 3:8). For example, consider what happened when the apostles Paul and Barnabas entered the city of Lystra to preach the good news:

> When the crowd saw what Paul had done, they shouted in the Lycaonian language, "The gods have come down to us in human form!" Barnabas they called Zeus, and Paul they called Hermes because he was the chief speaker. The priest of Zeus, whose temple was just outside the city, brought bulls and wreaths to the city gates because he and the crowd wanted to offer sacrifices to them.
>
> But when the apostles Barnabas and Paul heard of this, they tore their clothes and rushed out into the crowd, shouting: "Friends, why are you doing this? We too are only human, like you. We are bringing you good news, telling you to turn from these worthless things to the living God, who made the heavens and the earth and the sea and everything in them." (Acts 14:11–15 NIV)

The preconceived ideas of the people of Lystra were so strong that they misinterpreted the signs right in front of them and thought of Paul and Barnabas not as representatives of the living God, but little gods themselves.

Perhaps this is why Jesus got weary from doing "signs and wonders." We say we will believe if we see, but we don't. Even direct sensory evidence cannot always change a mind. If our minds are set on a reality, even though that reality is false, we may choose to double down on a belief system rather than open ourselves to the new ways God may be working.

Miracles don't precede faith; faith precedes miracles.

Then how do we read signs of Jesus in the present?

The Lord's Supper is a teleological meal, where endings are beginnings and beginnings are endings. As you discover in great environments such as Oxford and Cambridge, the ancient and the future happily sit side by side.

There is an ancient custom in Scandinavia that positions the communion rail around the altar in the form of a half-circle that stops at the back of the chancel. Beyond the chancel, on the other side of the wall, would lie the churchyard, the cemetery, where the members of that parish would be buried. The communion rail is only a half-circle inside the church because most of the church is underground, outside of the church. Their fellowship around the table continues, except that they are now partakers in the great communion hall in heaven. The small half-circle of communicants in the local church part of a circle widens and lengthens, reaching both back in time unto the first Lord's Supper and reaching forward into the world to come. In the Eucharist, the circle is completed. The sumptuous words of Lutheran pastor Charles Henrickson convey this teleological reality with power and passion:

> Shoulder by shoulder are they with us: our own faithful ancestors who once received the sacrament here at this altar, saints and martyrs elsewhere through the ages, and finally the Lord Himself and His apostles in the glorious kingdom in heaven above where the circle comes to its conclusion. This is "communio sanctorum," the communion of saints in Christ's kingdom of grace. Celebrating the Lord's Supper with my brothers and sisters in Christ, I am connected with the saints who sit at the Lord's Table in the heavenly kingdom. I am counted as one of God's holy people.[436]

God's love is both creative and re-creative: it brings into existence something new, and it gives new life to what once was but has died. We find signs of Jesus in the Lord's Supper and in our acts of love for one another.

But What about the Eschaton?

Perhaps you have read this entire book distinguishing the future-present *telos* from the present-future eschaton, and you still ask, "But what happens in 'the end,' i.e., the future?" Scriptures foretell of an eschaton, or a last days. If the kingdom begins now, what does that mean for the future?

The entire purpose of this book is to reorient ("O Oriens") your thinking from fascination and worry about the future to peace and joy in the present. Eschaton fixes us (humanity) in a linear story line that ends in a climactic moment to history. *Telos* fits us (humanity) into a nonlinear story line where we live simultaneously the past, present, and future, and where the timeless, the timely, and the time-full can be experienced in daily Maranatha moments of Christ has come, Christ is here, Christ is coming.

Perhaps time is linear, and history ends in a climactic moment. But events of the future are irrelevant to the promise of God, and our eschatological fixations have robbed us of the true joy of the resurrection, which is that the kingdom of heaven is available in the here and now. We serve a risen, rising, and regnant Lord. Jesus is not where heaven is. Heaven is where Jesus is.

But What Happens to Us When We Die?

Paul wrote, "But someone will ask, 'How are the dead raised? With what kind of body will they come?' How foolish! What you sow does not come to life unless it dies" (1 Cor 15:35–36 NIV). This is often preached as simply a "cost of discipleship" sermon, but what does it say about *telos*? If the kingdom of God is *telos*, and therefore it begins "in the now" when each spirit receives God's Spirit, and not just in the future, does that distinguish it from a place we enter after death?

English translations of the Scriptures hint at "realms"—such as the NIV in Romans 8:8–11, which describes two worlds or realms:

> Those who are in the realm of the flesh cannot please God.
>
> You, however, are not in the realm of the flesh but are in the realm of the Spirit, if indeed the Spirit of God lives in you. And if anyone does not have the Spirit of Christ, they do not belong to Christ. But if Christ is in you, then even though your body is subject to death because of sin, the Spirit gives life because of righteousness. And if the Spirit of him who raised Jesus from the dead is living in you, he who raised Christ from the dead will also give life to your mortal bodies because of his Spirit who lives in you.

With the gift of the Holy Spirit, do we enter a heavenly "realm" now, even while in the earthly realm, and then go through a transformation after death?

While Paul's writings imply two distinct bodies, an earthly body (the "flesh") and a heavenly body (the "spirit"), the world "realm" does not exist in the Greek. It is an English addition that creates a semiotic of space. These metaphors and metaphysics perhaps lead to the common idea that heaven is a spirit and not a physical place. But this is Gnostic and reflects the influence of Greek thinking on the early church. The story is clear—Jesus had a physical bodily post-resurrection. He ate with the disciples. "Matter participates in the resurrection transformation," writes physicist/priest John Polkinghorne.[437]

Further, as we wrote earlier, other people rose from the dead. In a passage almost no one preaches on, "the tombs broke open. The bodies of many holy people who had died were raised to life. They came out of the tombs after Jesus' resurrection and went into the holy city and appeared to many people" (Matthew 27:52–53 NIV). This weirdest of all passages implies something highly supernatural. The power of the kingdom inbreaking into the world was so strong at the moment, the veil so thin, that other people were affected like an electromagnetic pulse that regenerated all died bodies within a specific geographical region.

While the kingdom of God is a kingdom of the Spirit, this does not mean it is not a kingdom of the body. The distinct words are metaphors, not literal places. Scripture simply suggests two realities— "the flesh" and "the Spirit." These two realities— "flesh" and "Spirit"—are not literal, but metaphorical. Paul used them to describe the controlling agent: we were once controlled by the flesh, but we are now controlled by God's Spirit.

What we know is that we will have bodies, and they will be real, even more real than we have today and with greater fullness than our earthly bodies have been. To use Paul's metaphor, our heavenly bodies will be to our earthly bodies as a mature plant is to a seed. But heaven begins now. Heaven has never been better defined than by Jesus: "that where I am . . . you may be" (John 14:3). Heaven is the presence of Jesus. What happens to us when we die is we get to be with Jesus. That's why we can experience heaven in the here and now.

God's house may have many mansions, but heaven's mansions don't have penthouse suites, basement apartments, and rent-a-rooms. No classes (first or economy) exist in heaven. In fact, heaven is less about a place than a person.

Heaven is

less about pearly gates than about the Pearl of Great Price.

less about puffy white clouds than about the Lamb of God.

less about streets of gold than about the Great High Priest.

less about hilltop mansions than about the Son of the Most High.

less about crystal fountains than about the True Vine.

less about white robes than about the Light of the World.

less about glowing lampstands than about the Bright and Morning Star.

less about gemstone foundations than about the Chief Cornerstone.

less about jasper walls than about Wonderful Counselor, Mighty God, Everlasting Father, Prince of Peace.

Heaven is not where God is. God is heaven. Heaven is being with Jesus. And with Jesus, heaven begins now. It's heaven: Now or never.

> *Heaven is not where you are, it's who you're with. In other words, it's relationship.*
> **–founder/president of Cornerstone Forum Gil Bailie**

Life is more than about living. Life is about living with an end in mind. That end is Jesus. A happy life is living with an end in view from the start. That end is Jesus.

Every decision we make should have something in front of it–an end in mind. We want this book to help you live your life knowing what the end will be . . . and is. We begin with an end, or we quickly end every beginning. In fact, life is less about happy endings than about happy beginnings. Like cheese, wine, and slippers, some things just get better with age. Like the first question in the Westminster Shorter Catechism (1647), which was commissioned by the 1643 Assembly of Divines:

The chief end of man is to glorify God and enjoy him forever.

The End

The End

ENDNOTES

1   The "monomyth" is a form of comparative mythology that outlines a universal and is one of many structures that have been presented as the shape of stories. See Joseph Campbell, *Hero with a Thousand Faces*, 3rd ed. (Novato, CA: New World Library, 2008), 210. Campbell's first edition appeared in 1949, and his archetypal story thesis has been gold for screenwriters, playwrights, and novelists.

2   Robert McKee, Story: *Substance, Structure, Style, and the Principles of Screenwriting* (New York: HarperCollins, 1997), 9.

3   McKee, *Story*, 20.

4   Nancy Duarte, "Structure Your Presentation Like a Story," *Harvard Business Review*, October 31, 2012, https://hbr.org/2012/10/structure-your-presentation-li.

5   See Christopher Vogler, *The Writer's Journey: Mythic Structure for Writers* (Studio City, CA: Michael Wiese Productions, 1992).

6   Donald Miller, How to Tell a Story, *StoryBrand*, accessed July 12, 2022, https://storybrand.com/downloads/HowToTellAStory.pdf.

7   One of our favorite references for this appears at *Open Culture*, where a designer created visual versions of each story structure. See Josh Jones, "Kurt Vonnegut Diagrams the Shape of All Stories in a Master's Thesis Rejected by U. Chicago," *Open Culture*, February 18, 2014, http://www.openculture.com/2014/02/kurt-vonnegut-masters-thesis-rejected-by-u-chicago.html. See also Charles J. Shields, *And So It Goes: Kurt Vonnegut: A Life* (New York: Henry Holt, 2011).

8   Martyn Whittock, *The End Times, Again? 2000 Years of the Use & Misuse of Biblical Prophecy* (Eugene, OR: Cascade, 2021), 180.

9   C. S. Lewis, "Myth Became Fact," in *God in the Dock: Essays on Theology and Ethics*, ed. Walter Hooper (Grand Rapids: Eerdmans, 1970), 59. The Greek historian Sallustius is known for his conundrum "Now these things [myths] never happened, but always are." See Sallustius, "On the Gods and the Cosmos," sec. 4, in Gilbert Murray, *Five Stages of Greek Religion* (New York: AMS, 1925), https://sacred-texts.com/cla/fsgr/fsgr10.htm.

10   C. S. Lewis, "Rejoinder to Dr. Pittenger," *Christian Century* 75 (November 26, 1958): 1359–61.

11   This succinct summary comes from Joe Jackson, *Atlantic Fever: Lindbergh, His Competitors, and the Race to Cross the Atlantic* (New York: Farrar, Straus and Giroux, 2012), 181.

12   See Iain McGilchrist's two-volume treatise, *The Matter with Things: Our Brains, Our Delusions, and the Unmaking of the World* (London: Perspectiva, 2021).

13   Gustav Freytag, *Freytag's Technique of the Drama: An Exposition of Dramatic Composition and Art*, Authorized Translation from the Sixth German Edition, ed. Elias J. MacEwan (Chicago: S. C. Griggs, 1896), 114.

14   See Mary Frances Coady, Merton & Waugh: *A Monk, A Crusty Old Man, and the Seven Storey Mountain* (Buffalo: Paraclete, 2015).

15   Marianne Moore, *Complete Poems* (New York: Macmillan, 1967), 174.

16   McKee, *Story*, 16.

17   See Giles Gunn, *The Culture of Criticism and the Criticism of Culture* (New York: Oxford University Press, 1987).

18   At the end of Sigmund Freud's classic critique of culture, *Civilization and Its Discontent* (1930), there is this incredible moment where Freud admits that he has nothing positive to offer. He has no answers to the mystery of human existence and offers no healing from the agonies of life—except to grin and bear them. Here are some of his words: "I have not the courage to rise up before my fellow-men as a prophet, and I bow to their reproach that I can offer them no consolation." See Sigmund Freud, *Civilization and Its Discontents*: The Standard Edition, trans. and ed. James Strachey (New York: Norton, 1930), 145.

19   Scott Russell Sanders, *Staying Put: Making a Home in a Restless World* (Boston: Beacon, 1993), 154.

20   Karl Popper, *The Open Society and Its Enemies* (London: Routledge, 1945), 278.

21   Gene Blocker, *The Meaning of Meaninglessness* (The Hague, NL: Martinus Nijhoff, 1974).

22   Stephen Hawking and Leonard Mlodinow, *The Grand Design* (New York: Bantam, 2010), 5.

23   See Ross Douthat, *Bad Religion: How We Became a Nation of Heretics* (New York: Simon and Schuster, 2012).

24   MasterClass, "How to Use Seven-Point Story Structure in Your Writing," last updated July 28, 2021, https://www.masterclass.com/articles/how-to-use-seven-point-story-structure-in-your-writing.

25   Stephen E. Atkerson, *New Testament Church Dynamics: A Leader's Guide to Biblical Growth and Planting* (Atlanta: New Testament Reformation Fellowship, 2018), 809.

26   This is the contention of British New Testament scholar Ralph P. Martin in "The Lord's Supper," *The New Bible Dictionary*, ed. J. D. Douglas (Westmont, IL: InterVarsity Press, 1982), 709.

27   A recent manifesto from the authors' Wesleyan tradition, *The Faith Once Delivered: A Wesleyan Witness*, devotes 2 of 213 propositions, or less than 1 percent, to the kingdom of God. See *The Faith Once Delivered: A Wesleyan Witness* (Summit Document from the Next Methodism Summit, January 2022), The John Wesley Institute, accessed August 29, 2022, https://nextmethodism.org/summit-document/.

28   Andrew Stanton, "The Clues to a Great Story," filmed February 2012, TED video, 19.00, https://www.ted.com/talks/andrew_stanton_the_clues_to_a_great_story/transcript.

29   "The End," Google Trends, accessed June 12, 2020, https://trends.google.com/trends/explore?date=today%203-m&q=%22the%20end%22.

30   Martin Gurri, *The Revolt of the Public and the Crisis of Authority in the New Millennium* (San Francisco: Stripe Press, 2018), 80.

31   Adapted from *The Lion King*, directed by Roger Allers and Rob Minkoff (Walt Disney Pictures, 1994).

CHAPTER 1

32   Sean Martin, *The Black Death* (Harpenden, UK: Oldcastle Books, 2014), 20.

33   John Kelly, *The Great Mortality: An Intimate History of the Black Death, the Most Devastating Plague of All Time* (New York: Harper Perennial, 2005), 41.

34   Monica H. Green, ed. *Pandemic Disease in the Medieval World: Rethinking the Black Death* (Kalamazoo, MI: Arc Humanities Press, 2015), 9.

35   Kelly, *The Great Mortality*, 18.

36   Robert E. Lerner, "The Black Death and Western European Eschatological Mentalities," *American Historical Review* 86, no. 3 (1981):
533–52, https://doi.org/10.2307/1860369.

37   By comparison, COVID-19 had killed 4.6 million people as of
September 2021. As of August 2022, it had killed 6 million people.
See Coronavirus Resource Center: Johns Hopkins University & and
Medicine, accessed September 3, 2021, and August 29, 2022, https://
coronavirus.jhu.edu.

38   Kelly, *The Great Mortality*, 26.

39   Kelly, 13.

40   Maria A. Spyrou et al., "The Source of the Black Death in Fourteenth-Century Central Eurasia," *Nature* 606 (2022): 718–24, https://
doi.org/10.1038/s41586-022-04800-3.

41   Sidney Heath, *Pilgrim Life in the Middle Ages* (Port Washington, NY:
Kennikat, 1911), 96.

42   Thomas Robert Malthus, *An Essay on the Principle of Population* (Cambridge, UK: Cambridge University Press, 1992). The book was originally published anonymously in 1798.

43   For more on the story of Norman Borlaug and his work in prevent-
ing widespread famine during the worldwide population explosion
following the end of World War II, see Len Wilson, *Greater Things: The
Work of the New Creation* (Plano, TX: Invite Press, 2021).

44   Kelly, *The Great Mortality*, 3.

45   Kelly, 17.

46   Statistician Nassim Nicholas Taleb is known for his defense of black
swan theory, which describes an unexpected major cultural event
that is beyond the realm of scientific expectation. It is a response to
the rationalist and ancient Greek belief that black swans do not exist.
In agreement with Taleb, we believe the Greeks and rationalists were
wrong. Major events always have signs. See Nassim Nicholas Taleb,
Black Swan: The Impact of the Highly Improbable (New York: Random
House, 2010). The gray rhino comes from Michele Wucker, *The Gray
Rhino: How to Recognize and Act on the Obvious Dangers We Ignore* (New
York: St. Martin's Press, 2016).

47   Ronald Wright, *A Short History of Progress* (New York: Carroll & Graf,
2005), 113.

48   Johns Hopkins University of Medicine offers the best barometer of ongoing COVID-19 data. At the time of this writing, the mortality rate by country varied between 1.1–3.5 percent, with the odd exception of Mexico, at almost 9 percent. See https://coronavirus.jhu.edu.

49   "Ebola Outbreak 'Threatens Liberia's National Existence,'" BBC News, September 10, 2014, https://www.bbc.com/news/world-africa-29136594.

50   "Just Who Is Leading the Fight Against Ebola?," NBC News, September 12, 2014, https://www.nbcnews.com/storyline/ebola-virus-outbreak/just-who-leading-fight-against-ebola-n202221.

51   The figures on the number of doctors per population numbers can be misleading. In the island nation of Cuba, one doctor existed for every 200 people. Rachel Browne, "What Cuba Can Teach Canada about Vaccines," *MacLean's*, February 11, 2015, https://www.macleans.ca/society/health/what-cuba-can-teach-canada-about-vaccines/. But even Castro himself didn't want to get treated there.

52   "Situation Report: Ebola Virus Disease," World Health Organization, June 10, 2016, https://apps.who.int/iris/bitstream/handle/10665/208883/ebolasitrep_10Jun2016_eng.pdf;jsessionid=99A2D51EC27F56C79D7BF7C74F13A7F9?sequence=1.

53   Tal Axelrod, "WHO Deploys Team to Battle Ebola Outbreaks," *Hill*, February 18, 2021, https://thehill.com/policy/healthcare/539377-who-deploys-team-to-battle-ebola-outbreaks.

54   Michele Debczak, "5 People Who Were Amazingly Productive in Quarantine," *Mental Floss*, March 19, 2020, https://www.mentalfloss.com/article/620764/productive-people-in-quarantine. Shakespeare proved that periods such as the COVID-19 lockdown can be creative opportunities.

55   Daniel Defoe, *A Journal of the Plague Year* (London: Royal Exchange, 1722).

56   "Public's Mood Turns Grim: Trump Trails Biden on Most Personal Traits, Major Issues," Pew Research Center, June 30, 2020, https://www.pewresearch.org/politics/2020/06/30/publics-mood-turns-grim-trump-trails-biden-on-most-personal-traits-major-issues/.

57   Walter Benjamin, "The Work of Art in the Age of Mechanical Reproduction," in *The Cultural Studies Reader, 3rd ed.*, ed. Simon During (New York: Routledge, 2007), 74.

58   "Remarks of President Donald J. Trump—as Prepared for Delivery: Inaugural Address," White House Archives, January 20, 2017, https://trumpwhitehouse.archives.gov/briefings-statements/the-inaugural-address/.

59   Peggy Noonan, "The Nihilist in the White House," *Wall Street Journal*, November 21, 2014, https://www.wsj.com/articles/peggy-noonan-the-nihilist-in-the-white-house-1416533660.

60   Since 1992, the number of Americans who self-identify as conservative has remained remarkably consistent at about 36 percent. There has been a slight shift from moderate (43–35 percent) to liberal (17–24 percent). Of course, defining what these terms mean over time is another matter. See Lydia Saad, "The U.S. Remained Center-Right, Ideologically, in 2019," *Gallup*, January 9, 2020, https://news.gallup.com/poll/275792/remained-center-right-ideologically-2019.aspx.

61   In 2015, with a Democratic president, the Rasmussen poll registered just 31 percent of Americans who felt the country was headed in the right direction, long before the pandemic, mass protests, and mass unemployment of 2020. "31% Say U.S. Heading in Right Direction," *Rasmussen Reports*, July 13, 2015, https://www.rasmussenreports.com/public_content/archive/mood_of_america_archive/right_direction_or_wrong_track/july_2015/31_say_u_s_heading_in_right_direction.

62   Leonard Pitts Jr. "This Is the First July 4 on Which We Can Actually See the End of America Coming," *Miami Herald*, June 29, 2020, https://www.miamiherald.com/opinion/opn-columns-blogs/leonard-pitts-jr/article243770527.html.

63   The Martin Luther King, Jr. Center (@TheKingCenter), "In the final analysis, a riot is the language of the unheard. And what is it that America has failed to hear?" The Martin Luther King, Jr. Center, twitter post, May 28, 2020, 9:07 a.m., https://twitter.com/TheKingCenter/status/1266008254984982529.

64   Nihilism begins with the existing structure of a society but often leads to more existentially extreme conclusions.

65   Gerald O. Barney, *The Global 2000 Report to the President: Entering the 21st Century* (New York: Pergamon, 1980).

66   Peter Dunn-Warwick, "130+ Years of Steadily Increasing War," *Futurity*, June 29, 2011, http://www.futurity.org/society-culture/130-years-of-steadily-increasing-war/.

67   See Michael Shellenberger, *San Fransicko: Why Progressives Ruin Cities* (New York: Harper, 2021).

68   The Economist online, "Two thousand Years in One Chart," Graphic Detail (blog), June 28, 2011, http://www.economist.com/blogs/dailychart/2011/06/quantifying-history.

69   Almost all the countries that are above the 2.1 demarcation are Third World. Among developed countries, the only nation above 2.1 is Israel, at 2.75. (New Zealand is 2.1 and the United States is 2.05.)

70   Jonathan V. Last, "From the Archives of the Weekly Standard: America's One-Child Policy," *Washington Examiner*, September 27, 2010, https://www.washingtonexaminer.com/weekly-standard/americas-one-child-policy.

71   Daron Acemoglu et al., "A Dynamic Theory of Resource Wars," *Quarterly Journal of Economics* (February 2012): 127, http://doi.org/10.1093/qje/qjr048.

72   See Reinhart Koselleck, *Sediments of Time: On Possible Histories* (Stanford, CA: Stanford University Press, 2019).

73   Jacques Derrida, "Of an Apocalyptic Tone Recently Adopted in Philosophy," *Oxford Literary Review* 6 (December 1984): 3–37.

74   Thomas Hardy, *Wessex Poems and Other Verses: Poems of the Past and the Present* (London: MacMillan, 1919), 445.

75   Stephen Eric Bonner, *Critical Theory: A Very Short Introduction* (New York: Oxford University Press, 2017), 6.

76   David L. Barr, "John Is Not Daniel: The Ahistorical Apocalypticism of the Apocalypse," *Perspectives in Religious Studies* 40, no. 1 (2013): 49.

77   On Joachim's theology of history, see Marjorie Reeves, *The Influence of Prophecy in the Later Middle Ages* (New York: Oxford University Press, 1969), 17–21.

78   See Bernard McGinn, *The Calabrian Abbot: Joachim of Fiore in the History of Western Thought* (New York: Macmillan, 1985).

79   See James West Davidson, "The American Revolution," PBS, accessed August 29, 2022, https://www.pbs.org/wgbh/pages/frontline/shows/apocalypse/explanation/amrevolution.html.

80   The contemporary idea of apocalypse began with Friedrich Lücke, *Versuch einer vollständigen Einleitung in die Offenbarung des Johannes und in die apokalyptische Litteratur* (Bonn, DEU: E. Weber, 1852).

81 "Make Me A City," *Economist,* June 18, 2022, 70–71.

82 Rebecca Solnit, *A Paradise Built in Hell: The Extraordinary Communities That Arise in Disaster* (New York: Penguin, 2009), 22.

83 *Mission: Impossible—Fallout,* directed by Christopher McQuarrie (2018; Paramount Pictures, 2018), movie trailer.

CHAPTER 2

84 Lois Magner, *A History of Medicine* (New York: Marcel Dekker, 1992), 66–74.

85 A. E. Shipley, "Leeches," *British Medical Journal* 2, no. 2813 (November 28, 1914): 916–19.

86 Amelia Soth, "Why Did the Victorians Harbor Warm Feelings for Leeches?" *JSTOR Daily,* April 18, 2019, https://daily.jstor.org/why-did-the-victorians-harbor-warm-feelings-for-leeches/.

87 Shipley, "Leeches," 918.

88 Soth, "Why Did the Victorians Harbor Warm Feelings for Leeches?"

89 Howard Markel, "Dec. 14, 1799: The Excruciating Final Hours of President George Washington," PBS NewsHour, December 14, 2014, https://www.pbs.org/newshour/health/dec-14-1799-excruciating-final-hours-president-george-washington.

90 Philip E. Tetlock and Dan Gardner, *Superforecasting: The Art and Science of Prediction* (New York: Crown, 2015), 26.

91 Steven Pinker, *Enlightenment Now: The Case for Reason, Science, Humanism, and Progress* (New York: Viking, 2018), 11.

92 Pinker, 11.

93 Gerry Greenstone, "The History of Bloodletting," *BC Medical Journal* 52, no. 1 (January–February 2010): 12–14, https://www.bcmj.org/premise/history-bloodletting.

94 Lewis Henry Morgan, *Ancient Society; Or, Researches in the Lines of Human Progress from Savagery, through Barbarism to Civilization* (New York: H. Holt, 1877).

95 Greenstone, "The History of Bloodletting."

96   Noonan, "The Nihilist in the White House" (see chap. 1, n. XX).

97   Walter Isaacson, *The Innovators: How a Group of Hackers, Geniuses, and Geeks Created the Digital Revolution* (New York: Simon & Schuster, 2014), 33. While there is no agreed-upon inventor of the modern computer, Isaacson attempts in his book to give credit to Charles Babbage, an English mathematician whose prototype "Difference Engine" aimed to replace human tasks with machines.

98   Anthony Brandt and David Eagleman, *The Runaway Species: How Human Creativity Remakes the World* (New York: Catapult, 2017), 251.

99   Johan Norberg, *Progress: Ten Reasons to Look Forward to the Future* (London, UK: OneWorld, 2017), 78.

100   Norberg, 78.

101   Pinker, *Enlightenment Now*, 61.

102   Eric Metaxas, *Seven Men: And the Secret of Their Greatness* (Nashville: Thomas Nelson, 2013), 42.

103   Joel Mokyr, *A Culture of Growth: The Origins of the Modern Economy* (Princeton, NJ: Princeton University Press, 2017), 23.

104   Forrest Pool, interview by author Len Wilson, Plano, TX, April 2, 2018.

105   US president Lyndon Baines Johnson introduced the "Great Society" as an ambitious set of social reforms in 1964. *Public Papers of the Presidents of the United States: Lyndon B. Johnson, 1963–64*. Volume I, entry 357 (Washington, DC: Government Printing Office, 1965), 704–7.

106   Victor Dias, "St. Augustine on the Structure and Meaning of History" (master's thesis, Concordia University, 1996), 94.

107   Edward J. Larson, *Summer of the Gods: The Scopes Trial and America's Continuing Debate over Science and Religion* (New York: Basic Books, 1997), 23–24.

108   A. N. Wilson, *Charles Darwin: Victorian Mythmaker*, Kindle edition (New York: HarperCollins, 2017), loc. 1120.

109   Herbert Spencer, *The Principles of Biology*, vol. 1 (London: Williams and Norgate, 1864), 444.

110   As quoted in A. N. Wilson, *Charles Darwin*, 526.

111 Richard Dawkins, *The Blind Watchmaker: Why the Evidence of Evolution Reveals a Universe without Design* (New York: Norton, 1986), 6.

112 Daniel Gelernter, "Giving Up Darwin," *Claremont Review of Books* 19, no. 2 (Spring 2019): 104–9, https://www.claremont.org/crb/article/giving-up-darwin/.

113 Mircea Meliade, *The Quest: History and Meaning in Religion* (Chicago: University of Chicago Press, 1984), 39.

114 John T. Elson, "Is God Dead?," *Time*, April 8, 1966, https://content.time.com/time/subscriber/article/0,33009,835309,00.html.

115 Anthony Brandt and David Eagleman. *The Runaway Species: How Human Creativity Remakes the World* (New York: Catapault).

116 Chris Anderson, *Makers: The New Industrial Revolution* (New York: Crown Business, 2012).

117 Isaacson, *The Innovators*.

118 Barbara L. Fredrickson, *Positivity: Top-Notch Research Reveals the Upward Spiral That Will Change Your Life* (New York: Three Rivers Press, 2009). Fredrickson, a self-proclaimed "world's leading voice on emotional positivity," promises that happy thoughts will help readers "build their best future." This book appeared on Len Wilson's daughter's high school reading list.

119 For more on the relationship of progress and transhumanism, see Robert M. Geraci, "A Tale of Two Futures: Techno-Eschatology in the US and India," *Social Compass* 63, no. 3 (September 2016): 319–34, http://journals.sagepub.com/doi/10.1177/0037768616652332.

120 Yuval Noah Harari, *Homo Deus: A Brief History of Tomorrow* (New York: HarperCollins, 2017), 21.

121 Paul Kedrosky, "The Jesus Phone," *Wall Street Journal, Opinion,* June 29, 2007, https://www.wsj.com/articles/SB118308453151652551.

122 Fredrickson, *Positivity*, 27.

123 Barbara Ehrenreich, *Bright-Sided: How the Relentless Promotion of Positive Thinking Has Undermined America* (New York: Metropolitan Books, 2009), 8.

124 John Gray, "An Illusion with a Future," *Daedalus* 133, no. 3 (Summer 2004): 10, https://doi.org/10.1162/0011526041504542.

125 Gray, 10.

126 Ronald Wright, *A Short History of Progress*, 4.

127 A. N. Wilson, *Charles Darwin*, 577.

128 David Lempert, "The Myth of Social Progress, Revisited," *Human Figurations* 5, no. 1 (March 2016), http://hdl.handle.net/2027/spo.11217607.0005.107.

129 Isaacson, *The Innovators*, 9.

130 Matthew W. Slaboch, *A Road to Nowhere: The Idea of Progress and Its Critics* (Philadelphia: University of Pennsylvania Press, 2018), 15.

131 Slaboch, 15.

132 Slaboch, 16.

133 Slaboch, 17.

134 "The historical question was formulated by Lenin in two pronouns— "who whom?" Leon Trotsky, "Towards Capitalism or Towards Socialism?" *Labour Monthly* 7, no. 11 (November 1925): 659–66, https://www.marxists.org/archive/trotsky/1925/11/towards.htm.

135 James C. Scott, *Seeing Like a State: How Certain Schemes to Improve the Human Condition Have Failed* (New Haven, CT: Yale University Press, 1999), 6.

136 Scott, 310.

137 Computer Business Review lists the iPhone as one of the top five communication vehicles, along with Facebook, Skype, Bluetooth, and IBM Watson. I would have put it into a top two list. Tom Ball, "Top 5 Technological Advances of the 21st Century," Computer Business Review, February 8, 2018, https://techmonitor.ai/technology/emerging-technology/top-5-technological-advances-21st-century.

138 "Mobile Kids: the Parent, the Child, and the Smartphone," *Nielsen, February* 2017, https://www.nielsen.com/insights/2017/mobile-kids-the-parent-the-child-and-the-smartphone/.

139 Eric Andrew-Gee, "Your Smartphone Is Making You Stupid, Antisocial and Unhealthy. So Why Can't You Put It Down?!?" *Globe and Mail*, January 6, 2018, https://www.theglobeandmail.com/technology/your-smartphone-is-making-you-stupid/article37511900/.

140   David Graeber, *The Dawn of Everything: A New History of Humanity* (New York: Farrar, Strauss, and Giroux, 2021).

141   Steven Poole, *Rethink: The Surprising History of New Ideas* (New York: Scribner and Sons, 2016), 23.

142   "Exquisite 2300–Year-Old Scythian Woman's Boot Preserved in the Frozen Ground of the Altai Mountains," *Open Culture,* June 22, 2020, http://www.openculture.com/2020/06/exquisite-2300-year-old-scythian-womans-boot-preserved-in-the-frozen-ground-of-the-altai-mountains.html.

143   David Swisher, "Why Macchu Picchu Imagery?," Adventures in Missing the Point: A Journey Exploring the Semiotics of Communication (blog), December 27, 2012, https://semioticsignposts.blogspot.com/2012/12/why-macchu-picchu.html.

144   Bonner, *Critical Theory*, 70.

145   Bruno Macaes, "After Covid, Get Ready for the Great Acceleration," *Spectator*, March 13, 2021, https://www.spectator.co.uk/article/after-covid-get-ready-for-the-great-acceleration.

CHAPTER 3

146   Flavius Josephus, *The Antiquities of the Jews*, trans. William Whiston (Project Gutenberg, last updated August 9, 2017), bk. 17, chap 6, pars. 2–3, https://www.gutenberg.org/files/2848/2848-h/2848-h.htm.

147   King Herod had sons with ten different wives, and these sons fought incessantly for power, to the point where Herod had some of them killed, along with their mothers. Commenting on his local ruler's domestic life, Caesar Augustus once said, "I'd rather be Herod's pig than his son." Macrobius, The Saturnalia 2.4.11, https://penelope.uchicago.edu/Thayer/e/roman/texts/macrobius/saturnalia/home.html.

148   Flavius Josephus, *The Wars of the Jews*, trans. William Whiston (Project Gutenberg, last updated August 3, 2013), bk. 2, chap. 1, par. 2, https://www.gutenberg.org/files/2850/2850-h/2850-h.htm.

149   The Gospel of Luke records this moment as the marker for Jesus' birth, but Matthew's version aligns with other historical records, and most scholars agree that Jesus was likely born ten years earlier, in 4 BCE.

150 Josephus, *The Antiquities of the Jews*, 17.9.1.

151 Notably, this was younger than the eligible age of thirty for a Levite to enter the priesthood according to the Law (Numbers 4:3).

152 The Gospel of Luke describes local authority belonging to "Annas and Caiaphas" in 3:2, and this continued several years later as recorded in Acts 4:6, which describes Annas as the high priest even though the position belonged to Caiaphas.

153 Robert Glenn Johnson, *Jesus Unchained* (Plano, TX: Invite Press, 2022), 17.

154 Gabriel Josipovici, *What Ever Happened to Modernism?* (New Haven, CT: Yale University Press, 2010).

155 Gemma Simmonds, "The Baby and the Hat," *Tablet,* June 17, 2021, https://www.thetablet.co.uk/books/10/20178/the-baby-and-the-hat.

156 The most likely source we think is Sir John Denham (1615–1669), who wrote a poem with these lines that John Dryden loved to quote: "They but preserve the Ashes, thou the Flame, / True to his Sense, but truer to his Fame." See the quote in Tanya Caldwell, "John Dryden and John Denham," *Texas Studies in Literature and Language* 46, no. 1 (Spring 2004): 49–72.

157 "Ancients and Moderns in the Eighteenth Century," *Dictionary of the History of Ideas*, ed. Philip P. Wiener, vol. 1 (New York: Charles Scribner's Sons, 1968), 76–87.

158 Alain De Benoist, "A Brief History of the Idea of Progress," *Occidental Quarterly* 8 no. 1 (Spring 2008): 8.

159 Daniel Chernilo, "Social Change and Progress in the Sociology of Robert Nisbet," *Society* 52, no. 4 (July 9, 2015): 324–34, http://dx.doi.org/10.1007/s12115-015-9908-0.

160 Chernilo.

161 Mary Douglas, *Thinking in Circles: An Essay on Ring Composition, Terry Lecture Series* (New Haven, CT: Yale University Press, 2007), 6.

162 David Allen Brown, *Tradition and Imagination: Revelation and Change* (New York: Oxford University Press, 2004).

163 John T. Wixted et al., "Coding of Episodic Memory in the Human Hippocampus," *Proceedings of the National Academy of Sciences* 115, no. 5 (2018): 1093–98.

CHAPTER 4

164 Alissa Wilkinson, "The 'Left Behind' Series Was Just the Latest Way America Prepared for the Rapture," *Washington Post*, July 13, 2016, https://www.washingtonpost.com/news/act-four/wp/2016/07/13/the-left-behind-series-was-just-the-latest-way-america-prepared-for-the-rapture/.

165 Aaron Earls, "Signs of Jesus' Return?," *Lifeway Research*, April 7, 2020, https://research.lifeway.com/2020/04/07/vast-majority-of-pastors-see-signs-of-end-times-in-current-events/.

166 James D. Heiser, "The American Empire Should Be Destroyed": *Alexander Dugin and the Perils of Immanentized Eschatology* (Malone, TX: Repristination Press, 2014).

167 Ray Walters, "Ten Years of Best Sellers," *New York Times*, December 30, 1979, https://www.nytimes.com/1979/12/30/archives/ten-years-of-best-sellers-best-sellers.html.

168 Delf Rothe, "Governing the End Times? Planet Politics and the Secular Eschatology of the Anthropocene," *Millennium* 48, no. 2 (January 2020): 143–64, https://doi.org/10.1177/0305829819889138.

169 Leonard I. Sweet, "The Revelation of Saint John and History," *Christianity Today*, May 11, 1973, https://www.christianitytoday.com/ct/1973/may-11/revelation-of-saint-john-and-history.html.

170 See Norman Cohn, *The Pursuit of the Millennium, 2nd ed.* (New York: Harper Torchbooks, 1961), 103.

171 Leonard I. Sweet, "Christopher Columbus and the Millennial Vision of the New World," *Catholic Historical Review* 72, no. 3 (July 1986): 369–82.

172 Mircea Eliade, "Paradise and Utopia: Mythical Geography and Eschatology," *Mexico Documents*, uploaded November 24, 2014, https://vdocuments.mx/mircea-eliade-paradise-and-utopia.html?page=1.

173 Leonard Sweet has written extensively on millennialism with articles in *Christianity Today, Theology Today*, and *Theological Studies*. For example, see Leonard I. Sweet, "Millennialism in America: Recent Studies," *Theological Studies* 40, no. 3 (September 1979): 510–31, https://journals.sagepub.com/doi/10.1177/004056397904000305.

174 Florian Freistetter, *Isaac Newton: The Asshole Who Reinvented the Universe* (Amherst, NY: Prometheus, 2018), 143.

175 Michael Polanyi, *The Logic of Liberty* (New York: Routledge, 1951), 106.

176 For a thousand-page book arguing that the Bolshevik revolution was a millenarian movement, an apocalyptic sect, see *Yur Slezkine, The House of Government: A Saga of the Russian Revolution* (Princeton, NJ: Princeton University Press, 2017).

177 Emilio Gentile, *Politics as Religion* (Princeton, NJ: Princeton University Press, 2006), 112. See also A. James Gregor, *Totalitarianism and Political Religion: An Intellectual History* (Stanford, CA: Stanford University Press, 2012).

178 Jaroslav Pelikan, *The Vindication of Tradition* (Cambridge, MA: Yale University Press, 1984), 13.

179 C. S. Lewis, *The Collected Letters of C. S. Lewis, vol. 3* (New York: HarperCollins, 2004), 358.

180 Gary B. Ferngren, *Medicine and Health Care in Early Christianity* (Baltimore: Johns Hopkins University Press, 2016), 99.

181 See Eric Voegelin, T*he New Science of Politics: An Introduction* (Chicago: University of Chicago Press, 1952, 1987), xvi, 119–29, 163–66.

182 "'Our House Is On Fire': Greta Thunberg, 16, Urges Leaders to Act on Climate," *Guardian* (UK), January 25, 2019, https://www.theguardian.com/environment/2019/jan/25/our-house-is-on-fire-greta-thunberg16-urges-leaders-to-act-on-climate.

183 James G. Watt, testimony before the House Interior Committee, February 5, 1981.

184 Bill Moyers, "There Is No Tomorrow," *Star Tribune* (Minneapolis–St. Paul, MN), January 31, 2005, as quoted in Brian Carnell, "Bill Moyers, James Watt and the Creation of Media Myths," BrianCarnell.com, February 1, 2005, https://brian.carnell.com/articles/2005/bill-moyers-james-watt-and-the-creation-of-media-myths/.

185 See Howard Snyder, "How Free Methodists Got Left Behind: B. T. Roberts, Millennialism, and Dispensationalism," *Academia,* accessed September 16, 2022, https://www.academia.edu/12944577/How_Free_Methodists_Got_Left_Behind_B_T_Roberts_Millennialism_and_Dispensationalism.

186 Martyn Whittock, "The Day of the Lord," *Tablet,* May 21, 2022, 12.

CHAPTER 5

187 Emily Cockayne, *Rummage: A History of the Things We Have Reused, Recycled and Refused to Let Go* (London: Profile, 2020), 256.

188 Gavan Titley, *Is Free Speech Racist?*, *Debating Race* (Medford, MA: Politty, 2020), 34.

189 Anatoli Rybakov, *Children of the Arbat*, trans. Harold Shukman (New York: Dell, 1989), 526.

190 For the late Joseph Sherman, editor of *From Revolution to Repression: Soviet Yiddish Writing 1917–1952*, this was more than a human or literary tragedy. It spelled the end of European Yiddish.

191 Charles Wesley, "O For a Thousand Tongues to Sing" (1739), *The United Methodist Hymnal* (Nashville: United Methodist Publishing House, 1989), 57, verse 4.

192 Wesley, verse 4.

193 Søren Kierkegaard, as quoted in William H. Willimon, *On a Wild and Windy Mountain and 25 Other Meditations for the Christian Year* (Nashville: Abingdon, 1984), 65.

194 L. P. Hartley, *The Go-Between*, repr. ed. (New York: New York Review of Books, 2002), 17.

195 First outlined in R. G. Collingwood, *The Idea of History* [1946 Edition] (Eastford, CT: Martino Fine Books, 2014).

196 Edward Hallett Carr, *What Is History?* (New York: Vintage, 1967), 35.

197 Charles Darwin, *The Descent of Man and Selection in Relation to Sex, vol. 1* (London: John Murray, 1871), chap. 3.

198 Darwin, 100–101.

199 W.H. Auden, *City Without Walls and Other Poems* (New York: Random House, 1969), 67.

200 See C. S. Lewis, *Surprised by Joy: The Shape of My Early Life* (New York: Harcourt Brace, 1956), 193, 203.

201 Oxford Reference, s.v. "quiddity," accessed September 16, 2022, https://www.oxfordreference.com/view/10.1093/oi/authority.20110803100358893.

202 See J. K. Rowling on The Diane Rehm Show, WAMU Radio Washington, DC, October 20, 1999 (rebroadcast December 24, 1999).

203 Thomas Merton, *Seeking Paradise: The Spirit of the Shakers* (Maryknoll, NY: Orbis,), 40–41.

204 Lewis, *Surprised by Joy*, 193.

205 Boris Pasternak, *Doctor Zhivago* (New York: Knopf, 2010), 9.

206 Physis represents an "intrinsic pattern of growth through which everything that exists in the universe moves towards the fulfillment of its intrinsic ends." The difference between physis and progress is the application of natural growth to societal development. See Chernilo, "Social Change and Progress in the Sociology of Robert Nisbet".

207 Thomas Cahill, *The Gifts of the Jews: How a Tribe of Desert Nomads Changed the Way Everyone Thinks and Feels* (New York: Knopf, 1998), 5.

208 Henri-Charles Puech, quoted in Cahill, 5.

209 Frederic Raphael, *Antiquity Matters* (New Haven, CT: Yale University Press, 2017), 44.

210 J. B. Bury, *The Idea of Progress: An Inquiry into Its Origin and Growth* (London: Macmillan, 1920), 173–174.

211 Bury, 208–9.

212 Gray, "An Illusion with a Future."

213 Slaboch, *A Road to Nowhere*, 112.

214 Karl Marx, "The Eighteenth Brumaire of Louis Bonaparte," Liberte, Egalite, Fraternite: Exploring the French Revolution (website), accessed August 30, 2022, https://revolution.chnm.org/items/show/304.

215 Lempert, "The Myth of Social Progress, Revisited".

216 Vogler, *The Writer's Journey*, 187–88.

217 Douglas, *Thinking in Circles*, 6.

218 Douglas, 11.

219 Lempert, "The Myth of Social Progress, Revisited."

220 Benoist, "A Brief History of the Idea of Progress," 8.

221 Eliade, *The Quest* (1984), 88.

222 Benoist, "A Brief History of the Idea of Progress."

223 Douglas, *Thinking in Circles*, 10. The recognition of rings in ancient texts requires a macro analysis of long form writing, which runs counter to the micro emphasis of biblical criticism.

224 Dias, "St. Augustine on the Structure and Meaning of History," 83.

225 Augustine of Hippo, City of God, 11.6, trans. Marcus Dods, University of Central Florida Online, https://pressbooks.online.ucf.edu/ancientpoliticalphilosophy/chapter/augustine-the-city-of-god/.

226 Dias, "St. Augustine on the Structure and Meaning of History," iii.

227 Chernilo, "Social Change and Progress in the Sociology of Robert Nisbet".

228 Augustine, *City of God*, 5.2.

229 Benoist, "A Brief History of the Idea of Progress," 10.

230 Charles Lincoln Van Doren, *A History of Knowledge: Past, Present, and Future* (New York: Ballantine Books, 1993), 203.

231 René Descartes, *Discourse on the Method of Rightly Conducting the Reason, and Seeking Truth in the Sciences* (1637), trans. John Veitch, pt. 4, Project Gutenberg, last updated May 13, 2022, http://www.gutenberg.org/files/59/59-h/59-h.htm.

232 Diarmaid MacCulloch, *Christianity: The First Three Thousand Years*, (New York: Viking, 2010), 775.

233 Jack Hartnell, *Medieval Bodies: Life, Death, and Art in the Middle Ages* (London: Wellcome Collection, 2018), 15.

234 Ian Cooper, *The Cambridge Story: The Impact of Christianity in England* (Cambridge, UK: Christian Heritage, 2014), 4.

235 Jared Diamond, *Guns, Germs, and Steel: The Fates of Human Societies* (New York: Norton, 1997), 206.

236 David Brooks, "The Enlightenment Project," *New York Times, Opinion*, February 28, 2017, https://www.nytimes.com/2017/02/28/opinion/the-enlightenment-project.html.

237 Margaret A. Majumdar and Tony Chafer, "Progress: Its Visionaries and Its Malcontents," *Interventions* 19, no. 5 (July 4, 2017): 599–608, https://www.tandfonline.com/doi/full/10.1080/136980 1X.2017.1336459.

238 Slaboch, *A Road to Nowhere*, 77.

239 Slaboch, 89.

240 Slaboch, 111.

241 Slaboch, 17.

242 Mitchell Stephens, *The Rise of the Image, the Fall of the Word* (New York: Oxford University Press, 1998), 43.

243 Aleksandr Solzhenitsyn, quoted in Slaboch, *A Road to Nowhere*, 98.

244 Christopher Lasch, *The True and Only Heaven: Progress and Its Critics* (New York: Norton, 1991), 532.

245 Arthur M. Schlesinger Jr., *The Cycles of American History* (Boston: Houghlin Mifflin, 1999), vii.

246 Karl Mannheim, "The Problem of Generations," in *Essays on the Sociology of Knowledge: Collected Works*, vol. 5, ed. Paul Kecskemeti (New York: Routledge, 1952), 278.

247 Jane Pilcher, "Mannheim's Sociology of Generations: An Undervalued Legacy," *British Journal of Sociology 44*, no. 3 (1994): 481.

248 Brett McKay, "Podcast #236: What the Generational Cycle Theory Can Tell Us about Our Present Age," September 20, 2016, in The Art of Manliness, podcast, MP3 audio, 1.27.47, http://www.artofmanliness.com/2016/09/20/podcast-236-generational-cycle-theory-can-tell-us-present-age/.

249 William Strauss and Neil Howe, *Generations: The History of America's Future, 1584 to 2069* (New York: Quill), 1992.

250 Linette Lopez, "Steve Bannon's Obsession with a Dark Theory of History Should Be Worrisome," *Insider*, February 2, 2017, https://www.businessinsider.com/book-steve-bannon-is-obsessed-with-the-fourth-turning-2017-2.

251 Strauss and Howe, *Generations*, chap. 4.

252 Laura Spinney, "Human Cycles: History as Science," *Nature 488* (August 2012): 24–26, https://www.nature.com/news/human-cycles-history-as-science-1.11078.

253 Slaboch, *A Road to Nowhere*, 112.

254 Majumdar and Chafer, 599.

255 Len Wilson, *Greater Things*, 166.

256 Luigino Bruni and Stefano Zamagni, *Civil Economy: Efficiency, Equity, Public Happiness* (Bern, CH: Peter Lang AG, 2007).

257 Daniel Kahneman and Amos Tversky, "Prospect Theory: An Analysis of Decision under Risk," *Econometrica 47*, no. 2 (1979): 263–91, https://doi.org/10.2307/1914185.

258 Nassim Nicholas Taleb, *Antifragile: Things That Gain from Disorder* (New York: Random House, 2012), 5.

259 Malcolm Gladwell, "Blow Up," *New Yorker*, January 22, 1996, 32.

260 The words were originally Samuel Beckett's (Irish novelist and playwright). See Gregory Johns, *In the Dim Void: Samuel Beckett's Late Trilogy* (Kent, UK: Crescent Moon, 2016), 79.

261 "Winner Takes It All: How Markets Favor the Few at the Expense of the Many," Farnam Street (blog), September 2018, https://fs.blog/2018/09/mental-model-winner-take-all/.

262 Quentin Fottrell, "For the First Time, Young Americans Have Less Optimism Than Those Aged 55 and Older," *Market Watch*, April 3, 2018, https://www.marketwatch.com/story/for-the-first-time-ever-young-americans-are-less-optimistic-than-their-parents-2018-04-02.

263 James Hamblin, "Buy Experiences, Not Things," *Atlantic*, October 7, 2014, https://www.theatlantic.com/business/archive/2014/10/buy-experiences/381132/.

264 See Chris Taylor, "70% of Rich Families Lose Their Wealth by the Second Generation," *Money*, June 17, 2015, http://money.com/money/3925308/rich-families-lose-wealth/; Missy Sullivan, "Lost Inheritance," *Wall Street Journal*, March 8, 2013, https://www.wsj.com/articles/SB10001424127887324662404578334663271139552.

265 Eillie Anzilotti, "It's Time to Abandon Economic Growth as the Only Indicator of Success," *Fast Company*, April 12, 2018, https://amp.fastcompany.com/40557739/its-time-for-countries-to-abandon-economic-growth-as-the-only-indicator-of-success.

266 Anzilotti.

267 Noah Smith (@noahpinion), "1/OK, here's a thread about economic growth, technological progress, environmental sustainability, and political unrest!" Twitter, July 28, 2019, 9:28 a.m., https://twitter.com/Noahpinion/status/1155515380120449025.

268 Gray, "An Illusion with a Future," 5.

269 Talking Heads, "Road to Nowhere," by David Byrne, in Little Crea-
     tures Sire, October 1984, 33⅓ rpm.

270 See Thomas More, Utopia 1516 Libellus Vere Aureus Nec Minus
     Salutaris Quam Festivus de Optimo Rei Publicae Statu Deque
     Nova Insula Utopia, Wikimedia Commons, February 24, 2020,
     https://commons.wikimedia.org/wiki/File:Thomas_More_Uto-
     pia_1516_Libellus_vere_aureus_nec_minus_salutaris_quam_festi-
     vus._De_Optimo_reipublicae_Statu,_deque_nova_Insula_Utopia_
     (Biblioth%C3%A8que_Mazarine).jpg.

271 Edmund Burke, *A Letter from Edmund Burke, Esq; One of the Representa-
     tives in Parliament for the City of Bristol, to John Farr, and John Harris, Es-
     qrs. Sheriffs of That City, on the Affairs of America* (Farmington Hills, MI:
     Gale ECCO, 2006), 189–245. The original manuscript was printed in
     1777.

272 Schopenhauer, quoted in Slaboch, *A Road to Nowhere*, 18.

273 As quoted by Austrian neurologist Franz Seitelberger (1915–2007)
     in F. Seitelberger, "Lebensstufen des Gehirns: Neurobiologische
     Aspekte," in *Handbuch der Gerontopsychiatrie*, ed. H. G. Zapotoczky and
     P. K. Fischof (Vienna, AT: Springer Verlag, 1996), 19–42, https://doi.
     org/10.1007/978-3-7091-6563-8,_2.

274 Slaboch, *A Road to Nowhere*, 19.

275 John Gray, *Heresies: Against Progress and Other Illusions* (London:
     Granta Books, 2004), 5.

276 As cited by Tobie Lichtig in *Times Literary Supplement*, July 15, 2016,
     30.

277 Dan Allender, *To Be Told: Know Your Story, Shape Your Future* (Colorado
     Springs: Waterbrook, 2005), 1.

278 Mark Murray, "Poll: 80 Percent of Voters Say Things Are Out of
     Control in the US," *NBC News*, June 7, 2020, https://www.nbcnews.
     com/politics/meet-the-press/poll-80–percent-voters-say-things-are-
     out-control-u-n1226276.

279 "Emerging and Developing Economies Much More Optimistic Than
     Rich Countries about the Future," *Pew Research Center*, October 9,
     2014, https://www.pewresearch.org/global/2014/10/09/emerging-
     and-developing-economies-much-more-optimistic-than-rich-coun-
     tries-about-the-future/.

280 Spencer Wells (@spwells), "Just a head's up," *Twitter*, June 28, 2020,
     since deleted. See https://twitter.com/spwells.

281 Scott Sauls (@scottsauls), "Social justice without Jesus can be more Darwinian than just, fighting against unjust power only to assume and assert unjust power.," *Twitter*, June 27, 2020, 12:47 p.m., https://twitter.com/scottsauls/status/1276935076857745408.

282 Matt McNeil, Facebook post, June 28, 2020, https://www.facebook.com/matt.mcneil.50/posts/10221383553071236.

283 N. T. Wright, *Surprised by Hope: Rethinking Heaven, the Resurrection, and the Mission of the Church* (New York: HarperOne, 2007), 219.

284 See Thomas Aquinas, "On the First Man," First Article, "Whether Woman Should Have Been Made in the First Production of Things," citing Aristotle, De Gener. Anim., II, 3 (737a 27), in *Philosophy of Woman: An Anthology of Classic to Current Concepts*, ed. Mary Briody Mahowald, 3rd ed. (Indianapolis: Hackett, 1994), 54.

285 Aristotle, *The Politics*, trans. Benjamin Jowett, 1260a13, quoted in Mahowald, 361.

286 Thomas Aquinas, *Summa Theologiae*, "Treatise on Man": Question 92, "The Production of the Woman": Article 1, replies to objections 1 and 2, at http://summa-theologiae.org/question/09201.htm.

287 Mahatma Gandhi, quoted in Simone Painter-Brick, *Gandhi and the Middle East: Jews, Arabs and Imperial Interests* (London: I. B. Tauris, 2008), 63.

288 As quoted in the *Times Literary Supplement*, April 9, 2021, 13.

289 Andrew Sullivan, "What Happened to You? The Radicalization of the American Elite Against Liberalism," *Weekly Dish*, July 9, 2021, https://andrewsullivan.substack.com/p/what-happened-to-you-e5f

290 Sullivan.

CHAPTER 6

291 See Gideon Rachman, *The Age of the Strong-Man: How the Cult of the Leader Threatens Democracy around the World* (New York: Other Press, 2022).

292 Pierre Teilhard de Chardin, *The Phenomenon of Man*, trans. Sarah Appleton Weber, 2nd ed. (Eastbourne, UK: Sussex Academic Press, 2003), 7.

293 Pierre Teilhard de Chardin, *The Future of Man,* trans. Norman Denny (New York: Image Books, 2004), 31.

294 Pierre Teilhard de Chardin, *The Phenomenon of Man* (Glasgow, UK: Collins, 1959), 244–45.

295 Teilhard, *The Future of Man,* 298.

296 Teilhard, 267.

297 Teilhard, 51

298 Seymour Martin Lipset, "George Washington and the Founding of Democracy," *Journal of Democracy* 9, no. 4 (1998): 24–38, http://doi.org/10.1353/jod.1998.0066.

299 David Brooks, *The Second Mountain: The Quest for a Moral Life* (New York: Random House, 2019), 237.

300 The Who, "Won't Get Fooled Again," by Pete Townshend, London, Rolling Stones Mobile Studio, 1971, 45 rpm.

301 Claudia Springer, *James Dean Transfigured: The Many Faces of Rebel Iconography* (Austin: University of Texas Press, 2007), 16.

302 Jean-Jacques Rousseau, *On the Social Contract*

303 Biblically, rebellion began with the serpent. See Isaiah 14:13.

304 See John 15:13.

305 Jefferson Bethke, "Why I Hate Religion, but Love Jesus," January 10, 2012, YouTube video, 4:03, https://www.youtube.com/watch?v=1IAhDGYlpqY.

306 *The Breakfast Club,* directed by John Hughes (Universal City, CA: Universal, 1985), motion picture.

307 See Matthew 4:8; John 6:15.

308 Jurgen Moltmann, *The Coming of God: Christian Eschatology* (Minneapolis: Augsburg, 1996), 4.

309 See Bruce Clark, "The Philosophers Behind the Guns," *Tablet* 16 (April 2022): 19.

310 Brad Sylvester, "Fact Check: Did Henry Ford Say, 'If I Had Asked People What They Wanted, They Would Have Said Faster Horses'?" *Check Your Fact*, October 10, 2019, https://checkyourfact. com/2019/10/10/fact-check-henry-ford-quote-faster-horses/.

311 Malcolm Gladwell, "Focus Groups Should Be Abolished," *Ad Age*, August 8, 2005, https://adage.com/article/viewpoint/focus-groups-abolished/104151.

312 Dave Smith, "What Everyone Gets Wrong About This Famous Steve Jobs Quote, According to Lyft's Design Boss," *Business Insider*, April 19, 2019, https://www.businessinsider.com/steve-jobs-quote-misunderstood-katie-dill-2019-4.

313 The Daily Dish, "How Democracies Become Dictatorships," *Atlantic*, September 22, 2008, https://www.theatlantic.com/daily-dish/archive/2008/09/how-democracies-become-dictatorships/211352/.

314 Soren Kierkegaard, "That Individual": Two "Notes" Concerning My Work as an Author (1859), quoted in "The Crowd Is Untruth," Philosophical Society, accessed August 30, 2022, https://philosophicalsociety.com/Archives/The Crowd Is Untruth.htm#:~:text=The Crowd Is "Untruth" From Soren Kierkegaard%27s "That,need of having the crowd on its side.

315 This is true personally and socially. In the public sphere, every society has leaders. In the private sphere, as agnostic author David Foster Wallace noted, everyone worships something. David Foster Wallace, *This Is Water: Some Thoughts, Delivered on a Significant Occasion, about Living a Compassionate Life* (New York: Little, Brown, 2009), 99.

316 See Don Higgenbotham, *George Washington: Uniting a Nation* (New York: Ronan and Littlefield 2002).

317 John Cougar Mellencamp, "Authority Song," recorded October 23, 1983, track 3 on Uh-huh, Riva Records, studio album.

318 Pascal Boniface, "The Proliferation of States," *Washington Quarterly* 21, no. 3 (1998): 109–27, https://doi.org/10.1080/01636609809550335.

319 Franz von Sickingen, also known as "the Last Knight," provided the brawn for what turned out to be a prelude skirmish in 1522, five years after Martin Luther posted his famous Ninety-five Theses, while fellow knight Ulrich von Hutten, a devotee of the Renaissance humanist movement, provided the brain. Frederick Engels, the Prussian businessman/philosopher/historian who co-developed communist theory with Karl Marx, was the first to recognize the material role of the "wars of religion" that rocked Europe for over a century. See "The Peasant War in Germany," *Neue Rheinische Zeitung-Revue* (Summer 1850), *Works of Frederick Engels*, January 4, 1996, https://www.marxists.org/archive/marx/works/1850/peasant-war-germany/index.htm. Engels writes, "Hutten demanded nothing else than the elimination of all princes, the secularization of all church principalities and states, and the restoration of a democracy of the nobility." Let's remember that word demand, which we will return to later.

320 As quoted in Alex Christofi, *Dostoevsky in Love: An Intimate Life* (London: Bloomsbury, 2021), 196.

321 The Police, "Spirits in the Material World," by Sting, recorded 1981, track 1 on Ghost in the Machine, A&M, studio album.

322 Arthur C. Brooks, "The Lie We Tell Ourselves about Going to Bed Early," *Atlantic*, June 10, 2021.

323 Virgil, *Aeneid*, Book 2.

324 "'Magical' Moment," U2 website, November 27, 2009, https://www.u2.com/news/title/magical-experience/.

325 Langdon Hickman, "With No Line on the Horizon, U2 Delivered an Album of Future Hymns," Treble, February 8, 2022, https://www.treblezine.com/u2-no-line-on-the-horizon-future-hymns/.

HALF TIME

326 G. Scott Gleaves, *Did Jesus Speak Greek? The Emerging Evidence of Greek Dominance in First-Century Palestine* (Eugene, OR: Pickwick, 2015).

327 David Hume, *A Treatise of Human Nature*, Dover Philosophical Classics (Mineola, NY: Dover, 2003), 295, 296.

328 See Rowan Williams's translation of Waldo Williams's "In the Days of Caesar" as found in his *Collected Poems* (2022). Rowan Williams, *Collected Poems* (Manchester, UK: Carcanet, 2022).

329 James A. Lindsay, Peter Boghossian, and Helen Pluckrose, "Academic Grievance Studies and the Corruption of Scholarship," *Aero* magazine, February 10, 2018, https://areomagazine.com/2018/10/02/academic-grievance-studies-and-the-corruption-of-scholarship/. See also Helen Pluckrose and James Lindsay, "Cynical Theories," Philosophy Now, accessed August 30, 2022, https://philosophynow.org/issues/143/Cynical_Theories_by_James_Lindsay_and_Helen_Pluckrose.

330 Lindsay, Boghossian, and Pluckrose, "Academic Grievance Studies and the Corruption of Scholarship."

331 Carl F. H. Henry, *God, Revelation and Authority*, vol. 1 (Wheaton, IL: Crossway, 1976), 91.

332 "Race, Civil Rights and Photography," *Lens* (*New York Times* photojournalism blog), January 28, 2016, https://lens.blogs.nytimes.com/2016/01/18/race-civil-rights-and-photography/.

333 Malcolm Gladwell, "The Foot Soldier of Birmingham," Revisionist History, produced by Pushkin Industries, July 6, 2017, podcast, audio, 35:39, https://www.pushkin.fm/podcasts/revisionist-history/the-foot-soldier-of-birmingham.

334 *Eyes on the Prize: America's Civil Rights Years 1954–1965*, produced by Henry Hampton, aired 1987 on PBS, DVD Talk, April 6, 2010, https://www.dvdtalk.com/reviews/41906/eyes-on-the-prize-americas-civil-rights-years-1954-1965/.

335 Michael Polanyi, *Personal Knowledge: Towards a Post-Critical Philosophy* (Chicago: University of Chicago Press, 2015), 22.

336 Polanyi, 301.

337 N. T. Wright, *The New Testament and the People of God* (Minneapolis: Fortress, 1992), 32–33.

338 Wright, 33.

339 Wright, 33.

340 Stephens, *The Rise of the Image, the Fall of the Word*, 80.

341 See Jim Holt, "Time Bandits: What Were Einstein and Gödel Talking About?" *New Yorker*, February 20, 2005, https://www.newyorker.com/magazine/2005/02/28/time-bandits-2.

342 Daniel Kahneman, *Thinking, Fast and Slow* (New York: Farrar, Straus and Giroux, 2013).

343 Wright, *The New Testament and the People of God*, 33.

344 Wright, 35.

345 Cormac McCarthy, *Blood Meridian: Or the Evening Redness in the West* (New York: Vintage, 1985), 242.

346 McGilchrist, *The Matter with Things*, 199.

347 Karl Barth and Helmut Gollwitzer, *Church Dogmatics: A Selection with Introduction* (Louisville: Westminster John Knox Press, 1994), 67.

348 Michael Crichton, *Jurassic Park* (New York: Random House, 1990), 63.

349 Eric Peterson and Leonard Sweet, *Wade in the Water: Following the Sacred Stream of Baptism* (Eugene, OR: Wipf and Stock, 2018), xii.

350 Peterson and Sweet.

351 Umberto Eco, *The Name of the Rose* (New York: Mariner, 1980), 31.

352 Joshua Martin, *Nikola Tesla: How Energy, Frequencies and Vibrations Shape Reality* (N.p.: Amazon Digital Services–KDP Print US, 2022), n.p.

353 Robert A. Caro, *Working: Researching, Interviewing, Writing* (London: Bodley Head, 2019).

354 *Legendary Quotes of Benjamin Franklin* (n.p.: UB Tech, n.d.), 28, https://www.google.com/books/edition/Legendary_Quotes_of_Benjamin_Franklin/CE7sDwAAQBAJ?hl=en&gbpv=1&dq=Legendary+Quotes+of+Benjamin+Franklin&printsec=frontcover.

355 Matthew 11:25–30; Matthew 11:27: "No one knows the Father except the Son and those to whom the Son chooses to reveal him" (NIV).

CHAPTER 7

356 Claire Lehmann (@clairlemon), Twitter post, TWunroll, accessed September 21, 2022, https://twunroll.com/article/1345501448830795777.

357 Gurri, *The Revolt of the Public and the Crisis of Authority in the New Millennium*, 352.

358 Gurri, 358.

359 Fiske rejected the once-popular idea of a monolithic "public" shaped by an all-controlling media and instead argued for distinct audiences, each of whom receive messages differently—some passive, some with more active responses. John Fiske, *Television Culture* (London: Methuen, 1987), 236.

360 Gurri, *The Revolt of the Public and the Crisis of Authority in the New Millennium*, 359.

361 Gurri, 360.

362 Gurri, 361.

363 William Cummings, "Trump Sets Record for Most Tweets in a Single Day Since He Took Office, *USA Today*, last updated January 23, 2020, https://www.usatoday.com/story/news/politics/2020/01/23/trump-record-most-tweets-since-taking-office/4551815002/.

364 Mike McIntire, Karen Yourish, and Larry Buchanan, "In Trump's Twitter Feed: Conspiracy-Mongers, Racists and Spies," New York Times, November 2, 2019, https://www.nytimes.com/interactive/2019/11/02/us/politics/trump-twitter-disinformation.html.

365 Ben Smith, "Inside the Revolts Erupting in America's Big Newsrooms," *New York Times*, June 7, 2020, https://www.nytimes.com/2020/06/07/business/media/new-york-times-washington-post-protests.html.

366 Gurri, *The Revolt of the Public and the Crisis of Authority in the New Millennium*, 369–70.

367 Søren Kierkegaard, *Kierkegaard's Journals and Notebooks, vol. 5, Journals NB6–NB10* (Princeton, NJ: Princeton University Press, 2011), as quoted in Malcolm Muggeridge, *A Third Testament: A Modern Pilgrim Explores the Spiritual Wanderings of Augustine, Blake, Pascal, Tolstoy, Bonhoeffer, Kierkegaard, and Dostoevsky* (New York: Little, Brown, 1976), 82.

368 Muggeridge, 82.

369 Gurri, 385.

370 Gurri, 385. "Rather than chase after Nazis or other phantoms of history, those concerned with the future democracy should fix their attention on that young man: on the nihilist who believes, with passionate intensity, the destruction and slaughter are themselves a form of progress."

371 Gurri, 380.

372 See "Minneapolis Mayor Booed from Protest," Associated Press, June 8, 2020, YouTube video, 1.43, https://www.youtube.com/watch?v=3v0YLrQ8r4M; Ashley Green (@agreenphotog), "In an incredibly powerful moment, Police Chief Michael Shaw, urged by chanting, joins the crowd laying face down on the pavement," Twitter, June 6, 2020, 1:16 p.m., https://twitter.com/agreenphotog/status/1269332225499238400.

373 Gurri, 362.

374 See Robert M. Lindner, *Rebel Without a Cause* (New York: Penguin Random House, 1944).

375 Kris Rocke and Joel Van Dyke, *Geography of Grace: Doing Theology from Below* (Tacoma, WA: Center for Transforming Mission, 2012). Thanks to Teri Hyrkas for bringing this to our attention.

376 Bob Dylan, "Gotta Serve Somebody," by Bob Dylan, recorded May 4, 1979, track 1 on *Slow Train Coming*, Columbia, studio album; John Lennon, "Serve Yourself," recorded June 27, 1980, track 3 on disk 4 of *John Lennon Anthology*, Capitol/EMI, compact disc.

377 The enslavement of people for labor and sexual exploitation continues today. It generates $150 billion a year, even more than the drug trade.

378 See Clay Shirky, *Here Comes Everybody: The Power of Organizing Without Organizations* (New York: Penguin, 2009).

379 René Descartes, *Discourse on Method and Meditations*, trans. Elizabeth S. Haldane and G. R. T. Ross, Dover Philosophical Classics (Mineola, NY: Dover, 2003), 3.

380 Jeffrey Burton Russell, *Inventing the Flat Earth: Columbus and Modern Historians* (Santa Barbara, CA: Praeger, 1991), 37.

381 See David Tracy, *The Analogical Imagination: Christian Theology and the Culture of Pluralism* (New York: Crossroad, 1981).

382 Joel Gehrke, "Pope Francis Warns Russian Orthodox Patriarch Not to Be 'Putin's Altar Boy'," *Washington Examiner*, May 3, 2022, https://www.washingtonexaminer.com/policy/defense-national-security/pope-francis-warns-russian-orthodox-patriarch-not-to-be-putins-altar-boy.

CHAPTER 8

383 For more on this, see Jenna Silber Storey and Benjamin Storey, *Why We Are Restless: On the Modern Quest for Contentment* (Princeton, NJ: Princeton University Press, 2021).

384 Robert Badenas, "The Meaning of *Telos* in Romans 10:4" (PhD diss, Andrews University, 1983), https://digitalcommons.andrews.edu/dissertations/12.

385 See Mary Ann Getty, "Christ Is the End of the Law: Rom 10:4 in Its Context" (ThD diss, Katholieke Universiteat, Leuven, 1975), https://bib.kuleuven.be/english/pbib/collection/dissertations.

386 David H. Kelsey, "God and Teleology: Must God Have Only One 'Eternal Purpose'?" *Neue Zeitschrift Für Systematische Theologie* 54, no. 4 (2012): 369, http://doi.org/10.1515/nzsth-2012-0015.

387 Kelsey, 373.

388 Kelsey, 365.

389 T. S. Eliot, "Four Quartets," *The Complete Poems and Plays 1909–1950* (Orlando: Harcourt, Brace, 1952).

390 For example, see Frederick C. Grant, "The Permanent Value of the Primitive Christian Eschatology," *Biblical World: A Journal of the Awakening Church* 49, no. 1 (January 1917), https://www.journals.uchicago.edu/doi/pdfplus/10.1086/475712.

CHAPTER 9

391 See the book of Ezra.

392 See Douwe Draaisma's review "Seahorses in The Blob: What Gives Us Our Sense of Time" in *Times Literary Supplement,* May 6, 2022, commenting on the research reported on in Veronica O'Keane, *The Rag and Bone Shop: How We Make Memories And Memories Make U*s (New York: Allen Lane, 2022).

393 This is the most well-known English translation of Jesus' words.

394 For an analysis of Walter Rauschenbusch's conflation of God's kingdom with an ideology of progress, see Len Sweet's *Me and We: God's New Social Gospel* (Nashville: Abingdon, 2014) and Len Wilson's *Greater Things: The Work of the New Creation* (Plano, TX: Invite Press, 2021).

395 Barr, "John Is Not Daniel".

396 Moltmann, *The Coming of God,* 16.

397 See Exodus 33 for Moses; 1 Kings 19 for Elijah.

398 Robert Foster, "Why on Earth Use 'Kingdom of Heaven'?: Matthew's Terminology Revisited," *New Testament Studies* 48, no. 4, http://doi.org/10.1017/S0028688502000292.

399 Johnny Tabaie, "Iatrogenic Disease: The Silent Killer," The Holistic Sanctuary, April 13, 2020, https://www.theholisticsanctuary.com/holistic/iatrogenic-disease-the-silent-killer/.

400 Jeremy England, *Every Life Is On Fire: How Thermodynamics Explains the Origins of Living Things* (New York: Basic Books, 2020), 243.

401 For a philosophical definition of "reductionism," check out Lucy O'Brien's *Self-Knowing Agents* (Oxford, UK: Clarendon Press, 2008), in which she defines the reductionist view as one where "first-person contents are nothing more than systematically reflexive contents, and that an attitude has reflexive content just if the truth or satisfaction condition of the attitude depends in a certain systematic way upon the subject of the attitude. In particular, first-person contents are seen to be functions from context to truth or satisfaction conditions such that the subject of the attitude is the object of the truth or satisfaction conditions." We hope you understand this better than we do.

402 England, *Every Life Is On Fire*, 46.

403 Bernard Cooke, *Power and the Spirit of God: Toward an Experience-Based Pneumatology* (New York: Oxford UP, 2004), 7..

CHAPTER 10

404 Rachel Martin, "From Simple Exchange to Shakedown: The Evolution of 'Quid Pro Quo,'" NPR, October 26, 2019, https://www.npr.org/2019/10/26/773506497/from-simple-exchange-to-shakedown-the-evolution-of-quid-pro-quo.

405 Willie James Jennings, *The Christian Imagination: Theology and the Origins of Race* (New Haven, CT: Yale University Press, 2010), 9.

406 Samuel Chadwick, *The Way to Pentecost*, (Fort Washington, PA: CLC, 2007), about the author, emphasis in original.

407 Dallas Willard, *The Divine Conspiracy: Rediscovering Our Hidden Life in God* (New York: HarperCollins, 1998), 398.

408 Deuteronomy 8:17.

409 Kenneth E. Bailey, *Jesus Through Middle Eastern Eyes: Cultural Studies in the Gospels* (Downers Grove, IL: Intervarsity Press, 2008), 77.

410 Bailey, 81.

411 For the theological significance of the Greek word for "truth," which is *aletheia* and means "to come out of hiding," see Leonard Sweet, *Bad Habits of Jesus* (Carol Stream, IL: Tyndale, 2016).

412 For more on the chemistry of creativity, see Len Wilson, *Greater Things: The Work of the New Creation* (Invite Press, 2021).

CHAPTER 11

413 "The resurrection itself would be a meaningless doctrine, almost nonsensical, without the story that goes with it. 'The Birth of Christ,' wrote Tolkien, 'is the eucatastrophe of Man's history. The Resurrection is the euchatastrophe of the story of the Incarnation. This story begins and ends in joy.'" See J. R. R. Tolkien, *The Monsters and the Critics* (New York, NY: HarperCollins, 1997), 156.

414 See the Swedish film *As It Is in Heaven,* nominated for Best Foreign Film at the 2005 Academy Awards. *As It Is in Heaven,* directed by Kay Pollak, featuring Michael Nyqvist and Frida Hallgren (Lorber Films, 2014), https://www.amazon.com/As-Heaven-Michael-Nyqvist/dp/B002W1HBM0.

415 Song of Songs 4:12–14 describes seven incense-bearing trees and the components of the incense (v. 14).

416 John S. Bergsma, *The Jubilee from Leviticus to Qumran* (SUPPLEMENTS TO VETUS TESTAMENTUM, 115) (Leiden, NL: Brill, 2006). "But redemption is also to be accomplished through various representatives of the Lord, especially the mysterious one who is anointed with the Spirit (61:1). In Isa 61:1–4 this anointed one is given the task of proclaiming the eschatological jubilee, the 'year of the Lord 's favor,' which will involve liberation of the oppressed (v. 1), renewal of joy and optimism (v. 3), and economic restoration (v. 4). In this passage there is a clear convergence of the arrival of the redeemer figure—described here as . . . an anointed one—and the eschatological jubilee" (299–300).

417 Atkerson, *New Testament Church Dynamics*, 809.

418 Martin, "The Lord's Supper," 709.

419 Fanny Crosby, "Blessed Assurance" (1873), *The United Methodist Hymnal* (Nashville: United Methodist Publishing House, 1989), 369.

420 See e.g. Matthew 23:3.

421 Alexander Schmemann, *The Journals of Father Alexander Schmemann 1973–1983* (Yonkers, NY: St. Vladimir's Seminary Press, 2000), 292.

422 Zach Hunt, *Unraptured: How End Times Theology Gets It Wrong* (Scottdale, PA: Herald, 2019), 226–27.

423 Danish conductor Niels Gade composed only eight symphonies, despite living for another twenty years after completing his last. He is believed to have replied, when asked why he did not compose another symphony, "There is only one ninth," in reference to Beethoven.

424 Friedrich Schiller, "Ode to Joy" (1785), a paean to Jubilee.

425 Matthew 24:2.

426 See Glenn R. Storey, "The 'Skyscrapers' of the Ancient Roman World," *Latomus* 62, no. 1 (2003): 3–26, http://www.jstor.org/stable/41540040.

427 Thomas B. Slater, "Apocalypticism and Eschatology: A Study of Mark 13:3–37," *Perspectives in Religious Studies* 40, no. 1 (2013): 8.

428 "Meditation 17" is found in "Devotions upon Emergent Situations," and begins with words made even more famous by Ernest Hemingway, "Perchance he for whom this bell tolls may be so ill as that he knows not it tolls for him." The third paragraph begins with maybe the most famous lines in all of English literature: "No man is an island." See John Donne, "Devotions upon Emergent Occasions: Meditation XVII," in *The Works of John Donne,* ed. Henry Alford (London: John W. Parker, 1839), 574–75.

429 The first paragraph ends: "God employs several translators; some pieces are translated by age, some by sickness, some by war, some by justice; but God's hand is in every translation, and his hand shall bind up all our scattered leaves again, for that library where every book shall lie open to one another; as therefore the bell that rings to a sermon, calls not upon the preacher only, but upon the congregation to come; so this bell calls us all: but how much more me, who am brought so near the door by this sickness."

430 Ray Charles (vocalist), "What Kind of Man Are You?" by Ray Charles, recorded 1958 with Mary Ann Fisher, track 5 on *What'd I Say*, Atlantic, studio album.

Endnotes

431 Simon Sinek, *Start with Why: How Great Leaders Inspire Everyone to Take Action* (New York: Penguin, 2009).

432 Primo Levi, *If This Is a Man* (New York: Orion, 1959), 24.

433 Jonathan E. T. Kuwornu-Adjaottor and Patrick Yankyera, "The Meaning and Significance of Tetelestai in John 19:30," ResearchGate, https://www.researchgate.net/publication/337415360_THE_MEANING_AND_SIGNIFICANCE_OF_TETELESTAI_IN_JOHN_1930, p. 12. We have not found a more elegant tribute to this word than this one attributed to C. H. Spurgeon: "An ocean of meaning in a drop of language, a mere drop. It would need all the other words that ever were spoken, or ever can be spoken, to explain this one word. It is altogether immeasurable. It is high; I cannot attain to it. It is deep; I cannot fathom it. IT IS FINISHED is the most charming note in all of Calvary's music. The fire has passed upon the Lamb. He has borne the whole of the wrath that was due to His people. This is the royal dish of the feast of love." Charles Spurgeon, quoted in Sheila Walsh, *Holding ON When You Want to Let Go: Clinging to Hope When Life Is Falling Apart* (Grand Rapids: Baker, n.d.), chap. 1.

EPILOGUE

434 See "Apostles' Creed," on the website of the United Methodist Church, accessed September 24, 2022, https://www.umc.org/en/content/apostles-creed-traditional-ecumenical.

435 See Len Wilson, *Greater Things*.

436 Rev. Charles Henrickson at St. Matthew Lutheran Church in Bonne Terre, Missouri, as conveyed by Dr. David Wahlstedt, lead pastor, TheTableDallas.com.

437 John Polkinghorne, *The God of Hope and the End of the World* (New Haven, CT: Yale University Press, 2002), 113.

SELECT BIBLIOGRAPHY

Acemoglu, Daron, Mikhail Golosov, Aleh Tsyvinski, and Pierre Yared. "A Dynamic Theory of Resource Wars." *Quarterly Journal of Economics* (February 2012): 127, 283–331. http://doi.org/10.1093/qje/qjr048.

Adorno, Theodor, and Max Horkheimer. *Dialectic of Enlightenment*. Stanford, CA: Stanford University Press, 2007.

Allender, Dan. *To Be Told: Know Your Story, Shape Your Future*. Colorado Springs: Waterbrook, 2005.

"Ancients and Moderns in the Eighteenth Century." *Dictionary of the History of Ideas*. Edited by Philip P. Wiener. Volume 1. New York: Charles Scribner's Sons, 1968. 76–87.

Anderson, Chris *Makers: The New Industrial Revolution*. New York: Crown Business, 2012.

Ante-Nicene Fathers. Volume 1: Justin Martyr. "Dialogue with Trypho." Coptic Orthodox Church Heritage. https://st-takla.org/books/en/ecf/001/0010461.html.

As It Is in Heaven. Directed by Kay Pollak. Featuring Michael Nyqvist and Frida Hallgren.Lorber Films, 2014. 2 hr., 13 min.

Atkerson, Stephen E. *New Testament Church Dynamics: A Leader's Guide to Biblical Growth and Planting*. Atlanta: New Testament Reformation Fellowship, 2018.

Augustine of Hippo. *City of God*. Book 11.6. Translated by Marcus Dods. University of Central Florida Online. https://pressbooks.online.ucf.edu/ancientpoliticalphilosophy/chapter/augustine-the-city-of-god/.

Axelrod, Tal. "WHO Deploys Team to Battle Ebola Outbreaks." The Hill. February 18, 2021. https://thehill.com/policy/healthcare/539377-who-deploys-team-to-battle-ebola-outbreaks.

Badenas, Robert. "The Meaning of *Telos* in Romans 10:4." PhD diss., Andrews University, 1983. https://digitalcommons.andrews.edu/dissertations/12.

Bailey, Kenneth E. *Jesus Through Middle Eastern Eyes: Cultural Studies in the Gospels*. Downers Grove, IL: Intervarsity Press, 2008Bailey, Ronald. "Who Wants to Be Secretary of the Future?" *Reason* (June 2016): 16.

Barney, Gerald O. *The Global 2000 Report to the President: Entering the 21st Century.* New York: Pergamon, 1980.

Barr, David L. "John Is Not Daniel: The Ahistorical Apocalypticism of the Apocalypse." *Perspectives in Religious Studies* 40, no. 1 (2013): 49–63.

Barth, Karl, and Helmut Gollwitzer, *Church Dogmatics: A Selection with Introduction.* Louisville: Westminster John Knox, 1994.

Benoist, Alan de. "A Brief History of the Idea of Progress." *Occidental Quarterly* 8, no. 1 (Spring 2008): 8.

Bergsma, John S. *The Jubilee from Leviticus to Qumran* (Supplements To Vetus Testamentum, 115). Leiden, NL: Brill, 2006.

Blocker, Gene. *The Meaning of Meaninglessness.* The Hague, NL: Martinus Nijhoff, 1974.

Boniface, Pascal. "The Proliferation of States." *Washington Quarterly* 21, no. 3 (1998): 109–27. https://doi.org/10.1080/01636609809550335.

Bonner, Stephen Eric. *Critical Theory: A Very Short Introduction.* New York: Oxford University Press, 2017.

Brandt, Anthony, and David Eagleman. *The Runaway Species: How Human Creativity Remakes the World.* New York: Catapult, 2017.

Brooks, Arthur C. "The Lie We Tell Ourselves about Going to Bed Early." *Atlantic.* 10 June 2021.

Brooks, David. "The Enlightenment Project." *New York Times.* February 28, 2017. https://www.nytimes.com/2017/02/28/opinion/the-enlightenment-project.html.

Brooks, David. *The Second Mountain: The Quest for a Moral Life.* New York: Random House, 2019.

Brown, David Allen. *Tradition and Imagination: Revelation and Change.* New York: Oxford University Press, 2004.

Bruni, Luigino, and Stefano Zamagni. *Civil Economy: Efficiency, Equity, Public Happiness.* Bern, CH: Peter Lang AG, 2007.

Burke, Edmund. *A Letter from Edmund Burke, Esq; one of the Representatives in Parliament for the City of Bristol, to John Farr, and John Harris, Esqrs. Sheriffs of That City, on the Affairs of America.* Farmington Hills, MI: Gale ECCO, 2006.

Bury, J. B. *The Idea of Progress: An Inquiry into Its Origin and Growth.* London: Macmillan, 1920.

Cahill, Thomas. *The Gifts of the Jews: How a Tribe of Desert Nomads Changed the Way Everyone Thinks and Feels.* New York: Knopf, 1998.

Caldwell, Tanya. "John Dryden and John Denham." *Texas Studies in Literature and Language* 46, no. 1 (Spring 2004): 49-72.

Campbell, Joseph. *Hero with a Thousand Faces*. 3rd ed. Novato, CA: New World Library, 2008.

Caro, Robert A. *Working: Researching, Interviewing, Writing*. London: Bodley Head, 2019.

Chardin, Teilhard de. *The Future of Man*. Melbourne: Image Books, 1964.

———. *The Phenomenon of Man*. Glasgow: Collins, 1959.

Chernilo, Daniel. "Social Change and Progress in the Sociology of Robert Nisbet." *Society* 52, no. 4 (August 2015): 324–34. http://dx.doi.org/10.1007/s12115-015-9908-0.

Chesterton, Gilbert Keith. *Orthodoxy* (London: Bodley Head, 2016).

Christofi, Alex. *Dostoevsky in Love*. London: Bloomsbury Continuum, 2021.

Clark, Bruce. "The Philosophers Behind the Guns." *The Tablet* 16 (April 2022): 19.

Coady, Mary Frances. *Merton & Waugh: A Monk, A Crusty Old Man, and the Seven Storey Mountain*. Buffalo: Paraclete, 2015.

Cockayne, Emily. *Rummage: A History of the Things We Have Reused, Recycled and Refused to Let Go*. London: Profile, 2020.

Cohn, Norman. *The Pursuit of the Millennium*. 2nd ed. New York: Harper Torchbooks, 1961.

Collingwood, R. G. *The Idea of History [1946 Edition]*. Eastford, CT: Martino Fine Books, 2014.

Cooke, Bernard. *Power and the Spirit of God: Toward an Experience-Based Pneumatology*. New York: Oxford UP, 2004.

Cooper, Ian. *The Cambridge Story: The Impact of Christianity in England*. Cambridge: Christian Heritage, 2014.

Crichton, Michael. *Jurassic Park*. New York: Random House, 1990.

Darwin, Charles. *The Descent of Man*. Long Beach, NY: Facsimile, 1871.

Dawkins, Richard. *The Blind Watchmaker: Why the Evidence of Evolution Reveals a Universe Without Design*. New York: Norton, 1986.

Defoe, Daniel. *A Journal of the Plague Year*. London: Royal Exchange, 1722.

Derrida, Jacques. "Of an Apocalyptic Tone Recently Adopted in Philosophy." *Oxford Literary Review* 6 (December 1984): 3–37.

Descartes, René. *Discourse on the Method of Rightly Conducting the Reason, and Seeking Truthin the Sciences (1637)*. Part IV. Project Gutenberg. http://www.gutenberg.org/files/59/59h/59-h.htm.

Diamond, Jared. *Guns, Germs, and Steel: The Fates of Human Societies*. New York: W. W. Norton, 1997.

Dias, Victor. "St. Augustine on the Structure and Meaning of History." Master's thesis, Concordia University, 1996.

Donne, John. "Devotions upon Emergent Occasions: Meditation XVII." In *The Works of JohnDonne*. Edited by Henry Alford. London: John W. Parker, 1839.

Douglas, Mary. *Thinking in Circles: An Essay on Ring Composition*. Terry Lecture Series. New Haven, CT: Yale University Press, 2007.

Douthat, Ross. *Bad Religion: How We Became a Nation of Heretics*. New York: Simon and Schuster, 2012.

Duarte, Nancy. "Structure Your Presentation Like a Story." *Harvard Business Review*, October 31, 2012. https://hbr.org/2012/10/structure-your-presentation-li.

Earls, Aaron. "Signs of Jesus' Return?" Lifeway Research. April 7, 2020. https://research.lifeway.com/2020/04/07/vast-majority-of-pastors-see-signs-of-end-times-in-current-events/.

Eco, Umberto. *The Name of the Rose*. New York: Mariner, 1980.

Ehrenreich, Barbara. *Bright-Sided: How the Relentless Promotion of Positive Thinking Has Undermined America*. New York: Metropolitan Books, 2009.

Eliade, Mircea. "Paradise and Utopia: Mythical Geography and Eschatology." Scribd. https://www.scribd.com/document/49940919/Mircea-Eliade-Paradise-and-Utopia.

———. *The Quest: History and Meaning in Religion*. Chicago: University of Chicago Press, 1984.

Eliot, T. S. *Collected Poems, 1909–1962*. New York: Harcourt, Brace & World, 1963.

———. "Four Quartets," *The Complete Poems and Plays 1909–1950*. Orlando: Harcourt Brace, 1952.

Elson, John T. "Is God Dead?" *Time*. April 8, 1966.https://content.time.com/time/subscriber/article/0,33009,835309,00.html.

"Emerging and Developing Economies Much More Optimistic Than Rich Countries About the Future." Pew Research Center. October 9, 2014. https://www.pewresearch.org/global/2014/10/09/

emerging-and-developing-economies-much-more-optimistic-than-rich-countries-about-the-future.

Engels, Frederick. "The Peasant War in Germany." *Neue Rheinische Zeitung-Revue* (Summer 1850). Works of Frederick Engels. January 4, 1996. https://www.marxists.org/archive/marx/works/1850/peasant-war-germany/index.htm.

England, Jeremy. *Every Life Is On Fire: How Thermodynamics Explains the Origins of Living Things.* New York: Basic Books, 2020.

"The Faith Once Delivered: A Wesleyan Witness" (Summit Document from the Next Methodism Summit, January 2022), The John Wesley Institute, accessed August 29, 2022, https://nextmethodism.org/summit-document/.

Ferngren, Gary B. *Medicine and Health Care in Early Christianity.* Baltimore, MD: Johns Hopkins University Press, 2016.

Fiske, John. *Television Culture.* London: Methuen, 1987.

Foster, Robert. "Why on Earth Use 'Kingdom of Heaven'?: Matthew's Terminology Revisited." *New Testament Studies* 48, no. 4. http://doi.org/10.1017/S0028688502000292.

Fredrickson, Barbara L. *Positivity: Top-Notch Research Reveals the Upward Spiral That Will Change Your Life.* New York: Three Rivers Press, 2009.

Freistetter, Florian. *Isaac Newton: The Asshole Who Reinvented the Universe.* Amherst, NY: Prometheus, 2018.

Freud, Sigmund. *Civilization and its Discontents.* Standard Edition. Translated and edited by James Strachey. New York: W. W. Norton,1930.

Freytag, Gustav. *Freytag's Technique of the Drama: An Exposition of Dramatic Composition and Art.* Authorized Translation from the Sixth German Edition. Edited by Elias J. MacEwan. Chicago: S.C. Griggs, 1896.

Gardner, David. "An Evangelical Icon Finds Salvation in West Hollywood." *Los Angeles Magazine.* December 8, 2021. https://www.lamag.com/culturefiles/fallen-fundamentalist-rob-bell-venice-beach/.

Gelernter, Daniel. "Giving Up Darwin." *Claremont Review of Books* 19, no. 2 (Spring 2019): 104–9. https://www.claremont.org/crb/article/giving-up-darwin/.

Gentile, Emilio. *Politics as Religion.* Princeton, NJ: Princeton University Press, 2006.

Geraci, Robert M. "A Tale of Two Futures: Techno-Eschatology in the US and India." *Social Compass* 63, no. 3 (September 2016): 319–34. http://journals.sagepub.com/doi/10.1177/0037768616652332.

Getty, Mary Ann. "Christ is the End of the Law: Rom 10:4 in its Context." ThD diss, Katholieke Universiteat, Leuven, 1975. https://bib. kuleuven.be/english/pbib/collection/dissertations.

Gladwell, Malcolm. "Blow Up," *New Yorker,* January 22, 1996, 32.

Gladwell, Malcolm. "Focus Groups Should Be Abolished." Ad Age. August 8, 2005. https://adage.com/article/viewpoint/focus-groups-abolished/104151.

Gladwell, Malcolm. "The Foot Soldier of Birmingham," Revisionist History, produced by Pushkin Industries, July 6, 2017, podcast, audio, 35:39, https://www.pushkin.fm/podcasts/revisionist-history/the-foot-soldier-of-birmingham.

Gleaves, G. Scott. *Did Jesus Speak Greek? The Emerging Evidence of Greek Dominance in First-Century Palestine.* Eugene, OR: Pickwick Publications, 2015.

Graeber, David. *The Dawn of Everything: A New History of Humanity.* New York: Farrar, Strauss, and Giroux, 2021.

Grant, Frederick C. "The Permanent Value of the Primitive Christian Eschatology." *The Biblical World: A Journal of the Awakening Church* 49, no. 1 (January 1917). https://www.journals.uchicago.edu/doi/pdfplus/10.1086/475712.

Gray, John. "An Illusion with a Future." *Daedalus* 133, no. 3 (Summer 2004): 10. http://link.galegroup.com/apps/doc/A122376623/AONE?u=newb64238&sid=AONE&x d=005041ee.

———. *Heresies: Against Progress and Other Illusions.* London: Granta Books, 2004.

Green, Monica H., ed. *Pandemic Disease in the Medieval World: Rethinking the Black Death.* Kalamazoo, MI: Arc Humanities Press, 2015.

Gregor, A. James. *Totalitarianism and Political Religion: An Intellectual History.* Stanford, CA: Stanford University Press, 2012.

Gunn, Giles. *The Culture of Criticism and the Criticism of Culture.* New York: Oxford University Press, 1987.

Gurri, Martin. *The Revolt of the Public and the Crisis of Authority in the New Millennium.* San Francisco: Stripe Press, 2018.

Harari, Yuval Noah. *Homo Deus: A Brief History of Tomorrow.* New York: HarperCollins, 2017.

Hardy, Thomas. *Wessex Poems and Other Verses: Poems of the Past and the Present.* London: MacMillan, 1919.

Hartnell, Jack. *Medieval Bodies: Life, Death, and Art in the Middle Ages.* London: Wellcome Collection, 2018.

Hawking, Stephen. *The Grand Design.* New York: Bantam, 2010.

Heath, Sidney. *Pilgrim Life in the Middle Ages.* Port Washington, NY: Kennikat Press, 1911.

Heiser, James D. *"The American Empire Should Be Destroyed": Alexander Dugin and the Perils of Immanentized Eschatology.* Malone, TX: Repristination, 2014.

Henry, Carl F. H. *God, Revelation and Authority.* Volume 1. Wheaton, IL: Crossway, 1976.

Higgenbotham, Don. *George Washington: Uniting a Nation.* New York: Ronan and Littlefield 2002.

Hughes, Gerald W. *God in All Things.* London: Hodder & Stoughton, 2003.

Hunt, Zach. *Unraptured: How End Times Theology Gets It Wrong.* Scottdale, PA: Herald, 2019.

Isaacson, Walter. *The Innovators: How a Group of Hackers, Geniuses, and Geeks Created the Digital Revolution.* New York: Simon & Schuster, 2014.

Jackson, Joe. *Atlantic Fever: Lindbergh, His Competitors, and the Race to Cross the Atlantic.* New York: Farrar, Straus and Giroux, 2012.

Jennings, Willie James. *The Christian Imagination: Theology and the Origins of Race.* New Haven, CT: Yale University Press, 2010.

Johnson, Robert Glenn. *Jesus Unchained.* Plano, TX: Invite Press, 2022.

Jones, Josh. "Kurt Vonnegut Diagrams the Shape of All Stories in a Master's Thesis Rejected by U. Chicago." Open Culture. February 18, 2014. http://www.openculture.com/2014/02/kurt-vonnegut-masters-thesis-rejected-by-u-chicago.html.

Josephus, Flavius. *The Antiquities of the Jews.* Translated by William Whiston. Project Gutenberg. Last updated August 9, 2017. Book 17, chapter 6, number 2. https://www.gutenberg.org/files/2848/2848-h/2848-h.htm.

Josephus, Flavius. *The Wars of the Jews.* Translated by William Whiston. Project Perseus. Accessed August 29, 2022. Book 2, chapter 1, number 2. https://www.gutenberg.org/files/2850/2850-h/2850-h.htm.

Josipovici, Gabriel. *What Ever Happened to Modernism?* New Haven, CT: Yale University Press, 2010.

Kahneman, Daniel, and Amos Tversky. "Prospect Theory: An Analysis of Decision under Risk." *Econometrica* 47, no. 2 (1979): 263–91. https://doi.org/10.2307/1914185.

Kahneman, Daniel. *Thinking, Fast and Slow.* New York: Farrar, Straus and Giroux, 2013.

Kelly, John. *The Great Mortality: An Intimate History of the Black Death, the Most Devastating Plague of All Time.* New York: Harper Perennial, 2005.

Kelsey, David H. "God and Teleology: Must God Have Only One 'Eternal Purpose'?" *Neue Zeitschrift Für Systematische Theologie* 54, no. 4 (2012): 369. http://doi.org/10.1515/nzsth-2012-0015.

Kierkegaard, Soren. *Kierkegaard's Journals and Notebooks.* Volume 5. Journals *NB6-NB10.* Princeton, NJ: Princeton University Press, 2011. As quoted in Malcolm Muggeridge. *A Third Testament: A Modern Pilgrim Explores the Spiritual Wanderings of Augustine, Blake, Pascal, Tolstoy, Bonhoeffer, Kierkegaard, and Dostoevsky.* New York: Little, Brown, 1976.

Kierkegaard, Søren. *The Crowd Is Untruth.* n.p.: CreateSpace, 2015.

Koselleck, Reinhard. *Sediments of Time: On Possible Histories.* Stanford, CA: Stanford University Press, 2019.

Kuwornu-Adjaottor, Jonathan E. T., and Patrick Yankyera. "The Meaning and Significance of Tetelestai in John 19:30." ResearchGate. https://www.researchgate.net/publication/337415360_THE_MEANING_AND_SIGNIFCANCE_OF_TETELESTAI_IN_JOHN_1930.

Larson, Edward J. *Summer of the Gods: The Scopes Trial and America's Continuing Debate Over Science and Religion.* New York: Basic Books, 1997.

Lasch, Christopher. *The True and Only Heaven: Progress and Its Critics.* New York: W. W. Norton, 1991.

Lerner, Robert E. "The Black Death and Western European Eschatological Mentalities." *American Historical Review* 86, no. 3 (1981): 533–52. https://doi.org/10.2307/1860369.

Levi, Primo. *If This Is a Man.* New York: Orion, 1959.

Lewis, Alan. *Between Cross and Resurrection.* Grand Rapids: Eerdmans, 2003.

Lewis, C.S. "Myth Became Fact." In *God in the Dock: Essays on Theology and Ethics.* Edited by Walter Hooper. Grand Rapids: Eerdmans, 1970.

———. "Rejoinder to Dr. Pittenger." *Christian Century* 75 (November 26, 1958): 1359-61.

———. *Surprised By Joy.* Roermond, NL: 1955.

———. *The Collected Letters of C. S. Lewis.* Volume 3. New York: HarperCollins, 2004.

Lindner, Robert M. *Rebel Without a Cause.* New York: Penguin Random House, 1944.

Lindsay, James A.; Peter Boghossian; and Helen Pluckrose. "Academic Grievance Studies and the Corruption of Scholarship." *Aero Magazine.* February 10, 2018. https://areomagazine. com/2018/10/02/academic-grievance-studies-and-the-corruption-of-scholarship/.

Lipset, Seymour Martin. "George Washington and the Founding of Democracy." *Journal of Democracy* 9, no. 4 (1998): 24–38. http://doi.org/10.1353/jod.1998.0066.

Lücke, Friedrich. *Versuch einer vollständigen Einleitung in die Offenbarung des Johannes und in die apokalyptische Litteratur.* Bonn, DE: E. Weber, 1852.

Macaes, Bruno. "After Covid, Get Ready for the Great Acceleration." *Spectator.* March 13, 2021. https://www.spectator.co.uk/article/after-covid-get-ready-for-the-great-acceleration.

MacCulloch, Diarmaid. *Christianity: The First Three Thousand Years.* New York: Viking, 2010.

Macrobius. The *Saturnalia.* 2.4.11. https://penelope.uchicago.edu/Thayer/e/roman/texts/macrobius/saturnalia/home.html.

Magner, Lois. *A History of Medicine.* New York: Marcel Dekker, 1992.

Majumdar, Margaret A., and Tony Chafer. "Progress: Its Visionaries and Its Malcontents." *Interventions* 19, no. 5 (July 4, 2017): 599–608. https://www.tandfonline.com/doi/full/10.1080/1369801X.2017.1336459.

Malthus, Thomas Robert. *An Essay on the Principle of Population.* Cambridge, UK: 1992.

Mannheim, Karl. "The Problem of Generations." In *Essays on the Sociology of Knowledge: Collected Works.* Volume 5. Edited by Paul Kecskemeti. New York: Routledge, 1952.

Manzo, Bernard. "Our Patron Saint." *Times Literary Supplement.* 10 June 2011.

Markel, Howard. "Dec. 14, 1799: The Excruciating Final Hours of President George Washington." PBS News Hour. December 14, 2014. https://www.pbs.org/newshour/health/dec-14-1799-excruciating-final-hours-president-george-washington.

Martin, Ralph P. "The Lord's Supper." In *The New Bible Dictionary*. Edited by J. D. Douglas. Westmont, IL: InterVarsity Press, 1982.

Martin, Sean. *The Black Death*. Harpenden, UK: Oldcastle Books, 2014.

Marx, Karl. "The Eighteenth Brumaire of Louis Bonaparte." *Liberte, Egalite, Fraternite: Exploring the French Revolution*. Accessed August 30, 2022. https://revolution.chnm.org/items/show/304.

McCarthy, Cormac. *Blood Meridian: Or the Evening Redness in the West*. New York: Vintage, 1985.

McEntyre, Marilyn. "Holy Saturday in a Harrowing Time." *Christian Century* 18 (March 2021).

McGilchrist, Iain. *The Matter with Things: Our Brains, Our Delusions, and the Unmaking of the World*. London: Perspectiva, 2021.

McGinn, Bernard. *The Calabrian Abbot: Joachim of Fiore in the History of Western Thought*. New York: Macmillan, 1985.

McIntire, Mike; Karen Yourish; and Larry Buchanan. "In Trump's Twitter Feed: Conspiracy Mongers, Racists and Spies." *New York Times*. November 2, 2019. https://www.nytimes.com/interactive/2019/11/02/us/politics/trump-twitter-disinformation.html.

McKay, Brett. "What the Generational Cycle Theory Can Tell Us About Our Present Age." September 20, 2016. In *The Art of Manliness*. Podcast, MP3 audio, 1.27.47. http://www.artofmanliness.com/2016/09/20/podcast-236-generational-cycle-theory-can-tell-us-present-age/.

McKee, Robert. *Story: Substance, Structure, Style, and the Principles of Screenwriting*. New York: HarperCollins, 1997.

Meliade, Mircea. *The Quest: History and Meaning in Religion*. Chicago: University of Chicago Press, 1984.

Mencken, H. L. *Minority Report: H.L.Mencken's Notebooks*. Baltimore: The Johns Hopkins University Press, 1956.

Metaxas, Eric. *Seven Men: And the Secret of Their Greatness*. Nashville: Thomas Nelson, 2013.

Mokyr, Joel. *A Culture of Growth: The Origins of the Modern Economy*. Princeton, NJ: Princeton University Press, 2017.

Moltmann, Jurgen. *The Coming of God: Christian Eschatology*. Minneapolis: Augsburg, 1996.

Moore, Marianne. *Complete Poems*. New York: Macmillan, 1967.

Morgan, Lewis Henry. *Ancient Society; Or, Researches in the Lines of Human Progress from Savagery, through Barbarism to Civilization.* New York: H. Holt, 1877.

Muggeridge, Malcolm. *A Third Testament.* New York: Ballantine Books, 1976.

Noble, Alan. *You Are Not Your Own: Belonging to God in an Inhuman World.* Downers Grove, IL: InterVarsity Press, 2021.

Norberg, Johan. *Progress: Ten Reasons to Look Forward to the Future.* London: OneWorld, 2017.

O'Brien, Lucy. *Self-Knowing Agents.* Oxford, UK: Clarendon Press, 2008.

O'Keane, Veronica. *The Rag and Bone Shop: How We Make Memories and Memories Make Us.* New York: Allen Lane, 2022.

Pasternak, Boris. *Doctor Zhivago.* New York: Knopf, 2010.

Pelikan, Jaroslav. *The Vindication of Tradition.* Cambridge, MA: Yale University Press, 1984.

Peterson, Eric, and Leonard Sweet. *Wade in the Water: Following the Sacred Stream of Baptism.* Eugene, OR: Wipf and Stock, 2018.

Pilcher, Jane. "Mannheim's Sociology of Generations: An Undervalued Legacy." *British Journal of Sociology* 44, no. 3 (1994): 481.

Pinker, Steven. *Enlightenment Now: The Case for Reason, Science, Humanism, and Progress.* New York: Viking, 2018.

Polanyi, Michael. *The Logic of Liberty.* New York: Routledge, 1951.

Polanyi, Michael, and Mary Jo Nye. *Personal Knowledge: Towards a Post-Critical Philosophy.* Chicago: University of Chicago Press, 2015.

Polkinghorne, John. *The God of Hope and the End of the World.* New Haven, CT: Yale University Press, 2002.

Poole, Steven. *Rethink: The Surprising History of New Ideas.* New York: Scribner and Sons, 2016.

Popper, Karl. *The Open Society and Its Enemies.* London: Routledge, 1945.

Public Papers of the Presidents of the United States: Lyndon B. Johnson, 1963–64. Volume I, entry 357. Washington, DC: Government Printing Office, 1965. 704–7.

"Race, Civil Rights and Photography." Lens: Photography, Video and Visual Journalism. *New York Times.* January 28, 2016. https://lens.blogs.nytimes.com/2016/01/18/race-civil-rights-and-photography/.

Rachman, Gideon. *The Age of the Strongman: How the Cult of the Leader Threatens Democracy Around the World.* New York: Other Press, 2022.

Raphael, Frederic. *Antiquity Matters.* New Haven, CT: Yale University Press, 2017.

Reeves, Marjorie. *The Influence of Prophecy in the Later Middle Ages.* New York: Oxford University Press, 1969.

"Remarks of President Donald J. Trump – As Prepared for Delivery." The White House. January 20, 2017. https://www.archives.gov/presidential-libraries/archived-websites.

Rocke, Kris, and Joel Van Dyke. *Geography of Grace: Doing Theology from Below.* Tacoma, WA: Center for Transforming Mission, 2012.

Rothe, Delf. "Governing the End Times? Planet Politics and the Secular Eschatology of the Anthropocene." *Millennium* 48, no. 2 (January 2020): 143–64. https://doi.org/10.1177/0305829819889138.

Rowling, J. K. *The Diane Rehm Show,* WAMU Radio Washington, DC, October 20, 1999 (rebroadcast December 24, 1999).

Russell, Jeffrey Burton. *Inventing the Flat Earth: Columbus and Modern Historians.* Santa Barbara, CA: Praeger, 1991.

Sallustius. "On the Gods and the Cosmos." Part IV. In Gilbert Murray. *Five Stages of Greek Religion.* New York: AMS, 1925. https://sacredtexts.com/cla/fsgr/fsgr10.html.

Sanders, Scott Russell. *Staying Put: Making a Home in a Restless World.* Boston: Beacon Press, 1993.

Schmemann, Alexander. *The Journals of Father Alexander Schmemann* 1973-1983. Yonkers, NY: St. Vladimir's Seminary Press, 2000.

Scott, James C. *Seeing Like a State: How Certain Schemes to Improve the Human Condition Have Failed.* New Haven, CT: Yale University Press, 1999.

Seitelberger, F. "Lebensstadien des Gehirns: Neurobiologische Aspekte." In *Handbuch der Gerontopsychiatrie.* Edited by H.G. Zapotoczky and P. K. Fischof. Vienna, AT: Springer Verlag, 1996). https://doi.org/10.1007/978-3-7091-6563-8_2.

Shellenberger, Michael. *San Fransicko: Why Progressives Ruin Cities.* New York: Harper, 2021.

Shields, Charles, J. *And So It Goes. Kurt Vonnegut: A Life.* New York: Henry Holt, 2011.

Shipley, A. E. "Leeches." *British Medical Journal* 2, no. 2813 (November 28, 1914): 916–19.

Shirky, Clay. *Here Comes Everybody: The Power of Organizing Without Organizations*. New York: Penguin, 2009.

Sinek, Simon. *Start with Why: How Great Leaders Inspire Everyone to Take Action*. New York: Penguin, 2009.

Slaboch, Matthew W. *A Road to Nowhere: The Idea of Progress and Its Critics*. Philadelphia: University of Pennsylvania Press, 2018.

Slater, Thomas B. "Apocalypticism and Eschatology: A Study of Mark 13:3-37." *Perspectives in Religious Studies* 40, no. 1 (2013): 8.

Slezkine, Yur. *The House of Government: A Saga of the Russian Revolution*. Princeton, NJ: Princeton University Press, 2017.

Smith, Ben. "Inside the Revolts Erupting in America's Big Newsrooms." *New York Times*. June 7, 2020. https://www.nytimes.com/2020/06/07/business/media/new-york-times-washington-post-protests.html.

Solnit, Rebecca. *A Paradise Built in Hell: The Extraordinary Communities That Arise in Disaster*. New York: Penguin, 2009.

Spencer, Herbert. *The Principles of Biology*. Vol. 1. London: Williams and Norgate, 1864.

Spinney, Laura. "Human Cycles: History as Science." *Nature* 488 (August 2012): 24–26. https://www.nature.com/news/human-cycles-history-as-science-1.11078.

Springer, Claudia. *James Dean Transfigured: The Many Faces of Rebel Iconography*. Austin: The University of Texas Press, 2007.

Spyrou, Maria A., Lyazzat Musralina, and Guido A. Gnecchi Ruscone, et al. "The Source of the Black Death in Fourteenth-Century Central Eurasia." *Nature* 606 (2022): 718–24. https://doi.org/10.1038/s41586-022-04800-3.

Stanton, Andrew. "The Clues to a Great Story." Filmed February 2012. TED video, 19.00. https://www.ted.com/talks/andrew_stanton_the_clues_to_a_great_story/transcript.

Stephens, Mitchell. *The Rise of the Image, the Fall of the Word*. New York: Oxford University Press, 1998.

Storey, Glenn R. "The 'Skyscrapers' of the Ancient Roman World." *Latomus* 62, no. 1 (2003): 3–26. http://www.jstor.org/stable/41540040.

Storey, Jenna Silber, and Benjamin Storey. *Why We Are Restless: On the Modern Quest for Contentment*. Princeton, NJ: Princeton University Press, 2021.

Strauss, William, and Neil Howe. *Generations: The History of America's Future, 1584 to 2069*. New York: Quill, 1992.

Sweet, Leonard, *Bad Habits of Jesus*. Carol Stream, IL: Tyndale, 2016.

Sweet, Leonard I. "Christopher Columbus and the Millennial Vision of the New World." *Catholic Historical Review* 72, no. 3 (July 1986): 369–82.

Sweet, Leonard, and Frank Viola. *Jesus: A Theography*. Nashville: Thomas Nelson, 2012.

Sweet, Leonard. *Me and We: God's New Social Gospel*. Nashville: Abingdon Press, 2014.

———. "Millennialism in America: Recent Studies." *Theological Studies* 40, no. 3 (September 1979): 510–31. https://journals.sagepub.com/doi/10.1177/004056397904000305.

———. *Rings of Fire: Walking in Faith Through a Volcanic Future*. Colorado Springs: NavPress, 2019.

Taleb, Nassim Nicholas. *Antifragile: Things That Gain from Disorder*. New York: Random House, 2012.

———. *Black Swan: The Impact of the Highly Improbable*. New York: Random House, 2010.

Talking Heads. "Road to Nowhere." By David Byrne. Recorded October 1984. Little Creatures. Sire, 33 ⅓ rpm.

Tetlock, Philip E., and Dan Gardner. *Superforecasting: The Art and Science of Prediction*. New York: Crown, 2015.

The Breakfast Club. Directed by John Hughes. Featuring Emilio Estevez, Judd Nelson, and Molly Ringwald. Universal, 1985. 1hr. 37 min.

The Police. "Spirits in the Material World." *Ghost in the Machine*. A&M. 1981.

Tolkien, J. R. R. *The Monsters and the Critics*. New York: HarperCollins, 1997.

Trotsky, Leon. "Towards Capitalism or Towards Socialism?" *Labour Monthly* 7, no. 11 (November 1925): 659–66. https://www.marxists.org/archive/trotsky/1925/11/towards.htm.

Van Doren, Charles Lincoln. *A History of Knowledge: Past, Present, and Future*. New York: Ballantine Books, 1993.

Vogler, Christopher. *The Writer's Journey: Mythic Structure for Writers*. Studio City, CA: Michael Wiese Productions, 1992.

Volck, Brian. "A Conversation with Gil Bailie." *Image* 41 (Winter 2003): 63–77, 72.

Whittock, Martyn. "The Day of the Lord," *The Tablet*, 21 May 2022, 12.

———. *The End Times, Again? 2000 Years of the Use & Misuse of Biblical Prophecy.* Eugene, OR: Cascade, 2021.

Wilde, Oscar. *The Soul of Man under Socialism.* Boston, MA: John W. Luce, 1910.

Wilkinson, Alissa. "The 'Left Behind' Series Was Just the Latest Way America Prepared for the Rapture." *Washington Post.* July 13, 2016. https://www.washingtonpost.com/news/act-four/wp/2016/07/13/the-left-behind-series-was-just-the-latest-way-america-prepared-for-the-rapture/.

Willard, Dallas. *The Divine Conspiracy: Rediscovering Our Hidden Life in God.* New York: HarperCollins, 1998.

Williams, Rowan. *Collected Poems.* Manchester, UK: Carcanet, 2022.

Wilson, A. N. *Charles Darwin: Victorian Mythmaker.* New York: HarperCollins, 2017.

Wilson, Len. *Greater Things: The Work of the New Creation.* Plano, TX: Invite Press, 2021.

Wixted, John T., Stephen D. Goldinger, Larry R. Squire, Joel R. Kuhn, Megan H. Papesh, Kris A. Smith, David M. Treiman, and Peter N. Steinmetz. "Coding of Episodic Memory in the Human Hippocampus." *Proceedings of the National Academy of Sciences* 115, no. 5 (2018): 1093–98.

Wright, N. T. *God in Public: How the Bible Speaks Truth to Power Today.* London: Society for Promoting Christian Knowledge, 2016.

———. *Surprised by Hope: Rethinking Heaven, the Resurrection, and the Mission of the Church.* New York: HarperOne, 2007.

———. *The New Testament and the People of God.* Minneapolis: Fortress, 1992.

———. *What Saint Paul Really Said: Was Paul of Tarsus the Real Founder of Christianity?* Grand Rapids: Eerdmans, 2014.

Wright, Ronald. *A Short History of Progress.* New York: Carroll & Graf, 2005.

Wucker, Michele. *The Gray Rhino: How to Recognize and Act on the Obvious Dangers We Ignore.* New York: St. Martin's Press, 2016.

INDEX

Aquinas 94, 97, 127

Arche 48

Archelaus 41, 42

Aristotle xvi, 21, 81, 97, 132, 270

Armageddon 14, 55, 65

Ars Moriendi 4

Artifact xix, 35, 55

Ascension xxxiv, 13, 85, 166, 202, 237, 238

Augustine 13, 14, 27, 83, 84, 87

Author xxiii, xxvi, xxxiii, xxxiv, xxxv, 127, 141, 145, 153, 154, 157, 158, 159, 164, 191, 192, 225, 229, 230, 231, 232, 233, 234

Authority xxiii, xxvi, xxxiii, xxxiv, 23, 24, 32, 41, 42, 43, 48, 49, 50, 52, 67, 80, 82, 93, 97, 99, 101, 103, 104, 105, 106, 107, 108, 110, 111, 112, 113, 115, 116, 117, 118, 119, 120, 127, 131, 136, 139, 140, 145, 147, 148, 149, 150, 151, 152, 153, 154, 155, 156, 157, 158, 159, 177, 182, 184, 191, 197, 199, 200, 202, 203, 221, 225, 230, 231, 232, 233, 234

Absolute xxiii, xxvi

And authorship xxxiv, 153, 230, 233, 234

And social order 32, 127, 155

Control and 136

Crisis of 140, 147, 148

Historical 131

In Roman society 41, 42, 43, 50, 52

Jesus and xxxiii, xxxiv, 67, 105, 120, 153, 156, 157, 158, 159, 191, 197, 199, 200, 203, 221, 225, 230, 231, 232

Kingship and 118, 182, 191

Messianism and 99, 101, 103, 104, 111, 116

Philosophical shift in 23, 24, 48, 49, 107, 149, 150, 154, 177

Politics and 112, 113, 115

Power and xxxiii, 145, 153, 155, 202, 232

Progress and 32, 80, 82, 93

Rebellion and 106, 108, 110, 118, 151, 154

Caesar Augustus 42

Caiaphas 39, 41, 43, 44, 50, 51, 52, 177, 178

Calvin, John 58

Campbell, Joseph xv, xvi, 220

Cancel Culture 69, 71, 72, 73

Carr, E. H. 76

Cauthen, Kenneth 153, 154

Census 42

Chaos xv, 36, 86

Chardin, Teilhard de 102, 217

Chesterton, G. K. 28, 124, 223

Christian xv, xviii, xix, xxv, xxvi, xxviii, xxix, 13, 16, 23, 24, 27, 28, 29, 31, 32, 49, 50, 51, 55, 56, 57, 58, 60, 61, 62, 65, 66, 67, 72, 73, 79, 83, 84, 85, 88, 95, 96, 102, 108, 110, 113, 123, 124, 127, 135, 136, 137, 138, 139, 147, 155, 156, 158, 164, 166, 167, 168, 169, 177, 183, 188, 193, 203, 209, 210, 218, 223, 224, 227, 230, 236, 238

    Apocalypticism 13, 227

    Community 188, 209

    Doctrine 24

    Faith xxix, 28, 123, 135, 169, 224

    Gnostics 67

    Heresy 60

    History/Tradition xix, 50, 51, 58, 85, 96, 164, 169, 177, 183, 193

    Identity xix, xxv, 113

    Leaders 108

    Life xxix, 24, 167, 168, 224

    Ministry 79

    Nationalism 139

    Story 83, 102, 156

    Theology 31, 49, 56, 62, 230

    Thought 13, 27, 66, 88, 127, 147, 166

Christianity xxvii, xxviii, xxix, 14, 16, 29, 30, 46, 49, 50, 51, 55, 56, 59, 62, 74, 83, 85, 98, 108, 110, 124, 125, 127, 133, 151, 155, 177, 195,

Derrida, Jacques 10, 71

Descartes, René 48, 84, 94, 154

Disciple(s) xiii, xv, xvi, xxviii, xxxi, xxxii, xxxiii, xxxiv, 13, 44, 55, 68, 104,
    108, 114, 117, 118, 119, 127, 137, 157, 168, 169, 170, 176, 181,
    184, 185, 188, 189, 192, 205, 207, 211, 212, 219, 221, 222, 223,
    227, 228, 231, 237, 244

Dispensationalism 55, 56

Donne, John 230

Dostoevsky, Fyodor 119

Douglas, Mary 81, 82

Douthat, Ross xxix

Draaisma, Douwe 182

Duarte, Nancy xvi

Dunn, James D. R. 218

Dystopian xxxi, 7, 34, 88, 140

Earth Day 65

Ebola 6, 7, 10, 16, 24, 93, 94, 95

Eco, Umberto 11, 137, 157

Ehrenreich, Barbara 30

Einstein, Albert 134, 188, 224

Eliade, Mircea 58

Empire 14, 39, 57, 62, 81, 90, 96, 103, 110, 123, 177, 229

Empirical xxiii, 25, 26, 28, 128, 131, 133, 153

Empiricism xxiv, 24, 26, 48, 49, 84, 124

End xiii, xv, xvi, xvii, xviii, xix, xxi, xxii, xxiii, xxiv, xxv, xxvi, xxvii, xxviii,
    xxix, xxx, xxxi, xxxii, xxxiii, xxxiv, xxxv, 1, 3, 4, 5, 6, 7, 8, 11, 13,
    14, 16, 17, 20, 22, 23, 25, 27, 28, 29, 33, 34, 36, 44, 46, 48, 53, 55,
    56, 57, 59, 61, 62, 63, 64, 66, 67, 68, 69, 75, 76, 79, 80, 81, 82, 83,
    84, 85, 86, 88, 92, 93, 94, 95, 99, 102, 103, 104, 106, 110, 111, 112,
    113, 115, 116, 117, 118, 119, 120, 121, 125, 127, 135, 139, 140,
    141, 143, 145, 148, 153, 155, 157, 158, 159, 161, 163, 164, 165,
    166, 167, 168, 169, 170, 171, 172, 175, 177, 178, 179, 181, 182,
    183, 186, 187, 188, 190, 191, 192, 195, 196, 197, 199, 201, 202,
    203, 204, 205, 206, 207, 211, 215, 217, 218, 219, 220, 221, 222,
    224, 225, 227, 228, 229, 234, 235, 236, 237, 238, 241, 242, 243,

Grotius, Hugo 66

Growth 4, 5, 10, 30, 81, 85, 90, 91, 92, 93, 204

Gurri, Martin xxxiii, 148, 149, 150, 151, 152

Hardy, Thomas 11

Harrowing of hell xxxiii, 238

Harvey, Paul xxxiv

Harvey, William 23

Hawking, Stephen xxiii, 25

Hedonism 95

Hegel, Georg W. F. 32, 57, 85, 94

Heresy xxxii, 45, 46, 60, 79, 224

Hermeneutic 47, 157, 178, 220

Herod the Great 41, 42

Herodians 44

Hierarchical 117

Hippocrates 21

Historiographical 28, 86

History xviii, xix, xxi, xxii, xxiv, xxvii, xxviii, xxxi, xxxiii, 3, 5, 8, 9, 10, 13, 14, 16, 19, 22, 23, 24, 25, 27, 31, 32, 33, 35, 39, 48, 49, 51, 52, 53, 56, 57, 58, 59, 60, 62, 66, 69, 71, 73, 75, 76, 77, 78, 79, 80, 81, 82, 83, 84, 85, 86, 87, 88, 89, 90, 92, 93, 95, 96, 97, 98, 99, 105, 110, 111, 112, 113, 115, 117, 119, 120, 125, 130, 131, 134, 139, 151, 152, 153, 154, 155, 156, 158, 161, 163, 164, 165, 166, 169, 177, 178, 179, 182, 185, 187, 190, 206, 217, 218, 223, 229, 233, 234, 235, 238, 243, 244

    American 14, 53, 56, 66, 85, 90, 110, 152

    Apocalypse and 14

    As story xviii, xxi, xxii, xxxiii, 90

    Christian xix, 51, 96, 169

    End of xxiv, xxvii, xxviii, 27, 60, 113

    Eschaton and 56, 60, 62, 66

    Nihilism and 95

    Progress and 23, 24, 25, 31, 32, 33, 49, 56, 164, 185

Messianism xxxii, 13, 99, 105, 110, 116, 117, 145, 152

Metamorphosis xv

Metanoia xv

Metaphor xvi, xviii, xix, 13, 27, 28, 69, 78, 83, 87, 106, 136, 155, 184, 188, 204, 208, 227, 228, 230, 233, 244, 245

Methodism 177

Methodist Revolution 47

Millennialism xxxii, xxxiii, 13, 28, 53, 57, 58, 59, 60, 61, 62, 65, 66, 67, 140, 179

Miller, William 56

Milton, John 11, 58, 59

Moltmann, Jürgen 110, 186

Monarch 46, 48, 115, 117, 118, 184

More, Thomas 19, 46, 92

Mortality 3, 5, 6

Morton, Timothy 62, 63

Moses xxi, 42, 111, 114, 173, 187, 194, 205, 210, 211, 217, 233

Moyers, Bill 65

Muggeridge, Malcolm 150, 151

Müntzer, Thomas 57

Musk, Elon xxxi, 195

Myth xv, xvi, xviii, xxi, xxii, 14, 16, 34, 56, 60, 79, 91, 96, 103, 115, 128, 152, 177

Mystery xxix, 67, 78, 87, 138, 140, 167, 193, 212

Mysticism 23

Napier, John 59

Narrative xvi, xviii, xix, xx, xxix, xxxii, xxxiii, xxxv, 5, 27, 28, 50, 51, 52, 53, 60, 69, 75, 78, 79, 116, 118, 130, 132, 141, 153, 157, 163, 166, 185, 186, 188, 228, 231, 241

Nationalism 52, 73, 89, 93, 139, 178

Neo-Darwinism 28

New Left xviii

Newton, Isaac 58, 59

CPSIA information can be obtained
at www.ICGtesting.com
Printed in the USA
BVHW092034061222
653402BV00006B/20/J